THE
PRACTICE
OF
WRITING

Fourth Edition

THE
PRACTICE
OF
WRITING

Fourth Edition

ROBERT SCHOLES
Brown University

NANCY R. COMLEY
Queens College, CUNY

JANICE PERITZ
Queens College, CUNY

St. Martin's Press
New York

Senior editor: Karen J. Allanson
Development editor: Edward Hutchinson
Managing editor: Patricia Mansfield-Phelan
Project editor: Erica Appel
Production supervisor: Joe Ford
Art director: Sheree Goodman
Cover design: Rod Hernandez
Cover art: Picasso, Pablo. *Glass, Guitar, and Bottle*. Paris (early 1913). Oil, pasted paper, gesso, and pencil on canvas, 25 ¾″ × 21 ⅛″. The Museum of Modern Art, New York. The Sidney and Harriet Janis Collection. Photograph © 1993 The Museum of Modern Art, New York.

Library of Congress Catalog Card Number: 92-62777

For information, write:
St. Martin's Press, Inc.
175 Fifth Avenue
New York, NY 10010

ISBN: 0-312-10312-3

To Our Students,
who have taught us so much

Practice, practice. Put your hope in that.
W. S. MERWIN

Only where love and need are one,
And the work is play for mortal stakes,
Is the deed ever really done
For Heaven and the future's sakes.

ROBERT FROST

Give a man a mask and he will tell you the truth.

OSCAR WILDE

First question: who is speaking? Who, among the totality of speaking individuals, is accorded the right to use this sort of language? Who is qualified to do so? Who derives from it his own special quality, his prestige, and from whom, in return, does he receive if not the assurance, at least the presumption that what he says is true? What is the status of the individuals who—alone—have the right, sanctioned by law or tradition, juridically defined or spontaneously accepted, to proffer such a discourse?

MICHEL FOUCAULT

In our society, and probably in all others, capacity to bring off an activity as one wants to—ordinarily defined as the possession of skills—is very often developed through a kind of utilitarian make-believe. The purpose of this practicing is to give the neophyte experience in performing under conditions in which (it is felt) no actual engagement with the world is allowed, events having been "decoupled" from their usual embedment in consequentiality. Presumably muffing or failure can occur both economically and instructively. What one has here are dry runs, trial sessions, run-throughs—in short, "practicings."

ERVING GOFFMAN

A man knowing little or nothing of medical science could not be a good surgeon, but excellence at surgery is not the same thing as knowledge of medical science; nor is it a simple product of it. The surgeon must indeed have learned from instruction, or by his own inductions and observations, a great number of truths; but he must also have learned by practice a great number of aptitudes. Even where efficient practice is the deliberate application of considered prescriptions, the intelligence involved in putting the prescriptions into practice is not identical with that involved in intellectually grasping the prescriptions. There is no contradiction, or even paradox, in describing someone as bad at practising what he is good at preaching. There have been thoughtful and original literary critics who have formulated admirable canons of prose style in execrable prose. There have been others who have employed brilliant English in the expression of the silliest theories of what constitutes good writing.

GILBERT RYLE

T he way to write better is to write more—but not alone, not aimlessly, not without guidance and encouragement. This text is designed to facilitate the tasks of those engaged in learning and teaching about writing. It has been composed by three teachers who are themselves committed to writing as both a field of study and an occupation.

Our philosophy of composition is implicit in the epigraphs we have chosen for our book. As Frost says about all deeds, writing must be work *and* play, both serious *and* joyful, if it is to be done well. Any text in writing, then, must preserve the joy of composition for those who use it, even while providing the work that needs to be done.

We also believe, with Wilde, in the usefulness of masks. Nowhere in all their work are students so vulnerable as in their writing classes. Nowhere do they feel their personalities, their very selves, so open to criticism of a very painful sort. If the style is the person, to criticize the style is to wound the individual behind it. Many of our assignments are designed to free students from the burden of self by offering them personae, voices, and roles already chosen for their suitability to a given form of writing. The true self of a writer must be given space to grow in and should be protected while growing.

There is a public dimension to writing, as well. As Michel Foucault reminds us, certain forms of writing accompany certain social, economic, and political roles. In a society that encourages self-development and economic mobility, the skills of language—and foremost among them, writing— are the major path to advancement, whether personal, professional, or social. The language games and writing exercises presented here must be undertaken with the awareness that each individual's ability to develop and function socially will depend partly on the compositional skills of that individual. Our play at writing is for "mortal stakes" indeed.

Yet it is still play—what Goffman calls "utilitarian make-believe." In writing classes students are "neophytes" engaged in "dry runs, trial sessions . . . 'practicings'." As Gilbert Ryle points out, we learn some things by instruction, but the actual doing of anything must be learned by practice. For that reason we have provided models for analysis and discussion, short exercises for the classroom, and a range of longer assignments for homework papers. We take our motto from W. S. Merwin: "Practice, practice. Put your hope in that."

Users of previous editions may be interested in knowing the rationale for what we retained and what we changed in the present edition. As the table

of contents indicates, we have continued to use a framework that differentiates writing practices by discursive orientation and form. As pragmatists
whose primary commitment is to furthering the practice of writing, we took
seriously what instructors in the field had to say about our framework; since
most of them reported that it worked well in their classrooms, we were
inclined to retain it. That inclination was reinforced by our own experiences
as composition teachers. Although we support the recent turn to cultural
studies, it is our experience that students need a practical way to work
through questions about the discursive construction of identity, power, and
knowledge. And so, we decided to retain the arrangement by forms of
writing, while adding subtitles to Parts Two, Three, and Four that signal this
cultural emphasis.

Similar principles guided our review of each of the chapters. When
instructors in the field agreed that an assignment worked well in their
classrooms, we were inclined to retain it. Such was the case with the
readings on bilingual education and the punishment of crimes. Less successful or little-used assignments were either dropped or replaced with readings
and practices that are likely to be more effective and appealing. So, for
example, we dropped the "Not-So-Serious Job Letter"; we replaced Corta-
zar's rather abstract allegory with a more accessible but equally interesting
story by García Márquez; we exchanged Gould's critique of creationism for
his defense of the means and ends of modern science; and we substituted
Jane Tompkins's essay on "Fighting Words" for Plato's dialogue with Gor-
gias. Our interest in cultural studies prompted us to add more readings to
some popular assignments; to supplement the Reflection chapter with a new
reading and practice; and to revise quite thoroughly the one chapter we
found much too formalistic: Direction. By using conduct literature ranging
from Andreas Capellanus to Letitia Baldrige to exemplify directive writing,
the revised Direction chapter now poses power as a discursive, interpersonal, and sociocultural problem to be addressed and worked through in practice.

Since our commitment is to practice, we have followed instructors' responses and kept our introductions short, saying just enough to get students
started on the readings, questions, and practices that follow. In working
through this material, both teachers and students will find numerous opportunities to clarify, complicate, and challenge our introductory remarks about
a specific form of writing. As in prior editions, our general principle has been
to begin with a reading and practice that clarifies, to move through a set of
assignments that complicate, and to end with a reading and practice that
challenge. To better realize this dialectical principle, we not only revised
the order of some assignments in the chapters on Classification and Analysis
but also changed a number of readings, questions, and practices in other
chapters. So, for example, the Narration chapter now includes new readings
and questions that are designed first to clarify and then to complicate

our introductory remarks on level of detail, rhetorical effect, and point of view.

The chapter on Argumentation proceeds in a similar way. In the introduction to that chapter, we distinguish rational argument from persuasive manipulation; however, we do not buttress our distinction with either an abstract account of logical structure or an all-purpose list of logical fallacies. While our reviewers and colleagues usually appreciated the brevity of our chapter introductions, in this instance some requested us to say more about the logic of argument. Instead of acceding to this request, we decided to do something more in line with our commitment to practice and to the principle of dialectic. We chose instead to begin with a new reading: an argumentative essay in which Stephen Jay Gould exposes both the logical fallacies of a text he considers propagandistic and the kind of logical structure he considers reasonable. By working through this reading and its accompanying practice, students can clarify for themselves not only our introductory distinction between persuasion and argumentation, but also what counts as logical reasoning. Although subsequent assignments are designed to raise a number of complications, the most dialectical and therefore challenging assignment is the last one, which asks students to stage a dialogue between Jane Tompkins and Stephen Jay Gould on the means and ends of argumentation.

As the Argumentation chapter shows, we have tried to make this edition more explicitly dialogical as well as more implicitly dialectical. Also, we have updated and diversified the images, voices, and positions represented in the present edition. In the Persuasion chapter, Franklin Roosevelt's inaugural address has been replaced by Bill Clinton's. Instead of Buster Keaton, Marilyn Monroe appears in the Description chapter. The Synthesis chapter's project on photography now includes interviews with Robert Doisneau, Gordon Parks, and Eve Arnold; three photographs from the Vietnam War period; and a number of contemporary images. In place of the project on the elegy, the Synthesis chapter offers a new project, "Men and Women on Love: Some Poems." This project—like the present edition as a whole—was designed to be appealing to students, not only because it speaks to their interests, but also because the texts selected show how different people speak to and with others through the practice of writing.

We would like to thank our reviewers and other users of *Practice* for their helpful suggestions, in particular: Christine Bonnarigo, Pace University Westchester; Lurene Brooks, Golden West College; Flournoy Holland, University of Florida; Diane Le Blanc, University of Wyoming; Peggy Marron, University of Wyoming; Martin McKoski, University of Akron; Tracy T. Montgomery, Idaho State University; Martha Rainbolt, DePauw University; Doug Tedards, University of the Pacific; and Lisa Weston, California State University, Fresno.

As always, special thanks go to our colleagues and students at Brown University and Queens College of the City University of New York. Our experiences with them over three editions have taught us a lot about what our strengths and weaknesses are, which encouraged and enabled us to make the right changes this time. Indeed, one colleague, Janice Peritz of Queens College, had so many good ideas for revision that Scholes and Comley invited her to put them into *Practice*, and so to join RS and NRC as *Practice*'s "we."

Robert Scholes
Nancy R. Comley
Janice Peritz

About
THE PRACTICE
OF WRITING

This book is devoted to the practice of writing. It presents more opportunities for writing—"practices," as we call them—than anything else. The book also contains numerous "readings." This is so because we believe that, just as talking involves listening, and drawing involves looking, writing involves reading. The readings in this book are not meant to be put upon pedestals and admired, however admirable they may be. They are there to be worked with and responded to— in writing. They are there to be transformed, imitated, analyzed, argued with, and incorporated into new writing by the students who use this book.

Actually, there is more material here than anyone could possibly use in a single quarter or semester. The reason for this abundance is to provide instructors with options, choices, flexibility. After the first chapter, which is introductory, the writing opportunities move from the personal to the more impersonal and academic. The weight of the book, however, falls upon the more academic or critical kinds of writings, the forms and processes required for college courses. Thus, the last four chapters emphasize the kinds of analysis, argumentation, and synthesis required in research papers.

Obviously, we think that work in all the forms of writing is useful, or we would not have included them all in the book. But we understand also that there are many reasons why an instructor may wish to touch only lightly on the materials in Parts Two and Three, in order to concentrate heavily on Part Four. The book is designed to allow for this emphasis. There is, in fact, more material in every part than would be needed if all the parts were emphasized equally. The instructor will find that this text will support any emphasis that he or she chooses to make, though we have anticipated an emphasis on analysis, argument, and synthesis, providing the greatest depth in those chapters.

Within each chapter we present a particular form of writing, beginning with the most basic kinds of practice and moving toward more extended and demanding assignments. Using the chapter introduction, the first reading/ practice set, and one further set will allow an instructor to treat a particular chapter without lingering over it for too long; there is enough variety so that the second assignment can be chosen to suit the interests and capabilities of a given class.

However, this book also lends itself to a portfolio approach to the teaching of writing. After doing a number of different practices in a chapter or unit, the student writer might choose one to develop, revise, and edit as a paper for public presentation and evaluation.

Although we think the order in which we present the forms of writing in this book makes sense, we have tried not to be dogmatic. The forms of writing may in fact be introduced in any order, so long as the arrangement leads to synthesis at the end. In the chapter on synthesis, we have provided sufficient material so that library research is not necessary, but many of the suggested assignments there can be expanded and enriched by library work if the instructor desires it.

It is our conviction that writing is a way of thinking and that thinking is a pleasurable activity. Have fun.

C O N T E N T S

Preface   ix
About The Practice of Writing   xiii

PART ONE
Writing as a Human Act   1

1. PRACTICING WRITING   3
Situation, Form, Process

Communication and Language   3
Speaking and Writing   4
Practice: An Experience in Your Life   5
The Writing Situation   6
The Forms of Writing   7
Reading and Practice   11
Practice and Confidence   12
The Act of Writing: Experimenting, Drafting, Revising   13
The Writer as Role-Player   17

PART TWO
Writer-oriented Forms:
Discourse and the Self   19

2. EXPRESSION   21
Your Self as Subject

Reading: The Open-ended Writing Process   22
   Peter Elbow, from *Writing with Power*   22
Practice: Open-ended Writing   23

Reading: Expression through Association   23
  W. H. Gass, from *On Being Blue*   23

Practice: On Being ——————   24

Reading and Practice: Self-Expression through Art   25
  Edvard Munch, "The Cry"   26
  Erich Heckel, "Head of Girl"   27
  Wood Figure, Zaire   28

Reading: Two Expressions of Mood   29
  James Wright, "Lying in a Hammock at William Duffy's Farm in Pine Island, Minnesota"   29
  Sylvia Plath, from *The Bell Jar*   29

Practice: Mood in a Place   30

Reading: Ideas about the Telephone   31
  Ellen Goodman, from a newspaper column   31
  Federico Fellini, from *Fellini on Fellini*   32
  Roland Barthes, from *A Lover's Discourse*   33

Practice: Ideas about a Common Object   34

3. REFLECTION   35

Your Self as Object

Reading: Your Own Expressive Writing   36

Practice: Reflection as Revision   36

Reading: School Days Revisited   37
  Louise De Salvo, from "A Portrait of the *Puttana* as a Middle-Aged Woolf Scholar"   37
  Russell Baker, from *Growing Up*   40

Practice: Reflection on Your School Days   43

Reading: Looking at Pictures   43
  Gary Snyder, "Looking at Pictures to Be Put Away"   43
  Sharon Olds, "I Go Back to May 1937"   44
  Roland Barthes, "Looking for My Mother"   44

Practice: Reflecting on a Photograph   46

Reading: From Thing to Thought   47
  Isak Dinesen, "The Iguana"   47

Practice: Reflecting on Experience   48

Reading: From Experience to Thought   49
  Brent Staples, "Just Walk on By: A Black Man Ponders His Power to Alter Public Space"   49

Practice: Reflecting on Your Self Perceived   53

PART THREE
Reader-oriented Forms: Discourse and Power 55

4. DIRECTION 57
Guiding Your Reader

Practice: How to Make or Do Something   59

Reading: The Art of Eating Spaghetti   60

Practice: The Art of Eating _____   60

Reading: Direction through the Ages: How to Conduct Yourself   60
   Andreas Capellanus, from *The Art of Courtly Love*   61
   Christine de Pizan, from *The Mirror of Honor*   62
   Dr. John Gregory, from *A Father's Legacy to His Daughters*   63
   Constance Cary Harrison, from *The Well-Bred Girl in Society*   63
   Letitia Baldrige, from *Amy Vanderbilt's Everyday Etiquette*   64

Practice: How to Conduct Yourself   66

Reading: Indirection   66
   Fran Lebowitz, "How to Be a Directory Assistance Operator:
      A Manual"   66

Practice: How to Be a _____: A Manual   69

5. PERSUASION 70
Moving Your Reader

Reading: Persuasion in Advertising   71
   Fly-Tox Advertisement, 1926   71

Practice: The Ghastly Resort Hotel   74

Reading: Reaching a Different Audience   75

Practice: Changing the Persuasive Pattern   75

Reading: Political Persuasion   77
   Bill Clinton, "Inaugural Address"   77

Practice: An Enemy of the People   81

Practice: The Difficult Campaign Speech   82

Reading: The Job Letter and Résumé   83

Practice: The Job Letter   87

PART FOUR
Topic-oriented Forms: Discourse and Knowledge 91

6. NARRATION 93
Organizing Time

Reading and Practice 94
Willa Cather, "A Shooting" (from *O Pioneers!*) 95
Richard Wright, from "The Man Who Lived Underground" 96
Jamaica Kincaid, "The Tourist's Arrival" (from *A Small Place*) 98
Louise Erdrich, "Cousin Mary" (from *The Beet Queen*) 99
James Joyce, "The End of Molly's Soliloquy" (from *Ulysses*) 101

Reading and Practice: The Life of Stephen Crane 102

Practice: The Life of Yourself 109

Reading: Narrating an Event 110
Gabriel García Márquez, "A Very Old Man with Enormous Wings" 110

Practice: Suppose a ——————— Appeared in Your
Neighborhood 116

7. DESCRIPTION 117
Organizing Space

Reading: Point of View in Description 118
Marilynne Robinson, "A Kitchen" (from *Housekeeping*) 119
James Joyce, "A Restaurant" (from *Ulysses*) 119
Kate Simon, "A Street" (from *Bronx Primitive*) 120
M. Scott Momaday, "An Arbor" (from *The Way to Rainy Mountain*) 120

Practice: Organizing a Space 121

Reading: A Place with a History 121
Nikki Giovanni, from "400 Mulvaney Street" 122

Practice: Describing a Place with a History 126

Reading: Hogarth's "Noon" Described 127

Practice: Describing a Hogarth Street Scene 129

Reading: A Critic Describes a Face 131
Graham McCann, from *Marilyn Monroe* 131

Practice: Describing a Famous Face 132

Reading: "La Gioconda" 133
Walter Pater, from *The Renaissance* 134

Practice: "Il Giocondo" 134

8. CLASSIFICATION 136
Organizing Data

Reading: Social Groups in a Town 138
  Vance Packard, from *A Nation of Strangers* 138

Practice: Social Categories in an Institution 139

Practice: Social Types in a Particular Place 140

Reading: The Student Body 140
  Robert and Helen Lynd, from *Middletown* 141

Practice: Your Student Body 143

Reading: Classifying Commercials 144
  John W. Wright, from "TV Commercials That Move the
    Merchandise" 144

Practice: The Class of Full-Page Ads 148

Reading: Classifying Forms of Power 149
  Bertrand Russell, from *Power* 150

Practice: Power in an Institution You Know 151

Practice: From Abstract to Concrete 152

9. ANALYSIS 153
Taking Things Apart

Reading: Comparison and Contrast 154
  Stephen Crane, "The Last of the Mohicans" 154

Practice: Analysis of a Comparative Analysis 156

Practice: Fiction and Experience 156

Reading and Practice: Two Poets and a Painting 157
  W. H. Auden, "Musée des Beaux Arts" 160
  William Carlos Williams, "Landscape with the Fall of Icarus" 160

Reading: Analyzing an Advertisement 161

Practice: Analyzing a Magazine Advertisement 163

Reading: A Critic Theorizes about Advertising 163
  John Berger, from *Ways of Seeing* 164

Practice: Analyzing Images of Women in Advertising 165

10. ARGUMENTATION 176
Presenting a Thesis

Reading: A Scientist Argues about Means and Ends 178
  Stephen Jay Gould, "Integrity and Mr. Rifkin" 179

Practice: Reconstructing, Summarizing, and Evaluating Gould's Argument   187

Reading: A Feminist Discusses Women and Names   188
   Dale Spender, from *Man Made Language*   188

Practice: Arguing about Men and Women   193

Reading: An Educator Considers Class Myths and Realities   193
   Gregory Mantsios, from "Class in America: Myths and Realities"   194

Practice: Arguing from Statistics—The Education, Employment, and Income of Women   199

Reading: Two Positions on Bilingual Education   210
   Diane Ravitch, from "Politicization of the Schools: The Case of Bilingual Education"   210
   Angelo Gonzalez, "Bilingualism Pro: The Key to Basic Skills"   216

Practice: Arguing a Hypothetical Case of Bilingualism   218

Reading: Two Essays on Punishment of Crimes   219
   Karl Menninger, "The Crime of Punishment"   220
   C. S. Lewis, "The Humanitarian Theory of Punishment"   226

Practice: Arguing a Hypothetical Case of Punishment or Treatment for a Convicted Criminal   233

Reading: A Critic Reflects on the Violence of Western Reason   234
   Jane Tompkins, "Fighting Words: Unlearning to Write the Critical Essay"   235

Practice: Is There a Better Way?   240

11. SYNTHESIS   242
Putting Things Together

Reading and Practice: How Should Photographs Be "Read"?   243
   Jean Mohr, "A Photo and Some Reactions," from *Another Way of Telling*   244
   Allan Sekula, from "On the Invention of Photographic Meaning"   246
   John Berger Reads a Photograph (from *Another Way of Telling*)   247
   John Berger on the Use of Photography (from *About Looking*)   249

Reading: Three Photographs in Context   250
   Gisèle Freund on Doisneau's Photograph (from *Photography & Society*)   250
   From an Interview with Robert Doisneau (in *Dialogue with Photography*)   251
   Photograph: Robert Doisneau, A Parisian Café   252
   From an Interview with Gordon Parks (in *The Photographs of Gordon Parks*)   254
   Photograph: Gordon Parks, American Gothic   256

Martin Bush on Gordon Parks (from *The Photographs of Gordon Parks*) 258

Eve Arnold on Her Work (from *The Unretouched Woman*) 259

Photograph: Eve Arnold, Marlene Dietrich 260

From an Interview with Eve Arnold (in *Master Photographers*) 261

Practice: Writing about Photographs 263

Three More Photographs by Doisneau, Parks, and Arnold 265

Robert Doisneau, Sidelong Glance 265

Gordon Parks, Muslim School Children 266

Eve Arnold, A Literacy Teacher in Abu Dhabi 267

Three Pictures from the Vietnam War Period 268

Associated Press, A Paratrooper Works to Save the Life of a Buddy 268

John Paul Filo, Student Killed by National Guardsmen, Kent State University, May 4, 1970 269

Huynh Cong (Nick) Ut, Children Fleeing a Napalm Strike, June 8, 1972 270

A Picture Album 271

André Kertész, Elizabeth and I 271

Dorothea Lange, Drought Refugees Hoping for Cotton Work 272

Russian and American Troops Meet at Torgau on the Elbe, April 27, 1945 273

Henri Cartier-Bresson, Athens 274

Automatic Reconnaissance Camera, Mirage Jet 275

W. Eugene Smith, Tomoko in the Bath 276

Charles Martin, Window Dressing 277

Reading and Practice: Working People 278

Research: The Interview 278

Studs Terkel, from *Working* 279

Suzanne Seed, from *Saturday's Child* 283

Colin Henfrey, from *Manscapes* 283

Barbara Ehrenreich, from "Is Success Dangerous to Your Health?" 284

From Interviews by Students at the University of Oklahoma 285

Reading: The Western: Theory and Practice 288

John Cawelti, from *The Six-Gun Mystique* 288

Stephen Crane, "The Bride Comes to Yellow Sky" 303

Stephen Crane, "The Blue Hotel" 312

Practice: Stephen Crane and the Western Formula 336

Practice: Crane: The Man and the Stories 336

Reading and Practice: Men and Women on Love: A Collection of Poems 337

"Sonnet 138," William Shakespeare 338

"To My Dear and Loving Husband," Anne Bradstreet 338

"To His Coy Mistress," Andrew Marvell 339

"A Song," Charlotte Lennox 340

"Love's Philosophy," Percy Bysshe Shelley 341

CONTENTS

"Sonnet 43," from *Sonnets from the Portuguese,* Elizabeth Barrett Browning 341

"When You Have Forgotten Sunday: The Love Story," Gwendolyn Brooks 342

"Love Poem," John Frederick Nims 342

"Living in Sin," Adrienne Rich 343

"Love Song: I and Thou," Alan Dugan 344

"Now Ain't That Love?," Carolyn M. Rodgers 345

"Unabashed," Marie Ponsot 345

Index 353

THE
PRACTICE
OF
WRITING

Fourth Edition

Writing as a Human Act

1. PRACTICING WRITING

1. PRACTICING WRITING

Situation, Form, Process

COMMUNICATION AND LANGUAGE

Hand most human beings a baby and they will make faces at it. Why do they do that? Why do human beings talk to cats and dogs and even to babies in language far more complicated than an animal or a human infant could possibly understand? The answer is simple. Human beings need to communicate, and they will speak to any creature that appears to listen. To communicate with a baby, an adult will often make a face that imitates the face the baby is making. Baby sticks tongue out—adult sticks tongue out. Adults mimic babies all the time. In this way (and others) babies learn to mimic adults. And from the first simple sentences children hear, they develop a grammar—they acquire a language.

An extraordinary thing, language, yet every human being can learn one. In learning a language we learn not only the language itself, but also two ways of using it. One way is public. We call it "speech." The other way is private. We call it "thought." With language we give shape and meaning to our world. Words let us name the things we experience, as well as describe these things in relation to each other and to ourselves. They also help us to remember things we no longer have before us, and even to think of things we have never seen: unicorns, the universe, God, woman, man. We see men and women of course, and this man and that woman, but we do not see "man" or "woman." Those words name classes or categories, what the philosophers call *universals*. Language gives them to us and we use them to think with. "All humans are mortal," we think, along with other things that do not trouble the minds of cats, dogs, or babies.

Learning a language gives us the power to think and to express our thoughts in speech. But human development does not end here, because, at a certain point in the history of human culture, speaking is inevitably extended to include writing. Anthropologists have found isolated tribes that seem to be on the other side of that great linguistic divide, but even these "primitives" use signs of all sorts to produce and maintain their civilization. And civilization, as Sigmund Freud reminded us, has its discontents. For many people, writing is one of them.

SPEAKING AND WRITING

What is writing? It is not simply frozen speech. If you tape record a message, it can be played when you are gone and the message will still be supported by your voice, your accents, your emphasis. But if you write the same message for others to receive, they will have to read it, which means they will have to speak it to themselves in their own voices though not in their own words. Will it really be the same message under these circum-stances? Can you see how problems might arise?

You have perhaps heard of the experiment involving a circle of people in a room. One person writes down a message and holds it, whispering the message to the person to the left. That person then repeats it to the next person, and so on around the room. When the message returns to the sender, it is compared to the written text. If the message is long enough and the number of people large enough, the message returned never coincides with the message sent. If, on the other hand, the written message itself were passed around the circle, it would obviously remain the same, although it would probably not mean exactly the same thing to each person who reads it. The importance of this will become apparent if we take that circle of people in the room and imagine it stretched out over time, spanning many genera-tions.

Imagine a document written down hundreds of years ago and carefully preserved because its message was felt to be of great importance. Imagine, as well, a story, equally important, but instead of being written down, passed on from parent to child over many generations. Most scholars would agree about the fate of these two messages as they moved through the generations to the present. The written document would remain the same in its form, but because the language in which it had been written was itself changing over the years, the document would become more and more difficult to understand. It would require interpretation, commentary—perhaps even translation, such as texts written in Old English now receive. The oral text, however, the story transmitted from parent to child, would be thought of as the same story—"My mother told me this when I was little, and now, my child, I am telling you the same story." But actually, little changes would have crept in with every telling because one must always use the language as it is at a given moment. In face-to-face communication, the speaker always wants to be understood and will make any changes that are necessary to ensure that the listener understands.

In face-to-face communication, we have the luxury of a present audience, a listener we can see and who encourages us to make our message immediately understandable. Written communication doesn't offer this luxury. Every writer is always writing for a reader who is some distance away in space and time. For the writer there are no friendly smiles, nods, "uh-huhs"—nor any helpful questions like, "Hey, wait a minute, I don't get that." Writers must always imagine their audience and try to predict how a future reader will respond to the words being set down on a page.

PRACTICE

An Experience in Your Life

A. Assume that you are in a small group of people that you have just gotten to know and like. There are only three or four of you sitting around, relaxed. Maybe it is late at night. Because you are all getting to know one another, you have been taking turns telling about a memorable experience in your life—one you remember because you felt some strong emotion at the time, such as joy, sadness, anger, fear, confusion, or excitement.

Set this down on paper exactly as you would tell it to the group. Try to capture your ordinary conversational style as well as you can. If you have access to a tape recorder, you might try speaking this narrative first and then writing down what you have recorded. If not, try to write it the way it *would* come out if you had recorded it.

B. After you complete the first part of this assignment, exchange stories with one of your classmates. As you read your classmate's story, make notes of those parts that are unclear to you, or of people or events in the story that you'd like to know more about. For example, is it clear how the writer felt about the experience? If you had been present during the telling of the story, you could have asked, or you could have read his or her facial expressions and known something of what the speaker felt at the time.

You should then exchange these notes and discuss each other's stories, making more notes of what needs more development in your story and of what might be cut out. You should then revise your story, making sure that your written words will show your reader why this experience was memorable for you.

THE WRITING SITUATION

Every act of communication involves a sender who initiates a message and a receiver who interprets it: an adult making faces and a baby watching, a speaker telling a story and a listener paying attention, a writer explaining communication and a reader deciphering symbols on a page. But the elements that make up the situation in which communication takes place can be specified even further. All writing situations, for example, may be described by a simple diagram:

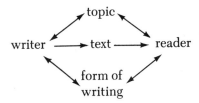

The central level of the diagram (writer → text → reader) describes the basic process of written communication. As the arrows indicate, the writer produces a written message (the *text*) that is transmitted to the reader. The reader reads it, interprets it, and understands it, thus completing the process. In order for this to happen, however, the writer and reader must share two kinds of knowledge, indicated on the diagram by the upper and lower terms (*topic* and *form of writing*). Both of these terms are connected to the writer and reader by double-ended arrows, indicating that this knowledge is shared by writer and reader from the beginning.

First of all, writer and reader must share some knowledge of the topic under discussion—the subject of the text—in order to communicate about it. A student's response to an essay question will be meaningless if the student has no familiarity with the subject of the question. A simple report of a football game will be incomprehensible to someone who has had absolutely no experience of football, who has never heard of a quarterback or a tackle or a scrimmage. Some knowledge of the topic—and of what has been communicated about that topic in the past—is essential if writer and reader are to complete the communication process.

Also essential is a shared knowledge of what we are calling a *form of writing*. At a fundamental level this means that reader and writer must be literate in the same language. If we write in Greek, you must read Greek to understand us. If we use a period, you must understand what such a symbolic marking may indicate.

At another level, a shared understanding of forms means something more immediately relevant to the practice of writing. Every writing task is done within a framework of expectations about the kind of words that will be used, the kinds of sentence structures that are appropriate, and the sort of organization that will make communication most effective. In other words, given a particular relationship between a writer and the intended reader and a particular topic with a history of its own, of which the participants inevitably have some awareness, the communication that results is likely to take a certain form—to have features in common with other communications occurring in similar circumstances. This helps to explain why, say, a letter from a seller to a prospective buyer sounds so unlike a funeral oration or an opinion of the Supreme Court, while a news article differs greatly from all three—and why we are able to make predictions about how any of these will sound before we have read them. Understanding the requirements of a writing situation allows us to choose a form appropriate to the particular writing task. In this book, our purpose is to help you gain such an understanding as well as to provide instruction and practice in the forms of writing that are most important for success in college and for participation in modern society.

THE FORMS OF WRITING

Although the number of possible writing situations is potentially infinite, they can, in fact, be reduced to a relatively small number that students of writing should actually practice. Let's look again at our diagram of the writing situation:

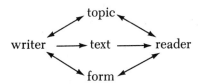

There are five units or elements in the diagram. The *text*, of course, is what the writer is going to produce. It is the thing all the fuss is about: the writing itself. The *form* is the set of conventional features that will guide the writer in writing and the reader in reading the text. In this book we are suggesting the study of ten basic forms of writing. These ten forms fall into three categories, oriented to the other three elements of the writing situation, giving us three types of form: those oriented to the writer, those oriented to the reader, and those oriented to the topic.

In actuality these ten forms are frequently mixed, but, for purposes of understanding and practice, it helps to isolate them. In this way we can concentrate on the prominent features of each form. It is our belief that a well-rounded writer should be capable of working in a range of forms, and that often a skill that is central in one form will prove useful in a form that emphasizes an entirely different aspect of writing.

Writer-oriented Forms

By *writer-oriented forms* we mean forms of writing in which the writer is the center of attention. These personal forms are the furthest removed from the kind of writing most often required in academic situations. They need feeling and thought, but they do not require research, documentation, or a structure of logical argument. If your most urgent need is to learn how to produce an acceptable term paper, it is quite proper to put most of your energy into learning other forms. But writing is not a mechanical process and you are not a machine. Writing is a way of thinking as well as a means of communication, and one of the things it can be used to think about is the self. Some writing must be impersonal. Some writing tasks demand that your personal feelings and values be restrained, if not suppressed. This demand is easier to negotiate if you know what counts as a personal form of writing—and if you understand what your feelings and values are.

We can readily recognize two main forms of writing that are writer-oriented: *expression* and *reflection*.

Expression.   In this form, the writer is most concerned with expressing certain feelings or thoughts for the sheer satisfaction of doing so. In a way, this is an emotionally self-centered form, an elaboration of such fundamental expressive gestures as a cry of rage or pain, a groan or sigh of depression, an "mmm" or "ah" of satisfaction. In writing expressively, we try to move from the basic feeling to some elaboration, some articulation of it in words. Putting things into words can make us feel better and help us to understand ourselves. Practice in expressive writing can also give our feelings and thoughts a chance to develop.

Reflection.   Reflection is quite different from expression. If you stand in front of a mirror your image will be doubled. You will be present in the flesh and your reflected image will be present also. In reflective writing, the writer's self is doubled. We don't simply write *from* ourselves, as in expression; we also write *about* ourselves. To do this we must get some distance from ourselves, some perspective. One way to do this is to look back—that is, our present, writing self looks back upon some previous self and measures, in some way, the distance between *then* and *now*. Reflection allows us to discover significance in the events of our own lives.

8

Reader-oriented Forms

All writing must be concerned with its reader. For over two thousand years, teachers of rhetoric have been admonishing their students: "Know your audience; imagine how they will respond to your words." This lesson is still valuable. The forms of writing that are oriented to the reader give us a chance to practice the principle of paying attention to the reader. Once this becomes a habit, it can help us in any writing situation.

There are two major types of reader-oriented writing: *direction* and *persuasion*.

Direction.   We are all familiar with directions. We find them in cookbooks, textbooks, exercise manuals, and all sorts of do-it-yourself pamphlets and self-help books.

Most directive writing must do two simple things: provide information and arrange that information in the most useful and comprehensible order. The lessons learned from practicing directive writing are simple but powerful: how to be concerned for the reader, and how to organize a process in time so that the procedures presented—the directions—can be followed with a minimum of confusion and complaint.

Persuasion.   In persuasion, too, the reader is the prime consideration, but instead of giving directions for something the reader is assumed to want already, persuasive writing is designed to create a want or motivate an action. The politician who wants your vote and the advertiser who wants your money are most likely to use persuasive techniques, but persuasion is not entirely absent from the writing of scientists and philosophers. Persuasion relies heavily on appeals to emotion. It often uses the same linguistic resources as poetry to achieve its end: vivid images, careful control of connotations, repetition, rhythm, even rhyme. In our society, highly persuasive writing is so frequently encountered and so skillfully deployed that every citizen should understand it thoroughly, if only to avoid being victimized by it.

Topic-oriented Forms

Most academic situations call for topic-oriented forms of writing, where the personality of the writer is not a central concern and few direct appeals to the reader are made. Instead, the topic itself is examined and presented to the reader for the sake of informing or for thoughtful consideration. The careful reporting of observations, the clear organization of a body of knowledge, the reasoned examination of alternatives are the virtues of topic-oriented writing, and skill in using these forms is one of the distinguishing marks of an educated person.

The six major types of topic-oriented writing are *narration*, *description*, *classification*, *analysis*, *argumentation*, and *synthesis*.

Narration.   A narrative is a report on an event, a happening that unfolds in time. Narration is a form of writing shared by the creative writer, who invents the events to be narrated, and the reporter or researcher who seeks to record or recover some actual sequence of events. In this book, we are not concerned with the art of writing fictional narratives, but with narration as a form of reporting observation or research. From practice in narration we learn to manage time—to organize language so as to capture events and display them clearly with the emphasis falling where we want it to. In actual writing, narration is often blended with other forms; for example, a story may be told to illustrate a point in an argument. But narration is sufficiently distinct as a form to be studied in itself.

Description.   In description, we take a scene or an object and capture it in language. That is, we organize the details of the object or scene we wish to describe in the way that will most effectively convey the sensual image. Just as work in narration is practice in the organization of *time* in writing, work in description is practice in the organization of *space*. This is important not only because description is used in other forms of writing, but because what is being learned from practicing narration and description is organization itself. In the topic-oriented forms, organization is crucial. It is a skill that must be learned.

Classification.   Classification is another form that puts a premium on organization. In classification, we organize our material not by time or space, but by a principle of logic: all things with these features belong in this category, and this category is a subcategory of this larger class of things. In a form like classification, we can see just how closely writing and thinking are related. Although we almost never encounter an entire piece of writing that consists of nothing but classification, we encounter very little writing in the academic disciplines that does not depend upon some system of classifying the material under discussion.

Analysis.   Analysis is both a way of observing and a way of writing about what we have observed. In particular, it involves taking things apart and seeing how the parts are related, so as to understand how the object of analysis *works*. This taking apart, of course, is done mentally, not physically. The tools of analysis are comparing and contrasting, connecting and distinguishing, and the discovery of causes and effects. When the results of analysis are organized to make and support a thesis, analysis moves toward argument.

Argumentation.   Argumentation differs from persuasion by being more rational. It is aimed at clarifying a topic rather than at moving a reader. Its function is to make the reader *see* things in a particular way rather than to make the reader *do* something. Argumentation is especially important for college students because it demonstrates the principles of organization that inform most academic writing: the formulation of a thesis, the presentation of evidence to support and develop the thesis, and the deployment of specific ways of reasoning such as the logic of cause and effect. In the humanities, the social sciences, and the natural sciences, these organizing principles are so important that they often inform research as well as writing. In consequence, written research often relies on argumentation for its skeletal structure, even though it is fleshed out with features drawn from the other forms of writing.

Synthesis. Synthesis—which means "putting together"—is the fullest and most complete kind of academic writing. In synthesis, the writer uses the data provided by research and analysis to formulate and explore a hypothesis about some complex body of material. The different academic subjects are concerned with the study of very different kinds of material, and they may present their results in different manners (using mathematical symbols, pictures, charts, graphs, and other modes of presentation), but the ultimate goal of all academic research projects is the production of a synthetic text: a text that interweaves various forms of writing to make sense of the materials studied.

READING AND PRACTICE

These, then, are the forms that one must understand in order to become a successful writer. But how does one know when a particular form is appropriate, and how does one achieve the necessary proficiency in these forms? The most effective way is through reading and practice.

Before every act of writing comes a reading. First, we must "read" the writing situation. (We are thinking here of the way a quarterback "reads" the opposing defense, or how a doctor "reads" a patient's symptoms.) Reading in this way is a means of diagnosing what will be required, of determining the course our writing should take: What will my reader know about the topic, and what will be my reader's attitude? What can I, as a writer, discover about the topic? What form of writing will be suitable, given the topic itself, my particular concerns, and the expectations of my reader? Reading the writing situation will mean finding answers to questions like these.

As these questions suggest, reading the situation effectively will generally require other kinds of reading as well. Of course, there is always the possibility of researching the topic in some way; as suggested earlier, you cannot write well on a subject you know nothing about. Just as important, though, is reading in order to become familiar with how people usually write about a topic, to discover the kind of writing a particular task requires, to understand the form that will be expected in the given situation.

Writing is like entering a conversation that is already going on before you start to speak. If you want readers to appreciate what you have to say, then you must demonstrate your understanding of the appropriate conventions.

Such conventions begin with matters like ending a sentence with a period and move through the proper method of documenting sources for a term paper or the differences between reporting on a sports event for a newspaper column and reporting on a similar event for a sociological study. How do you learn such forms? Babies learn the conventions of speech by observing and imitating the activities of adults; writers learn the conventions of a particular writing situation by reading and understanding how others have successfully approached the task.

Think for a moment about the many conventions of writing you already know. Even something as simple as a note to a friend involves a fairly complicated set of conventions, but such conventions more than likely come easily to you because you are familiar with the forms of writing such a situation requires—you have read many similar notes written by others and have had many occasions to write notes yourself. But imagine being faced with writing a different kind of note: on your first day of a new job, your boss asks you to compose a memo to be circulated among the staff. Even if you've been given the topic and told fairly specifically what should be said, the task will pose significant problems until you have a sense of the conventions that you are expected to follow. The obvious solution to these problems will be to check the files for examples of how memos have been written in the past. Then, with the benefit of reading, imitation, and practice, writing a memo will begin to come as naturally to you as writing an informal note, so much so that you may soon find yourself modifying the received form, trying to discover a more effective means of communication for yourself.

In any field, we learn the conventions of particular forms of writing by reading and practicing those forms. This does not mean that all writing is imitation, but to achieve originality we must read the work of our predecessors. Originality, then, begins as imitation and moves on to recombination, finally emerging as something new and different enough to be called original. Those who do not read and practice are condemned to repeat the work of those that they have not read, to reinvent the wheel when what is needed is the invention of the axle, the bearing, or the differential gear.

PRACTICE AND CONFIDENCE

In this book we will offer you some help in understanding what is required in different writing situations, we will provide examples of the various forms of writing for you to read, and, most important, we will give you a chance to practice these forms for yourself. But you must remember, practicing writing is not like football practice, where everybody goes out together with a lot of group support and encouragement. It is more like practicing tennis, where you bang a ball against a wall for hours, or practicing the guitar or the piano, where you make no progress from one lesson to the next if you don't put in time alone playing the instrument. Only you can do it. You should also remember that in your writing class all your writing is practicing. You are trying things out, seeing where your strengths are, finding out what you need to work on so that in time you can gain confidence in your writing skills.

Such confidence is essential, for every writing task brings with it a certain amount of anxiety. Confronted with a blank piece of paper and the prospect of setting down a part of oneself for others to read, perhaps to reject, and certainly to judge, one is bound to feel at least some slight nervousness. This is the same kind of nervousness that every performer feels: the actress before going on stage, the football player before the kickoff, the politician before a speech. Even the best performers feel it, and most of them say that they need it and use it. With the confidence that comes from understanding and practice, writers, like performers, can convert their nervousness into excellence in the performance itself.

As writers know, however, this nervousness can also cause one to freeze up, to lose concentration, to go blank, particularly when the audience one writes for is made up of strangers. Such debilitating fear is really a fear of the end of writing, of being read and evaluated, but it creeps back to inhibit the beginning. Inexperienced writers sometimes assume that writing works this way: First you have an idea; then you put it down on paper. But this is not the case with good writing. Writing is not only a tool for communication, for transmitting ideas or transcribing what has already been thought: It is itself a way of thinking, of developing ideas, trying them out, arranging them, testing them. It is a way of separating your thoughts from yourself—making them take a visible form outside your mind—so that you can think about them and improve them. It is, in fact, always practice, and realizing this can make you a stronger, more confident writer.

THE ACT OF WRITING: EXPERIMENTING, DRAFTING, REVISING

There is no one way to write, no magic process guaranteed to produce a perfect piece of writing if followed step by step. Not all writers work in the same way, and even an individual writer approaches different tasks in different ways, depending on his or her writing habits and on the writing situation. But experienced writers can point to particular moves that generally occur in the act of writing, even though these moves may be combined in different ways. In addition to the basic psychomotor act of writing—the way the hand, eye, and brain work so that we can put words on paper—we can distinguish three moves in the practice of writing: experimenting, drafting, and revising. These moves are not isolated states in a strict sequence, since writing is a complex, interwoven process like a hooked rug, not a set of distinct compartments like a freight train. But each of these moves does represent a particular kind of work that writers do.

Experimenting

Your most productive way of beginning almost any writing task will be to try out and test your thoughts on paper without the pressure of structuring your expression into its final form. (Even a thank-you note to Aunt Bessie can be less difficult if you simply jot down various things you might say *before* you write "Dear Aunt Bessie.") If you consider your first words on paper as something tentative, as a way of starting to think rather than as a monument to perfected thought, you will be able to explore whatever subject you approach more deeply and fully, and you will go a long way toward taking the initial nervousness out of writing. Such experimenting is your chance to practice what you have to say before you begin to worry about how your audience will judge the eventual form of your work.

This is not to say that experimenting doesn't involve some sense of form and audience. Indeed, all writers begin by considering these two aspects of the writing situation along with their topic as they go about preparing to compose a text.

A writer must begin, of course, by choosing a subject to write about. Sometimes your choices will be fairly narrow, sometimes seemingly infinite; but in any case it will be important to give some thought to your possibilities. This may mean making a list of potential subjects, or experimenting with the sort of open-ended writing that will be discussed in Chapter 2. However you proceed, your purpose is to discover a focus that will allow you to work productively. Once you have chosen a focus, you may need to do some research—either by reading or by firsthand observation—and to take notes about what you learn; this may lead you to refocus your work or to refine your initial approach. Only rarely will a fully realized topic come immediately to mind: You can only know what will work by trying things out, by testing your thoughts in writing.

During this process of experimenting, you will need to give some attention to the possible forms your writing will take and what those forms will require. The practice you do throughout this course will help you learn more about the features of various forms of writing, and this understanding will, in turn, help you recognize the sort of experimenting that will be most useful for a particular assignment. If you're preparing to write a narrative, for example, your experimenting may involve a chronological outline of a sequence of actions: First this happened, then this happened, then this happened, etc. You may also give yourself a chance to discover and develop the significant details that will make your narration more than a shorthand reporting of events. Classification, on the other hand, will require that you spend some time describing the important features or characteristics of the objects you wish to classify. Then, by listing similarities and differences among these objects, you can begin to determine categories or classes into which the objects can be placed; writing out statements to see the kind of information you can squeeze from one set of classes may lead you to try another set of classes, then another, that will provide increasingly useful information about the objects themselves. For an argument you will want to define a tentative thesis—a position on a particular issue—and then, perhaps, to test your thesis by listing all the evidence you can come up with to support that thesis, as well as the evidence that might be used against it. Then you can go on to develop your evidence in more detail, to find the information that will make your evidence most convincing, maybe even to modify your thesis according to available evidence. Eventually, you will need to rank your evidence and to decide the most effective way of ordering that evidence as you structure your full argument.

As you try out and test your ideas within the conventions of particular forms, you will also need to take account of your eventual audience: What will they need to know? What are their likely preconceptions about this topic? Will they expect my writing to take a particular form? How can I interest them in what I have to say? Your answers to questions like these will be important in determining the choices you make during the writing process.

Experimenting, then, is essential to the practice of writing. Much of it will take place before drafting; but even as you write your first draft, you may find yourself jotting down ideas to use later or stopping to explore ways of working through a difficult section. And, of course, some experimenting may be done in your head. However, capturing those experiments on paper gives you a way of working through—rather than worrying about—the problem of getting started. It is natural to want to put off the anxiety of drafting; experimenting lets you do so productively.

Drafting

Drafting is the point at which you begin to put your ideas in some kind of order and to envision a potential shape for the work you will produce: a beginning, a middle, and an end. Before they begin drafting, some writers make an outline to remind themselves of how they wish to order their ideas. Such an outline is usually quite rough and may be frequently rearranged and amended during the drafting process. Making an extensive formal outline before drafting is difficult because, as with experimenting, much of what you will say will be discovered during the act of writing and not beforehand. The process of putting words on paper is a process of thinking in which you should frequently look back at what you have written to see if what you are about to write will follow logically from what you wrote earlier. Pausing and rereading at frequent intervals will not cause you to forget the point you wanted to make; such pauses can spark new ideas for developing your point more effectively. Often, such ideas will not relate to the section you are working on, so you should jot them in the margin or on your outline to return to at the appropriate time. Remember that the first draft is still an experiment and new discoveries can still be made.

If you are writing a fairly long paper, you may, after a few pages of writing, want to pause and outline what you've written to see more clearly what points you have made and whether you have left anything out or are repeating yourself. Then continue on toward your proposed destination, and when you think you have finished your first draft, stop. You are now ready to begin revising.

Revising

Imagine a speaker halfway through a political talk stopping and saying, "Actually, I've begun this all wrong. Now I see what I really want to say. Forget what you've just heard. I'm going to start over." Ridiculous, is it not? Or imagine a football team watching movies of their last game and one of them saying, "I missed a block on that last play; run it again and I'll do it right this time." Impossible! But in writing this is exactly what we do all the time. We run the instant replay and correct our mistakes—not only the mistakes in execution, such as spelling or punctuation, but also the mistakes in conception. That is, if we see that one play isn't working, we can call another play entirely. Think what a tremendous advantage that would give a quarterback. It is an advantage we can all have if we *revise and rewrite*. If you are the sort of writer who never revises, who never writes a second draft, who thinks of every word as a finished product, you are a prime candidate for writer's block. You may also be doomed to remain at a superficial level of understanding about your subject. To refuse revision is to refuse thought itself.

The professional writer's secret is revision and revision and revision. Some of the greatest writers—poets, essayists, scholars—have begun their work with ordinary thoughts in sloppy language and refined it only through numerous revisions. Revision comes not only when a draft is complete, but at every stage of writing. Whenever you put the work down for a walk around the room or a trip down the hall, and especially when you are away from it for any length of time, you should reread it when you pick it up and make revisions where they are needed.

What guides you in revising? How can you tell when changes are necessary and what sort of changes must be made? This requires critical perspective. You must try to see your writing in terms of the form you are trying to achieve. If it is an argument, is it clear, honest, well-reasoned? Does it need more evidence? Should you concede something or change your thesis? If it is a description, have you emphasized the right things, found the right words for them, put them in the right order?

You must also try to get outside of yourself and see things from another perspective, as you would in writing a reflective essay. Certain kinds of practice can help you achieve this critical distance. In some situations, particularly a writing class, you may very well have an opportunity to critique the drafts of other writers, as well as to consider revisions of your own drafts based on the comments you receive from your peers. You may also be given a chance to make revisions based on the comments of your instructor. You can learn a great deal from such opportunities. First, as a reader, you must articulate why you do or do not find certain aspects of someone else's draft effective; if you take your role as a reader/critic seriously, you can develop critical powers that you can then transfer to your own work. In addition, the feedback you receive from other readers of your drafts can make you more aware of the needs of an audience of strangers. This awareness can lead you to imagine more clearly how those strangers, your readers, will react to a particular piece of writing. What will they find confusing or distracting in this work? If you can find the problems, you can fix them.

The last act of rewriting must be proofreading, a check for mechanical errors in spelling and punctuation. Your reader can accept last-minute corrections better than outright errors and will be grateful to you for taking the trouble to correct the errors. Keep that stranger grateful if you can.

THE WRITER AS ROLE-PLAYER

As we have emphasized, confidence in yourself as a writer can come from thinking of your work as practice: first, from using your writing class as an opportunity to practice different kinds of writing tasks, and second, from realizing that the act of writing always allows you the opportunity to practice what you have to say before you present it to an audience of strangers.

Finally, we must consider another aspect of the writing situation, one that especially pertains to confidence: the notion of the writer as an actor.

The existentialist philosopher Jean-Paul Sartre once observed that a waiter in a café was handling the most difficult part of his job—the strain of being shouted at, hurried, always referred to as *garçon* ("boy")—by a simple but beautiful trick. He was *imagining* that he was a waiter in a café. Instead of presenting his real, vulnerable self to the abuse of customers and boss, he was acting out the role of waiter. He put the *role* of waiter between his actual self and his function as waiter. This enabled him to perform the job with a high degree of skill, without the anxiety of feeling that his real self was always on display.

Writers can learn a lesson from this. Even in writing tasks that involve our real selves—such as composing an application for a job we really desire—we may function better, may represent ourselves better, if we accept the task as a role to play, rather than if we conceive of the situation as bringing our true selves forward for judgment and criticism.

You don't need any special training for role-playing, because you do it all the time. In a single day, you may play the role of attentive student in the classroom, irate driver in a traffic jam, affectionate child at home, romantic lover with a special friend. You move in and out of these roles almost unconsciously, and this skill you have in social situations can be transferred to writing situations.

When the idea of the writer as role-player is combined with the idea that the reader must be imagined by the writer, the stage is set for a certain kind of practice. By imagining yourself in a variety of situations, addressing a variety of readers, you can in fact increase the range of your imaginative skill. You can become a better actor as a writer. This text will provide opportunities for this sort of practice.

Writer-oriented Forms: Discourse and the Self

2. EXPRESSION

3. REFLECTION

2. EXPRESSION

Your Self as Subject

In a sense, all writing is expressive. At some level, we express ourselves in every act of writing, even if it is only by writing carelessly because we are not interested in the assigned topic. But in another sense, writing is never completely expressive, because its rules and practices are part of a social system over which we have little control. In writing, we can only say what the system of writing will let us say.

Whether or not you have thought about the problem in exactly this way, you have probably encountered it. Because modern life is so complicated, there are many barriers to full expression. We all feel a kind of censorship that prevents us from expressing things that might expose our weaknesses or show us to be different from our fellows, from leaving a durable record that may say more about ourselves than we had meant to say. We may also have trouble expressing ourselves because our language is full of ready-made expressions, clichés that can falsify and standardize whatever may be unique in our unshaped thoughts and feelings. This mixture of feelings—fear of being misunderstood and fear of being understood too well—is a major part of the anxiety about writing that most of us have.

Practice in expression is designed to ease both aspects of the writer's anxiety and to provide opportunities for thoughts to grow and deepen. Freedom of expression is particularly important, because it is what makes the activity of experimenting so productive, allowing writers to explore what is in their minds as elaborately or outrageously as they wish without holding back for fear something is "wrong" or not within acceptable social limits. Eventually, of course, the limits must be considered. Writers must become more self-critical and disciplined and should work to refine the discoveries of expression within the constraints imposed by the writing situation. Such discipline, however, is not the first concern of expression.

Thus, the first writing opportunities that follow here are simply chances for you to write for yourself, to get started, to stretch your possibilities before you think about presenting your thoughts and feelings to anyone else. The forms of practice presented later in this chapter will begin to ask for a more public kind of expression, in which you must consider the problem of expressing *your* self *to* some other self. The purpose of expression, after all, is to broaden your powers of communication.

READING

The Open-ended Writing Process

Here is some good advice from an expert on how to get started in expressing yourself.

Peter Elbow, from *Writing with Power*

The open-ended writing process is ideal for the situation where you 1 sense you have something to write but you don't quite know what. Just start writing about anything at all. If you have special trouble with that first moment of writing—that confrontation with a blank page—ask yourself what you *don't* want to write about and start writing about it before you have a chance to resist. First thoughts. They are very likely to lead you to what you are needing to write.

Keep writing for at least ten or twenty or thirty minutes, depending 2 on how much material and energy you come up with. You have to write long enough to get tired and get past what's on the top of your mind. But not so long that you start pausing in the midst of your writing.

Then stop, sit back, be quiet, and bring all that writing to a point. 3 That is, by reading back or just thinking back over it, find the center or focus or point of those words and write it down in a sentence. This may mean different things: you can find the main idea that is there; or the new idea that is trying to be there; or the imaginative focus or center of gravity—an image or object or feeling; or perhaps some brand new thing occurs to you now as very important—it may even seem un-related to what you wrote, but it comes to you now as a result of having done that burst of writing. Try to stand out of the way and let the center or focus itself decide to come forward. In any event don't worry

22

about it. Choose or invent something for your focus, and then go on. The only requirement is that it be a single thing. Skip a few lines and write it down. Underline it or put a box around it so you can easily find it later. (Some people find it helpful to let themselves write down two or three focusing sentences.)

PRACTICE

Open-ended Writing

Start writing, following Elbow's advice as closely as you can. That is, write as he suggests you do, read your writing, and find your point or focus. That's all you have to do. Save this material, however, for you may return to it later in the course.

READING

Expression through Association

Here is the opening of a book on blueness and blue things by a philosopher who is also a fiction writer (or vice versa). You may find it difficult to follow every mention of blue as you read, but you can't help but get the idea. The piece is simply a list of things that are blue or that can have the word *blue* applied to them. You may be surprised by some, feel a shock of recognition at others, and find some just too tricky to decipher. As you read, just try to follow along, noting how the word *blue* goes with everything mentioned.

W. H. Gass, from *On Being Blue*

Blue pencils, blue noses, blue movies, laws, blue legs and stockings, the language of birds, bees, and flowers as sung by longshoremen, that lead-like look the skin has when affected by cold, contusion, sickness, fear; the rotten rum or gin they call blue ruin and the blue devils of its delirium; Russian cats and oysters, a withheld or imprisoned breath, the blue they say that diamonds have, deep holes in the ocean and the blazers which English athletes earn that gentlemen may wear; afflictions of the spirit—dumps, mopes, Mondays—all that's dismal—low-down gloomy music, Nova Scotians, cyanosis, hair rinse, bluing, bleach; the rare blue dahlia like that blue moon shrewd things happen only once in, or the call for trumps in whist (but who remembers whist or what the death of unplayed games is like?), and correspondingly the flag, Blue Peter, which is our signal for getting under way; a swift pitch, Confederate money, the shaded slopes of clouds and mountains, and so the constantly increasing absentness of Heaven (*ins Blaue hinein*, the Germans say), consequently the color of everything that's empty: blue bottles, bank accounts, and compliments, for instance, or, when the sky's turned turtle, the blue-green bleat of ocean (both the same), and, when in Hell, its neatly landscaped rows of concrete huts and gas-blue flames; social registers, examination booklets, blue bloods, balls, and bonnets, beards, coats, collars, chips, and cheese . . . the pedantic, indecent and censorious . . . watered twilight, sour sea: through a scrambling of accidents, blue has become their color, just as it's stood for fidelity. Blue laws took their hue from the paper they were printed on. Blue noses were named for a potato.

PRACTICE

On Being _____

Looking back at the passage by Gass, can you find examples of things in the world that are literally blue: things we perceive as having that color? Can you also find examples of things that are blue only in some figurative or metaphorical way? Gass is fascinated by the way language works, by the way that the name of a color is applied to all sorts of things that actually have no color at all. In the last two sentences, he explains how two things that are not literally blue came to be called blue: laws and noses. Although many of his blue things are so called for reasons lost in the history of language, Gass invents nothing here. In this passage he takes an inventory of the English language as he understands it, trying to summon up all the things that are regularly called blue. Their strange combinations, ordered by his own mind's patterns of association, make a kind of prose poem. By concentrating on the *word* "blue," in all its applications, he frees his mind to roam around, to make connections that are startling, to be creative, expressive.

It is important to note that Gass is not being merely personal and arbitrary here. He is not calling things blue just because he wants to (like the French poet who called oranges blue). This passage is a collaboration between Gass and his language. He is thus free to associate all things that have been called blue often enough to make their blueness part of the language.

Your job is simply to work as Gass has worked, but with another color. We suggest a primary color, one that has spread throughout the language, so that you can combine in your paragraph things that are literally that color with things that we only speak of figuratively as being that color. Save this exercise. You may be returning to it later.

Self-Expression through Art

Art takes many forms and has many uses. One use is to provide a vehicle for the expression of feelings that many of us have but cannot express as well as an artist can. Considered in this way (which, of course, is not the only way it can be considered), art helps us to organize and understand aspects of ourselves. In the following exercise, we ask you to consider three works of visual art, each of which depicts a figure in a different state of mind or feeling.

It would be possible, in an analytic exercise, to ask you to interpret what the artist intends the work to mean. But we are definitely *not* asking you that kind of question. Instead, we ask you to imagine that each work expresses some aspect of your own personality or some thoughts or feelings that you recognize as moods you have experienced or might experience. In short, use each picture as a stimulus to your own self-expression. You will find it easier to do this, however, if you do not write *as yourself* but instead use the pictures as masks that you put on in order to speak.

For each piece of art, then, write out what the figure in the picture seems to you to be feeling. You may choose to write in any grammatical person (I, you, he, or she), but write about what feelings the picture brings out in you. We suggest using the present tense, but if you are more comfortable with the past, use that. Just be consistent. For instance, looking at the first picture, you might begin in any of several ways: 1) He is frightened; 2) You are suffering; 3) I am in agony. Once you get started, you may look at the picture occasionally for stimulation, but do not be afraid to follow your own thoughts and feelings. If one word leads to another, write them all down.

The purpose of this exercise, like that of others in this chapter, is to help you loosen up as a writer, to break through some of the resistances that inhibit you and prevent you from writing as expressively as you can. There is no question of "the right answer" here, but only of writing more or less expressively. Don't quit after a few words. Keep on thinking, feeling, and writing until you have really expressed yourself about each picture. You can stop writing, think about something else for a while, and then come back to your picture. You may be surprised at how much your subconscious will dredge up while you are not thinking about the picture consciously. Number each of your expressions to correspond with the picture you are using as your stimulus to expression.

© Edvard Munch, "The Cry" (1895) (*William Francis Warden Fund, Courtesy Museum of Fine Arts, Boston*)

© Erich Heckel, "Head of Girl" (1912)

Wood figure, Zaire.

Two Expressions of Mood

Consider the following poem. Reading it aloud once or twice would be a good idea. Then proceed to the questions.

Lying in a Hammock at William Duffy's Farm in Pine Island, Minnesota

Over my head, I see the bronze butterfly,
Asleep on the black trunk,
Blowing like a leaf in green shadow.
Down the ravine behind the empty house,
The cowbells follow one another   5
Into the distances of the afternoon.
To my right,
In a field of sunlight between two pines,
The droppings of last year's horses
Blaze up into golden stones.   10
I lean back, as the evening darkens and comes on.
A chicken hawk floats over, looking for home.
I have wasted my life.

—JAMES WRIGHT

Questions

1. Note the movement of the speaker's eyes. What does he see? What other senses are involved?
2. How would you evaluate the images he presents to us? Are they pleasant, unusual, shocking? What kind of mood do they convey?
3. Consider the last line of the poem. Do you think the speaker is being ironic? How might you rephrase the last line?

In the following passage, a young woman is expressing the feelings and thoughts she experienced on a visit to a doctor's office, where she looked at a baby magazine and at a real mother and child. Read the passage and consider the questions that follow it.

Sylvia Plath, from *The Bell Jar*

I leafed nervously through an issue of *Baby Talk*. The fat, bright 1
faces of babies beamed up at me, page after page—bald babies, choco-

late-colored babies, Eisenhower-faced babies, babies rolling over the first time, babies reaching for rattles, babies eating their first spoonful of solid food, babies doing all the little tricky things it takes to grow up, step by step, into an anxious and unsettling world.

I smelt a mingling of Pablum and sour milk and salt-cod-stinky 2
diapers and felt sorrowful and tender. How easy having babies seemed to the women around me! Why was I so unmaternal and apart? Why couldn't I dream of devoting myself to baby after fat puling baby like Dodo Conway?

If I had to wait on a baby all day, I would go mad. 3

I looked at the baby in the lap of the woman opposite. I had no idea 4
how old it was, I never did, with babies—for all I knew it could talk a blue streak and had twenty teeth behind its pursed, pink lips. It held its little wobbly head up on its shoulders—it didn't seem to have a neck—and observed me with a wise, Platonic expression.

The baby's mother smiled and smiled, holding that baby as if it were 5
the first wonder of the world. I watched the mother and the baby for some clue to their mutual satisfaction, but before I had discovered anything, the doctor called me in.

Questions

1. The voice in the passage belongs to Esther Greenwood. How would you describe the mood or moods she experiences in the doctor's office? What is the most appropriate word for her mood? What words in the passage are doing the most work in the expression of mood?
2. How would you describe Esther's personality as it is revealed in this passage? What details convey this most strongly?
3. Esther's mood is presented partly as a contrast to other possible responses to babies and motherhood. How are the other responses conveyed? How is an attitude toward them established?
4. Are ideas, as well as a mood or moods, expressed here? Make a summary statement of what you take to be the main idea of the passage—if you feel that it does convey or imply any ideas.
5. At one point Esther says she "felt sorrowful and tender." Are these the words you would have chosen to describe her mood? Explain any discrepancy.
6. Consider the longest and shortest sentences in the passage. What does each contribute to the expressiveness of the text?

PRACTICE

Mood in a Place

You have just considered two examples of the expression of a mood or feeling inspired by being in a particular place at a particular time. In both cases, the things that are there to be experienced become the basis for the expression of a mood or feeling.

Your task in this exercise is to pick a place and use its details selectively to convey a mood or feeling of your own. Put yourself in a place where there are things to be seen and heard and even smelled that encourage your feelings to seek expression: a playground, for example, or an empty gymnasium or a noisy disco. You may come up with a subtle but unified feeling or a flow of contradictory or contrary feelings. But remember to use your chosen place as the source of expressive details.

READING

Ideas about the Telephone

In the three passages that follow, an American woman, an Italian man, and a Frenchman speak of their personal feelings about the telephone. As you read each passage, follow the expression of ideas in it.

Ellen Goodman, from a newspaper column

Sometimes I think that the telephone call is as earthbound as daily 1
dialogue, while a letter is an exchange of gifts. On the telephone you
talk; in a letter you tell. There is a pace to letter writing and reading
that doesn't come from the telephone company but from our own inner
rhythm.

We live mostly in the hi-tech, reach-out-and-touch-someone mod- 2
ern world. Communication is an industry. It makes demands of us. We
are expected to respond as quickly as computers. A voice asks a
question across the ocean in a split second, and we are supposed to
formulate an answer at this high-speed rate of exchange.

But we cannot, blessedly, "interface" by mail. There is leisure and 3
emotional luxury in letter-writing. There are no obvious silences to
anxiously fill. There are no interruptions to brook. There are no
nuances and tones of voice to distract.

A letter doesn't take us by surprise in the middle of dinner, or 4
intrude when we are with other people, or ambush us in the midst of
other thoughts. It waits. There is a private space between the give and
the take for thinking.

I have known lovers, parents and children, husbands and wives who 5
send each other letters from one room to another simply for the chance
to complete a story of events, thoughts, feelings. I have known people
who could not "hear" what they could read.

There is this advantage to slowing down the pace of communica- 6
tions. The phone demands a kind of simultaneous satisfaction that is as
elusive in words as in sex. It's letters that let us take turns, let us sit and
mull and say exactly what we mean.

Today we are supposed to travel light, to live in the moment. The 7
past is, we are told, excess baggage. There is no question that the
phone is the tool of these times. As fine and as ephemeral as a good
meal.

But you cannot hold a call in your hands. You cannot put it in a 8
bundle. You cannot show it to your family. Indeed, there is nothing to
show for it. It doesn't leave a trace. Tell me: How can you wrap a
lifetime of phone calls in a rubber band for a summer's night when you
want to remember?

Federico Fellini, from *Fellini on Fellini*

Frankly, I don't see myself as the fanatical telephone user that 1
friends and colleagues have been calling me for years, with mis-
chievous amusement. My work brings me into contact with a large
number of people, which means I'm involved in an endless network of
relationships, and so it's natural that a fair part of my day should be
spent on the telephone. Like everyone else I consider and use the
telephone as an indispensable, fast and practical means of communication. And yet this daily use of it hasn't yet managed to remove my
astonishment at the fundamentally fantastic aspect of telephoning, that
is, of communication at a distance. Apart from any hackneyed ideas
about communication by telephone being the modern technical equivalent of ancient means of communication—telepathy, for instance—I
want to make just a few odd, hurried remarks about it. I wonder, for
instance, why it is easier to get out of an unexpected visit than to
withstand the temptation to pick up the telephone when it keeps
ringing? Just because the person speaking isn't physically present,
communication on the telephone is more tenuous but more authentic,
less real but more precise, more temporary but more spontaneous,
more delicate but at the same time more intense. As a rule one pays
more attention both to oneself and to the other person when talking on
the telephone, one participates more. Feeling and impressions expand: good news becomes more exciting because right away it is more
privately taken in. A disaster becomes unbearable, because the imagination is fully stretched.

Terror is terror in its purest form: nothing is more chilling than a 2
threat or a damning criticism pronounced on the telephone. Even the
dullest, silliest joke on the telephone loses its dullness and pointless-
ness and takes on a disarming charm. For my part, I think solitude

filled with voices is far preferable and far more joyful than the physical presence of others, when it has no meaning or point to it.

Roland Barthes, from *A Lover's Discourse*

My anxieties as to behavior are futile, ever more so, to infinity. If 1 the other, incidentally or negligently, gives the telephone number of a place where he or she can be reached at certain times, I immediately grow baffled: should I telephone or shouldn't I? (It would do no good to tell me that I *can* telephone—that is the objective, reasonable meaning of the message—for it is precisely this *permission* I don't know how to handle.)

What is futile is what apparently has and will have no consequence. 2 But for me, an amorous subject, everything which is new, everything which disturbs, is received not as a fact but in the aspect of a sign which must be interpreted. From the lover's point of view, the fact becomes consequential because it is immediately transformed into a sign: it is the sign, not the fact, which is consequential (by its *aura*). If the other has given me this new telephone number, what was that the sign of? Was it an invitation to telephone *right away*, for the pleasure of the call, or only *should the occasion arise*, out of necessity? My answer itself will be a sign which the other will inevitably interpret, thereby releasing, between us, a tumultuous maneuvering of images. *Everything signifies:* by this proposition, I entrap myself, I bind myself in calculations, I keep myself from enjoyment.

Sometimes, by dint of deliberating about "nothing" (as the world 3 sees it), I exhaust myself; then I try, in reaction, to return—like a drowning man who stamps on the floor of the sea—to a *spontaneous* decision (spontaneity: the great dream: paradise, power, delight): *go on, telephone, since you want to!* But such recourse is futile: amorous time does not permit the subject to align impulse and action, to make them coincide: I am not the man of mere "acting out"—my madness is tempered, it is not seen; it is *right away* that I fear consequences, any consequence: it is my fear—my deliberation—which is "spontaneous."

Questions

1. Try to describe the speaker suggested by each of the three voices. What kind of personality is suggested by each passage? What specific elements in each text are most expressive of the speaker's individuality? Which text is most revealing of its speaker's personality?
2. Consider the situation of each speaker in relation to the telephone. Does the speaker consider himself or herself mainly a caller, or a person likely to be called? Which passage develops the speaker's situation most elaborately?

3. Reduce each passage to its main idea or ideas about the telephone. Do the three passages express contradictory or complementary ideas? Which expresses views most compatible with your own?
4. Which passage is easiest to read? Why? Which one presents ideas that are least familiar to you? Which seems richest in ideas, most thoughtful? Which is most difficult? Why?
5. The telephone is a common subject in all three passages—but are they *about* the telephone? If not, what are they about?

PRACTICE

Ideas about a Common Object

Using one of the two passages on telephones as an example, write a short expressive piece conveying your ideas about the telephone or about some other common piece of modern technology: the answering machine, the fax machine, the remote control, the computer, the Walkman, the boom box. You might begin by writing the name of the object at the top of a page. Then jot down a list of thoughts about that object as they occur to you, or focus on the topic through the kind of open-ended writing described in the first reading of this chapter (p. 22). Based on these notes, write a draft that will clearly convey your thoughts to a reader.

3. REFLECTION

Your Self as Object

Reflection, like expression, is oriented to the writer. Unlike expression, however, it is not an immediate presentation of thought or feeling. It is mediated—by time, by distance, by experience and maturity. It is a *re-flection*, a looking-*back*. If expression is naturally a young person's form, reflection is the opposite: a form for those who have enough perspective to look back on things and see them differently from the way they seemed to be at the time. For a child, reflection is almost an impossibility. But as soon as we are old enough to remember childhood itself as a time when we were "different"—or are able to look across the gap of any great event, like a death in the family, the loss of a friend, or a danger experienced—we can begin to reflect on our experience. Being able to think reflectively is itself a sign of maturity.

Reflection usually depends on the difference between two moments: the time of the event or situation and the time of the writing—in other words, *then* and *now*. The writer of reflection must use this difference in time to express the feelings and thoughts of *now* by recalling or imagining the emotions and ideas present *then*. Reflection is not simply the telling of a tale or describing of a scene. These things may enter into it, but they are there for the sake of what they are only *now* seen to mean.

Reflection also has a crucial role to play in the writing process itself. Writing is not an instantaneous event. Not only does it take a certain amount of time to write even a single sentence, but any serious writing project may extend over a considerable period of time. During the time of writing, there are many moments of reflection in which the writer examines the words already there on the page, sometimes thinking, "But that's not what I meant to say. I really meant. . . ." We feel the same way about deeds often enough ("I didn't mean to do *that*"), but deeds cannot be undone. Words, however, can be unwritten. We call this process *revision,* and it is an aspect of reflection that we can use in all the other forms of writing. Just as the process of revision is often helped by seeing our writing from the perspective of others, so too is the process of self-reflection. From another person's perspective we may not look as we think we do.

READING

Your Own Expressive Writing

If you accepted our earlier invitation to follow Peter Elbow's advice and produce some open-ended writing—or to express yourself through a color or by discussing pictured moods—you are eligible to participate in this exercise. The first step is to find the writing you did there and read it over. This kind of reflection on previous writing is crucial to every person's development of thought through the process of rewriting.

Read over your work, then, whether you did all three of the expressive exercises or only one or two. Try to read it with eyes that are both critical and creative. Don't be critical in a nit-picking way, looking for little errors. Read as a writer reads, looking for the expressions that are most revealing, most vigorous, that seem to capture something in language that is expressively equal to the idea or feeling that lies behind the language. Above all, look for patterns. If you have done all three exercises, look for any ideas or feelings or key words that appear in all three. If you only did the Elbow exercise, look for the "point" that Elbow suggested you would find.

It would be good to exchange your writing with a few others to find out what pattern or point they may find in your work. When you have discussed and considered your expressive writing thoroughly, you will be ready to use it as the basis for more practice in writing.

PRACTICE

Reflection as Revision

The idea of this assignment is to use your earlier writing as raw material for a more finished, polished piece of work. In the expressive exercises, you allowed things to drift up into your consciousness without trying to pursue them and explore their implications. Reading over that work, you should now find one or more topics that are important to you, about which you have opinions, feelings, thoughts. Having located such a topic, you are now in a position to consider it more carefully, to reflect upon it, to develop your thoughts in a coherent way. That is exactly what we ask you to do. Beginning from your previous expressive writing, even using phrases from it where appropriate, *use* writing as a way of working toward your best answer to the question, "What do I really think about _____?" Keep on writing, reflecting, and revising until you are satisfied with your reflections. If you were assigned the earlier practice, "An Experience in Your Life," consider that as another option for revision.

READING

School Days Revisited

In the following selections from their autobiographies, the writers recall incidents from their school careers. Louise De Salvo reflects on her college experience and career choice, and Russell Baker reflects on a high school teacher who helped him make a career choice. De Salvo became a well-known scholar and Baker became a well-known journalist.

Louise De Salvo, from "A Portrait of the *Puttana* as a Middle-Aged Woolf Scholar"

Autumn 1963.

I am a senior at Douglass College. In 1963 Douglass College is the kind of school a bright young working-class woman can afford. Douglass, I think, is filled with brilliant women, and I have never seen brilliant women before. I have studied Shakespeare with Doris Falk, the novel with Anna Wells, philosophy with Amelie Rorty. I now have Twentieth-Century Fiction with Carol Smith. 1

Carol Smith is lecturing on Virginia Woolf's *To the Lighthouse*. She is talking about the relationship between Mr. and Mrs. Ramsay in "The Window" section of the novel. I have never in my life heard such genius. I am taking notes, watching her talk, and watching her belly. She is very pregnant. She is wearing a beige maternity dress. I take down every word, while watching to see when the baby she is pregnant with will kick her again. 2

I learn to love Virginia Woolf. I observe that it is possible to be a woman, to be brilliant, to be working, to be happy, and to be pregnant. And all at the same time. 3

I am interviewed about how an Italian-American woman like me 4
became a Woolf scholar. I search my memory, think of studying with
Carol Smith, and suddenly remember my fascination with the figure of
Cam Ramsay in *To the Lighthouse*. Cam Ramsay, the child Mrs.
Ramsay virtually ignores, so busy is she with her son James; Cam
Ramsay, the child who is "wild and fierce." The child who clenches her
fist and stamps her feet. The child who is always running away,
running away. The child who will not let anyone invade the private
space that she has created to protect herself in this family with a
tyrannical father who strikes out with a beak of brass.

I remember my own adolescence. Could it be that I have seen 5
something of myself in Cam those many years ago and that in trying to
understand the relationship between Cam Ramsay and her creator,
Virginia Woolf, I am also trying to learn something about my own past?
Aren't I now in the middle of a long essay about Virginia Woolf as an
adolescent, reading her 1897 diary, a tiny brown gilt leather volume,
with a lock and key, that must be read with a magnifying glass, so tiny
and spidery is the hand, an essay that has given me more satisfaction to
write than anything I have written yet about Virginia Woolf? And
haven't I been stressing Woolf's capacity to cope, rather than her
neurosis, in that difficult year? Could it be that in concentrating on
Woolf's health, I am also trying to heal myself?

I am married, and enduring my husband's medical internship as 6
best I can, on next to no money, with a baby who never sleeps and who
cries all the time. Although I am twenty-five, I look fifty. I have deep
circles under my eyes. I have no figure. I am still wearing maternity
clothes.

I had put my husband through medical school. (According to him, I 7
helped put him through medical school—his parents paid his tuition
and gave him a small allowance, and I worked as a high school English
teacher and paid for everything else.) In that internship year, we came
very close to a divorce. Your basic doctor-in-training-meets-gorgeous-
nurse-and-wants-to-leave-his-wife-and-small-baby story.

One day, I look into the bathroom mirror and decide that I will 8
either kill myself or that I will go back to graduate school and become
economically independent as quickly as I can. I look into the medicine
chest, thinking that if my husband leaves me with this baby, I will
probably be young, gifted, and on welfare. After wondering whether
you could kill yourself by taking a year's supply of birth control pills
and fantasying that, with the way my luck is running, I might grow
some hair on my chest, but I probably wouldn't die, I decide that I will
go back to school, get a Ph.D., and go into college teaching. I also

realize that I might buy some time by squelching the young-doctor-leaves-his-young-wife-for-nurse script, at least temporarily, by announcing to my husband that if he leaves me, *he* can have the baby. Then he and his sweet young nurse can contemplate how romantic their life together will be with this baby who cries and throws up all the time.

He tells me he doesn't believe that I can part with my child.   9

I say, "Wanna bet?"   10

Shortly thereafter, he decides to hang around for a while longer. 11

. . . .

When I first learned that Virginia Woolf had spent seven years in 12 the creation of *The Voyage Out,* her first novel, I thought that surely she must have been mad for that, if for no other reason. But as I carted off copies of *Melymbrosia,* my reconstruction of the earlier version of that novel, to the Editor's Office of The New York Public Library some seven years after *I* had begun working with her novel, I reflected that I have come to share a great deal with this woman. I have come to be a great deal like her in her attitudes toward the male establishment and art and feminism and politics; have learned from living for seven years with her to take the very best from her while managing, through the example of her life and her honesty about it, to avoid the depths of her pain.

She has been very good to me, this woman.   13

In looking back over my life, I realize that my work on Virginia 14 Woolf has helped me make some important changes.

Before I worked on Virginia Woolf, I wasn't a feminist. Before I 15 worked on Virginia Woolf, I didn't know how strong a woman I was. Before I worked on Virginia Woolf, I whined a lot, like my Italian foremothers, about how men got all the breaks and about the ways they abused their women, like I felt I had been abused, but I didn't really understand that there was a social structure that was organized to keep men dominant and women subservient, and I really didn't understand how important it was for women to be economically independent and the potentially horrifying consequences if they were not.

Before I worked on Virginia Woolf, I would ask the young doctors 16 who came to our house for dinner if I could get them another cup of coffee, being careful to wait until there was a break in the conversation. Now my husband, Ernie, and our children—Jason and Justin—get up to cook me breakfast. Virginia Woolf has, in many ways, created a monster in me, and I am proud to give her partial credit for it. I like to think that she would have been pleased that my reading *A Room of One's Own* has been a very important part of my emancipation from the tradition of the suffering woman. Now I am a hell-raiser, a spitfire, and I buy and wear "Mean Mother," "Nurture Yourself," and "I Am a Shameless Agitator" buttons. And I have recently started to pump iron (much to the amusement of fifteen-year-old Jason—the would-be writer, the one who used to throw up all the time, who has turned out to be a very nice kid after all—and eleven-year-old Justin, who has something to say about everything I do). But sometimes, when I'm feeling really good and have the time, I make them a bread pudding.

Questions

1. Reflection involves the manipulation of time. Look at the first three paragraphs and try to determine exactly how many different moments in time can be distinguished. Note especially all the words that help keep the reader clearly oriented in time. How many sentences in these paragraphs are entirely lacking in markers that indicate some change or shift in time?

2. The essential feature of the management of time in reflective writing is a distinction between the time of the events being reflected upon and the moment of reflection itself. Read through these paragraphs noting every phrase that indicates a difference between time of the events and the time of reflection. What effect has De Salvo tried to attain through use of the present tense?

Russell Baker, from *Growing Up*

The notion of becoming a writer had flickered off and on in my head 1 since the Belleville days, but it wasn't until my third year in high school that the possibility took hold. Until then I'd been bored by everything associated with English courses. I found English grammar dull and baffling. I hated the assignments to turn out "compositions," and went at them like heavy labor, turning out leaden, lackluster paragraphs that were agonies for teachers to read and for me to write. The classics thrust on me to read seemed as deadening as chloroform.

When our class was assigned to Mr. Fleagle for third-year English 2 I anticipated another grim year in that dreariest of subjects. Mr. Fleagle was notorious among City students for dullness and inability to inspire. He was said to be stuffy, dull, and hopelessly out of date. To me he looked to be sixty or seventy and prim to a fault. He wore primly severe eyeglasses, his wavy hair was primly cut and primly combed. He wore prim vested suits with neckties blocked primly against the collar buttons of his primly starched white shirts. He had a primly pointed jaw, a primly straight nose, and a prim manner of speaking that was so correct, so gentlemanly, that he seemed a comic antique.

I anticipated a listless, unfruitful year with Mr. Fleagle and for a 3 long time was not disappointed. We read *Macbeth*. Mr. Fleagle loved *Macbeth* and wanted us to love it too, but he lacked the gift of infecting others with his own passion. He tried to convey the murderous ferocity of Lady Macbeth one day by reading aloud the passage that concludes

. . . I have given suck, and know
How tender 'tis to love the babe that milks me.
I would, while it was smiling in my face,
Have plucked my nipple from his boneless gums. . . .

The idea of prim Mr. Fleagle plucking his nipple from boneless gums was too much for the class. We burst into gasps of irrepressible snickering. Mr. Fleagle stopped.

"There is nothing funny, boys, about giving suck to a babe. It is 4 the—the very essence of motherhood, don't you see."

He constantly sprinkled his sentences with "don't you see." It wasn't 5 a question but an exclamation of mild surprise at our ignorance. "Your pronoun needs an antecedent, don't you see," he would say, very primly. "The purpose of the Porter's scene, boys, is to provide comic relief from the horror, don't you see."

Late in the year we tackled the informal essay. "The essay, don't you 6 see, is the. . . ." My mind went numb. Of all forms of writing, none seemed so boring as the essay. Naturally we would have to write informal essays. Mr. Fleagle distributed a homework sheet offering us a choice of topics. None was quite so simpleminded as "What I Did on My Summer Vacation," but most seemed to be almost as dull. I took the list home and dawdled until the night before the essay was due. Sprawled on the sofa, I finally faced up to the grim task, took the list out of my notebook, and scanned it. The topic on which my eye stopped was "The Art of Eating Spaghetti."

This title produced an extraordinary sequence of mental images. 7 Surging up out of the depths of memory came a vivid recollection of a night in Belleville when all of us were seated around the supper table—Uncle Allen, my mother, Uncle Charlie, Doris, Uncle Hal— and Aunt Pat served spaghetti for supper. Spaghetti was an exotic treat in those days. Neither Doris nor I had ever eaten spaghetti, and none of the adults had enough experience to be good at it. All the good humor of Uncle Allen's house reawoke in my mind as I recalled the laughing arguments we had that night about the socially respectable method for moving spaghetti from plate to mouth.

Suddenly I wanted to write about that, about the warmth and good 8
feeling of it, but I wanted to put it down simply for my own joy, not for
Mr. Fleagle. It was a moment I wanted to recapture and hold for
myself. I wanted to relive the pleasure of an evening at New Street. To
write it as I wanted, however, would violate all the rules of formal
composition I'd learned in school, and Mr. Fleagle would surely give it
a failing grade. Never mind. I would write something else for Mr.
Fleagle after I had written this thing for myself.

When I finished it the night was half gone and there was no time left 9
to compose a proper, respectable essay for Mr. Fleagle. There was
no choice next morning but to turn in my private reminiscence of
Belleville. Two days passed before Mr. Fleagle returned the graded
papers, and he returned everyone's but mine. I was bracing myself for
a command to report to Mr. Fleagle immediately after school for
discipline when I saw him lift my paper from his desk and rap for the
class's attention.

"Now, boys," he said, "I want to read you an essay. This is titled 10
'The Art of Eating Spaghetti.' "

And he started to read. My words! He was reading *my words* out 11
loud to the entire class. What's more, the entire class was listening.
Listening attentively. Then somebody laughed, then the entire class
was laughing, and not in contempt and ridicule, but with open-hearted
enjoyment. Even Mr. Fleagle stopped two or three times to repress a
small prim smile.

I did my best to avoid showing pleasure, but what I was feeling was 12
pure ecstasy at this startling demonstration that my words had the
power to make people laugh. In the eleventh grade, at the eleventh
hour as it were, I had discovered a calling. It was the happiest moment
of my entire school career. When Mr. Fleagle finished he put the final
seal on my happiness by saying, "Now that, boys, is an essay, don't you
see. It's—don't you see—it's of the very essence of the essay, don't you
see. Congratulations, Mr. Baker."

For the first time, light shone on a possibility. It wasn't a very 13
heartening possibility, to be sure. Writing couldn't lead to a job after
high school, and it was hardly honest work, but Mr. Fleagle had
opened a door for me. After that I ranked Mr. Fleagle among the finest
teachers in the school.

Questions

1. What periods of time are being reflected upon in the first two paragraphs?
2. Mr. Fleagle is described and presented to us primarily through the eyes of the
   sixteen-year-old Baker. Why? What do you think of Mr. Fleagle?
3. What statement is being made about reflective writing in this reflective piece?

Reflection on Your School Days

Choose an event or situation from your elementary or high school years. It may be an event similar to one of those in the De Salvo and Baker pieces concerning a teacher or a subject you remember well. It may be an event of brief duration or a situation that extended over a period of time. You might list a number of events before you choose one to focus on.

Write out the event as you experienced it *then*, as if you were expressing your thoughts in a diary or in a letter to a close friend at the time the event took place. Read over what you have written, and reconsider the event from your present perspective. Then revise what you have written to emphasize this present perspective, being sure to provide a conclusion in which you reflect on what the event means to you *now*. Before you begin your draft, you might want to do some brainstorming to see what particular details you can remember—about the people involved and what they did or said, about the place where the event occurred, about your expectations, and about what you learned.

Looking at Pictures

We live in the age of mechanical reproduction of images: photographs, photoprinting, cinema, video, computer graphics. All of these, in their turn, may become the object of transformation into words. The following selections illustrate this process with three instances of writers looking at photographs and recording the moment with their own apparatus, the written word.

Looking at Pictures to Be Put Away

Who was this girl
In her white night gown
Clutching a pair of jeans

On a foggy redwood deck.
She looks up at me tender,   5
Calm, surprised,

What will we remember
Bodies thick with food and lovers
After twenty years.

—GARY SNYDER

I Go Back to May 1937

I see them standing at the formal gates of their colleges,
I see my father strolling out
under the ochre sandstone arch, the
red tiles glinting like bent
plates of blood behind his head, I   5
see my mother with a few light books at her hip
standing at the pillar made of tiny bricks with the
wrought-iron gate still open behind her, its
sword-tips black in the May air,
they are about to graduate, they are about to get married,   10
they are kids, they are dumb, all they know is they are
innocent, they would never hurt anybody.
I want to go up to them and say Stop,
don't do it—she's the wrong woman,
he's the wrong man, you are going to do things   15
you cannot imagine you would ever do,
you are going to do bad things to children,
you are going to suffer in ways you never heard of,
you are going to want to die. I want to go
up to them there in the late May sunlight and say it,   20
her hungry pretty blank face turning to me,
her pitiful beautiful untouched body,
his arrogant handsome blind face turning to me,
his pitiful beautiful untouched body,
but I don't do it. I want to live. I   25
take them up like the male and female
paper dolls and bang them together
at the hips like chips of flint as if to
strike sparks from them, I say
Do what you are going to do, and I will tell about it.   30

—SHARON OLDS

Roland Barthes, "Looking for My Mother"

There I was, alone in the apartment where she had died, looking at   1
these pictures of my mother, one by one, under the lamp, gradually
moving back in time with her, looking for the truth of the face I had
loved. And I found it.

The photograph was very old. The corners were blunted from   2
having been pasted into an album, the sepia print had faded, and the
picture just managed to show two children standing together at the end
of a little wooden bridge in a glassed-in conservatory, what was called a

Winter Garden in those days. My mother was five at the time (1898), her brother seven. He was leaning against the bridge railing, along which he had extended one arm; she, shorter than he, was standing a little back, facing the camera; you could tell that the photographer had said, "Step forward a little so we can see you"; she was holding one finger in the other hand, as children often do, in an awkward gesture. The brother and sister, united, as I knew, by the discord of their parents, who were soon to divorce, had posed side by side, alone, under the palms of the Winter Garden (it was the house where my mother was born, in Chennevières-sur-Marne).

I studied the little girl and at last rediscovered my mother. The distinctness of her face, the naïve attitude of her hands, the place she had docilely taken without either showing or hiding herself, and finally her expression, which distinguished her, like Good from Evil, from the hysterical little girl, from the simpering doll who plays at being a grownup—all this constituted the future of a sovereign *innocence* (if you will take this word according to its etymology, which is: "I do no harm"), all this had transformed the photographic pose into that untenable paradox which she had nonetheless maintained all her life: the assertion of a gentleness. In this little girl's image I saw the kindness which had formed her being immediately and forever, without her having inherited it from anyone; how could this kindness have proceeded from the imperfect parents who had loved her so badly—in short: from a family? Her kindness was specifically *out-of-play*, it belonged to no system, or at least it was located at the limits of a morality (evangelical, for instance); I could not define it better than by this feature (among others): that during the whole of our life together, she never made a single "observation." This extreme and particular circumstance, so abstract in relation to an image, was nonetheless present in the face revealed in the photograph I had just discovered. "Not a just image, just an image," Godard says. But my grief wanted a just image, an image which would be both justice and accuracy—*justesse:* just an image, but a just image. Such, for me, was the Winter Garden Photograph.

Questions

1. The camera is mechanical. What it records is fixed. But human memory is selective and changes as we move through time. Snyder's poem is about forgetting: "Who?" "What?" How are the poem's two questions related?
2. Why does Snyder use the present tense in line 5? How are past, present, and future considered in the nine lines of the poem?
3. What does "thick with food and lovers" mean? Why "thick"?
4. Who are "we"? Where are "we"? When are "we"? What are "we" doing?

5. What kinds of innocence is Olds evoking in this poem?
6. How would you describe the imagery she uses? Note especially lines 5 and 9, as well as the "paper dolls" in the final lines.
7. How would you characterize Olds's reflection on these pictures? In other words, what sort of "picture" does her poem create?
8. Barthes says that his mother (even in her childhood picture) was characterized by "the assertion of a gentleness." He calls this phrase a "paradox." What does he mean by that?
9. In paragraph 3 what does Barthes mean by saying that his mother never made an "observation," putting the word into quotation marks? What do you suppose he means by "observation"?
10. What is a "just" image?

PRACTICE

Reflecting on a Photograph

Snyder shows us one way of writing about a photograph that preserves the image of someone no longer remembered by the writer—a way of reflecting on an image left behind by the process of mechanical reproduction. Olds shows us how a photograph can suspend its subject in a moment of time, inducing in the writer the desire to engage in dialogue with the past. Barthes shows us one way of writing about a photograph of someone very close to the writer, someone remembered so well that the writer's reflections overwhelm the image, either filling it with the writer's feelings or noticing in it the absence of those qualities most important in the person whose image it is.

All three of these writers show how naturally photographs put us into a reflective mood. Because they freeze a moment of time, they force us to reflect in order to connect the flow of life to the frozen image reproduced by the camera. Taking these writers not as models but as inspiration, select a single photograph from your personal collection, and reflect upon it. Try to make your writing as serious and thoughtful as what you have just read. Here are some things to remember as you prepare to write:

A. The reader will *not* have the picture, so you will not be able to depend on the visual image to work for you. You will have to put into words whatever you want the reader to know about the image you are reflecting upon. You might begin by listing the important things that are in the picture, and those that are left out. Your essay may well turn upon the difference between these two lists.

B. Think of the image as unchanging while everything around it changes. How does the presence of the image before you as you prepare to write affect you? Where does the image direct your thoughts? Close your eyes and think about the image. Where do your thoughts want to go? What is *there?*

C. What do you remember, what have you forgotten, what will become of this image? If you have chosen a photograph of a person (as we suggest you do), try to determine what things about the person are important to you (you might list them), and compare these with what the camera has caught and what it has missed. Here is space for reflection.

D. Qualities caught and missed, time frozen and moving, the simplicities of mechanism and the complexities of life—these are your starting points.

READING

From Thing to Thought

This is a complete reflection by the Danish writer Isak Dinesen, who lived in Africa for many years. She published her reminiscences in a book called *Out of Africa,* from which this selection has been taken. In reading the selection, we ask you to be especially alert to three things: (1) its management of time, (2) its use of descriptive and illustrative language, and (3) its organization.

Isak Dinesen, "The Iguana"

In the Reserve I have sometimes come upon the Iguana, the big 1 lizards, as they were sunning themselves upon a flat stone in a riverbed. They are not pretty in shape, but nothing can be imagined more beautiful than their coloring. They shine like a heap of precious stones or like a pane cut out of an old church window. When, as you approach, they swish away, there is a flash of azure, green and purple over the stones, the color seems to be standing behind them in the air, like a comet's luminous tail.

Once I shot an Iguana. I thought that I should be able to make some 2 pretty things from his skin. A strange thing happened then, that I have never afterwards forgotten. As I went up to him, where he was lying dead upon his stone, and actually while I was walking the few steps, he faded and grew pale, all color died out of him as in one long sigh, and by the time that I touched him he was grey and dull like a lump of concrete. It was the live impetuous blood pulsating within the animal, which had radiated out all that glow and splendor. Now that the flame was put out, and the soul had flown, the Iguana was as dead as a sandbag.

Often since I have, in some sort, shot an Iguana, and\ I have 3
remembered the one of the Reserve. Up at Meru I saw a young Native
girl with a bracelet on, a leather strap two inches wide, and embroi-
dered all over with very small turquoise-colored beads which varied a
little in color and played in green, light blue and ultramarine. It was an
extraordinarily live thing; it seemed to draw breath on her arm, so that
I wanted it for myself, and made Farah buy it from her. No sooner had
it come upon my own arm than it gave up the ghost. It was nothing
now, a small, cheap, purchased article of refinery. It had been the play
of colors, the duet between the turquoise and the "nègre"—that quick,
sweet, brownish black, like peat and black pottery, of the Native's
skin—that had created the life of the bracelet.

In the Zoological Museum of Pietermaritzburg, I have seen, in a 4
stuffed deep-water fish in a showcase, the same combination of coloring, which there had survived death; it made me wonder what life can
well be like, on the bottom of the sea, to send up something so live and
airy. I stood in Meru and looked at my pale hand and at the dead
bracelet, it was as if an injustice had been done to a noble thing, as if
truth had been suppressed. So sad did it seem that I remembered the
saying of the hero in a book that I had read as a child: "I have
conquered them all, but I am standing amongst graves."

In a foreign country and with foreign species of life one should take 5
measures to find out whether things will be keeping their value when
dead. To the settlers of East Africa I give the advice: "For the sake of
your own eyes and heart, shoot not the Iguana."

Questions

1. Make an outline of Dinesen's five-paragraph essay. What is covered in each
   paragraph?
2. Note all the major shifts in time of events or grammatical tense in the essay.
   How does the time structure compare to your organizational outline?
3. In this essay, reflection on individual experiences is brought to the point of
   generalization and advice. How is this accomplished? How does reflection turn
   into advice? How does the care for description contribute to the strength of the
   advice?

PRACTICE

Reflecting on Experience

Reflect on two or three events in your life from which you learned
something. Try to draw a conclusion, a generalization, or, like Dinesen,

some sort of advice from your experiences. You might begin by listing events that were memorable because of your mistaken or thoughtless behavior. (We all have had experiences of this kind.) After making your list, try to find two or three items that show a similar pattern of behavior. That is, look for different occasions that can be seen as versions of the "same learning process" or the "same mistake." Using these items from your list as an outline, then write about the events, not just telling what happened but reflecting on the way what happened represents a typical kind of experience, something that you have learned from and that other people may learn from if you can make clear what is typical in your personal experience.

Remember that Dinesen does not simply reach a conclusion for herself ("I shouldn't have done that," or "I won't do that again"). She generalizes her experience as widely as she can. Try to move in the direction she indicates, from yourself to others who are like you.

READING

From Experience to Thought

This essay by Brent Staples, who is on the editorial board of the *New York Times*, originally appeared in *Ms.* magazine. As you read it, note how the movements from experience to reflection on experience are organized.

Brent Staples, "Just Walk on By: A Black Man Ponders His Power to Alter Public Space"

My first victim was a woman—white, well dressed, probably in her 1 early twenties. I came upon her late one evening on a deserted street in Hyde Park, a relatively affluent neighborhood in an otherwise mean, impoverished section of Chicago. As I swung onto the avenue behind her, there seemed to be a discreet, uninflammatory distance between us. Not so. She cast back a worried glance. To her, the youngish black man—a broad six feet two inches with a beard and billowing hair, both hands shoved into the pockets of a bulky military jacket—seemed menacingly close. After a few more quick glimpses, she picked up her pace and was soon running in earnest. Within seconds she disappeared into a cross street.

That was more than a decade ago. I was twenty-two years old, a 2 graduate student newly arrived at the University of Chicago. It was in the echo of that terrified woman's footfalls that I first began to know the unwieldly inheritance I'd come into—the ability to alter public space in ugly ways. It was clear that she thought herself the quarry of a mugger, a rapist, or worse. Suffering a bout of insomnia, however, I was stalking sleep, not defenseless wayfarers. As a softy who is scarcely able to take a knife to a raw chicken—let alone hold it to a person's throat—I was surprised, embarrassed, and dismayed all at once. Her flight made me feel like an accomplice in tyranny. It also made it clear that I was indistinguishable from the muggers who occasionally seeped into the area from the surrounding ghetto. That first encounter, and those that followed, signified that a vast, unnerving gulf lay between nighttime pedestrians—particularly women—and me. And I soon gathered that being perceived as dangerous is a hazard in itself. I only needed to turn a corner into a dicey situation, or crowd some frightened, armed person in a foyer somewhere, or make an errant move after being pulled over by a policeman. Where fear and weapons meet—and they often do in urban America—there is always the possibility of death.

In that first year, my first away from my hometown, I was to become 3 thoroughly familiar with the language of fear. At dark, shadowy intersections in Chicago, I could cross in front of a car stopped at a traffic light and elicit the *thunk, thunk, thunk, thunk* of the driver—black, white, male, or female—hammering down the door locks. On less traveled streets after dark, I grew accustomed to but never comfortable with people who crossed to the other side of the street rather than pass me. Then there were the standard unpleasantries with police, doormen, bouncers, cab drivers, and others whose business it is to screen out troublesome individuals *before* there is any nastiness.

I moved to New York nearly two years ago and I have remained an 4 avid night walker. In central Manhattan, the near-constant crowd cover minimizes tense one-on-one street encounters. Elsewhere—visiting friends in SoHo,[1] where sidewalks are narrow and tightly spaced buildings shut out the sky—things can get very taut indeed.

Black men have a firm place in New York mugging literature. 5 Norman Podhoretz[2] in his famed (or infamous) 1963 essay, "My Negro Problem—And Ours," recalls growing up in terror of black males; they "were tougher than we were, more ruthless," he writes—and as an adult on the Upper West Side of Manhattan, he continues, he cannot constrain his nervousness when he meets black men on certain streets. Similarly, a decade later, the essayist and novelist Edward Hoagland extols a New York where once "Negro bitterness bore down mainly on other Negroes." Where some see mere panhandlers, Hoagland sees "a mugger who is clearly screwing up his nerve to do more than just *ask* for money." But Hoagland has "the New Yorker's quick-hunch posture for broken-field maneuvering," and the bad guy swerves away.

---

[1]A district of lower Manhattan known for its art galleries.
[2]A literary critic and editor of *Commentary* magazine.

I often witness that "hunch posture," from women after dark on the 6
warrenlike streets of Brooklyn where I live. They seem to set their
faces on neutral and, with their purse straps strung across their chests
bandolier style, they forge ahead as though bracing themselves against
being tackled. I understand, of course, that the danger they perceive is
not a hallucination. Women are particularly vulnerable to street violence, and young black males are drastically overrepresented among
the perpetrators of that violence. Yet these truths are no solace against
the kind of alienation that comes of being ever the suspect, against
being set apart, a fearsome entity with whom pedestrians avoid making
eye contact.

It is not altogether clear to me how I reached the ripe old age of 7
twenty-two without being conscious of the lethality nighttime pedestrians attributed to me. Perhaps it was because in Chester, Pennsyl-
vania, the small, angry industrial town where I came of age in the
1960s, I was scarcely noticeable against a backdrop of gang warfare,
street knifings, and murders. I grew up one of the good boys, had
perhaps a half-dozen fist fights. In retrospect, my shyness of combat
has clear sources.

Many things go into the making of a young thug. One of those things 8
is the consummation of the male romance with the power to intimidate. An infant discovers that random flailings send the baby bottle
flying out of the crib and crashing to the floor. Delighted, the joyful
babe repeats those motions again and again, seeking to duplicate the
feat. Just so, I recall the points at which some of my boyhood friends
were finally seduced by the perception of themselves as tough guys.
When a mark cowered and surrendered his money without resistance,
myth and reality merged—and paid off. It is, after all, only manly to
embrace the power to frighten and intimidate. We, as men, are not
supposed to give an inch of our lane on the highway; we are to seize the
fighter's edge in work and in play and even in love; we are to be valiant
in the face of hostile forces.

Unfortunately, poor and powerless young men seem to take all this 9
nonsense literally. As a boy, I saw countless tough guys locked away; I
have since buried several, too. They were babies, really—a teenage
cousin, a brother of twenty-two, a childhood friend in his mid-
twenties—all gone down in episodes of bravado played out in the
streets. I came to doubt the virtues of intimidation early on. I chose,
perhaps even unconsciously, to remain a shadow—timid, but a sur-
vivor.

The fearsomeness mistakenly attributed to me in public places often 10
has a perilous flavor. The most frightening of these confusions occurred
in the late 1970s and early 1980s when I worked as a journalist in
Chicago. One day, rushing into the office of a magazine I was writing

for with a deadline story in hand, I was mistaken for a burglar. The office manager called security and, with an ad hoc posse, pursued me through the labyrinthine halls, nearly to my editor's door. I had no way of proving who I was. I could only move briskly toward the company of someone who knew me.

Another time I was on assignment for a local paper and killing time 11 before an interview. I entered a jewelry store on the city's affluent Near North Side. The proprietor excused herself and returned with an enormous red Doberman pinscher straining at the end of a leash. She stood, the dog extended toward me, silent to my questions, her eyes bulging nearly out of her head. I took a cursory look around, nodded, and bade her good night. Relatively speaking, however, I never fared as badly as another black male journalist. He went to nearby Waukegan, Illinois, a couple of summers ago to work on a story about a murderer who was born there. Mistaking the reporter for the killer, police hauled him from his car at gunpoint and but for his press credentials would probably have tried to book him. Such episodes are not uncommon. Black men trade tales like this all the time.

In "My Negro Problem—And Ours," Podhoretz writes that the 12 hatred he feels for blacks makes itself known to him through a variety of avenues—one being his discomfort with that "special brand of paranoid touchiness" to which he says blacks are prone. No doubt he is speaking here of black men. In time, I learned to smother the rage I felt at so often being taken for a criminal. Not to do so would surely have led to madness—via that special "paranoid touchiness" that so annoyed Podhoretz at the time he wrote the essay.

I began to take precautions to make myself less threatening. I move 13 about with care, particularly late in the evening. I give a wide berth to nervous people on subway platforms during the wee hours, particularly when I have exchanged business clothes for jeans. If I happen to be entering a building behind some people who appear skittish, I may walk by, letting them clear the lobby before I return, so as not to seem to be following them. I have been calm and extremely congenial on those rare occasions when I've been pulled over by the police.

And on late-evening constitutionals along streets less traveled by, I 14 employ what has proved to be an excellent tension-reducing measure: I whistle melodies from Beethoven and Vivaldi and the more popular classical composers. Even steely New Yorkers hunching toward nighttime destinations seem to relax, and occasionally they even join in the tune. Virtually everybody seems to sense that a mugger wouldn't be warbling bright, sunny selections from Vivaldi's *Four Seasons*. It is my equivalent of the cowbell that hikers wear when they know they are in bear country.

Questions

1. How many shifts in time do you find in this essay?
2. How does Staples use Norman Podhoretz's essay?
3. Staples tells how he has had to alter his behavior. Would you say there is a larger message in this essay? How would you describe it?

Reflecting on Your Self Perceived

Reflect on two or three events in your life when you became aware of how others perceived you. These might be experiences that made you feel "surprised, embarrassed and dismayed," just as Brent Staples felt, or you may have felt surprised and pleased. You should not only tell what happened, but reflect on what difference, if any, the experience made in your self-perception and actions.

Reader-oriented Forms: Discourse and Power

4. DIRECTION

5. PERSUASION

4. DIRECTION

Guiding Your Reader

In writing directions, we assume that the reader wants to follow them. We do not have to engage in persuasion. All we have to do is make our verbal presentation so clear that the reader can get all the necessary information from our words. This is not as easy as it sounds. If you have ever tried to follow the directions that come with various unassembled products, you know something about how difficult it is. Inadequate directions are extremely frustrating and can almost always be traced to one problem: the writer's failure to imagine the reader clearly and to understand what the reader already knows and what new information must be provided.

The writer of directions has to imagine the reader out there somewhere, holding the directions in one hand and coming back to them every step of the way. How much explanation does the reader need? How much can be taken for granted? Cookbooks, for instance, often take a lot for granted. Here are some directions from *The New York Times Cook Book:*

BASIC PIE PASTRY   Pastry for 9-inch pie or 6 tarts

2 cups sifted all-purpose flour   ⅓ **cup cold water, approximately**
1 teaspoon salt
⅔ **cup shortening**

1. Sift together the flour and salt.
2. Using a pastry blender or two knives, chop in the shortening until the mixture resembles coarse cornmeal.

3. Sprinkle water slowly over the top of the flour, while tossing the mixture up from the bottom of the bowl with a fork. After about three-quarters of the water has been added, press the dampened part of the dough into a ball and set aside. Add only enough water to dampen the remaining flour mixture. Press all the dough together and divide into two portions, one slightly larger than the other. If the kitchen is hot, chill the dough for one-half hour before rolling.
4. Place the larger ball of dough on a lightly floured pastry cloth or board, pat in all directions with a floured rolling pin and then roll from the center out in all directions, loosening the pastry and reflouring the cloth and rolling pin as necessary. Roll into a round one-eighth inch thick and two inches larger in diameter than the top of the pie pan.
5. Fold gently into quarters, place in the pan and unfold. Fit the dough into the pan loosely and press against the pan without stretching it. Trim the edge slightly larger than the outside rim of the pan. Add desired filling.
6. Stack the pastry trimmings on the remaining dough and roll until about one inch larger than the top of the pan. Fold gently into quarters and cut several small gashes to allow steam to escape.
7. Moisten the rim of the lower crust, place top crust on the filled pan and unfold. Do not stretch the pastry. Tuck the rim of the top beneath the edge of the undercrust and flute with the fingers, making a tight seal.
8. Bake as directed for the filling used.

For the uninitiated, there will be some mysteries here. How does one "chop in" shortening? What does coarse cornmeal look like? Why is the dough dampened in two steps, then pressed together, and then divided? What temperature must the kitchen be to be "hot"? Are the "pastry trimmings" the same thing as the dough cut off the edge of the pan? If so, when does "dough" become "pastry"? Moisten the rim with what? How do you "flute with the fingers"?

This cookbook is for those who don't need to ask such questions. Another book might proceed in a more elementary way. And someone just learning to cook might well prefer the more elementary book. All kinds of writing must be adjusted to the level of the potential reader, but directive writing is most sensitive to this because the reader has to do more than read it. He or she must act out the directions. Failures of communication that might go unnoticed in other kinds of writing will quickly become apparent when the reader tries to turn directions into deeds.

Here are a few rules (or directions) for you to follow when writing directions.

1. Always imagine the reader trying to perform your words, depending on them.

2. Give the reader as much information and explanation as is necessary—and no more.
3. Go step by step, following the order of procedure with your words so that the reader can follow the words with deeds.
4. Consider the morale of the reader, and offer encouragement when needed, as well as information.

How to Make or Do Something

This exercise has three stages: writing, testing, and revising.

A. *Writing.* Think of something that you know more about than the average person. It can't simply be "knowledge of" in this case; it must be "knowing how to" make something or do something. It must also be something that another person might conceivably want to learn how to do. It can be anything from how a football guard should pull out of the line and block the opposing linebacker or safety on a sweep, to how to change a diaper, tune a guitar, braid hair, paper-train a dog, or figure out a statistical mean.

The first part of your task is to describe clearly the person or the sort of person you are writing this for. How familiar or unfamiliar is he or she with the background? In choosing your audience try not to make your task either too hard or too easy. Choose some type of person who knows something about the subject but doesn't know how this particular thing is done. Remember to write a description of this person first. Then name your project: How to _____. Make a list of all the steps required to complete the task. Next, consider this list in terms of the audience you have described: Will any further explanation be necessary? Can any explanations be simplified? Are there places where you will need to consider your reader's morale? Finally, produce the best set of directions you can for the task you have chosen.

B. *Testing.* Exchange your set of directions with another person in your class. Then, each of you should mark every point at which you feel in doubt about the writer's intentions or feel that you could not follow the directions. Do this, imagining that each of you is exactly the type of person named as audience. Ideally, you should give your paper to the person in the class who fits your audience profile the most closely, but do the best you can in any case. Your reader should provide you with a set of written directions for the revision of your directions.

C. *Revising*. Follow your reader's directions and revise your original directions as well as you can. Resubmit them to your reader for approval. If you ran into problems following your reader's directions for revision, just tell him or her about them. Don't write directions for revising the directions. Enough is enough.

READING

The Art of Eating Spaghetti

In an earlier selection, Russell Baker reflected on his first successful English composition, "The Art of Eating Spaghetti" (pages 40–42). Go back and read that section of the Baker selection and then return to the assignment below.

PRACTICE

The Art of Eating ―――――――

We are told that Baker and his relatives discussed the "socially respectable method for moving spaghetti from plate to mouth," but we aren't told what that method is. Consider your experience with spaghetti and write a socially respectable method for eating it. Or, if you prefer, you may write directions for eating another "difficult" food, such as a triple-decker ice cream cone, barbecued spare ribs, an artichoke, or a long hot dog with relish, onions, catsup, and sauerkraut on a short roll.

Whatever food you choose, remember that you are writing for an audience that is inexperienced in eating this particular food, does not have money to spare for dry-cleaning bills, and is easily embarrassed in public.

READING

Direction through the Ages: How to Conduct Yourself

Since the Middle Ages, conduct literature has been an important forum for directive writing. Such literature tells how to act in various social situations. In so doing, it also promotes certain cultural ideals or virtues. Until the end of the seventeenth century, most conduct literature was addressed to male members of the aristocracy. In the eighteenth and nineteenth centuries, the amount and popularity of such literature increased as women became the preferred audience for conduct-book writers. During the twentieth century, etiquette manuals, self-help books, and advice columns in newspapers and magazines proliferated. As a result, conduct literature is now very specialized in both the readers it addresses and the topics it takes up. Nevertheless, it continues to imply a reader who is—or should be—concerned with self-presentation and self-improvement.

Andreas Capellanus, from *The Art of Courtly Love* (1174–86)

The man who wants to keep his love affair for a long time untroubled should above all things be careful not to let it be known to any outsider, but should keep it hidden from everybody; because when a number of people begin to get wind of such an affair, it ceases to develop naturally and even loses what progress it has already made. Furthermore a lover ought to appear to his beloved wise in every respect and restrained in his conduct, and he should do nothing disagreeable that might annoy her. Moreover every man is bound, in time of need, to come to the aid of his beloved, both by sympathizing with her in all her troubles and by acceding to all her reasonable desires. Even if he knows sometimes that what she wants is not so reasonable, he should be prepared to agree to it after he has asked her to reconsider. And if inadvertently he should do something improper that offends her, let him straightway confess with downcast face that he has done wrong, and let him give the excuse that he lost his temper or make some other suitable explanation that will fit the case. And every man ought to be sparing of praise of his beloved when he is among other men; he should not talk about her often or at great length, and he should not spend a great deal of time in places where she is. When he is with other men, if he meets her in a group of women, he should not try to communicate with her by signs, but should treat her almost like a stranger, lest some person spying on their love might have opportunity to spread malicious gossip. Lovers should not even nod to each other unless they are sure that nobody is watching them. Every man should also wear things that his beloved likes and pay a reasonable amount of attention to his appearance—not too much because excessive care for one's looks is distasteful to everybody and leads people to despise the good looks that one has. If the lover is lavish in giving, that helps him retain a love he has acquired, for all lovers ought to despise all worldly riches and should give alms to those who have need of them. Nothing is considered more praiseworthy in a lover than to be known to be generous, and no matter how worthy a man may be otherwise, avarice degrades him, while many faults are excused if one has the virtue of liberality. Also, if the lover is one who is fitted to be a warrior, he should see to it that his courage is apparent to everybody, for it detracts very much from the good character of a man if he is timid in a fight. A lover should always offer his services and obedience freely to every lady, and he ought to root out all his pride and be very humble. He ought to give a good deal of attention to acting toward all in such fashion that no one may be sorry to call to mind his good deeds or have reason to censure anything he has done. Then, too, he must keep in mind the general rule that lovers must not neglect anything that good manners demand or good breeding suggests, but they should be very careful to do everything of this sort.

Christine de Pizan, from *The Mirror of Honor* (1405)

A lady loving honor, or any woman in the estate of marriage, must 1 love her husband and live with him in peace. Otherwise she already has encountered the torments of Hell, where storms rage perpetually. Although doubtlessly women of all sorts may love their husbands dearly, either they do not know all of these rules or, because of their youth, do not know how to demonstrate their love. This lesson will teach them how.

The noble princess wishing to love according to the rules of honor 2 will conduct herself toward her lord, whether he is young or old, in all ways expected for good faith and true love. She will be humble toward him in deed, word, and attitude. She will obey him without complaint and will keep her peace as punctiliously as did Good *Queen Esther* in the Bible's first chapter of her book, where her lord so loved and honored her that she had no wish he would not grant. The lady will show her love by lavishing care and attention on all matters pertaining to his welfare, that of his soul as well as of his body. In order to attend to his soul she will win the confidence of his confessor, to whom she can turn if she sees in her lord any indication of sin whose practice could lead to his perdition. She might hesitate to mention such frailty to her husband for fear of displeasing him; instead, she will have his confessor admonish him, begging him to serve Our Lord faithfully. And, when giving alms and doing good works, she always will say: "Pray God for my lord and me."

Parallel to her concern for her lord's soul is the lady's concentration 3 on his bodily needs. She must assure that his health is maintained and his life preserved from threat. Therefore she will wish to talk frequently with his physicians, inquiring about the state of his health, sometimes being present at their consultations, and wisely heeding their opinions. Similarly, she will want to be sure her husband's servants serve him well. If need be, she will not hesitate to take personal charge, no matter who has been appointed to this duty. Because it is not customary for royal ladies to be in such close contact with their *husbands* as other women are with theirs, the lady frequently will inquire for information about him from chamberlains and others of his suite. She will see him as often as possible, always expressing joy at their meeting. In his presence she will show a joyful face and say things which she knows will please him.

Dr. John Gregory, from *A Father's Legacy to His Daughters* (1774)

Consider every species of indelicacy in conversation as shameful in itself, and as highly disgusting to us. All double *entendre* is of this sort. The dissoluteness of men's education allows them to be diverted with a kind of wit, which yet they have delicacy enough to be shocked at when it comes from your mouths, or even when you hear it without pain and contempt. Virgin purity is of that delicate nature, that it cannot hear certain things without contamination. It is always in your power to avoid these. No man, but a brute or a fool, will insult a woman with conversation which he sees gives her pain; nor will he dare to do it if she resent the injury with a becoming spirit. There is a dignity in conscious virtue which is able to awe the most shameless and abandoned of men.

You will be reproached, perhaps, with prudery: by prudery is usually meant, an affectation of delicacy. Now I do not wish you to affect delicacy; I wish you to possess it. At any rate, it is better to run the risk of being thought ridiculous than disgusting.

The men will complain of your reserve; they will assure you that a franker behaviour would make you more amiable; but, trust me, they are not sincere when they tell you so. I acknowledge, that on some occasions it might render you more agreeable as companions, but it would make you less amiable as women—an important distinction which many of your sex are not aware of. After all, I wish you to have great ease and openness in your conversation. I only point out some considerations which ought to regulate your behaviour in that respect.

Constance Cary Harrison, from *The Well-Bred Girl in Society* (1898)

A fashion safe to stamp a young girl in general society as but ill-equipped with knowledge of good form is that of "vanishing" in company with her attendant after a dance and remaining in unfrequented corners until remark is thereby created. Such is the young woman whose chaperon is in continual speculation as to her whereabouts, or else in active exercise to find her. She is no doubt often innocent of intention to offend, but at large and mixed entertainments the better part of wisdom in a woman is to keep in view of her fellows. A witty Frenchwoman, Mme. de Girardin, once wrote, "Amuse yourselves, O young beauties, but flutter your wings in the broad light of day. Avoid shadows in which suspicion hides." The "vanishing woman" act, made famous by a clever Hungarian magician in fashionable séances in drawing-rooms last season, should be limited in performance to a platform in full view of the audience. The prompt return of a young woman to the side or vicinity of her chaperon after dancing is not only a graceful and well-bred action, but affords an opportunity to the man, who too often is embarrassed in this respect, to withdraw and fulfil some other engagement.

Conspicuous mannerisms in dancing are offensive to good form. I   2
refer to certain tricks of holding the left arm and hand, of carrying the train of the dress (which should be what is called "dancing length," and then forgotten utterly), of dipping the knees when waltzing, etc. These habits, contracted through heedlessness, perhaps, have been seen to mar the otherwise charming grace of maidens whose youth and beauty called attention to their movements on the floor. A dancing-master in New York, whose pupils are known throughout Europe for their admirable form, would never tolerate an approach to either affectation or hoydenism among the young ladies of his classes. Most of these girls had afterward occasion to discover that what he thus taught them was of the first importance in shaping the verdict of the jury of chaperons, who, sitting on the benches around the ball-room walls, make or mar a maiden's claim to a place in the front ranks of good society.

Letitia Baldridge, from *Amy Vanderbilt's Everyday Etiquette* (1978)

Our fourteen-year-old son wants to begin dating. He is shy and awk-   1
ward, an only child, and we ourselves are confused about the mores of today's dating. How can we help him launch forth into the dating world?

The first thing to master is how to make the date in the first place.   2
Sometimes asking a girl for a date on the telephone is easier for a young man than in a face-to-face meeting.

Before he makes that call, he should jot down on a piece of paper all   3
the information he must communicate, so that no important details will be omitted: the occasion, where is it, when is it, what will everyone be wearing, is a meal included, what time will she be picked up, by whom, how, and when will she be taken home?

When the big night arrives, he should give special attention to his 4
grooming. If he's paying for the whole date, he should have his money
safely in hand; if they are splitting the costs, all of that should have
been arranged ahead of time, so that no embarrassing moments occur.

He should be on time to pick up his date. He should not sit in the 5
car with whoever is driving and simply honk to announce his arrival; he
should go up to her house or apartment and ring the bell. Her parents
will probably ask him inside, and he should sit down with them to
make conversation until she arrives on the scene. If sports, for example, is the only subject about which he talks with ease, he should ask
her parents what they think of such and such a team. That conversation
might last well beyond the time she appears, ready to go.

During their date, he should not leave her alone or go off with other 6
friends. He should make sure she has enough to eat and drink (unless
she's the independent type who takes care of that herself). If it's a
dance, he should see to it she's not standing alone on the sidelines.

He should get her home on time, exactly. If anything happens, such 7
as transportation problems, he should assure that her parents are
called immediately with an explanation of the delay.

At the end of the evening he should say, "Thank you for coming with 8
me tonight." If the young woman doesn't thank him in return and say
that *she* had a great time, then she is the one who needs to look to her
manners!

Questions

1. Most conduct books are divided into subsections, each bearing a subtitle that
   indicates what's at issue. Assume for the moment that each of the excerpts
   above constitutes a complete subsection; give each excerpt a "How to _____"
   or "The Art of _____" subtitle. What problems did you have in coming up
   with subtitles? How did you deal with these problems? Compare your subtitles
   with those composed by your classmates; which subtitles do you like best?
   Why?
2. Which of these excerpts is most like basic directive writing as we have
   described it on pages 58–59? Which excerpt is least like basic directive writing? Do any of the excerpts strike you as nondirective in form or purpose?
3. Which excerpt seems most attentive to the reader? How is this attention
   expressed? Are some parts of each excerpt aimed more at the reader's morale
   than at information or instruction? Which parts? How important are these
   parts?
4. Directive writing aims at influencing its reader's actions. Presumably, it succeeds in being informative when the reader acts out the directions. We doubt,
   however, that you will act out all the directions in these excerpts. Must we
   then conclude that for you, these directive pieces of writing are not informative? What, if anything, do you know now that you didn't know before
   reading these samples of directive writing?

How to Conduct Yourself

The dean of students has asked you to help put together a "Social Survival Skills Manual" for newcomers to the college. You will be working on the manual with some twenty other students, each of whom has the same general task as you do: to choose some particular social situation that is likely to pose a problem for the incoming student and to compose a directive piece of writing that will enable the newcomer to act appropriately. Since the project interests you—and pays well—you agree to draft a contribution for consideration by both the student group and the dean. But what to write about? Meeting people? Getting a date? Dressing for campus success? Making the grade with professors or with a particular group of peers? Dealing with campus police? librarians? roommates? Cafeteria etiquette? Although there are many possibilities, you decide to do the one that you think is really important. So do it.

Indirection

The format and grammar of the following essay are typical of directive writing. Its title is informative; it proceeds step by step with a subsection devoted to each step; and it uses the imperative form of the verb. But is it really a serious piece of directive writing? Does Lebowitz really want directory assistance operators to follow her directions? It doesn't seem so, does it? Maybe this piece of writing is antidirective or undirective; maybe Lebowitz has no intention of guiding the acts of directory assistance operators. But then why bother to write a "how to" manual for them? It seems to us that Lebowitz's manual is neither simply directive nor merely undirective; rather, it is what Shakespeare's Polonius called "a bait of falsehood" that "by indirections find[s] directions out" (*Hamlet* II.i. 60, 63). What do you think?

Fran Lebowitz, "How to Be a Directory Assistance Operator: A Manual"

Introduction

    Uppermost in your mind should be the fact that as a Directory 1 Assistance Operator your job is to serve the public. You must be helpful and courteous, of course, but serving the public is a grave responsibility and consists of a good deal more than might be immediately apparent. Give them the number, sure, but it must be remembered that the public is made up largely of people, and that people have needs far beyond mere telephone numbers. Modern life is such that the public has come to rely rather heavily on convenience, often forgetting the value and rewards of difficult, sustained labor. The human animal has an instinctive need for challenge, and you, as a Directory Assistance Operator, can be instrumental in reintroducing this factor to the lives of your charges. So serve the public, by all means, but do not make the mistake of thinking that serving the public compels you to indulge its every whim—for that, future Directory Assistance Operator, would be not only an error in perception but also a tacit admission of irresponsibility.

Lesson One: Is That a Business or a Residence?

When a member of the public (henceforth to be referred to as the   2 Caller) asks you for a number, do not even think about looking it up before you have inquired in a pleasant yet firm tone of voice, "Is that a business or a residence?" This procedure is never to be omitted, for doing so would display an improper and quite unforgivable pre-sumptuousness on your part. Just because the Russian Tea Room doesn't sound like someone's name to *you* doesn't mean that it isn't. Americans *often* have strange names, a fact that has no doubt come to your attention no matter how short a time you may have been in our country.

Lesson Two: Do You Have the Address?

This lesson is of primary importance as it serves a twofold purpose.   3 The first of these is to facilitate the process of finding the number in cases where there are many parties with the same name. Note that this is not the case in the aforementioned Russian Tea Room, who seems, poor man, to have no living relatives, at least not in Manhattan. The second and more important reason for asking this question is to make certain that the Caller is really interested in the *telephone number,* and is not imposing on your time and energy in a sneaky attempt to weasel out of you, the Directory Assistance Operator, an exact street address. You are, after all, employed by the New York Telephone Company, and are not under any circumstances to allow yourself to be badly used by some larcenous Caller trying to pull a fast one.

Lesson Three: Could You Spell That, Please?

The Caller will frequently respond to this query with an audible and   4 unpleasant sigh, or in extreme cases an outright expletive. Ignore him absolutely. You are just doing your job, and anyway, what good reason could he possibly have for wanting to telephone someone whose name he won't or can't even spell?

Lesson Four: Is That "B" as in Boy?

In recent times this traditional, even classic, question has presented 5 a rather touchy problem. Marches have been marched, laws have been passed, rights have been won. The sensitivity of the average member of the Third World has been heightened to the point where asking, no matter how respectfully, "Is that 'B' as in boy?" is apt to provoke an unseemly response. But since it is quite impossible, no matter how empathetic one may be, to logically inquire, "Is that 'B' as in man?," the modern Directory Assistance Operator is pretty much on her own here. Do, however, avoid "Is that 'B' as in black?" because you can never tell these days. And times being what they are, male Directory Assistance Operators assisting female callers are cautioned strongly against even thinking of risking, "Is that 'B' as in baby?"

Lesson Five: You Can Find That Number Listed in Your Directory

This last procedure, coming as it does at the end of your long, often 6 stressful association with the Caller, is the one most commonly neglected, particularly by the novice. Its importance should, however, not be underestimated, as it is well known that last impressions are lasting impressions. The Directory Assistance Operator is, as has been frequently illustrated in this manual, subjected to every sort of unattractive and condescending human behavior. "You can find that number listed in your directory" is your opportunity to establish once and for all that the Directory Assistance Operator is nobody's fool. "You can find that number listed in your directory" lets the Caller know, in no uncertain terms, that you have no intention of being pushed around by *anyone*, let alone anyone who, it seems, cannot even read the telephone book. So, for heaven's sake, never forget "You can find that number listed in your directory." It gets them every time.

Addendum: Have a Nice Day

The truly dedicated Directory Assistance Operator never fails to 7 conclude the call with a sprightly rendition of "Have a nice day." "Have a nice day" is the perfect parting shot, not only because it shows once and for all which of you is the bigger person, but also because it has the eminently satisfying effect of causing the Caller to forget the number.

Questions

1. Which of our rules for directive writing (pages 58–59) does Lebowitz follow in her essay? Which rules does she break? How does she break these rules?
2. In reading this "manual," when did you know for sure that it was not to be taken literally as a set of straightforward directions for directory assistance operators? What words, phrases, or passages made you so sure?

3. As you see it, what are the directions that Lebowitz implicitly gives to directory assistance operators? to the public who deals with such operators?
4. Lebowitz's "manual" appears in a collection of her essays called *Social Studies*. To what extent is her "manual" a study of our society? What, if anything, did you learn about our society by considering this example of indirection?

PRACTICE

How to be a _____: A Manual

Our society is full of people whose job is to serve some segment of the public. There are police officers, social workers, waiters, sales personnel, political representatives, guidance counselors, professors, lawyers, librarians, directive writers, and many others. Sometimes, members of the public feel themselves ill-served by those in a position to serve them well. Has this ever happened to you? If so, this practice offers you the chance to get back at those who have served you ill—but only by indirection. Using Lebowitz's essay as a model, write a set of directions for some specific kind of public servant that not only exposes how the public can be ill-served but also suggests—by indirection—how we might be better served.

5. PERSUASION

Moving Your Reader

In a democratic and capitalistic society, we depend upon persuasion to do what coercion does in a totalitarian society. Thus persuasion is used to move us to vote in certain ways and to spend in certain ways. We are, in fact, bombarded with persuasive texts, visual as well as verbal, by all the media of mass communication: newspapers, magazines, radio, and television. Written persuasion is also used in more personal ways: to seek employment, to redress grievances, to make changes in an organization or group. In public life, persuasion pervades our law courts as well as our halls of government.

Although many political speeches and some advertisements do, in fact, mix rational argument with the emotional appeal of persuasive language, we can make a clear distinction between argument and persuasion. Argument seeks to make an informed case for or against something; it tries to prove by logical connection that one view of a topic is right and another is wrong. It does not necessarily seek to motivate the reader to action. Persuasion, on the other hand, is always concerned with action and motivation: "trust me," "fear them," "buy this product," "vote for this candidate." At its most insidious, persuasion can even spur readers to action that is contrary to reason.

Every citizen needs to be able to deal with persuasion in two ways: to produce it when necessary and to defend oneself against it constantly. For purposes of defense, it is best to know how persuasion is put together from the inside. One who has written it knows firsthand how it works. These persuasive exercises, then, are designed with a double purpose: to improve your writing skills and to make you a more alert and critical reader of persuasive texts.

There are certain aspects of persuasion that are neither nice nor fair. Persuasion tries to subdue thought by appealing to emotion, and persuasive writing, in its most extreme forms, tries to ignore the alternatives to whatever cause it is pleading. Advertisers of cigarettes are not happy to include that little message from the Surgeon General in their ads. They would much prefer to ignore the dangerous side of their product. As it is, they will do everything they can to counter those ominous words about ill-health by projecting images of healthy outdoor life associated with the product.

In some of these assignments you will be asked to think in this same one-sided way, because this is the best way to learn how persuasive discourse works. These are language games we are playing here, to help develop your verbal abilities. We are not "playing for keeps." So enter into them with good will, adopting the roles that are assigned. But be wary of learning these lessons too well. Persuasion is a dangerous toy.

READING

Persuasion in Advertising

The persuasive manner of the following ad may seem ludicrously obvious now, but its techniques are still used. Notice how the visual and verbal aspects of the ad reinforce one another. Few contemporary ads would rely so heavily on verbal copy. (Because the verbal print is so small in our reduced copy, we have reproduced the language of the fine print from the ad.) After you have examined the pictures and text, consider the questions that follow them.

Fly-Tox Advertisement, 1926

In many finely appointed homes spraying every room with Fly-Tox 1 is a daily summertime accomplishment. This is not just an exceptional refinement. Indeed, it is considered a requisite to good housekeeping.

Spraying the entire room with Fly-Tox reaches and kills offensive 2 household insects even in their places of hiding. That insures unmolested summer comfort. Musty, fly-tainted odors are displaced by an atmosphere of cleanliness. The draperies are unsoiled, spotless, beautiful. The upholstery fresh and bright, radiant with cleanliness. In the absence of unclean household insects, every room in the house

What is your baby worth?

Priceless! A great gift that can never be replaced! Innocent and defenseless. Its comfort and health, even life itself, depend on little duties that constitute vigilant care and loving thoughtfulness.

In the summertime no greater service can be rendered than to shield the child and its food from the perilous contact with flies and mosquitoes.

The fly is the filthiest insect known. Literally hundreds—some scientists say, thousands—of deadly bacteria swarm in the putrescent ooze of a fly's spongy foot. It contaminates everything it touches. Sows the germs of disease on the very delicacies a child likes to eat.

The mosquito is no less an assassin. Whole epidemics have been traced by its ravages. Penetrating a child's tender skin, the bite is bitterly painful. And with the germ of fever firing their blood, little bodies writhe in the burning torture of flaming torment. The end—sometimes is tragic.

Flies and mosquitoes transmit typhoid fever, dysentery infantile paralysis. Safety is only possible when these insects are killed. That is why devoted parents in millions of homes use Fly-Tox. It destroys flies and mosquitoes. It safeguards the health and comfort of our most precious possession—little children.

Wherever there are flies, use Fly-Tox

In many finely appointed homes spraying every room with Fly-Tox is a daily summertime accomplishment. This is not just an exceptional refinement. Indeed, it is considered a requisite to good housekeeping.

Spraying the entire room with Fly-Tox reaches and kills offensive household insects even in their places of hiding. That insures unmolested summer comfort. Musty, fly-tainted odors are displaced by an atmosphere of cleanliness. The draperies are unsoiled, spotless, beautiful. The upholstery fresh and bright, radiant with cleanliness. In the absence of unclean household insects, every room in the house glows with a refreshing, cleanly charm—a charm in which every housewife enjoys a rightful pride.

The Modern Safeguard to Health and Comfort

Fly-Tox is an established, efficient household insecticide. It was developed at Mellon Institute of Industrial Research. Stainless. Harmless to humans. Yet when its cleanly fragrant spray touches them these insect enemies to man's health and comfort crumple up and die. Fly-Tox has brought to millions of homes a new summer comfort—a house without flies or mosquitoes. Most people prefer the hand sprayer. It gives better satisfaction. However, a trial sprayer is given free with every small bottle.

HALF PINT · 50C   PINT · 75C   QUART · $1.25   GALLON · $4.00

Gallons in glass jugs are especially suitable for hotels, restaurants, summer camps, institutions

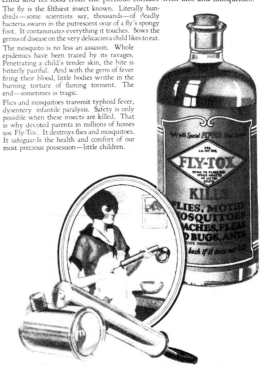

FLY-TOX
KILLS FLIES
MOSQUITOES
MOTHS. ROACHES, ANTS, FLEAS

glows with a refreshing, cleanly charm—a charm in which every house-wife enjoys a rightful pride.

Fly-Tox is an established, efficient household insecticide. It was 3 developed at Mellon Institute of Industrial Research. Stainless. Harm-less to humans. Yet when its cleanly fragrant spray touches them these insect enemies to man's health and comfort crumple up and die. Fly-Tox has brought to millions of homes a new summer comfort—a house without flies or mosquitoes.

Most people prefer the hand sprayer. It gives better satisfaction. 4 However, a trial sprayer is given free with every small bottle.

In the summertime no greater service can be rendered than to 5 shield the child and its food from the perilous contact with flies and mosquitoes. The fly is the filthiest insect known. Literally hundreds—some scientists say, thousands—of deadly bacteria swarm in the putrescent ooze of a fly's spongy foot. It contaminates everything it touches. Sows the germs of disease on the very delicacies a child likes to eat.

The mosquito is no less an assassin. Whole epidemics have been 6 traced by its ravages. Penetrating a child's tender skin, the bite is bitterly painful. And with the germ of fever firing their blood, little bodies writhe in the burning torture of flaming torment. The end—sometimes is tragic.

Flies and mosquitoes transmit typhoid fever, dysentery, infantile 7 paralysis. Safety is only possible when these insects are killed. That is why devoted parents in millions of homes use Fly-Tox. It destroys flies and mosquitoes. It safeguards the health and comfort of our most precious possession—little children.

Questions

1. Advertising is usually aimed at a specific audience. How would you describe the target group for this ad? What details in the ad indicate the audience the copywriter had in mind?
2. Persuasion often appeals to "absolutes" or accepted standards of value or behavior. How many different appeals of this sort can you detect in the Fly-Tox ad? What emotions are most directly evoked by the text?
3. Consider the use of connotative language in the text of the ad. What connotations are most frequently and powerfully evoked? How are contrasting connotations used to motivate the prospective buyer? How much information about the composition of the product is actually given? Where do you suspect the ad to be farthest from the truth? Where is it most accurate?
4. How do the visual images work to persuade? What is the function of each of the five separate pictures presented? Can you link certain images with specific words in the text?

READER-ORIENTED FORMS

PRACTICE

The Ghastly Resort Hotel

You have just landed a job writing advertising copy for a resort hotel on a small island off the coast of the United States. The hotel management has brought you to the island for a few days of exploration, during which you have noted the following features:

1. The hotel seems made of plastic. It features shiny, new, bright, loud colors and wildly patterned wallpaper.
2. The rooms are very small, the walls are thin, and music from the hotel bar can be heard all night long.
3. Hot water for bathing is seldom available.
4. The hotel band, a group of local kids playing on garbage can lids and harmonicas, seems to know only three songs.
5. The island is run by a dictator whose soldiers are everywhere. You saw three of them savagely beat a ragged child who tried to steal a loaf of bread.
6. The one town on the island is really a small village full of battered shacks with outdoor plumbing facilities.
7. The beach consists of a small amount of imported white sand spread over the local mud.
8. A swimmer at the beach was recently attacked and badly wounded by a barracuda.
9. At two minutes after sunset, hordes of large, vicious mosquitoes come out.
10. It is blazing hot while the sun is out but damp and cold at night.
11. The hotel owns one large motor launch. Every few days, when the launch is in good repair, it takes a crowded group of tourists to a small sand bar where they look for shells but mostly find cans and bottles left by other tourists.
12. The food in the hotel is highly flavored with some mysterious local herb that lingers in your taste buds for days. The most frequently featured dish is a local specialty: squid.

All in all, this is not a place you would choose for yourself or recommend to a friend. But the job is important to you, and you have already run up a large bill that you cannot pay until you receive your fee for writing the copy. You decide that you will not leave out any of the material from the above list (to satisfy your conscience), but you will try to put everything in the most favorable light possible (to appease your employer). You sit down in your room to write the most attractive copy you can. You can hear the band playing one of their three tunes. You begin to write. . . .

But before you begin, let us give you some technical advice. You have several problems to contend with here. One is organizational. The twelve items you have to cover must be grouped in paragraphs according to some system. You must look for natural groupings and then organize your writing accordingly, with an appropriate introduction and conclusion. Another problem is connotation. Nothing in your copy must have an unpleasant connotation. The word *barracuda*, for instance, would be as out of place as the word *cancer* in a cigarette ad. This problem, in turn, leads to a denotative problem. To satisfy what is left of your conscience, you must use some word or phrase that points to the barracuda you happen to know about, although this reference must be disguised or prettied-up in some way. And so it is for every detail.

READING

Reaching a Different Audience

The advertisement on page 76 appeared in 1954, in a campaign designed to change the image of Marlboro cigarettes. Marlboro cigarettes were identified as a "feminine high-style cigarette" when the company decided to go masculine. This is the way that marketing researcher Pierre Martineau described that campaign in *Motivation in Advertising* (1957): "1. No women were shown in the advertising. 2. All models were very virile men. . . . 3. The models were also chosen as successful, forceful personalities to inspire emulation, identification with an admirable figure. . . . 4. To reinforce the notion of virility and also to hint of a romantic past, each man had a plainly visible tattoo on his hand. . . . This symbol gave richness to the product image, bringing it all into focus."

PRACTICE

Changing the Persuasive Pattern

Pierre Martineau's analysis makes clear the motivation behind the Marlboro Man ad. Your job in this assignment is to produce an ad for a different but similar advertising campaign.

First find a product that is clearly associated with one particular type of person (a certain sex, age, class, race, profession). Then construct an ad designed to make that same product appeal to a very different type of person. Make an entire full-page ad, with visual and verbal material laid out in the most effective way. (This is a cut-and-paste job.)

Along with the ad, submit a paragraph in which you explain what you

The Marlboro Man

A lot of man . . . a lot of cigarette

"He gets a lot to like—filter, flavor, flip-top box." The works.
A filter that means business. An easy draw that's all
flavor. And the flip-top box that ends crushed cigarettes.

(MADE IN RICHMOND, VIRGINIA, FROM A PRIZED RECIPE)

NEW "SELF-STARTER"

Marlboro

Just pull the tab
slowly and the
cigarettes pop
up. No digging.
No trouble.

POPULAR FILTER PRICE

have done. Describe the association pattern you are trying to change, and the sort of consumer you are trying to persuade to buy your product.

READING

Political Persuasion

On January 20, 1993, Bill Clinton delivered the following speech at his inauguration as President of the United States. During the presidential campaign, Clinton had declared himself an agent of "change"—a "New Democrat" determined to do what was necessary to revitalize both the economy and the society of the United States. Voter turnout for the 1992 presidential election was higher than it had been for the preceding thirty years. But even though Clinton won the electoral college vote quite handily, the results of the popular vote were less clear-cut: 43 percent of the popular vote went to Bill Clinton, 38 percent to George Bush, and 19 percent to Ross Perot. For the first time in twelve years, a Democrat was elected president; but that Democrat did not receive a majority of the popular vote.

In Clinton's inaugural speech, you will see how one contemporary politician goes about appealing to an audience for their support in the difficult times that lie ahead. As far as we know, most public commentators considered the speech a solid piece of persuasion rather than either a *tour de force* or a weak performance. What do you think? Do you find Clinton's speech appealing and persuasive?

The two practices that follow Clinton's speech give you the chance to try your hand at political persuasion. The first is adapted from a century-old play by Henrik Ibsen, and the other has been invented for this occasion, but each offers you the opportunity to practice one of the most important features of persuasive writing: getting the audience on your side.

Bill Clinton, Inaugural Address

My fellow citizens, today we celebrate the mystery of American   1
renewal. This ceremony is held in the depth of winter, but by the words we speak and the faces we show the world, we force the spring. A spring reborn in the world's oldest democracy that brings forth the vision and courage to reinvent America.

When our founders boldly declared America's independence to the   2
world and our purposes to the Almighty, they knew that America to endure would have to change. Not change for change sake but change to preserve America's ideals—life, liberty, the pursuit of happiness. Though we march to the music of our time, our mission is timeless.

Each generation of Americans must define what it means to be an American.

On behalf of our nation, I salute my predecessor, President Bush, 3 for his half-century of service to America.

And I thank the millions of men and women whose steadfastness 4 and sacrifice triumphed over depression, fascism and communism. Today, a generation raised in the shadows of the cold war assumes new responsibilities in a world warmed by the sunshine of freedom but threatened still by ancient hatreds and new plagues.

Raised in unrivaled prosperity, we inherit an economy that is still 5 the world's strongest but is weakened by business failures, stagnant wages, increasing inequality and deep divisions among our own people.

When George Washington first took the oath I have just sworn to 6 uphold, news traveled slowly across the land by horseback and across the ocean by boat. Now the sights and sounds of this ceremony are broadcast instantaneously to billions around the world. Communications and commerce are global, investment is mobile, technology is almost magical, and ambition for a better life is now universal. We earn our livelihood in America today in peaceful competition with people all across the earth. Profound and powerful forces are shaking and remaking our world. And the urgent question of our time is whether we can make change our friend and not our enemy.

This new world has already enriched the lives of millions of Amer- 7 icans who are able to compete and win in it. But when most people are working harder for less, when others cannot work at all, when the cost of health care devastates families and threatens to bankrupt our enterprises great and small, when the fear of crime robs law-abiding citizens of their freedom, and when millions of poor children cannot even imagine the lives we are calling them to lead, we have not made change our friend. We know we have to face hard truths and take strong steps, but we have not done so. Instead, we have drifted, and that drifting has eroded our resources, fractured our economy and shaken our confidence.

Though our challenges are fearsome, so are our strengths. Amer- 8 icans have ever been a restless, questing, hopeful people, and we must bring to our task today the vision and will of those who came before us. From our Revolution to the Civil War, to the Great Depression, to the civil rights movement, our people have always mustered the determination to construct from these crises the pillars of our history.

Thomas Jefferson believed that to preserve the very foundations of 9 our nation we would need dramatic change from time to time. Well my fellow Americans, this is our time. Let us embrace it.

Our democracy must be not only the envy of the world but the 10 engine of our own renewal. There is nothing wrong with America that cannot be cured by what is right with America. And so today we pledge an end to the era of deadlock and drift, and a new season of American renewal has begun.

To renew America we must be bold. We must do what no genera- 11 tion has had to do before. We must invest more in our own people—in their jobs and in their future—and at the same time cut our massive debt. And we must do so in a world in which we must compete for every opportunity. It will not be easy. It will require sacrifice. But it can be done and done fairly. Not choosing sacrifice for its own sake, but for our own sake. We must provide for our nation the way a family provides for its children.

Our founders saw themselves in the light of posterity. We can do no 12 less. Anyone who has ever watched a child's eyes wander into sleep knows what posterity is. Posterity is the world to come. The world for whom we hold our ideals, from whom we have borrowed our planet and to whom we bear sacred responsibility. We must do what America does best: offer more opportunity to all and demand more responsibility from all.

It is time to break the bad habit of expecting something for nothing 13 from our Government or from each other. Let us all take more responsibility not only for ourselves and our families but for our communities and our country.

To renew America we must revitalize our democracy. This beautiful 14 capital, like every capital since the dawn of civilization, is often a place of intrigue and calculation. Powerful people maneuver for position and worry endlessly about who is in and who is out, who is up and who is down, forgetting those people whose toil and sweat sends us here and pays our way.

Americans deserve better, and in this city today there are people 15 who want to do better. And so I say to all of you here, let us resolve to reform our politics so that power and privilege no longer shout down the voice of the people. Let us put aside personal advantage so that we can feel the pain and see the promise of America. Let us resolve to make our Government a place for what Franklin Roosevelt called bold, persistent experimentation, a Government for our tomorrows, not our yesterdays. Let us give this capital back to the people to whom it belongs.

To renew America, we must meet challenges abroad as well as at 16 home. There is no longer a clear division between what is foreign and what is domestic. The world economy, the world environment, the world AIDS crisis, the world arms race—they affect us all.

Today, as an old order passes, the new world is more free but less 17 stable. Communism's collapse has called forth old animosities and new dangers. Clearly, America must continue to lead the world we did so much to make.

While America rebuilds at home, we will not shrink from the 18 challenges nor fail to seize the opportunities of this new world. Together with our friends and allies we will work to shape change lest it engulf us. When our vital interests are challenged or the will and conscience of the international community is defied, we will act, with peaceful diplomacy whenever possible, with force when necessary.

The brave Americans serving our nation today in the Persian Gulf 19 and Somalia, and wherever else they stand, are testament to our resolve.

But our greatest strength is the power of our ideas, which are still 20 new in many lands. Across the world we see them embraced and we rejoice. Our hopes, our hearts, our hands are with those on every continent who are building democracy and freedom. Their cause is America's cause.

The American people have summoned the change we celebrate 21 today. You have raised your voices in an unmistakable chorus, you have cast your votes in historic numbers, and you have changed the face of Congress, the Presidency and the political process itself. Yes, you, my fellow Americans, have forced the spring.

Now we must do the work the season demands. To that work I now 22 turn with all the authority of my office. I ask the Congress to join with me. But no President, no Congress, no government can undertake this mission alone. My fellow Americans, you, too, must play your part in our renewal.

I challenge a new generation of young Americans to a season of 23 service; to act on your idealism by helping troubled children, keeping company with those in need, reconnecting our torn communities. There is so much to be done. Enough, indeed, for millions of others who are still young in spirit to give of themselves in service, too.

In serving, we recognize a simple but powerful truth: We need each 24 other and we must care for one another. Today we do more than celebrate America, we rededicate ourselves to the very idea of Amer-ica: An idea born in revolution and renewed through two centuries of challenge; an idea tempered by the knowledge that but for fate we, the fortunate and the unfortunate, might have been each other; an idea ennobled by the faith that our nation can summon from its myriad diversity the deepest measure of unity; an idea infused with the conviction that America's long, heroic journey must go forever up-ward.

And so, my fellow Americans, as we stand at the edge of the 21st 25 century, let us begin anew with energy and hope, with faith and discipline. And let us work until our work is done. The Scripture says,

"And let us not be weary in well-doing, for in due season we shall reap if we faint not."

From this joyful mountaintop of celebration we hear a call to service 26 in the valley. We have heard the trumpets, we have changed the guard. And now each in our own way, and with God's help, we must answer the call.

Thank you, and God bless you all. 27

Questions

1. This speech is not so much a case of persuasion to action—to buy something or vote for someone—as it is persuasion to believe in something. What, exactly, is the audience being asked to believe?
2. Consider the ways in which the speaker establishes a positive relationship with the audience. Note, for example, his use of the pronouns "I," "me," "you," "we," and "us." Which pronoun is most often used? Why isn't it used all the time?
3. Compare the structure, style, and point of paragraphs 1 and 5. In what ways are these two paragraphs similar? In what ways are they different? Why do you think Clinton began with paragraph 1 instead of paragraph 5? Are many other paragraphs in this speech structured like paragraph 1? What about style? Which paragraphs are most like paragraph 1 in style?
4. Political persuasion often appeals to widely accepted standards, values, traditions, and authorities. Hence, appeals to nationalism and religious belief are common in American political discourse. To what standards, values, traditions, and authorities does Clinton appeal? Does he use one kind of appeal more than others?
5. The persuasive force of a political speech is often measured by the quotable maxims, slogans, or sound-bites it contains. Many commentators on Clinton's speech cited the following line as quotable: "There is nothing wrong with America that cannot be cured by what is right with America." Can you find other such quotable lines or phrases? What makes these lines or phrases so quotable?

PRACTICE

An Enemy of the People

Assume that you are a doctor in a small resort town. The economy of the town depends heavily on the seasonal business of tourists who come to swim in clean waters and enjoy cool breezes. You have just made some tests and discovered that sewage from the town has begun to pollute the beach water, posing a danger to the health of bathers. In your judgment, the town must either close the beach to swimming or put in expensive equipment to treat the sewage before it is pumped into the water.

News of your discovery has leaked out, some of it in wildly exaggerated form. Since closing the beach would hurt many people financially, you are rapidly becoming an unpopular person. You have been getting obscene phone calls, and garbage has been dumped on your doorstep. Your children say they don't want to go to school but won't say why—though they never were reluctant to go to school in the past.

Some of the owners of small hotels along the shore have found another doctor who will swear that the beach is perfectly healthy. Someone is spreading a rumor that you have been trying to scare people and drive real estate prices down so that you can make a profit for yourself. This is complicated by the fact that you *have* been looking for a larger house to buy, closer to the beach.

The situation is very ugly. At this point the mayor calls a town meeting to discuss the water and sewage problem. You know the other doctor will be there. You have received a threatening letter telling you to stay away. But you have resolved to take your case to the people. You know that you will have to be very persuasive to get a fair hearing. You sit down to write your speech. . . .

PRACTICE

The Difficult Campaign Speech

Persuasive discourse is important in all elections for public office, from dogcatcher to President of the United States. The following assignment is designed to let you try your hand at writing a political speech under certain specific conditions.

You are running for the office of mayor (or some other office in local government) in your hometown. Your opponent is one of the richest and most influential members of the community. His family has been prominent for generations. He attended private school and graduated from Harvard College with highest honors and then from Yale Law School. He is now the senior partner in your community's most prestigious law firm.

You went to the local public schools and the state or city college, where your record was relatively undistinguished. In your teens, you hung around with a group that was often in minor trouble with the police. As a college student, you and a group of friends were busted for possession of marijuana but charges against you were dropped for lack of evidence. Some of your friends were not so fortunate. After graduating from college, you held a number of sales positions in local businesses. You got married and had two children; after fifteen years of marriage, you and your spouse decided to divorce each other. At present, you are well-to-do through part ownership of a used-car lot and a chain of neighborhood hairdressing establishments.

Your opponent has just told the public about your arrest, some twenty years ago, for drug possession. He has also questioned your family values as well as your business acumen. You are scheduled to make a speech at a local community college. The audience will be composed of students who live in your town and are eligible to vote. Many, but not all, of these students are in their late teens or early twenties.

In writing your speech, you must decide how to deal with your own record, with your opponent, and with your audience. You may choose to ignore some things, but remember that it might be better to deal with them than to leave them undiscussed. In particular, you must work to leave this audience feeling good about you—not merely sympathetic, but convinced that you have qualities that will make you the better official from the point of view of their attitudes and interests. You may promise things, as all politicians do, but if you promise too much you may lose credibility. Above all, you must leave the audience with faith in your ability and integrity. In an actual situation, your clothing, posture, voice, gestures, gaze, and other things would help or hinder you. Here, you have only words to work with. Make them work for you.

READING

The Job Letter and Résumé

When you apply for a job, most business and professional organizations require you to submit a letter of application and a résumé of your educational and work experience. On the basis of these two documents, they decide whether or not to grant you an interview, so it's important that your letter of application be direct, sincere, persuasive, and well written, and that your résumé be factual and neat in appearance.

The Résumé

On page 84 is a sample résumé presenting the facts about Jennifer Hazard, who is seeking a position in a bank. Her résumé follows one of the standard formats. In drawing up your own résumé, you may want to check with the job placement office at your school for suggestions or consult one of the many books on writing résumés that are now available.

The Letter

Your letter of application should elaborate on the information in your résumé that is most pertinent to the job for which you are applying. Letters of application also follow a fairly standard format:

Résumé

JENNIFER HAZARD

63 Bridge Road
Warlock, Rhode Island 02885
Phone: 401-247-8694

Education:

| 1985–1989 | Warlock High School, Warlock, Rhode Island |

1989–1991 Ocean State Junior College, Cranberry, Rhode
           Island
           Major: Accounting

1991–1993 Pawtuxet College, Providence, Rhode Island;
           will graduate May 21, 1988 with a B.A. degree.
           Minor: Sociology

Extracurricular Activities:

1991–1993 Pawtuxet College Women's Swim Team

1992–1993 Business Manager, Pawtuxet College Clarion

Experience:

1988–1989 Cashier, Joe's Family Drive-In, Warlock, Rhode
           Island

1989   Counselor, Swimming Instructor, Stone Hill Camp,
           Rumstick, Rhode Island

1991–1992 Bookkeeper, Mercury Hardware Store, Warlock,
           Rhode Island

1992–present Teller, Warlock Town Bank, Warlock, Rhode
              Island

References:

Professor John McNulty, Department of Economics,
Pawtuxet College, Providence, Rhode Island 02903

Professor Marilyn Vargas, Department of Sociology,
Pawtuxet College, Providence, Rhode Island 02903

Mr. Joseph DiSano, Manager, Warlock Town Bank,
Warlock, Rhode Island 02885

Paragraph 1: State the job for which you are applying. Explain where you saw the advertisement or who told you about the job.

Paragraph 2: Describe your college training, stressing those courses and activities most relevant to the job for which you are applying.

Paragraph 3: Describe your previous work experience and how it relates to the position you want.

Paragraph 4: Tell why you'd like to work for the particular company or organization.

Paragraph 5: State that your résumé is enclosed (and any other material requested, such as letters of recommendation), and that you are available for an interview.

Following are a sample job advertisement and a letter from Jennifer Hazard.

BRANCH MANAGER TRAINEES

Friendly National Bank seeks recent college graduates interested in a challenging career as Branch Managers in our rapidly expanding bank. If you are hard-working, self-starting, enjoy responsibility, and love working with people, you will be right for our training program. Some experience in banking, or training in economics, management, or accounting preferred.

Send letter and résumé to:
Harold O'Brien
Personnel Department
Friendly National Bank
Providence, Rhode Island 02905

```
                                    65 Bridge Road
                                    Warlock, Rhode Island
                                    May 1, 19--


Mr. Harold O'Brien
Personnel Department
Friendly National Bank
Providence, Rhode Island   02905

Dear Mr. O'Brien:
```

　　I wish to apply for the position as Branch Manager Trainee which was advertised in the <u>Providence</u> <u>Daily</u> <u>Bugle</u> on April 30.

　　This month I shall be graduating from Pawtuxet College, where I've been majoring in economics. Because I've been interested in a career in banking, I decided to research the functions of the two banks in my hometown of Warlock for my economics honors thesis. I wanted to know what services were most used by the customers of these banks and how the banks were working with small businesses to help them expand or to improve their facilities. Warlock, like so many older towns, has had to revitalize its downtown business area in order to compete with the new malls outside town. Such renewal has been possible because of the cooperation of the banks, the town planning committee, and the businesspeople. Writing this thesis showed me how important a part of a community a bank can be when it takes an active interest in the growth of that community.

　　I've had practical experience in financial affairs as Business Manager of the college newspaper and in my summer and part-time work as a bookkeeper and as a teller. In fact, doing the books for a small hardware store which wanted to expand gave me a good picture of small busisness problems. It was this experience that started my thesis research.

　　I'd especially enjoy working for Friendly National Bank because of the innovations in banking you've introduced and because I am looking for a challenging position in a bank that gives the same attention to the small businessperson as to a large corporation.

　　I have enclosed my résumé, and if my credentials interest you, I am available for an interview at your convenience.

```
                                    Sincerely yours,

                                    Jennifer Hazard

                                    JENNIFER HAZARD
```

The Job Letter

We have provided six job advertisements adapted from advertisements that appeared in various newspapers. Choose one of these advertisers as a prospective employer, or if you prefer, find an advertisement in your local newspaper for a job you would like.

First, you should draw up a résumé following the model in this book or another standard format. You can list your own qualifications or imagine you are someone else and invent some suitable qualifications for the job you're interested in.

Second, write a letter applying for the job. Remember, be direct and sincere, and be sure to read the job advertisement very carefully. For example, look at the Byron Badway advertisement for video game designers. This company stresses its "creative design group" and development of electronic games, so you should show in your letter that you have held creative, developmental positions either at work or at school. Also, this company produces "sensational" games. Therefore they want to hire people with a strong background in their field ("avid and experienced game-player") and related areas ("computers, animation, technical drawing"). In other words, you'll have to convince them that you're knowledgeable, creative, ambitious, deeply interested in what they manufacture, and that you work well with others.

Choose your job, and start writing.

VIDEO GAME DESIGNER

The Byron Badway Company has an opening for a Video Game Designer. Join our creative design group and help us develop new games as sensational as our latest hit, VENUSIAN VELCRO WARS. In addition, you will participate in the developing of electronic games and toys and traditional board and 3-D games.

The person we seek should have a BSID degree or the equivalent, and experience in such related fields as computers, film animation, or technical drawing. He or she should also be an avid and experienced game-player.

Send your letter and résumé to:
Personnel Manager
Byron Badway Co.
615 Circuit Drive
North Melba, New Jersey 05697

PHYSICAL THERAPIST

Full time position available for Registered Physical Therapist in growing department of a 250-bed accredited general hospital.

Excellent opportunity for the right individual to help develop new therapy program. If you are creative, resourceful, people-oriented, and would like to live and work in one of Florida's finest recreational areas on the blue water coast of the beautiful Gulf, apply now.

Salary based on potential and experience, plus excellent benefits. Contact the Personnel Department, Luxor General Hospital, Luxor Beach, Florida 32509.

Fragrance Evaluator

Lucretia Borgia Cosmetics, maker of Spring Mist, Ravishing, and Ariel fragrances, offers an excellent opportunity for a qualified individual to function as an in-house expert in the evaluation of Lucretia Borgia Fragrances, as well as our health and beauty products.

Two years of fragrance evaluation experience, coupled with an extensive knowledge and appreciation of fine fragrances and fragrance products, is required. The individual we seek should also possess well-developed communication and interpersonal skills in order to deal with all types of personnel.

We offer a highly competitive salary, and excellent benefits including major medical, life insurance, pension plan, and paid relocation expenses.

Qualified individuals should send letter and résumé to: Personnel Department,

Lucretia Borgia Cosmetics, Inc.
Ripley Industrial Park
Ripley, New York 10612

District Manager

Texas Taco, America's biggest and most successful chain of taco shops, has just celebrated another outstanding year of incredible growth.

We seek a highly motivated district manager whose responsibilities will include marketing, financial planning, work plans and profit objectives for Texas Taco shops in your district. Involvement with franchising and direct line duties with top level executives are also important aspects of this position.

Your personal qualities are of more interest to us than your specific background. A Bachelor's degree and 3-5 years of general business experience are required. We offer an excellent starting salary, a full range of fringe benefits, and a thorough, stimulating training program.

If you are seeking a position of importance and high visibility, one which impacts significantly on the future of Texas Taco, submit letter, résumé, and salary history to:

Personnel Department
Texas Taco, Inc.
150 Sam Houston Blvd.
Dallas, Texas 80653

Topic-oriented Forms: Discourse and Knowledge

6. NARRATION

7. DESCRIPTION

8. CLASSIFICATION

9. ANALYSIS

10. ARGUMENTATION

11. SYNTHESIS

6. NARRATION

Organizing Time

To narrate is to give an account—in speech or in writing—of a process or series of events that take place over a period of time. The period of time may be large or small, years or seconds, but time is the heart of narrative. Speech and writing themselves take time. It takes a certain amount of time to utter a sequence of sentences, or even a single sentence. It also takes time to write or to read a sentence. The art or craft of writing narrative prose depends upon how the writer manages these two times—the time of events and the time of reading. It is possible, for instance, to describe a whole baseball season in a few sentences ("The Red Sox started out well in April but faded in September—a familiar story."); but it is also possible to spend a lot of time—and a lot of words—describing a single pitch to a single batter. If you write about a single pitch, of course, you will break down that event (the pitch) into a series of sub-events (little movements of the pitcher and the batter—or even their thoughts and feelings) in order to make your account into a narrative.

A big part of the writer's task in producing narrative prose, then, is choosing a suitable level of detail for the events being recounted and arranging those details in a sequence that will present events clearly. The writer of narrative must also solve a few other problems. One is the problem of emotional affect. Every narrative generates some emotional affect. Often, in academic writing such as assignments in courses, the effect sought is one of cold, dispassionate clarity. It is possible to think of this as the absence of emotion—as a pure, "natural" kind of writing. But the absence of emotion is far from natural. It is an effect achieved by writers through a considerable act of self-discipline. It is, in fact, something that every student of writing must work to achieve in order to satisfy the requirements of certain courses or instructors. The best way to gain control over the whole range of emotional possibilities in narration—from engaged to detached, from hot to cold—is to practice narrating the "same" events with different emotional coloration. In preparation for this kind of work, you should learn to read narrative prose with one eye on the way the writer shapes the reader's feelings about what is narrated.

Another problem facing the writer of narrative is that of point of view. From whose perspective will the events be recounted? As you are no doubt aware, viewpoint is closely related to the emotional quality of a narration. It is possible to tell events from the perspective of a detached observer, like a god or a scientist, but it is also possible to use the perspective of someone emotionally involved in the events. If you want to achieve an unemotional perspective about some experiments on a guinea pig, you do not recount them from the viewpoint of the guinea pig. One of the skills you should develop with respect to narrative is the ability to recount the "same" events from different points of view.

Rather than continuing to discuss narration in this abstract way, we think it will be better to move to some examples of narrative prose written by accomplished writers. Each of these samples is a short section from a longer work. They are not presented as complete texts, with beginnings, middles, and ends, but as demonstrations of how a good writer produces narrative prose. We ask you to look at them more slowly and carefully than you might if you were racing through a long book, and to think about the way in which each of them has been constructed.

READING AND PRACTICE

Example 1

The following paragraph is taken from Willa Cather's novel, *O Pioneers!* In this paragraph, Cather recounts an episode in which a jealous husband murders his wife and her lover. As you read the paragraph, try to pay particular attention to two things: first, how the narrator sometimes focuses your attention on the mind and thoughts of Frank and sometimes on objects and events that exist outside of Frank; and, second, how Cather varies the level of detail and, with it, the pace of events. For example, how little things (like resting the butt of the gun on the ground) and big things (like shooting the gun) are narrated.

Willa Cather, "A Shooting" (from *O Pioneers!*)

At the wheatfield corner, where the orchard hedge ended and the path led across the pasture to the Bergsons', Frank stopped. In the warm, breathless night air he heard a murmuring sound, perfectly inarticulate, as low as the sound of water coming from a spring, where there is no fall, and where there are no stones to fret it. Frank strained his ears. It ceased. He held his breath and began to tremble. Resting the butt of his gun on the ground, he parted the mulberry leaves softly with his fingers and peered through the hedge at the dark figures on the grass, in the shadow of the mulberry tree. It seemed to him that they must feel his eyes, that they must hear him breathing. But they did not. Frank, who had always wanted to see things blacker than they were, for once wanted to believe less than he saw. The woman lying in the shadow might so easily be one of the Bergsons' farm-girls. . . . Again the murmur, like water welling out of the ground. This time he heard it more distinctly, and his blood was quicker than his brain. He began to act, just as a man who falls into the fire begins to act. The gun sprang to his shoulder, he sighted mechanically and fired three times without stopping, stopped without knowing why. Either he shut his eyes or he had vertigo. He did not see anything while he was firing. He thought he heard a cry simultaneous with the second report, but he was not sure. He peered again through the hedge, at the two dark figures under the tree. They had fallen a little apart from each other, and were perfectly still—No, not quite; in a white patch of light, where the moon shone through the branches, a man's hand was plucking spasmodically at the grass.

Questions

1. Describe Frank's state of mind as these events take place. Discuss your evidence and the way you have interpreted it. In other words, consider how you know what you think you know. Is your conclusion something you have reached on your own, or has the writer directed your thinking in some way?
2. As an experiment, rewrite this paragraph either in a cold, detached manner or in an impassioned, confessional manner. If you choose the first alternative, imagine that you are a police officer reporting this sequence of events; begin your report as follows: "The suspect walked to the corner of the wheatfield. He. . . ." If you choose the second alternative, imagine that you are Frank unburdening yourself to your closest friend; begin your confession as follows: "As I got to the corner of the wheatfield—you know, where the orchard hedge ends and the path goes off to the Bergsons'—I. . . ."
3. Consider the differences between your rewrite and the original. Did you find it necessary to change the level of detail or pace of the original? What details did you leave out or add? Why?

Example 2

Richard Wright begins one of his best known short stories with the following four paragraphs. As you can see, the paragraphs differ in length, with the second and fourth paragraphs being shorter than the first and third. Are there differences other than length between the longer and shorter paragraphs? As you read each paragraph, try to pay attention to what Wright does to get you involved in the feelings and actions of "the man." How does each paragraph affect you emotionally?

Richard Wright, from "The Man Who Lived Underground"

I've got to hide, he told himself. His chest heaved as he waited, 1
crouching in a dark corner of the vestibule. He was tired of running and dodging. Either he had to find a place to hide, or he had to surrender. A police car swished by through the rain, its siren rising sharply. They're looking for me all over . . . He crept to the door and squinted through the fogged plate glass. He stiffened as the siren rose and died in the distance. Yes, he had to hide, but where? He gritted his teeth. Then a sudden movement in the street caught his attention. A throng of tiny columns of water snaked into the air from the perforations of a manhole cover. The columns stopped abruptly, as though the perforations had become clogged; a gray spout of sewer water jutted up from underground and lifted the circular metal cover, juggled it for a moment, then let it fall with a clang.

He hatched a tentative plan: he would wait until the siren sounded 2
far off, then he would go out. He smoked and waited, tense. At last the siren gave him his signal; it wailed, dying, going away from him. He stepped to the sidewalk, then paused and looked curiously at the open manhole, half expecting the cover to leap up again. He went to the center of the street and stooped and peered into the hole, but could see nothing. Water rustled in the black depths.

He started with terror; the siren sounded so near that he had the 3
idea that he had been dreaming and had awakened to find the car upon him. He dropped instinctively to his knees and his hands grasped the rim of the manhole. The siren seemed to hoot directly above him and with a wild gasp of exertion he snatched the cover far enough off to admit his body. He swung his legs over the opening and lowered himself into watery darkness. He hung for an eternal moment to the rim by his finger tips, then he felt rough metal prongs and at once he knew that sewer workmen used these ridges to lower themselves into manholes. Fist over fist, he let his body sink until he could feel no more prongs. He swayed in dank space; the siren seemed to howl at the very rim of the manhole. He dropped and was washed violently

into an ocean of warm, leaping water. His head was battered against a wall and he wondered if this were death. Frenziedly his fingers clawed and sank into a crevice. He steadied himself and measured the strength of the current with his own muscular tension. He stood slowly in water that dashed past his knees with fearful velocity.

He heard a prolonged scream of brakes and the siren broke off. Oh, God! They had found him! Looming above his head in the rain a white face hovered over the hole. "How did this damn thing get off?" he heard a policeman ask. He saw the steel cover move slowly until the hole looked like a quarter moon turned black. "Give me a hand here," someone called. The cover clanged into place, muffling the sights and sounds of the upper world. Knee-deep in the pulsing current, he breathed with aching chest, filling his lungs with the hot stench of yeasty rot. 4

Questions

1. What is your emotional reaction as you read this narrative of going underground? Do your feelings change from one moment to another? Does paragraph 1 affect you differently than paragraph 4?
2. As an experiment, rewrite this sequence of events in a cool, direct manner. Imagine that you are "the man" and that you are now in police custody. You've confessed to having committed the crime but the police won't end the interrogation session until you tell them how you eluded arrest in the first place. You are tired and want the interrogation session to end as quickly as possible; so you tell them what they want to know.
3. How does your rewrite differ from the original? Did you change the level of detail? What about word choice? Compare paragraph 3 of the original with your rendition of the act of entering the sewer. What verbs did you use? What verbs does Wright use? What adjectives did you use? What adjectives does Wright use?
4. Compare Cather's narration of a murder with Wright's narration of going underground. Is one more detached—or cool—than the other? Is one more detailed than the other? Does one emotionally involve you more than the other? In both cases, how much of the emotion results from the events recounted and how much from the words in which the events are recounted?

Example 3

The following passage is taken from Jamaica Kincaid's book about Antigua, *A Small Place*. As you read this passage try to think about the point of view from which the sequence of events is being narrated. Point of view is often defined in terms of the grammatical person and the tense of the verbs. However, it can also be considered as a question of position and perspective: whose experiences, feelings, and ideas inform and shape the narration of events?

Jamaica Kincaid, "The Tourist's Arrival" (from *A Small Place*)

You disembark from your plane. You go through customs. Since you are a tourist, a North American or European—to be frank, white—and not an Antiguan black returning to Antigua from Europe or North America with cardboard boxes of much needed cheap clothes and food for relatives, you move through customs swiftly, you move through cutsoms with ease. Your bags are not searched. You emerge from customs into the hot, clean air: immediately you feel cleansed, immediately you feel blessed (which is to say special); you feel free. You see a man, a taxi driver; you ask him to take you to your destination; he quotes you a price. You immediately think that the price is in the local currency, for you are a tourist and you are familiar with these things (rates of exchange) and you feel even more free, for things seem so cheap, but then your driver ends by saying, "In U.S. currency." You may say, "Hmmmm, do you have a formal sheet that lists official prices and destinations?" Your driver obeys the law and shows you the sheet, and he apologises for the incredible mistake he has made in quoting you a price off the top of his head which is so vastly different (favouring him) from the one listed. You are driven to your hotel by this taxi driver in his taxi, a brand-new Japanese-made vehicle. The road on which you are travelling is a very bad road, very much in need of repair. You are feeling wonderful, so you say, "Oh, what a marvellous change these bad roads are from the splendid highways I am used to in North America." (Or, worse, Europe.) Your driver is reckless; he is a dangerous man who drives in the middle of the road when he thinks no other cars are coming in the opposite direction, passes other cars on blind curves that run uphill, drives at sixty miles an hour on narrow, curving roads when the road sign, a rusting, beat-up thing left over from colonial days, says 40 MPH. This might frighten you (you are on your holiday; you are a tourist); this might excite you (you are on your holiday; you are a tourist), though if you are from New York and take taxis you are used to this style of driving: most of the taxi drivers in New York are from places in the world like this. You are looking out the window (because you want to get your money's worth); you notice that all the cars you see are brand-new, or almost brand-new, and that they are all Japanese-made. There are no American cars in Antigua— no new ones, at any rate; none that were manufactured in the last ten years. You continue to look at the cars and you say to yourself, Why, they look brand-new, but they have an awful sound, like an old car—a very old, dilapidated car. How to account for that? Well, possibly it's because they use leaded gasoline in these brand-new cars whose engines were built to use non-leaded gasoline, but you mustn't ask the person driving the car if this is so, because he or she has never heard of unleaded gasoline. You look closely at the car; you see that it's a model of a Japanese car that you might hesitate to buy; it's a model that's very expensive; it's a model that's quite impractical for a person who has to work as hard as you do and who watches every penny you earn so that you can afford this holiday you are on. How do they afford such a car? And do they live in a luxurious house to match such a car? Well, no. You will be surprised, then, to see that most likely the person driving this brand-new car filled with the wrong gas lives in a house that, in comparison, is far beneath the status of the car; and if you were to ask why you would be told that the banks are encouraged by the government to make loans available for cars, but loans for houses not so easily available; and if you ask again why, you will be told that the two main car dealerships in Antigua are owned in part or outright by ministers in government. Oh, but you are on holiday and the sight of these brand-new cars driven by people who may or may not have really passed their driving test (there was once a scandal about driving licenses for sale) would not really stir up these thoughts in you.

Questions

1. Grammatically speaking, what is the point of view in this passage? Why do you think Kincaid uses the verb tense and person that she does?
2. In terms of position and perspective, what is the point of view of this paragraph? Is the paragraph informed and shaped by experiences, feelings, and ideas of a tourist? an Antiguan? both? neither? What is the relationship between this perspective and the grammatical person and tense of the paragraph?
3. As an experiment, try narrating the tourist's taxi ride in a way that represents it either as exciting or as frightening. Feel free to change the verb tense, person, perspective, level of detail, and pace of Kincaid's narrative; just do what you need to do to make it seem either exciting or frightening.

Example 4

In the following two paragraphs from Louise Erdrich's novel, *The Beet Queen*, Sita Kozka recounts a sequence of events that began one morning and ended twenty-four hours later. As you read Sita's narrative, try to notice how specific words and phrases signal the temporal sequence of events, how the focus shifts from one person to another, and how different details affect you.

Louise Erdrich, "Cousin Mary" (from *The Beet Queen*)

My cousin Mary came in on the early freight train one morning, 1
with nothing but an old keepsake box full of worthless pins and

buttons. My father picked her up in his arms and carried her down the hallway into the kitchen. I was too old to be carried. He sat her down, then my mother said, "Go clean the counters, Sita." So I don't know what lies she told them after that.

Later on that morning, my parents put her to sleep in my bed. 2 When I objected to this, saying that she could sleep on the trundle, my mother said, "Cry sakes, you can sleep there too, you know." And this is how I ended up that night, crammed in the trundle, which is too short for me. I slept with my legs dangling out in the cold air. I didn't feel welcoming toward Mary the next morning, and who can blame me?

Questions

1. What features make this example of narration seem clear and simple—or, at least, clearer and simpler than the prior examples? What features make this seemingly simple narrative interesting instead of just simpleminded?
2. How did Sita's narrative affect you? Did your feelings change from one moment in the narrative to another? Do you consider this a hot or a cold piece of writing? Is the narrative point of view detached or emotionally involved?
3. As an experiment, rewrite this sequence of events from the mother's perspective. Imagine that you are Sita's mother writing a letter to your best friend about what happened when "poor orphaned Mary" first came to live with you.

Example 5

Our final example of narration consists of the last page (more or less) of James Joyce's famous novel *Ulysses*. This is not narration by a detached narrator, but what is called "stream-of-consciousness" narrative. In these lines we read the unpunctuated thoughts of Molly Bloom as she falls asleep on the night of June 16, 1904. She is thinking of her past, and in particular she recalls two different but similar events: the time she agreed to marry her husband, Leopold Bloom, while they lay together on the Hill of Howth outside of Dublin, Ireland, and an earlier moment, when she was a girl in Gibraltar, and said "Yes" to her first lover. The events narrated here are the thoughts themselves, and their order controls the order of the writing; but they are thoughts of these other two important events, each of which was a sequence leading up to the word *Yes*, so that we have a narrative within a narrative. To get the proper feeling from these lines, you should listen to them read aloud. As you study this text, try to see how the language conveys the excitement of the climactic events narrated. Pay particular attention to the use of the little words *and* and *yes*.

James Joyce, "The End of Molly's Soliloquy" (from *Ulysses*)

the sun shines for you he said the day we were lying among the rhododendrons on Howth head in the grey tweed suit and his straw hat the day I got him to propose to me yes first I gave him the bit of seedcake out of my mouth and it was leapyear like now yes 16 years ago my God after that long kiss I near lost my breath yes he said I was a flower of the mountain yes so we are flowers all a womans body yes that was one true thing he said in his life and the sun shines for you today yes that was why I liked him because I saw he understood or felt what a woman is and I knew I could always get round him and I gave him all the pleasure I could leading him on till he asked me to say yes and I wouldnt answer first only looked out over the sea and the sky I was thinking of so many things he didnt know of Mulvey and Mr Stanhope and Hester and father and old captain Groves and the sailors playing all birds fly and I say stoop and washing up dishes they called it on the pier and the sentry in front of the governors house with the thing round his white helmet poor devil half roasted and the Spanish girls laughing in their shawls and their tall combs and the auctions in the morning the Greeks and the jews and the Arabs and the devil knows who else from all the ends of Europe and Duke street and the fowl market all clucking outside Larby Sharons and the poor donkeys slipping half asleep and the vague fellows in the cloaks asleep in the shade on the steps and the big wheels of the carts of the bulls and the old castle thousands of years old yes and those handsome Moors all in white and turbans like kings asking you to sit down in their little bit of a shop and Ronda with the old windows of the posadas 2 glancing eyes a lattice hid for her lover to kiss the iron and the wineshops half open at night and the castanets and the night we missed the boat at Algeciras the watchman going about serene with his lamp and O that awful deepdown torrent O and the sea the sea crimson sometimes like fire and the glorious sunsets and the figtrees in the Alameda gardens yes and all the queer little streets and the pink and blue and yellow houses and the rosegardens and the jessamine and geraniums and cactuses and Gibraltar as a girl where I was a Flower of the mountain yes when I put the rose in my hair like the Andalusian girls used or shall I wear a red yes and how he kissed me under the Moorish wall and I thought well as well him as another and then I asked him with my eyes to ask again yes and then he asked me would I yes to say yes my mountain flower and first I put my arms around him yes and drew him down to me so he could feel my breasts all perfume yes and his heart was going like mad and yes I said yes I will Yes.

Questions

1. Try to retell in your own words the process of Molly's thoughts, beginning in this way: "First she thinks of what her husband said to her the day she got him to propose to her ('the sun shines for you') and then she remembers how they were lying among the rhododendrons. . . ." Discuss with your fellow students any parts you have difficulty understanding.

2. Listen to some different versions of the passage read aloud. What is the right way to read it? That is, what emotional tone suits the passage best? Choose some portion of the passage and rewrite it in grammatically correct sentences that change as little of the original phrasing as possible. Does your rewrite change the emotional effect of the original? If so, how so?

3. Imagine that you are Molly Bloom's psychoanalyst, and that the passage you have just read is the transcription of her free association at your last session. For a paper you are planning to deliver at a forthcoming meeting of the Society for Psychoanalytic Study, you wish to include a description of Molly's case (with the name changed, of course). Write a version of Molly's thoughts that will be suitable for inclusion in your professional paper. If you don't know exactly what a professional paper at a psychoanalytic meeting would be like, don't worry. Use your imagination, and do your best to produce something that sounds more like a scientist and less like Molly Bloom, but that covers the material in the passage. You don't have to diagnose her case or cure her of anything. You only need to translate her free associations into a scientific summary. You might begin something like this: "The patient while free-associating returned obsessively to certain scenes of her youth. . . ."

The Life of Stephen Crane

After a long search for employment, you've just landed a job as an editorial assistant in a large publishing company. During your second day on the job, the editor you work for discovers a problem with the company's new edition of Stephen Crane's *The Red Badge of Courage*. Although the edition is due to go to the printer tomorrow, something is missing: the "About the Author" preface that your company always includes in editions of literary classics that it plans to market for college use. It appears that your predecessor never got around to writing the preface; maybe that's why he was fired. In any event, it's your job now and the preface must be written by the end of the day.

Unfortunately, you don't know much about Crane; you haven't read any of his fiction, poetry, or journalism and there's no time to do so now. Nor is there time to do library research on Crane's life. However, the editor does give you a file of material collected by your predecessor. In that file, you find a chronology of Crane's life, some comments about the man and his work by

Crane's contemporaries, and one of Crane's articles on the Spanish-American War. (These materials are reprinted below.)

The editor expects an account of Crane's life that college students will find both interesting and useful. He reminds you that the "About the Author" preface must give readers an idea of Crane's character, motivation, and accomplishments as well as an assessment of his life. You don't have enough information to cover all the events in the chronology; and anyway, it wouldn't be appropriate to do so. Instead, you must analyze the data you have, looking for patterns of events that will enable you to narrate the story of Crane's life in two to three pages.

Read through all the material several times, making notes to yourself about what information seems most significant and where you see important connections. Then, compose an "About the Author" preface that fulfills the editor's expectations.

Stephen Crane: A Chronology

1871 Birth of Stephen Crane on November 1 at 14 Mulberry Place, Newark, New Jersey. The fourteenth and last child of Reverend Jonathan Townley Crane, graduate of the College of New Jersey (later Princeton University) and presiding elder for the Newark district of Methodism; and his wife Mary Helen, daughter of a well-known Methodist minister, George Peck. 1

1876 Family moves to Paterson, New Jersey, where Dr. Crane is appointed to Cross Street Church. 2

1878 Dr. Crane is appointed pastor at Port Jervis, New York. In September, Stephen begins his public school education here, the locale of his later *Whilomville Stories* and "The Monster." 3

1880 Death of Dr. Crane in Port Jervis on February 16. Mrs. Crane supports family by writing for Methodist papers and the New York *Tribune* and the Philadelphia *Press*. 4

1883 Mrs. Crane moves to Asbury Park, New Jersey, where Stephen attends school. 5

1885 Stephen writes his first story, "Uncle Jake and the Bell-Handle," never published during his lifetime. Enrolls at Pennington Seminary, Pennington, New Jersey. Withdraws from Pennington, probably December 1887, in protest of hazing charge. 6

1888 In January, Stephen enrolls at Hudson River Institute (Claverack College) in Claverack, New York, and remains here until 1890. Publishes his first sketch, "Henry M. Stanley," in school magazine *Vidette* (February 1890), and is promoted to captain in military drill. Probably hears Civil War tales from history teacher, retired General Van Petten. During the summer 7 months (1888–92), Stephen assists his brother Townley who operates a news bureau at Asbury Park.

1890 Stephen enters Lafayette College in September as mining 8 engineering student. Poor class attendance.

1891 Transfers to Syracuse University in January. Correspondent for 9 the New York *Tribune* in Syracuse. Presumably sells sketches to the Detroit *Free Press;* publishes his first story, "The King's Favor," in May issue of the Syracuse *University Herald;* and begins writing *Maggie: A Girl of the Streets.* Spends little time in the classroom; ends college career in June. During the summer, he meets Hamlin Garland at Avon-by-the-Sea and reports his lecture on William Dean Howells (August 18). In love with Helen Trent. Mother dies in Paterson on December 7.

1892 First substantial publication of his short fiction; five of his *Sulli-* 10 *van County Sketches* appear in the New York *Tribune* (July 3, 10, 17, 24, 31). First of his New York City sketches published, "The Broken-Down Van" (July 10). Fired as reporter by *Tribune* for writing sardonic article on parading Junior Order of United American Mechanics at Asbury Park (August 21). In love with Lily Brandon Munroe.

1893 *Maggie: A Girl of the Streets* is rejected by various publishers; 11 Crane publishes it at his own cost under pseudonym Johnston Smith. Receives encouragement from Garland and Howells. Begins writing *The Red Badge of Courage.*

1894 Sells abridged version (18,000 words) of *The Red Badge* to 12 Bachellor-Johnson Syndicate for ninety dollars; it appears first in the Philadelphia *Press* (December 3–8). Short stories and sketches on social issues appear in *The Arena* and New York *Press.*

1895 In January, meets and falls in love with Nelly Crouse. This same 13 month he begins his trip to the American West and Mexico, writing special features for the Bacheller-Johnson Syndicate. Meets Willa Cather in Lincoln, Nebraska. Publishes volume of free verse in March, *The Black Riders.* . . . The complete version (50,000 words) of *The Red Badge* is published by Appleton in October and becomes a best seller and wins a large following in England.

1896 *George's Mother* and revised version of *Maggie* published in May 14 and June, respectively. In September, Crane defends Dora Clark, arrested for "soliciting"; this incident makes him continual target of New York City police. Publishes his first collection of stories, *The Little Regiment and Other Episodes of the American Civil War,* in November, his "last thing dealing with battle." Meets Cora Taylor (Howorth) in November in Jacksonville, Florida, at her establishment, Hotel de Dream.

1897 Shipwrecked off Florida coast on January 2 on *Commodore,* 15 carrying contraband to Cuban insurgents; this incident is source of "The Open Boat," which appears in June. With Cora Taylor he covers short-lived Greco-Turkish War (April–May) as war correspondent for New York *Journal* and *Westminister Gazette.* Publishes *The Third Violet* in May (serialized the previous year). Resides at Ravensbrook villa (Oxted, Surrey) in England with Cora; no evidence that they were ever legally married. Friendships with Joseph Conrad, Henry James, Ford Madox Ford, Harold Frederic, and others. Travels to Ireland in September.

1898 To Cuba and the Spanish-American War as correspondent for 16 Pulitzer's New York *World* and later Hearst's New York *Journal;* first dispatches in April, and last in November. Richard Harding Davis names him the best of the war correspondents in Cuba. Publishes *The Open Boat and Other Tales of Adventure* (April). At the peak of his short story craft, with the appearance of "The Bride Comes to Yellow Sky" (February), "Death and the Child" (March), "The Monster" (August), and "The Blue Hotel" (November–December).

1899 Crane returns to England and to Cora in January; resides at 17 Brede Place (Sussex), legend-filled castle. Publishes second book of poems, *War is Kind; The Monster and Other Stories;* and *Active Service,* a novel based on his Greek experiences. Writes at feverish pace to pay off many debts; plans a novel on the American Revolution, never finished; and starts *The O'Ruddy,* his last novel.

1900 Recurrence of earlier tubercular attacks in January and periodi- 18 cally until his death on June 5 in a sanitorium at Badenweiler, Germany. Buried at Hillside, New Jersey. Appearance of *Whilomville Stories* and Cuban war stories, *Wounds in the Rain.*

—THOMAS A. GULLASON

1891 Crane at Syracuse University

Clarence Loomis Peaslee, a classmate of Crane's:

He has a deep regard for true learning, but not for the rubbish that 19 often passes under that name, and if he has not burned the midnight oil in search of "school" knowledge, he has worked as but few men have in the field of observation and the study of mankind. In college Crane was an omnivorous reader and sat up late at night, diligently poring over the masterpieces of literature or trying to put upon paper his own peculiar views of man and life . . . He wanted to produce something that would make men think, that would make men feel as he felt, and to do this he early realized that for him it must come through hard work.

Another classmate:

He gloried in talking with shambling figures who lurked in the dark [20] doorways on deserted slum streets, and his love for adventure constantly kept his feet on ill-lighted thoroughfares honeycombing the city.

1895 Reviews of Crane's novel *The Red Badge of Courage*

From the Boston Transcript:

It is a tremendous grasping of the glory and carnage of all war; it is the [21] rendering, in phrases that reveal like lightning flashes, of the raw fighter's emotions, the blind magnificent courage and the cowardice equally blind of a youth first possessed by the red sickness of battle.

From Outlook *magazine (December 21, 1895):*

The story is not pleasant by any means, but the author seems to lay [22] bare the very nerves of his character; practically, the book is a minute study of one man's mind in the environment of war in all its horrible detail.

From Book Buyer *magazine (April 1896):*

A note from Stephen Crane: "I have never been in battle, of course, [23] and I believe that I got my sense of the rage of conflict on the football field. The psychology is the same. The opposing team is an enemy tribe."

1896 Publication of *Maggie: A Girl of the Streets*

From a note Crane wrote on the cover of Hamlin Garland's copy of Maggie:

It is inevitable that you will be greatly shocked by this book, but [24] continue please with all possible courage to the end. For it tries to show that environment is a tremendous thing in the world and frequently shapes lives regardless. If one proves that theory one makes room in heaven for all sorts of souls (notably an occasional street girl) who are not confidently expected to be there by many excellent people. It is probable that the reader of this small thing may consider the author to be a bad man; but obviously that is a matter of small consequence.

From an English review:

Maggie is a study of life in the slums of New York, and of the hopeless 25 struggle of a girl against the horrible conditions of her environment; and so bitter is the struggle, so black the environment, so inevitable the end, that the reader feels a chill at his heart, and dislikes the book even while he admires it. Mr. Crane's realism is merciless and unsparing; in these chapters are set before us in cold blood hideous phases of misery, brutality, drunkenness, vice; while oaths and blasphemies form the habitual speech of the men and women who live and move in this atmosphere of vileness. Yet every scene is alive and has the unmistakable stamp of truth upon it. The reader does not feel that he is reading about these horrors; he feels as if the outer walls of some tenement houses in the slums had been taken away and he could see—and see with comprehension—the doings of the teeming inmates. Over the whole grimly powerful tragedy is the redeeming grace of the author's implied compassion; but he never mars the effect of the story by speaking this compassion or by pointing a moral. He has drawn a vivid picture of life at its lowest and worst; he has shown us the characters as they would be, with no false glamor of an impossible romance about them; and the moral may confidently be left to look after itself, since it stares from every page. Maggie herself is a wonderfully well-drawn character, and the book, repellent though it is, is in its way a triumph.

1897   The *Commodore* disaster

From the New York Press, *January 5, 1897:*

CRANE'S SPLENDID GRIT

"That man Crane is the spunkiest fellow out," said Captain Murphy 26 tonight to The Press correspondent, in speaking of the wreck and incidents pertaining to it. "The sea was so rough that even old sailors got seasick when we struck the open sea after leaving the bar, but Crane behaved like a born sailor. He and I were about the only ones not affected by the big seas which tossed us about. As we went south he sat in the pilot house with me, smoking and telling yarns. When the leak was discovered he was the first man to volunteer aid.

JOKES AMID DANGER

"His shoes, new ones, were slippery on the deck, and he took them off 27 and tossed them overboard, saying, with a laugh: 'Well, captain, I guess I won't need them if we have to swim.' He stood on deck with me all the while, smoking his cigarette, and aided me greatly while the boats were getting off. When in the dinghy he suggested putting up the overcoat for a sail, and he took his turn at the oars or holding up the oar mast.

TRIES TO SAVE HIGGINS

"When we went over I called to him to see that his life preserver was 28 on all right and he replied in his usual tones, saying that he would obey orders. He was under the boat once, but got out in some way. He held up Higgins when the latter got so terribly tired and endeavored to bring him in, but the sailor was so far gone that he could hardly help himself. When we were thrown up by the waves, Crane was the first man to stagger up the beach looking for houses. He's a thorough-bred," concluded the captain, "and a brave man, too, with plenty of grit."

1898   Crane as correspondent in the Spanish-American War

From Langdon Smith in Cosmopolitan *magazine, September 1898:*

Crane was standing under a tree calmly rolling a cigarette; some leaves 29 dropped from the trees, cut away by the bullets; two or three men dropped within a few feet. Crane is as thin as a lath. If he had been two or three inches wider or thicker through, he would undoubtedly have been shot. But he calmly finished rolling his cigarette and smoked it without moving away from the spot where the bullets had suddenly become so thick.

From Crane's report of the battle of San Juan in the New York World, *July 14, 1898:*

The road from El Paso to San Juan was now a terrible road. It should 30 have a tragic fame like the sunken road at Waterloo. Why we did not later hang some of the gentry who contributed from the trees to the terror of this road is not known.

The wounded were stringing back from the front, hundreds of 31 them. Some walked unaided, an arm or shoulder having been dressed at a field station. They stopped often enough to answer the universal hail "How is it going?" Others hobbled or clung to a friend's shoulders. Their slit trousers exposed red bandages. A few were shot horribly in the face and were led, bleeding and blind by their mates.

And then there were the slow pacing stretcher-bearers with the 32 dead or the insensible, the badly wounded, still figures with blood often drying brick color on their hot bandages.

Prostrate at the roadside were many others who had made their way 33 thus far and were waiting for strength. Everywhere moved the sure-handed, invaluable Red Cross men.

Over this scene was a sort of haze of bullets. They were of two kinds. 34 First, the Spanish lines were firing just a trifle high. Their bullets swept over our firing lines and poured into this devoted roadway, the single exit, even as it had been the single approach. The second fire was from guerillas concealed in the trees and thickets along the trail. They had come in under the very wings of our strong advance, taken good positions on either side of the road and were peppering our line of communication whenever they got a good target, no matter, apparent-ly, what the target might be.

Red Cross men, wounded men, sick men, correspondents and 35 attaches were all one to the guerilla. The move of sending an irregular force around the flanks of the enemy as he is making his front attack is so legitimate that some of us could not believe at first that the men hidden in the forest were really blazing away at the non-combatants or the wounded. Viewed simply as a bit of tactics, the scheme was admirable. But there is no doubt now that they intentionally fired at anybody they thought they could kill.

You can't mistake an ambulance driver when he is driving his 36 ambulance. You can't mistake a wounded man when he is lying down and being bandaged. And when you see a field hospital you don't mistake it for a squadron of cavalry or a brigade of infantry.

PRACTICE

The Life of Yourself

Following the example of the biographical material presented for Stephen Crane in the previous assignment, draw up a chronology of ten to fifteen important events in your life from your birth to the present. Also provide five short paragraphs elaborating on those events you consider the most important. For example, your first day in kindergarten may have been an exciting or terrifying experience, and you should briefly describe that event. You should bring this material to class and exchange it with a student you don't know very well. You and this student will then write each other's biographies.

In analyzing the other student's material, remember that you are writing the *story* of a person's life. In arranging this story, you don't have to begin with the person's birth (unless something extraordinary occurred). You might start with what you consider the most outstanding event and trace it back. To do this, you should look for related events in the material. For example, if the person is a football player, can you trace this competitive interest back to elementary school days? Or if the person is majoring in pre-med or nursing, look for a reason—perhaps volunteer work in a hospital or a death or illness in the family has been influential.

Now write a short biography of this other student. Your instructor can decide whether or not this material should be presented anonymously.

READING

Narrating an Event

Here is a complete work of fiction by the Latin American writer Gabriel Garcia Márquez. Although it may be an example of the kind of fiction that some critics call "magic realism," we ask you to read it as a simple narrative that might give you an idea for some writing of your own.

Gabriel García Márquez, "A Very Old Man with Enormous Wings"

A Tale for Children

On the third day of rain they had killed so many crabs inside the house that Pelayo had to cross his drenched courtyard and throw them into the sea, because the newborn child had a temperature all night and they thought it was due to the stench. The world had been sad since Tuesday. Sea and sky were a single ash-gray thing and the sands of the beach, which on March nights glimmered like powdered light, had become a stew of mud and rotten shellfish. The light was so weak at noon that when Pelayo was coming back to the house after throwing away the crabs, it was hard for him to see what it was that was moving and groaning in the rear of the courtyard. He had to go very close to see that it was an old man, a very old man, lying face down in the mud, who, in spite of his tremendous efforts, couldn't get up, impeded by his enormous wings. 1

Frightened by that nightmare, Pelayo ran to get Elisenda, his wife, who was putting compresses on the sick child, and he took her to the rear of the courtyard. They both looked at the fallen body with mute stupor. He was dressed like a ragpicker. There were only a few faded hairs left on his bald skull and very few teeth in his mouth, and his pitiful condition of a drenched great-grandfather had taken away any sense of grandeur he might have had. His huge buzzard wings, dirty and half-plucked, were forever entangled in the mud. They looked at him so long and so closely that Pelayo and Elisenda very soon overcame their surprise and in the end found him familiar. Then they dared speak to him, and he answered in an incomprehensible dialect with a 2 strong sailor's voice. That was how they skipped over the inconvenience of the wings and quite intelligently concluded that he was a lonely castaway from some foreign ship wrecked by the storm. And yet, they called in a neighbor woman who knew everything about life and death to see him, and all she needed was one look to show them their mistake.

"He's an angel," she told them. "He must have been coming for the 3 child, but the poor fellow is so old that the rain knocked him down."

On the following day everyone knew that a flesh-and-blood angel 4 was held captive in Pelayo's house. Against the judgment of the wise neighbor woman, for whom angels in those times were the fugitive survivors of a celestial conspiracy, they did not have the heart to club him to death. Pelayo watched over him all afternoon from the kitchen, armed with his bailiff's club, and before going to bed he dragged him out of the mud and locked him up with the hens in the wire chicken coop. In the middle of the night, when the rain stopped, Pelayo and Elisenda were still killing crabs. A short time afterward the child woke up without a fever and with a desire to eat. Then .they felt magnanimous and decided to put the angel on a raft with fresh water and provisions for three days and leave him to his fate on the high seas. But when they went out into the courtyard with the first light of dawn, they found the whole neighborhood in front of the chicken coop having fun with the angel, without the slightest reverence, tossing him things to eat through the openings in the wire as if he weren't a supernatural creature but a circus animal.

Father Gonzaga arrived before seven o'clock, alarmed at the strange 5 news. By that time on-lookers less frivolous than those at dawn had already arrived and they were making all kinds of conjectures concerning the captive's future. The simplest among them thought that he should be named mayor of the world. Others of sterner mind felt that he should be promoted to the rank of five-star general in order to win all wars. Some visionaries hoped that he could be put to stud in order to implant on earth a race of winged wise men who could take charge of the universe. But Father Gonzaga, before becoming a priest, had been a robust woodcutter. Standing by the wire, he reviewed his catechism in an instant and asked them to open the door so that he could take a close look at that pitiful man who looked more like a huge decrepit hen among the fascinated chickens. He was lying in a corner drying his open wings in the sunlight among the fruit peels and breakfast leftovers that the early risers had thrown him. Alien to the impertinences of the world, he only lifted his antiquarian eyes and murmured something in his dialect when Father Gonzaga went into the chicken coop and said good morning to him in Latin. The parish priest had his first suspicion of an imposter when he saw that he did not understand the language of

God or know how to greet His ministers. Then he noticed that seen close up he was much too human: he had an unbearable smell of the outdoors, the back side of his wings was strewn with parasites and his main feathers had been mistreated by terrestrial winds, and nothing about him measured up to the proud dignity of angels. Then he came out of the chicken coop and in a brief sermon warned the curious against the risks of being ingenuous. He reminded them that the devil had the bad habit of making use of carnival tricks in order to confuse the unwary. He argued that if wings were not the essential element in determining the difference between a hawk and an airplane, they were even less so in the recognition of angels. Nevertheless, he promised to write a letter to his bishop so that the latter would write to his primate so that the latter would write to the Supreme Pontiff in order to get the final verdict from the highest courts.

His prudence fell on sterile hearts. The news of the captive angel 6 spread with such rapidity that after a few hours the courtyard had the bustle of a marketplace and they had to call in troops with fixed bayonets to disperse the mob that was about to knock the house down. Elisenda, her spine all twisted from sweeping up so much marketplace trash, then got the idea of fencing in the yard and charging five cents admission to see the angel.

The curious came from far away. A traveling carnival arrived with a 7 flying acrobat who buzzed over the crowd several times, but no one paid any attention to him because his wings were not those of an angel but, rather, those of a sidereal bat. The most unfortunate invalids on earth came in search of health: a poor woman who since childhood had been counting her heartbeats and had run out of numbers; a Portu-guese man who couldn't sleep because the noise of the stars disturbed him; a sleepwalker who got up at night to undo the things he had done while awake; and many others with less serious ailments. In the midst of that shipwreck disorder that made the earth tremble, Pelayo and Elisenda were happy with fatigue, for in less than a week they had crammed their rooms with money and the line of pilgrims waiting their turn to enter still reached beyond the horizon.

The angel was the only one who took part in his own act. He spent 8 his time trying to get comfortable in his borrowed nest, befuddled by the hellish heat of the oil lamps and sacramental candles that had been placed along the wire. At first they tried to make him eat some mothballs, which, according to the wisdom of the wise neighbor woman, were the food prescribed for angels. But he turned them down, just as he turned down the papal lunches that the penitents brought him, and they never found out whether it was because he was an angel or because he was an old man that in the end he ate nothing but eggplant mush. His only supernatural virtue seemed to be patience. Especially during the first days, when the hens pecked at him, searching for the stellar parasites that proliferated in his wings, and the cripples pulled out feathers to touch their defective parts with, and even the most merciful threw stones at him, trying to get him to rise so they could see him standing. The only time they succeeded in arousing him was when they burned his side with an iron for branding steers, for he had been motionless for so many hours that they thought he was dead. He awoke with a start, ranting in his hermetic language and with tears in his eyes, and he flapped his wings a couple of times, which brought on a whirlwind of chicken dung and lunar dust and a gale of panic that did not seem to be of this world. Although many thought that his reaction had been one not of rage but of pain, from then on they were careful not to annoy him, because the majority understood that his passivity was not that of a hero taking his ease but that of a cataclysm in repose.

Father Gonzaga held back the crowd's frivolity with formulas of 9 maidservant inspiration while awaiting the arrival of a final judgment on the nature of the captive. But the mail from Rome showed no sense of urgency. They spent their time finding out if the prisoner had a navel, if his dialect had any connection with Aramaic, how many times he could fit on the head of a pin, or whether he wasn't just a Norwegian with wings. Those meager letters might have come and gone until the end of time if a providential event had not put an end to the priest's tribulations.

It so happened that during those days, among so many other carni- 10 val attractions, there arrived in town the traveling show of the woman who had been changed into a spider for having disobeyed her parents. The admission to see her was not only less than the admission to see the angel, but people were permitted to ask her all manner of questions about her absurd state and to examine her up and down so that no one would ever doubt the truth of her horror. She was a frightful tarantula the size of a ram and with the head of a sad maiden. What was most heart-rending, however, was not her outlandish shape but the sincere affliction with which she recounted the details of her misfortune. While still practically a child she had sneaked out of her parents' house to go to a dance, and while she was coming back through the woods after having danced all night without permission, a fearful thunderclap rent the sky in two and through the crack came the lightning bolt of brimstone that changed her into a spider. Her only nourishment came from the meatballs that charitable souls chose to toss into her mouth. A spectacle like that, full of so much human truth and with such a fearful lesson, was bound to defeat without even trying that of a haughty angel who scarcely deigned to look at mortals. Besides, the few miracles attributed to the angel showed a certain mental disorder, like the blind man who didn't recover his sight but grew three new teeth, or the paralytic who didn't get to walk but almost won the lottery, and the leper whose sores sprouted sunflowers. Those consolation miracles, which were more like mocking fun, had already ruined the angel's reputation when the woman who had been changed into a spider finally crushed him completely. That was how Father Gonzaga was cured forever of his insomnia and Pelayo's courtyard went back to being as empty as during the time it had rained for three days and crabs walked through the bedrooms.

The owners of the house had no reason to lament. With the money 11 they saved they built a two-story mansion with balconies and gardens and high netting so that crabs wouldn't get in during the winter, and with iron bars on the windows so that angels wouldn't get in. Pelayo also set up a rabbit warren close to town and gave up his job as bailiff for good, and Elisenda bought some satin pumps with high heels and many dresses of iridescent silk, the kind worn on Sunday by the most desirable women in those times. The chicken coop was the only thing that didn't receive any attention. If they washed it down with creolin and burned tears of myrrh inside it every so often, it was not in homage to the angel but to drive away the dungheap stench that still hung everywhere like a ghost and was turning the new house into an old one. At first, when the child learned to walk, they were careful that he not get too close to the chicken coop. But then they began to lose their fears and got used to the smell, and before the child got his second teeth he'd gone inside the chicken coop to play, where the wires were falling apart. The angel was no less standoffish with him than with other mortals, but he tolerated the most ingenious infamies with the patience of a dog who had no illusions. They both came down with chicken pox at the same time. The doctor who took care of the child couldn't resist the temptation to listen to the angel's heart, and he found so much whistling in the heart and so many sounds in his kidneys that it seemed impossible for him to be alive. What surprised him most, however, was the logic of his wings. They seemed so natural on that completely human organism that he couldn't understand why other men didn't have them too.

When the child began school it had been some time since the sun 12 and rain caused the collapse of the chicken coop. The angel went dragging himself about here and there like a stray dying man. They would drive him out of the bedroom with a broom and a moment later find him in the kitchen. He seemed to be in so many places at the same time that they grew to think that he'd been duplicated, that he was reproducing himself all through the house, and the exasperated and unhinged Elisenda shouted that it was awful living in that hell full of angels. He could scarcely eat and his antiquarian eyes had also become so foggy that he went about bumping into posts. All he had left were the bare cannulae of his last feathers. Pelayo threw a blanket over him and extended him the charity of letting him sleep in the shed, and only then did they notice that he had a temperature at night, and was delirious with the tongue twisters of an old Norwegian. That was one of the few times they became alarmed, for they thought he was going to die and not even the wise neighbor woman had been able to tell them what to do with dead angels.

And yet he not only survived his worst winter, but seemed im- 13 proved with the first sunny days. He remained motionless for several days in the farthest corner of the courtyard, where no one would see him, and at the beginning of December some large, stiff feathers began to grow on his wings, the feathers of a scarecrow, which looked more like another misfortune of decrepitude. But he must have known the reason for those changes, for he was quite careful that no one should notice them, that no one should hear the sea chanteys that he sometimes sang under the stars. One morning Elisenda was cutting some bunches of onions for lunch when a wind that seemed to come from the high seas blew into the kitchen. Then she went to the window and caught the angel in his first attempts at flight. They were so clumsy that his fingernails opened a furrow in the vegetable patch and he was on the point of knocking the shed down with the ungainly flapping that slipped on the light and couldn't get a grip on the air. But he did manage to gain altitude. Elisenda let out a sigh of relief, for herself and for him, when she saw him pass over the last houses, holding himself up in some way with the risky flapping of a senile vulture. She kept watching him even when she was through cutting the onions and she kept on watching until it was no longer possible for her to see him, because then he was no longer an annoyance in her life but an imaginary dot on the horizon of the sea.

—TRANSLATED BY GREGORY RABASSA

Questions

1. Briefly summarize the sequence of events in "A Very Old Man with Enormous Wings."
2. Over what period of time do the events in this story occur? How does Márquez manage to "cover" this length of time in such a short story? Does the level of detail vary? What events are recounted with lots of detail? What events are recounted with little detail? What kind of events are not recounted?
3. From whose perspective is this narrative told? the old man's? Pelayo's and Elisenda's? Father Gonzaga's? the crowd's? the child's? none of these? all of these?
4. Márquez subtitles this piece "A Tale for Children." Do you think this story

would be a good one to read to a child? Is the vocabulary appropriate for a child? What about the syntax? How might this story affect a child emotionally? What emotional and intellectual effects did it have on you? In what way is this "a tale for children"?

PRACTICE

Suppose a _____ Appeared in Your Neighborhood

In Márquez's story, you have seen what happens when a strange old man with enormous wings appears in a family's yard. Imagine that someone or something equally strange is discovered in a neighborhood that you know well. Where might it appear? What might it be? What would happen? How would people in and out of the neighborhood react? How would you feel about it?

Try narrating such an imaginary possibility as if it had really happened.

7. DESCRIPTION

Organizing Space

In a sense, narration is easy because events unfolding in time have a linear shape or structure. When someone is having difficulty in reporting an event to us, we say, "Just begin at the beginning." We can do this because both events and narratives have beginnings. Descriptions have beginnings, too. The problem is that the things being described often do not. We may describe what we hear, taste, smell, or feel, but because human beings are sight-dominated creatures, we most often describe what we see. That is, we translate our perceptions of space-bound objects with no perceivable beginning or end into a time-bound, linear form: writing.

For the writer, description of a visual object poses a number of problems: where to begin? what to include next? where to end? All these problems can be reduced to one: the problem of order. How should description be arranged? There is, however, another problem hiding behind this one: what information should be selected for inclusion in a written description? Even a blank wall presents a nearly infinite amount of information for anyone who inspects it closely enough. Selection and arrangement, the twin problems of descriptive writing, can be solved in the same way. The writer must have a *point of view* about the object being described. That is, as a writer you must see something in the object that will enable you to make a statement about it—which will in turn help you to organize the impressions you are receiving from the object. Once you have a point of view, you will know what to look for, what to record; and you will have the option of moving from one item to another according to the way the objects relate to your point of view.

A scientist describing a specimen will leave out certain irrelevant details. A poet or essayist describing the same object might include much that the scientist would consider irrelevant and exclude the data of most concern to the scientist. The purpose shapes the presentation and helps to generate the point of view required for good description. Some of the following assignments are designed to develop your awareness of the way in which point of view shapes description. In others we have posed problems in translation from a visual text to a verbal one or even more complicated problems in the imitation of a verbal style and description of a visual object simultaneously.

Point of View in Description

Here are examples of four notable writers at work describing things. The four selections serve to illustrate how a writer can organize an interior space like a bedroom or a restaurant, an exterior urban space such as a city, and finally, an exterior rural space, such as cultivated fields.

In reading each selection you should consider in particular each writer's point of view. How has the writer actually organized the space to get it on paper? What has been included? What has been excluded? For instance, every room has a floor, a ceiling, and four walls. Which of these has Robinson included and excluded? Of the things that the writer has chosen to include, which are mentioned first? What pattern can you find in the movement from one object to the next? Can you tell how the writer has decided upon a particular order? If you were going to make a film based on the description of the place, could you do it with a single location? Could your camera capture everything in one steady movement, or would it have to hop around, frequently changing position, distance, and angle? You might also ask what aspects of the written description a camera could not capture.

The writer's point of view requires some consistent feeling or attitude toward the scene being described. You should try to reduce the attitude in each of the following descriptions to the shortest possible expression—a single word if you can—that expresses the dominant feeling conveyed by the description. Which of the following words best suits the Robinson selection: pleasure, displeasure, fascination, disgust, disapproval, sympathy? Can you find words or phrases that sum up the point of view that is used to unify each of the other three examples?

After reading and discussing all four examples, you should try to articulate the general principles of descriptive writing. What features do all four of these different writers employ in their descriptions? What is unique to each one?

Marilynne Robinson, "A Kitchen" (from *Housekeeping*)

. . . Lucille had startled us all, flooding the room so suddenly with light, exposing heaps of pots and dishes, the two cupboard doors which had come unhinged and were propped against the boxes of china. The tables and chairs and cupboards and doors had been painted a rich white, layer on layer, year after year, but now the last layer had ripened to the yellow of turning cream. Everywhere the paint was chipped and marred. A great shadow of soot loomed up the wall and across the ceiling above the stove, and the stove pipe and the cupboard tops were thickly felted with dust. Most dispiriting, perhaps, was the curtain on Lucille's side of the table, which had been half consumed by fire once when a birthday cake had been set too close to it. Sylvie had beaten out the flames with a back issue of *Good Housekeeping*, but she had never replaced the curtain. It had been my birthday, and the cake was a surprise, as were the pink orlon cardigan with the imitation seed pearls in the yoke and the ceramic kangaroo with the air fern in its pouch. Sylvie's pleasure in this event had been intense, and perhaps the curtain reminded her of it.

James Joyce, "A Restaurant" (from *Ulysses*)

His heart astir he pushed in the door of the Burton restaurant. Stink 1 gripped his trembling breath: pungent meatjuice, slop of greens. See the animals feed.

Men, men, men. 2

Perched on high stools by the bar, hats shoved back, at the tables 3 calling for more bread no charge, swilling, wolfing gobfuls of sloppy food, their eyes bulging, wiping wetted moustaches. A pallid suet-faced young man polished his tumbler knife fork and spoon with his napkin. New set of microbes. A man with an infant's saucestained napkin tucked round him shovelled gurgling soup down his gullet. A man spitting back on his plate: halfmasticated gristle: no teeth to chewchewchew it. Chump chop from the grill. Bolting to get it over. Sad booser's eyes. Bitten off more than he can chew. Am I like that? See ourselves as others see us. Hungry man is an angry man. Working tooth and jaw. Don't! O! A bone! That last pagan king of Ireland Cormac in the schoolpoem choked himself at Sletty southward of the Boyne. Wonder what he was eating. Something galoptious. Saint Patrick converted him to Christianity. Couldn't swallow it all however.

—Roast beef and cabbage. 4

—One stew. 5

Smells of men. His gorge rose. Spaton sawdust, sweetish warmish 6
cigarette smoke, reek of plug, spilt beer, men's beery piss, the stale of
ferment.

Couldn't eat a morsel here. Fellow sharpening knife and fork, to eat 7
all before him, old chap picking his tootles. Slight spasm, full, chewing
the cud. Before and after. Grace after meals. Look on this picture then
on that. Scoffing up stewgravy with sopping sippets of bread. Lick it off
the plate, man! Get out of this.

Kate Simon, "A Street" (from *Bronx Primitive*)

We lived at 2029 Lafontaine, the last house on the west side of the
street from 178th to 179th, a row of five-story tenements that ended at
a hat factory. To the north and solidly, interminably, along the block to
180th there stretched a bitter ugliness of high walls of big stones that
held a terminal point and service barns of El trains. (It may be that my
recoil from early Renaissance palaces, their pugnacious blocks of stone
and fortress grimness, stems from these inimical El walls.) Across from
the factory were a garage and the Italian frame houses that lined that
side of the street down to 178th Street. At the corner of 178th Street,
on our Jewish-German-Polish-Greek-Hungarian-Rumanian side, was
Mrs. Katz's candy store. The only other store I knew at first was the
grocery run by a plodding elderly couple at the corner of 179th Street
and Arthur Avenue, the street to the east. In spite of their lack of
English and my frail Yiddish, I eagerly ran errands there to watch their
feet slide and pat in their brown felt slippers and to admire the
precision with which the old man cut once, twice, into a tub of butter
to dig out exactly a quarter pound. And on their side of 179th Street,
about midway between Arthur and Lafontaine, there was a big tree,
the only street tree in the neighborhood, which showered me, and
only me, with a million white blossoms. It was my tree and I watched
and touched it as carefully as the Italian grandfathers watched and
touched the tomato plants in their backyards.

Scott Momaday, "An Arbor" (from *The Way to Rainy Mountain*)

Some of my earliest memories are of the summers on Rainy Mountain Creek, when we lived in the arbor, on the north side of my
grandmother's house. From there you could see downhill to the pecan
grove, the dense, dark growth along the water, and beyond, the long
sweep of the earth itself, curving out on the sky. The arbor was open on
all sides to the light and the air and the sounds of the land. You could

see far and wide even at night, by the light of the moon; there was nothing to stand in your way. And when the season turned and it was necessary to move back into the house, there was a sense of confinement and depression for a time. Now and then in winter, when I passed by the arbor on my way to draw water at the well, I looked inside and thought of the summer. The hard dirt floor was dark red in color—the color of pipestone.

Organizing a Space

A. Describe a place that you know. Choose a place you can look at as you write or a place so strong in your memory that you don't need to look at it. Begin by just jotting down details of the scene or words that capture your feeling about it. Don't hurry yourself, but take some time accumulating bits of language that serve to capture some aspect of the place for you.

When you have enough material, read it over and then begin drafting your written description. As you write, ask yourself if you are making the right choices for selection and arrangement of details. Are you leaving out something important? Are you mentioning things that are not necessary to convey the impression you want to convey? What impression *do* you want to convey?

B. Let another person or a group read your description, and, without any coaching from you, tell you the impression they received from your writing. If they seem to be missing something, getting a confused impression, or getting an impression different from what you wished to convey, you should undertake a revision of your description that will eliminate as many of these problems as possible.

A Place with a History

In the following selection from her autobiography, *Gemini*, Nikki Giovanni gives us an example of how knowledge of the history of a place can make that place interesting. In this case, personal and family history are interwoven with urban history. She also provides an example of how physical details are integrated with historical information. As you read her essay, be thinking about some place of historical interest that you might describe and pay particular attention to the ways she has found to include the past—what is *not* there now—with what is present.

Nikki Giovanni, from "400 Mulvaney Street"

When we were growing up Knoxville didn't have television, let 1 alone an airport. It finally got TV but the airport is in Alcoa. And is now called Tyson Field. Right? Small towns are funny. Knoxville even has a zip code and seven-digit phone numbers. All of which seems strange to me since I mostly remember Mrs. Flora Ford's white cake with white icing and Miss Delaney's blue furs and Armetine Picket's being the sharpest woman in town—she attended our church—and Miss Brooks wearing tight sweaters and Carter-Roberts Drug Store sending out Modern Jazz Quartet sounds of "Fontessa" and my introduction to Nina Simone by David Cherry, dropping a nickel in the jukebox and "Porgy" coming out. I mostly remember Vine Street, which I was not allowed to walk to get to school, though Grandmother didn't want me to take Paine Street either because Jay Manning lived on it and he was home from the army and very beautiful with his Black face and two dimples. Not that I was going to do anything, because I didn't do anything enough even to think in terms of not doing anything, but according to small-town logic "It looks bad."

The Gem Theatre was on the corner of Vine and a street that runs 2 parallel to the creek, and for 10 cents you could sit all day and see a double feature, five cartoons and two serials plus previews for the next two weeks. And I remember Frankie Lennon would come in with her gang and sit behind me and I wanted to say, "Hi. Can I sit with you?" but thought they were too snooty, and they, I found out later, thought I was too Northern and stuck-up. All of that is gone now. Something called progress killed my grandmother.

Mulvaney Street looked like a camel's back with both humps bulg- 3 ing—up and down—and we lived in the down part. At the top of the left hill a lady made ice balls and would mix the flavors for you for just a nickel. Across the street from her was the Negro center, where the guys played indoor basketball and the little kids went for stories and nap time. Down in the valley part were the tennis courts, the creek, the bulk of the park and the beginning of the right hill. To enter or leave the street you went either up or down. I used to think of it as a fort, especially when it snowed, and the enemy would always try to sneak through the underbrush nurtured by the creek and through the park trees, but we always spotted strangers and dealt. As you came down the left hill the houses were up on its side; then people got regular flat front yards; then the right hill started and ran all the way into Vine and Mulvaney was gone and the big apartment building didn't have a yard at all.

Grandmother and Grandpapa had lived at 400 since they'd left 4 Georgia. And Mommy had been a baby there and Anto and Aunt Agnes were born there. And dated there and sat on the swing on the front porch and fussed there, and our good and our bad were recorded there. That little frame house duplicated twice more which overlooked the soft-voiced people passing by with "Evening, 'Fessor Watson, Miz Watson," and the grass wouldn't grow between our house and Edith and Clarence White's house. It was said that he had something to do with numbers. When the man tried to get between the two houses and the cinder crunched a warning to us, both houses lit up and the man was caught between Mr. White's shotgun and Grandfather's revolver, trying to explain he was lost. Grandpapa would never pull a gun unless he intended to shoot and would only shoot to kill. I think when he reached Knoxville he was just tired of running. I brought his gun to New York with me after he died but the forces that be don't want anyone to keep her history, even if it's just a clogged twenty-two that no one in her right mind would even load.

Mr. and Mrs. Ector's rounded the trio of houses off. He always wore 5 a stocking cap till he got tied back and would emerge very dapper. He was in love with the various automobiles he owned and had been seen by Grandmother and me on more than one occasion sweeping the snow from in front of his garage before he would back the car into the street. All summer he parked his car at the bottom of the hill and polished it twice a day and delighted in it. Grandmother would call across the porches to him, "Ector, you a fool 'bout that car, ain't cha?" And he would smile back. "Yes, ma'am." We were always polite with the Ectors because they had neither children nor grandchildren so there were no grounds for familiarity. I never knew Nellie Ector very well at all. It was rumored that she was a divorcée who had latched on to him, and to me she became all the tragic heroines I had read about, like *Forever Amber* or the *All This and Heaven Too* chick, and I was awed but kept my distance. He was laughs, though. I don't know when it happened to the Ectors but Mr. White was the first to die. I considered myself a hot-shot canasta player and I would play three-hand with Grandmother and Mrs. White and beat them. But I would drag the game on and on because it seemed so lonely next door when I could look through my bedroom window and see Mrs. White dressing for bed and not having to pull the shade anymore.

You always think the ones you love will always be there to love you. 6 I went on to my grandfather's alma mater and got kicked out and would have disgraced the family but I had enough style for it not to be considered disgraceful. I could not/did not adjust to the Fisk social life and it could not/did not adjust to my intellect, so Thanksgiving I rushed home to Grandmother's without the bitchy dean of women's permission and that dean put me on social probation. Which would have worked but I was very much in love and not about to consider her punishment as anything real I should deal with. And the funny thing about that Thanksgiving was that I knew everything would go down just as it did. But I still wouldn't have changed it because Grandmother and Grandpapa would have had dinner alone and I would have had dinner alone and the next Thanksgiving we wouldn't even have him and Grandmother and I would both be alone by ourselves, and the only change would have been that Fisk considered me an ideal student, which means little on a life scale. My grandparents were surprised to see me in my brown slacks and beige sweater nervously chain-smoking and being so glad to touch base again. And she, who knew everything, never once asked me about school. And he was old so I lied to him. And I went to Mount Zion Baptist with them that Sunday and saw he was going to die. He just had to. And I didn't want that. Because I didn't know what to do about Louvenia, who had never been alone in her life.

I left Sunday night and saw the dean Monday morning. She asked where I had been. I said home. She asked if I had permission. I said I didn't need her permission to go home. She said, "Miss Giovanni," in a way I've been hearing all my life, in a way I've heard so long I know I'm on the right track when I hear it, and shook her head. I was "released from the school" February 1 because my "attitudes did not fit those of a Fisk woman." Grandpapa died in April and I was glad it was warm because he hated the cold so badly. Mommy and I drove to Knoxville to the funeral with Chris—Gary's, my sister's, son—and I was brave and didn't cry and made decisions. And finally the time came and Anto left and Aunt Agnes left. And Mommy and Chris and I stayed on till finally Mommy had to go back to work. And Grandmother never once asked me about Fisk. We got up early Saturday morning and Grandmother made fried chicken for us. Nobody said we were leaving but we were. And we all walked down the hill to the car. And kissed. And I looked at her standing there so bravely trying not to think what I was trying not to feel. And I got in on the driver's side and looked at her standing there with her plaid apron and her hair in a bun, her feet hanging loosely out of her mules, sixty-three years old, waving goodbye to us, and for the first time having to go into 400 Mulvaney without John Brown Watson. I felt like an impotent dog. If I couldn't protect this magnificent woman, my grandmother, from loneliness, what could I ever do? I have always hated death. It is unacceptable to kill the young and distasteful to watch the old expire. And those in between

7

our link commit the little murders all the time. There must be a better way. So Knoxville decided to become a model city and a new mall was built to replace the old marketplace and they were talking about convention centers and expressways. And Mulvaney Street was a part of it all. This progress. . . .

Gay Street is to Knoxville what Fifth Avenue is to New York. 8 Something special, yes? And it looked the same. But Vine Street, where I would sneak to the drugstore to buy *Screen Stories* and watch the men drink wine and play pool—all gone. A wide, clean military-looking highway has taken its place. Austin Homes is cordoned off. It looked like a big prison. The Gem Theatre is now some sort of nightclub and Mulvaney Street is gone. Completely wiped out. Assassinated along with the old people who made it live. I looked over and saw that the lady who used to cry "HOT FISH! GOOD HOT FISH!" no longer had a Cal Johnson Park to come to and set up her stove in. Grandmother would not say, "Edith White! I think I'll send Gary for a sandwich. You want one?" Mrs. Abrum and her reverend husband from rural Tennessee wouldn't bring us any more goose eggs from across the street. And Leroy wouldn't chase his mother's boyfriend on Saturday night down the back alley anymore. All gone, not even to a major highway but to a cutoff of a cutoff. All the old people who died from lack of adjustment died for a cutoff of a cutoff.

And I remember our finding Grandmother the house on Linden 9 Avenue and constantly reminding her it was every bit as good as if not better than the little ole house. A bigger back yard and no steps to climb. But I knew what Grandmother knew, what we all knew. There was no familiar smell in that house. No coal ashes from the fireplaces. Nowhere that you could touch and say, "Yolande threw her doll against this wall," or "Agnes fell down these steps." No smell or taste of biscuits Grandpapa had eaten with the Alaga syrup he loved so much. No Sunday chicken. No sound of "Lord, you children don't care a thing 'bout me after all I done for you," because Grandmother always had the need to feel mistreated. No spot in the back hall weighted down with lodge books and no corner where the old record player sat playing Billy Eckstine crooning, "What's My Name?" till Grandmother said, "Lord! Any fool know his name!" No breeze on dreamy nights when Mommy would listen over and over again to "I Don't See Me in Your Eyes Anymore." No pain in my knuckles where Grandmother had rapped them because she was determined I would play the piano, and when that absolutely failed, no effort on Linden for us to learn the flowers. No echo of me being the only person in the history of the family to curse Grandmother out and no Grandpapa saying, "Oh, my," which was serious from him, "we can't have this." Linden Avenue was pretty but it had no life.

And I took Grandmother one summer to Lookout Mountain in 10 Chattanooga and she would say I was the only grandchild who would take her riding. And that was the summer I noticed her left leg was shriveling. And she said I didn't have to hold her hand and I said I liked to. And I made ice cream the way Grandpapa used to do almost every Sunday. And I churned butter in the hand churner. And I knew and she knew that there was nothing I could do. "I just want to see you graduate," she said, and I didn't know she meant it. I graduated February 4. She died March 8.

And I went to Knoxville looking for Frankie and the Gem and 11 Carter-Roberts or something and they were all gone. And 400 Mulvaney Street, like a majestic king dethroned, put naked in the streets to beg, stood there just a mere skeleton of itself. The cellar that had been so mysterious was now exposed. The fireplaces stood. And I saw the kitchen light hanging and the peach butter put up on the back porch and I wondered why they were still there. She was dead. And I heard the daily soap operas from the radio we had given her one birthday and saw the string beans cooking in the deep well and thought how odd, since there was no stove, and I wanted to ask how Babbi was doing since I hadn't heard or seen "Brighter Day" in so long but no one would show himself. The roses in the front yard were blooming and it seemed a disgrace. Probably the tomatoes came up that year. She always had fantastic luck with tomatoes. But I was just too tired to walk up the front steps to see. Edith White had died. Mr. Ector had died, I heard. Grandmother had died. The park was not yet gone but the trees looked naked and scared. The wind sang to them but they wouldn't smile. The playground where I had swung. The courts where I played my first game of tennis. The creek where our balls were lost. "HOT FISH! GOOD HOT FISH!" The hill where the car speeding down almost hit me. Walking barefoot up the hill to the center to hear stories and my feet burning. All gone. Because progress is so necessary. General Electric says, "Our most important product." And I thought Ronald Reagan was cute.

PRACTICE

Describing a Place with a History

Provide a description, long or short as your instructor prefers, of a place that is interesting partly because of its history. Ideally, there should be some visible remains of that history, but also some things that would be quite unperceivable without your historical knowledge.

Your job is to integrate what *is* there with what *was* there, to describe both the present and the absent, the present and the past. Before you write, take another look at the way Nikki Giovanni solved the problem of integrating past and present in her essay. For instance, you might examine paragraphs 8 and 9, where she uses negative constructions to put into her text what is no longer *there* in the place she is describing. Note how much emphasis is placed on what people did and what they no longer do as well as on places and things that are gone or changed.

READING

Hogarth's "Noon" Described

William Hogarth was England's leading caricaturist and visual satirist in the eighteenth century. He is famous for his series of engravings depicting male and female degeneration and disaster, called *The Rake's Progress* and *The Harlot's Progress*. The engraving we are reprinting here is from a much milder series, called *The Four Times of Day*. This one is "Noon," first printed in 1738. Along with the engraving we are providing a sample description of it, to give you some ideas on how to write your own description.

This is a picture of a street scene in a bustling city, full of people in eighteenth-century clothing. The street itself is made of cobblestones, and has an open sewer or gutter running down the middle of it. A dead cat lies in the gutter near some broken stones.

The right side of the picture is dominated by a large brick building with windows of leaded glass. A crowd is emerging from a small door in the building, half of them coming closer to our viewpoint, the other half walking away with their backs turned. Some of this crowd have severe expressions on their faces and carry black books. They may be coming from a rather puritanical church after service.

In the right foreground, among this crowd, are a man, woman, and child dressed in what must have been the height of fashion. The man is wearing shoes with buckles, stockings, knee-britches, an immense bowtie and a long coat with frills and over twenty buttons. He is making elegant gestures with his hands, pointing his feet like a dancer, with a cane dangling by a ribbon from his ruffled wrist, and a sword hanging from his other side.

This elegant fop is speaking to a richly dressed lady, while in front of them is a creature like a midget, but probably a small boy, dressed like a miniature of the man, complete with a cane, a wig, and a toy sword. He has a hand inside his long vest as he gazes downward, smiling, possibly at the dead cat. These three seem to be a family group.

On the other side of the gutter there is a group of people who have obviously not been to church. They stand in front of a sign that says "Good

NOON

Eating" between two very large teeth topped with a picture of a man's head on a platter. From a window above a woman is throwing an old piece of meat from a platter toward the gutter, while a man grabs for it from behind her, and misses. Near the window hangs a sign with a picture of a woman standing so that the top of the sign is at the level of her neck, leaving her headless.

Down below in the street a boy is scratching his bushy head and bellowing over a huge pie he has apparently just dropped, while a poorly dressed girl scrambles at his feet for the broken pieces, stuffing them into her mouth. Just behind these two stand another couple, a woman holding a hot pie with her apron, while a black man reaches around her from behind to fondle her breasts and kiss her cheek. She seems to be encouraging this but her pie is tilting, dripping its liquid center towards the cobblestones. The whole pie may soon be headed that way.

The gutter seems to divide the well-to-do from the less affluent, the pious from the boisterous. This division gives a sense of the diversity of city life. But it is a very unflattering picture. There are no attractive people in the picture, except the young woman who is losing her pie and perhaps more than that. Even a building in the background has a huge crack, parallel to the gutter, running down its side.

PRACTICE

Describing a Hogarth Street Scene

On page 130 is a London street scene done by Hogarth a few years after the one just presented and discussed. Your assignment is to write a description of this scene that is about as complete and accurate as our description of the other engraving by Hogarth.

You should not try to follow the other description. That one was organized partly by the gutter that Hogarth used to divide his picture. (Such gutters were called "kennels" in Hogarth's day.) You must find an organizing principle in this engraving that will guide you in making your description of it.

This one seems to tell a bit more of a story than the first. Certainly it offers a thematic way of organizing the material. There is no single correct way of doing this, but rather several possible ways. Your job is to find one and use it here.

A Critic Describes a Face

Here are two excerpts from Graham McCann's book, *Marilyn Monroe*. In these two paragraphs, McCann conjectures about Monroe's photographic image, and describes her face and what her look seems to promise to the spectator. McCann describes Monroe's as a "celebrity body" and then describes what he means by that. As you read, try to analyze how McCann achieves his effect. What physical features does he describe? Notice how he links description with his analysis of Monroe's body image.

Graham McCann, from *Marilyn Monroe*

Select a typical photograph of Marilyn Monroe. Study it, scrutinize   1
its features, sense its execution. Was this one pose unique, snapped
between its forming and dissolving, or was it an achingly familiar pose,
shot successively, here as merely one amongst many? Monroe, as a still
image, excites the most intense reaction from the spectator: what
happened before, after, who was in the room with her, who was behind

George Barris, from *Marilyn*

the camera, what was she thinking, saying, feeling? The single image sparks off a series of questions (every caption trails off into three dots . . .). A typical pose displays her with glistening blonde hair, brightly dressed, her face set with half-closed eyes and half-opened mouth (not quite seeing, not quite speaking)—a picture of sheer promise. Parts of her body—the dark red lips, the long black eyelashes, the shaped and elongated eyebrows—are heavily outlined, whilst other parts—her neck and torso—are traced with trinkets and clothing that accentuate the roundness and fullness of her figure. The bent-forward attitude of her head and upper body, the slanting seductiveness of the eyes and lips, fashion an alluring self-image quite distinct from the cryptic off-camera self Monroe spent her life striving to define. As seen in portraits, Monroe intrigues us, invites us to ponder on our peculiar relationship to her. . . .

In her early stills, Monroe is seen as interesting because of her body; in later portraits, it is a "celebrity body" that is the interesting sight. In the silent movies stylization of both gesture and looks was necessary for narrative, and prompted not only new ways of walking, sitting and using the hands, but also the development of styles to suit personalities. Fashions became part of a mammoth tie-up between the cinema and big business; the two influenced each other in the interests of the "image industry." Glamour contains a charm enhanced by means of illusion. A glamour image of a woman is particularly impressive in that it plays on the desire of the viewer in a peculiarly pristine way: beauty or sexuality is desirable exactly to the extent that it is idealized and unattainable. Monroe suffered because of this image: "People expected so much of me, I sometimes hated them. It was too much of a strain . . . Marilyn Monroe has to look a certain way—be *beautiful*— and act in a certain way, be talented. I wondered if I could live up to their expectations." [W. J. Weatherby, *Conversations with Marilyn*. London: Robson Books, 1976, 146.]

PRACTICE

Describing a Famous Face

Using what you have learned from studying McCann's techniques, write a description of your own. Select a well-known figure who appears regularly in the media—a rock star, an actress, an athlete, an anchorperson, a politician—and try to capture the special qualities of his or her performance, particularly those that can be treated in terms of facial expressions and posture (rather than voice or language). The idea is to include the necessary minimum of physical details, but to go beyond such details to the impression they convey. Make your description about as long as McCann's.

READING

"La Gioconda"

"La Gioconda" ("The Smiling Woman"), better known as "Mona Lisa" ("Lady Lisa"), is perhaps the most famous painting in the world. Walter Pater's elaborate and impressionistic descriptive meditation on the painting (written a century ago) is also famous.

If you look closely at Pater's prose, you will see that it begins as a description and then moves away from the painting to a kind of meditation on what the painting symbolizes (in this case, the eternal feminine). Various meanings are "read into" the Mona Lisa by the writer. What he knows and what he imagines about the painting are all introduced to make this image bear a great symbolic burden.

The Mona Lisa
by Leonardo Da Vinci
(*Louvre*)

Walter Pater, from *The Renaissance*

The presence that rose thus so strangely beside the waters, is expressive of what in the ways of a thousand years men had come to desire. Hers is the head upon which all "the ends of the world are come," and the eyelids are a little weary. It is a beauty wrought out from within upon the flesh, the deposit, little cell by cell, of strange thoughts and fantastic reveries and exquisite passions. Set it for a moment beside one of those white Greek goddesses or beautiful women of antiquity, and how would they be troubled by this beauty, into which the soul with all its maladies has passed! All the thoughts and experience of the world have etched and molded there, in that which they have of power to refine and make expressive the outward form, the animalism of Greece, the lust of Rome, the mysticism of the middle age with its spiritual ambition and imaginative loves, the return of the Pagan world, the sins of the Borgias. She is older than the rocks among which she sits; like the vampire, she has been dead many times, and learned the secrets of the grave; and has been a diver in deep seas, and keeps their fallen day about her; and trafficked for strange webs with Eastern merchants: and, as Leda, was the mother of Helen of Troy, and as Saint Anne, the mother of Mary; and all this has been to her but as the sound of lyres and flutes, and lives only in the delicacy with which it has molded the changing lineaments, and tinged the eyelids and the hands. The fancy of a perpetual life, sweeping together ten thousand experiences, is an old one; and modern philosophy has conceived the idea of humanity as wrought upon by, and summing up in itself, all modes of thought and life. Certainly Lady Lisa might stand as the embodiment of the old fancy, the symbol of the modern idea.

PRACTICE

"Il Giocondo"

In recent times we have come to know other smilers. We present two of them here for your consideration: the irrepressible Bart (Ay caramba!) Simpson; and John Goodman as Dan, the loveable husband and father of the TV show "Roseanne." Your assignment is to provide a meditation on one of these two contemporary smilers, in the manner of Pater (whose writing, you will no doubt have noticed, is as strange and highly wrought as his ideas). While we would not like you to write this way as a regular habit, we encourage you to try it just this one time. Follow Pater's sentence structure as closely as you can, while letting your imagination go on the deep significance of your chosen face.

Bart Simpson by Matt Groening
© and ™Twentieth Century Fox Film
Corporation. All rights reserved.

Dan, played by John Goodman

The purpose of this sort of exercise is twofold. The movement from description to symbolism is an important mental process, one well worth mastering. And the experience of matching your thoughts to an unfamiliar sentence structure will make you more aware of stylistic possibilities in your future writing. This is an exercise in the *form* of thought.

8. CLASSIFICATION

Organizing Data

Classification consists of organizing things according to categories. When we don't like it we call it pigeon-holing, implying that things are being stuffed into categories whether they fit or not. But this kind of organization is basic to language itself. Nouns like *sheep* and *goats* or adjectives like *red* and *green* are themselves categories that help us organize our world. What we are calling "classification" is simply a more systematic use of the power that language gives us to arrange and organize the flood of information or data that we encounter every day.

Classification is based on our ability to compare and contrast, to find common features that link all the members of one group of things, along with other features that distinguish all the members of *this* group from all the members of *that* group. This way of thinking is as old as Aristotle, but was developed extensively during the period when biology was becoming a science. Accurate classification enabled the modern theories of evolution and the origin of species to be generated. In other areas of study, especially the social sciences, a good classification system enables an investigator to perceive relationships that were not apparent earlier and, in fact, to give data meaning. Classification is especially important during the research and experimenting phase of a project.

If you look carefully, you will find classification used in all the readings included in our chapters on analysis and argument. Stephen Jay Gould, for instance, classifies one kind of argument as scholarship and another as propaganda, so that he can make his own argument against propaganda. In order to analyze how "publicity" works, John Berger must first define "publicity" as a kind of language or discourse. And Gregory Mantsios needs the categories of "myth" and "reality" to make his case that class is a category that really matters. To begin composing an analysis or argument, we need categories. The act of writing may then reveal that we haven't got the best categories for our purposes. We then must revise our thinking so that we can revise our writing.

One of the most important research skills is the ability to *play* with the data we are collecting. This is true of the most serious professional projects as well as of amateur practicing. But perhaps we should clarify what we mean by *play*. We are not suggesting fakery or carelessness, but rather that one should play as a child plays with blocks or tinker-toys, trying different arrangements to see what can be made of them. In academic research, *play* means trying out various systems of classification, and the basic move in classification is finding categories that enable you to bring together a group of things that would have been separated without these concepts (or categories) that unite them.

In biology, for example, the basic category is life itself, which brings all living things together and excludes stones, machines, and all those things that we call inorganic. The basic class is then refined and refined, yielding smaller groups at every level until the smallest biological group (the species) is reached. Thus, human beings are classified this way:

Kingdom: Animalia
  Phylum: Chordata
    Subphylum: Vertebrata
      Class: Mammalia
        Subclass: Eutheria
          Order: Primates
            Family: Hominidae
              Genus: Homo
                Species: Sapiens

It is possible to divide Homo sapiens into smaller groups, but once we get below the level of species, we are moving into areas of less interest to biologists and more interest to anthropologists and other social scientists: races, nations, classes, tribes, occupational groups, kinship groups, and so on. For any classifier, the first question is how many levels of classification are needed, and the second is how many categories at each level are required to cover all the material.

Let us look a little more closely at the way the biological classification system works. At the fourth level, *Class*, mammals are distinguished from all the other creatures in the category above it—that is, all the other living things that have vertebrae or backbones (fish, birds, reptiles, and amphibia).

Mammals, the Class mammalia, are defined in biology books as "warm-blooded animals whose skin is covered with hair; the females have mammary glands that secrete milk for the nourishment of the young." Within the class of mammals there are three subclasses that are distinguished by the ways they give birth: eggs, like the platypus; pouches, like the possum; or a womb or uterus, like the rat, bat, whale, human, and many others. This third subclass, *Eutheria*, is then broken down into twelve orders, so that even-toed mammals with hooves (cows and hippopotamuses, for instance) can be distinguished from odd-toed mammals with hooves (horses and rhinoceroses, for instance). One of these twelve orders is distinguished as the first, the highest, and is therefore called *primate*. This order includes humans, who devised the whole system, and there is a moral in this: those who write, rank. The "highest" order, primate, is distinguished by having hands and large brains, both of which may be used to "grasp" things. The human brain grasps powerfully by naming and classifying things. The "highest" primate—Genus, Homo; Species, sapiens—is the classifying primate.

Classification can be used in many ways on many topics, as you will see from the Readings and Practices that follow.

READING

Social Groups in a Town

This is a very short excerpt, but it illustrates the way in which a professional social scientist will try to make the casual classifications he encounters into more systematic and complete groupings.

Vance Packard, from *A Nation of Strangers*

A Darien businessman who has lived there all his life said: "The 1 town is divided between commuters and locals and they seldom cross paths except in the stores; and there is a certain amount of resentment." The wife of a transferee who had lived in Darien two years told me: "You feel you are not really accepted here because they expect you to move and so they don't care about getting acquainted."

A somewhat more precise picture of the divisions would show three 2 major groups, with little interaction between them:

1. The locals—people who were raised in Darien and make their 3 living there, as merchants, contractors, etc. Some are of old Irish-Yankee stock, many are of Italian ancestry.

2. The Darien people—families from somewhere else who have 4
made it by living in Darien more than five years. They dominate the
town socially.

3. The transients—who will be moving on after one to four years of 5
residence.

Questions

1. What are the main differences between the classification suggested by the
   businessman and Packard's "more precise picture"?
2. Assume that Packard started with the genus of "all residents of Darien." On
   what basis has he distinguished the three species he finds within that genus?
3. Packard says of his first group that they "make their living" in Darien. How
   does this distinguish them from the others?
4. Packard's second group is said to "dominate the town socially." What does this
   mean? How does this relate to what the businessman and the transferee's wife
   told Packard? Are the businessman and the wife distinguishable in terms of
   Packard's categories?
5. One of the uses of classification is to prepare the way for interesting questions.
   For instance, if Packard's grouping is accurate and his information is correct,
   we are now in a position to ask *why* Group 2 dominates. We may not be able to
   answer on the basis of the information we have, but we now can formulate our
   need for more information—or we can speculate and suggest answers on the
   basis of what we already know.

   Two questions: Why do you suppose Group 2 dominates? What additional
   information might help you answer this question?

PRACTICE

Social Categories in an Institution

This practice is meant to be a thought experiment rather than an occasion
for polished prose.

1. Using Packard's sample as a model, construct a relatively brief and
   general classification of all the people in your college or university.
2. Consider the following questions: What principle did you use to construct your classes? What other classifying principles are possible? Is
   your classification system complete? Is there a category for all the
   people a visitor to your campus might see? Do any of the categories
   overlap?
3. Try one or two alternative classifications or compare your set of classes
   with those devised by a few of your classmates. Try to come up with
   the most complete and logically clear set of categories that you can.

4. Take one of the general categories you've constructed and subdivide it to account for distinct groups within that category. What principles did you use to subdivide members of the category? What other principles of subdivision are possible?
5. Which level of classification do you think would be most useful to an incoming student? Why?

PRACTICE

Social Types in a Particular Place

All classifications entail some kind of articulation between the general and the specific. However, in constructing a system of classification, we sometimes begin with large, general categories that we then subdivide, working our way down toward more and more specific groupings. At other times, we work in the opposite direction, beginning with the specifics we observe and then grouping those specifics into distinct types which can, in turn, be considered in terms of more general categories—and so on.

In the previous practice, you probably worked from the top down. In this practice, you are to work from the bottom up—from observation to classification into types. Begin by choosing one of the following scenes to observe: a college cafeteria, a college sports event, a college library, a college fraternity party, or a college class session. Then, based on your observations, classify and discuss one of the following:

1. the eating habits of students in a college cafeteria
2. the spectatorial habits of people who attend a college sports event
3. the study habits of students in a college library
4. the interpersonal habits of students at a college fraternity party
5. the in-class habits of students in a college course

READING

The Student Body

Here is a sample of classification done by a team of sociologists in the 1920s. We invite you to read it before you undertake your own essay in classification of a student body. Remember, this study was done about seventy years ago and was concerned with a high school population. You should not expect to follow it closely in your own work, but it may give you some ideas.

Robert and Helen Lynd, from *Middletown*

Less spectacular than athletics but bulking even larger in time 1
demands is the network of organizations that serve to break the nearly
two thousand individuals composing the high school microcosm into
the more intimate groups human beings demand. These groups are
mainly of three kinds: the purely social clubs, in the main a stepping
down of the social system of adults; a long distance behind in point of
prestige, clubs formed around curriculum activities; and, even farther
behind, a few groups sponsored by the religious systems of the adults.

In 1894 the high school boasted one club, the "Turemethian Liter- 2
ary Society." According to the early school yearbook:

> The Turemethian Society makes every individual feel that practically
> he is free to choose between good and evil; that he is not a mere straw
> thrown upon the water to mark the direction of the current, but that he
> has within himself the power of a strong swimmer and is capable of
> striking out for himself, of buffeting the waves, and directing, to a
> certain extent, his own independent course. Socrates said, "Let him who
> would move the world move first himself." . . . A paper called The
> Zetetic is prepared and read at each meeting. . . . Debates have created
> . . . a friendly rivalry. . . . Another very interesting feature of the
> Turemethian Society is the lectures delivered to us. . . . All of these
> lectures help to make our High School one of the first of its kind in the
> land. The Turemethian Society has slowly progressed in the last year.
> What the future has in store for it we can not tell, but must say as Mary
> Riley Smith said, "God's plans, like lilies pure and white, unfold; we
> must not tear the close-shut leaves apart; time will reveal the calyxes of
> gold."

Six years later, at the turn of the century, clubs had increased to the
point of arousing protests in a press editorial entitled "Barriers to
Intellectual Progress." Today clubs and other extracurricular activities
are more numerous than ever. Not only is the camel's head inside the
tent but his hump as well; the first period of the school day, often
running over into the next hour, has recently, at the request of the
Mothers' Council, been set aside as a "convocation hour" dedicated to
club and committee meetings.

The backbone of the purely social clubs is the series of unofficial 3
branches of former high school fraternities and sororities; Middletown
boasts four Alpha chapters. For a number of years a state law has
banned these high school organizations, but the interest of active
graduate chapters keeps them alive. The high school clubs have harm-
less names such as the Glendale Club; a boy is given a long, impressive
initiation into his club but is not nominally a member of the fraternity
of which his club is the undergraduate section until after he graduates,

when it is said that by the uttering of a few hitherto unspoken words he comes into his heritage. Under this ambiguous status dances have been given with the club name on the front of the program and the fraternity name on the back. Two girls' clubs and two boys' clubs which every one wants to make are the leaders. Trailing down from them are a long list of lesser clubs. Informal meetings are usually in homes of members but the formal fall, spring, and Christmas functions are always elaborate hotel affairs.

Extracurricular clubs have canons not dictated by academic standards of the world of teachers and textbooks. Since the adult world upon which the world of this intermediate generation is modeled tends to be dominated primarily by getting a living and "getting on" socially rather than by learning and "the things of the mind," the bifurcation of high school life is not surprising. 4

> "When do you study?" some one asked a clever high school Senior who had just finished recounting her week of club meetings, committee meetings, and dances, ending with three parties the night before. "Oh, in civics I know more or less about politics, so it's easy to talk and I don't have to study that. In English we're reading plays and I can just look at the end of the play and know about that. Typewriting and chemistry I don't have to study outside anyway. Virgil is worst, but I've stuck out Latin four years for the Virgil banquet; I just sit next to _____ and get it from her. Mother jumps on me for never studying, but I get A's all the time, so she can't say anything."

The relative status of academic excellence and other qualities is fairly revealed in the candid rejoinder of one of the keenest and most popular girls in the school to the question, "What makes a girl eligible for a leading high school club?"

> "The chief thing is if the boys like you and you can get them for the dances," she replied. "Then, if your mother belongs to a graduate chapter that's pretty sure to get you in. Good looks and clothes don't necessarily get you in, and being good in your studies doesn't necessarily keep you out unless you're a 'grind.' Same way with the boys—the big thing there is being on the basketball or football team. A fellow who's just a good student rates pretty low. Being good-looking, a good dancer, and your family owning a car all help."

The clubs allied to curricular activities today include the Dramatic Club—plays by sophomore, junior, and senior classes in a single spring have replaced the "programs of recitations, selections, declamations, and essays" of the old days; the Daubers, meeting weekly in school hours to sketch and in evening meetings with graduate members for special talks on art; the Science Club with its weekly talks by members and occasional lectures by well-known scientists; the Pickwick Club, 5 open to members of English classes, meeting weekly for book reviews and one-act plays, with occasional social meetings; the Penmanship Club; and the Virgil Club, carrying with it some social prestige. Interest in the work of these clubs is keen among some students. All have their "pledges," making their rituals conform roughly to those of the more popular fraternities and sororities.

On the periphery of this high school activity are the church and   6 Y.M.C.A. and Y.W.C.A. clubs. All these organizations frankly admit that the fifteen- to twenty-one-year person is their hardest problem. The Hi-Y club appears to be most successful. The Y.M.C.A. controls the extracurricular activities of the grade school boys more than any other single agency, but it maintains itself with only moderate success in the form of this Hi-Y Club among the older boys. A Hi-Y medal is awarded each commencement to the boy in the graduating class who shows the best all-round record, both in point of scholarship and of character. The Y.W.C.A. likewise maintains clubs in the grades but has rough sledding when it comes to the busy, popular, influential group in high school. According to one representative senior girl:

> "High School girls pay little attention to the Y.W. and the Girl Reserves. The boys go to the Y.M. and Hi-Y club because it has a supper meeting once a month, and that is one excuse for getting away from home evenings. There aren't any supper meetings for the girls at the Y.W. It's not much good to belong to a Y.W. club; *any one* can belong to them."

All manner of other clubs, such as the Hiking Club and the Boys'   7 and Girls' Booster Club and the Boys' and Girls' Pep Club, hover at the fringes or even occasionally take the center of the stage.

PRACTICE

Your Student Body

Squire magazine is putting together an issue devoted to the college scene in the United States today. They have asked you to contribute an article on your school's student body—an article that will give their readers a sense of the current social scene at one American college. You realize that one of the best ways to organize your thinking and writing is to classify the student body into different groups and types. But you still have to figure out how this classifying can best be done.

One possibility is to start with two large divisions, such as fraternity and nonfraternity groups or resident and commuter groups. But is this division really significant to the social scene in your college? Would some other initial grouping be better? Then, there's the issue of types in each of the general categories. For example, each fraternity might be identified with a particular type of student, such as the prep school type, the athletic type, the studious type, and so on. Maybe it would be better to begin your classifying with specific types and then to work up from there to more general categories that include some types but not others. You can proceed in a number of ways, but you should remember that your goal is to construct a classification system that will give *Squire*'s readers a sense of the current social scene at your college.

Once you've decided on a classification system, we suggest that you make an outline that includes the name and distinguishing features of each group in your system. These features might include dress, social behavior, study habits, and so on. Then, you should take this outline and transform it into a short article. If it's a good article, *Squire* might just offer you a permanent job.

READING

Classifying Commercials

This is a fairly long example of the use of classification to organize a large body of material. As you read, look for the way the writer has organized the information into two major classes and several subclasses.

John W. Wright, from "TV Commercials That Move the Merchandise"

Speaking in New York recently at one of a series of advertising 1 seminars sponsored by *Advertising Age*, [Harry W.] McMahan railed against the malady of "Festivalitis," a disease of the ego which infected many advertising men during the sixties and drove them to seek creative awards for themselves rather than financial rewards for their clients. Inflation, unemployment, and a couple of energy shortages, however, combined to produce the no-nonsense atmosphere of the seventies in which sales results have been restored to their rightful place at the head of all other criteria. The once glamorous notion of the Mass Consumption Society working with well-oiled precision while elaborate and expensive TV commercials gently stroked the nation's collective subconscious has given way to the dull workaday task of discovering why some commercials actually succeed in establishing the end-all and be-all of contemporary American business, "brand preference."

Over the last ten years McMahan has examined literally tens of 2 thousands of commercials, not in the simpleminded fashion of the dilettante, but in the manner of the structuralist who tries to reveal the essential but often hidden elements in a society, or a literary genre, or even an art form. Anthropologists have used the method for decades to delineate and codify the morals and mores of primitive tribes and this approach seems to work just as well when applied to successful television advertising. According to McMahan's tabulations, seventy-five percent of today's money-making commercials employ either one of two traditional advertising techniques: forty-two percent use a jingle, while thirty-three percent plant the face of a familiar personality on the screen in very close proximity to the product. (Occasionally there are commercials which use both, such as the one in which Petula Clark sings and dances for Burlington Mills.)

Jingles have been popular in broadcast advertising ever since the 3 Ralston Straight Shooters sang the opening commercial to the *Tom Mix* radio program in 1933, the same year that the Wheaties Quartet introduced "Have You Tried Wheaties?" to the audience for *Jack Armstrong, the All-American Boy*. Everyone who grew up in the forties or fifties knows dozens of jingles, including "Pepsi-Cola Hits the Spot," "My Beer Is Rheingold, the Dry Beer," "You Get a Lot to Like with a Marlboro," "Winston Tastes Good Like a Cigarette Should." And they'll no doubt remember them till their dying day since each was constantly repeated for years on both radio and television. According to McMahan, the simple, melodic jingle has evolved into the sophisticated, fully orchestrated contemporary sound, which has become associated with the leading brands of consumer products such as Coke ("Coke Adds Life"), McDonald's ("We Do It All For You"), Budweiser ("Here Comes the King"), Cheerios ("You're Gonna Get a Powerful Start"), and Chevrolet ("Baseball, Hot Dogs, Apple Pie, and Chevrolet"). Most could be called hard-driving, foot-tapping, easy-to-hum, memorable tunes which, in ad-talk, help to define the product's "personality." Obviously some products have different requirements. Kodak, for example, uses the gentle, one might say bathetic, "Times of Your Life"—a shameless exploitation of our deepest emotional relationships—to sell film and cameras to young parents or new grandparents. Pine-Sol, too, took the quiet route but still landed on top of its field. They all have, McMahan says, "the look of the leader."

But McMahan notes that the jingle can be a powerful tool in 4 introducing new products as well. The stripteasing housewife singing "I've been sweet, and I've been good" helped to make Aviance the best selling new fragrance in less than six months. And in spectacular fashion the memorable production number for Leggs panty hose (featuring women dancing around a supermarket singing the slightly erotic "Our Leggs fit your legs, they'll hold you, they'll squeeze you, they'll never let you go") gave this Hanes brand name a thirty percent share of the panty hose market where just a few years before the leader had only four percent.

Not all advertisers find it necessary or even desirable to have a song   5
written and arranged expressly for their product. As audience segmenting grows more sophisticated, the use of established popular songs can help to make the advertising relevant to the target group. For example a diet product called Figurines used the melody of *Tangerine*, a hit from the big band era, to sell to women over forty. (Some advertising people, said McMahan, believe the commercial was successful because women associated the song with their earliest romantic experiences.) On the other hand Clairol's Herbal Essence Shampoo recently used the Beach Boys' tune about California girls to reach the younger set, the increasingly important eighteen- to thirty-five-year-olds.

If good use of music can actually get consumers to sing about an   6
advertiser's products, the use of a star or celebrity helps to catch the viewer's attention immediately and allows the advertiser to reinforce his arguments in magazines and at the point-of-purchase with posters and other pictorial material. Associating your product or service with a star enables you to stand out from the crowd, so celebrities are especially good in highly competitive markets such as airline travel (Robert Morley has made British Airways the leader in transatlantic flights so it comes as no surprise that Gene *An American in Paris* Kelly was hired by Air France), perfume (Catherine Deneuve for Chanel started a trend that now includes Margaux Hemingway for Babe and Candice Bergen for Cie), even automatic coffee makers (Joe Di-Maggio's success for the number one Mr. Coffee must have induced Norelco to hire a coffee "expert" like Danny Thomas).

Several years ago the FTC foolishly tried to clamp down on the use   7
of stars and celebrities but, as so often happens, the advertisers have been able to circumvent or ignore the regulations. The new rules failed, in part, because the FTC assumed that the American people were so naive they actually had to be told that celebrities were paid for giving endorsements. But the use of famous athletes, opera singers, prima ballerinas, writers, generals, admirals, socialites, and the stars of stage and screen dates back to the turn of the century when Sarah Bernhardt, Enrico Caruso, and the suffragette Elizabeth Cady Stanton lent their names and reputations to help sell manufactured goods. Even folk heroes such as Charles Lindbergh and Ernest Hemingway, or political heroes like General MacArthur or Lillian Hellman, found their way into the advertising pages of our leading magazines. During radio's heyday the biggest stars (including Benny, Vallee, Allen, Kate Smith) always took a big part in promoting the sponsor's product and this "tradition" carried over into early television. So, historically speak-

ing, the public has been conditioned for a long time and through all of the media to accept the notion that in America, one of the perquisites due to a top flight athlete, artist, or popular performer is the money from endorsements.

McMahan claims that today twenty-one percent of all moneymaking 8 TV commercials use stars and celebrities and chances are very good that the percentage will grow. Ironically, the FTC's increasingly stringent regulations on advertisers will help this to happen because, as McMahan says: "Stars are especially useful when there are limitations on what you can say about the product." That's one reason why Bobby *Baretta* Blake doesn't tell us what STP actually does, he only guarantees that it works. And so potentially effective is his promise that he allegedly received twenty thousand dollars for one ten-second spot. This isn't much when compared to the multimillion dollar deals given to O. J. Simpson (Hertz, TreeSweet Orange Juice), Joe Namath (Brut, Hamilton Beach), and Bill Cosby (Ford, Jell-O, Del Monte), but it indicates that the cost factor can be a major drawback to any advertiser considering the endorsement technique.

Television is the one medium which allows advertisers to counter- 9 act this problem. Because so many Americans watch TV so frequently (it's on over six hours a day in the *average* home) advertisers have been able to create their very own thirty-second programs starring characters who are just as well known and just as one-dimensional as Kojak, Columbo, or John-Boy Walton. At a fraction of the cost of a star presenter, Madge the Manicurist, now in her twelfth year for Palmolive Dishwashing Liquid, or the longlasting, "lonely" Maytag Repairman bring with them that very important recognition factor necessary if consumers are to remember the brand name. It's known in the business as the "continuing central character," and McMahan estimates that twelve percent of the money makers have taken this route.

The technique was first used on television more than twenty years 10 ago. At that time everyone involved with the fledgling medium was obsessed with animation and trick photography so "Speedy" Alka-Seltzer, Tony the Tiger, and Manners the Butler were typical as well as famous and successful. Today commercial stars run the personality gamut from a finicky feline like Morris the Cat (who helped 9-Lives get twenty-five percent of the canned cat food market), to a smart-ass company president such as Frank Perdue, whose brand-name chickens clearly rule the roost. Of course animated characters are still around and some, like the Keebler Elves, or the Pillsbury Doughboy, are very effective. In fact, one of the biggest advertising success stories of the last decade is the stork who talks like Groucho Marx and delivers Vlasic pickles instead of babies. In just about five years this small Detroit-based company has taken over twenty-four percent of the pickle market, more than double that of the gigantic, century-old Heinz corporation.

But if there's a trend, it's more toward true-to-life, trustworthy 11 characters like Pete the Butcher who does Shake 'n Bake, or Maxwell House's Cora (played by Margaret Hamilton, who earlier achieved believability and immortality as the Wicked Witch in *The Wizard of Oz*). It just may be, however, that these types seem pleasing only because of the constant presence of offensive characters, although this kind can also do the job of selling the goods. The continually revolting Mr. Whipple, for example, has made Charmin the number-one "single-ply" toilet tissue, while the depressingly wholesome Mr. Goodwin helps Crest maintain a staggering forty percent of the toothpaste market. Meanwhile their female counterparts, Aunt Bluebell and Rosie, lend particularly irksome vocal qualities to the great paper-towel battle currently raging between Scott, the leader, and Bounty, the challenger. Rosie, played by Nancy Walker (who, as Rhoda's mother, could not be considered a star presenter), has given Bounty over twenty percent of the paper towel market even though the product is not yet distributed nationally. (Aunt Bluebell, interestingly enough, is played by Mae Questel, who first gained fame in the thirties doing the voices of Betty Boop and of Popeye's girl friend, Olive Oyl.)

Questions

1. Wright uses only two main classes (music and personality), but introduces many more subdivisions to order his data. Make an outline of Wright's system, including all levels and subclasses, noting the refinements he uses to categorize types of commercials rather than simply naming the different ads.
2. How does Wright's classification system relate to the organization and paragraphing of his text?
3. Since Wright finished his essay (1979), many new commercials have appeared. Can you supply new data that will fit into his categories? How well have the categories themselves lasted? Can you improve them in any way?

PRACTICE

The Class of Full-Page Ads

A. You will need a magazine for this assignment. Choose one issue of a recent magazine with wide popular appeal, such as *People*, *Time*, *Ebony*, *Newsweek*, *Sports Illustrated*, or the *New Yorker*. Start with the back cover and work forward from there. Pick out the first thirty full-page advertisements. (If there aren't thirty, you don't have the right kind of magazine.)

Let your thirty samples represent the class of Full-Page Ads. Then find a method of dividing the ads into subclasses and orders. You may or may not need further subdivision into genus and species. Try not to make things too complicated for yourself. When you have finished making your classification, write a paragraph or two in which you discuss the reasons for your selection of categories and the problems you encountered in assigning the individual ads to them. Cut out and include the thirty ads with your paper.

In developing your categories, you may wish to emphasize formal qualities (color vs. black and white, amount of pictures vs. words, presence or absence of human figures), or you may prefer to emphasize subject matter (goods vs. services, food vs. beverages, luxury vs. necessity).

Remember, the point of this assignment is to test the possibilities of classification, not to achieve perfection. If you run into difficulties in classifying, then use these very difficulties in your discussion.

B. You and your classmates should break into small groups of three or four. Make sure each person in the group worked on a different magazine. Then, as a group, work out a classification system that will cover the ads from all three or four magazines, and produce a report on the different patterns of advertising you detect in each of the magazines. This report should be written, but suitable for oral presentation and discussion in class. The point is to *use* the classification system as a way of describing the differences in the magazines. You may wish, finally, to speculate on the reasons behind the differences.

READING

Classifying Forms of Power

The following material first appeared as the opening to Chapter 3 of the philosopher Bertrand Russell's book *Power*. We present it to you as an excellent example of classification in action. In reading it, you should pay particular attention to the way it is organized. Russell is exceptionally careful to name the processes of thought he is using:

First Paragraph: "Power may be defined. . . ."
Second: "There are various ways of classifying. . . ."
Third: "Power . . . may be classified. . . ."
Fifth: "These forms of power are . . . displayed. . . ."
Sixth: "All these forms . . . are exemplified. . . ."
Seventh-tenth: "illustrates," "typifies," "show," "are illustrative"
Eleventh: "Let us apply these . . . analogies. . . ."
Twelfth: ". . . organizations are . . . distinguishable. . . ."

Bertrand Russell, from *Power*

Power may be defined as the production of intended effects. It is 1
thus a quantitative concept: given two men with similar desires, if one
achieves all the desires that the other achieves, and also others, he has
more power than the other. But there is no exact means of comparing
the power of two men of whom one can achieve one group of desires,
and another another; e.g., given two artists of whom each wishes to
paint good pictures and become rich, and of whom one succeeds in
painting good pictures and the other in becoming rich, there is no way
of estimating which has the more power. Nevertheless, it is easy to say,
roughly, that A has more power than B, if A achieves many intended
effects and B only a few.

There are various ways of classifying the forms of power, each of 2
which has its utility. In the first place, there is power over human
beings and power over dead matter or nonhuman forms of life. I shall
be concerned mainly with power over human beings, but it will be
necessary to remember that the chief cause of change in the modern
world is the increased power over matter that we owe to science.

Power over human beings may be classified by the manner of 3
influencing individuals, or by the type of organization involved.

An individual may be influenced: A. By direct physical power over 4
his body, e.g., when he is imprisoned or killed; B. By rewards and
punishments as inducements, e.g., in giving or withholding employment; C. By influence on opinion, i.e., propaganda in its broadest
sense. Under this last head I should include the opportunity for
creating desired habits in others, e.g., by military drill, the only
difference being that in such cases action follows without any such
mental intermediary as could be called opinion.

These forms of power are most nakedly and simply displayed in our 5
dealings with animals, where disguises and pretenses are not thought
necessary. When a pig with a rope round its middle is hoisted squeal-
ing into a ship, it is subject to direct physical power over its body. On
the other hand, when the proverbial donkey follows the proverbial
carrot, we induce him to act as we wish by persuading him that it is to
his interest to do so. Intermediate between these two cases is that of
performing animals, in whom habits have been formed by rewards and
punishments; also, in a different way, that of sheep induced to embark
on a ship, when the leader has to be dragged across the gangway by
force, and the rest then follow willingly.

All these forms of power are exemplified among human beings. 6
The case of the pig illustrates military and police power. 7
The donkey with the carrot typifies the power of propaganda. 8
Performing animals show the power of "education." 9

The sheep following their unwilling leader are illustrative of party 10 politics, whenever, as is usual, a revered leader is in bondage to a clique or to party bosses.

Let us apply these Aesopian analogies to the rise of Hitler. The 11 carrot was the Nazi program (involving, e.g., the abolition of interest); the donkey was the lower middle class. The sheep and their leader were the Social Democrats and Hindenburg. The pigs (only so far as their misfortunes are concerned) were the victims in concentration camps, and the performing animals are the millions who make the Nazi salute.

The most important organizations are approximately distinguishable 12 by the kind of power that they exert. The army and the police exercise coercive power over the body; economic organizations, in the main, use rewards and punishments as incentives and deterrents; schools, churches, and political parties aim at influencing opinion. But these distinctions are not very clear-cut, since every organization uses other forms of power in addition to the one which is most characteristic.

Questions

1. Try diagramming Russell's classification scheme for power. Do you think Russell used a top-down or a bottom-up method to generate his set of classifications?
2. In paragraph 4, Russell identifies three ways "an individual may be influenced." After defining the third way as "by influence on opinion," Russell notes that in cases such as "military drill," habits are formed without the "mental intermediary . . . called opinion." Why doesn't Russell posit a fourth type of power to account for such cases? Do you think he should have? Why or why not?
3. Although Russell says that he is concerned with forms of "power over human beings," he uses animal analogies to explain his classifications. In this context, do you think animal analogies are appropriate? To what extent do people who are treated like pigs, donkeys, performing animals, or sheep become pigs, donkeys, performing animals, or sheep? Do people have powers that are not available to these animals? Do these animals have powers that remain unaccounted for in Russell's taxonomy of power? In short, is Russell's taxonomy of power complete or does it leave out important forms of power?

PRACTICE

Power in an Institution You Know

Classify and discuss the forms of power that are characteristic of an institution you know well such as a school, a family, a youth group, a military organization, or a business. In developing your classification, you might want to use Russell's categories as a point of departure. However, if you do so, then be sure that you test their applicability to your topic and modify them as necessary to fit your purpose. In planning and organizing your essay, you should remember that Russell's work not only classifies but also defines and exemplifies. What definitions and examples do you need to make your classifications informative and interesting?

PRACTICE

From Abstract to Concrete

Using Russell's very clear structure as a model (definition, classification, exemplification), write a short essay in which you take some other large abstraction—love, faith, service, education—and produce your own discussion of it. To get started, brainstorm by writing down your definitions of the abstraction you have chosen. Compare your definitions with a dictionary's way of defining your chosen term. Then, work out the definition that will best suit your project. It is quite likely that you will want to revise your definition once you start the process of classifying the forms of the abstraction you have selected. You will, in fact, be testing the usefulness of your definition in the process of classification. Remember to follow the pattern of Russell's essay, in which the definition of power is followed by classification, and classification is supported by illustration and exemplification.

Title your essay "Forms of _____."

9. ANALYSIS

Taking Things Apart

Analysis is a systematic way of studying things by examining how the parts that make up the whole function and relate. We can analyze most things in a systematic way, including living creatures, machines, events, social groups, ecosystems, and texts. A written analysis is a way of reporting your systematic study so that others can see and understand what you've discovered.

But writing analytically is not only a way of reporting what you've discovered; it is also a way of discovering and recording what is worth reporting to others. So, for example, you might begin your study of something by writing an outline that indicates the parts you will examine and the order in which you will analyze them. As you fill in your outline with specific observations, you may discover complex units that need to be broken down into smaller units, specifics that require you to add new categories to your original outline, and patterns or relationships that are worth recording for possible use in your final report or written analysis. Analysis is a way of using writing to improve observation. It is not just a report on a finished set of observations; it is a *way* of observing.

Generally speaking, analysis proceeds in two ways: comparatively and dialectically. In a comparative analysis, you examine the parts of two or more specific things in order to discover, record, and report significant similarities and differences between those things. In a dialectical analysis, you examine the parts of one specific thing in order to discover, record, and report the extent to which it can be understood in terms of a more general framework or theory. The practices in this chapter offer opportunities for both kinds of analysis. The first practice asks you to examine a specific comparative analysis in terms of its formal features, while the next two practices invite you to try your hand at comparative analysis. The last two practices challenge you to undertake a dialectical analysis of advertising, first by examining one advertisement in terms of a rhetorical framework and, second, by examining one aspect of a number of advertisements in terms of John Berger's theory of "publicity."

READING

Comparison and Contrast

The following brief essay appeared in the New York *Tribune* in February of 1892. It was the work of Stephen Crane, a young man of twenty, who had recently left college to pursue a career as a writer. This was the first of a series of "sketches" of Sullivan County in New York's Catskill Mountains, which began Crane's career.

Stephen Crane, "The Last of the Mohicans"

Few of the old, gnarled and weather-beated inhabitants of the pines 1 and boulders of Sullivan County are great readers of books or students of literature. On the contrary, the man who subscribes for the county's weekly newspaper is the man who has attained sufficient position to enable him to leave his farm labors for literary pursuits. The historical traditions of the region have been handed down from generation to generation, at the firesides in the old homesteads. The aged grandsire recites legends to his grandson; and when the grandson's head is silvered he takes his corncob pipe from his mouth and transfixes his children and his children's children with stirring tales of hunter's exploit and Indian battle. Historians are wary of this form of procedure. Insignificant facts, told from mouth to mouth down the years, have been known to become of positively appalling importance by the time they have passed from behind the last corncob in the last chimney corner. Nevertheless, most of these fireside stories are verified by books written by learned men, who have dived into piles of moldy documents and dusty chronicles to establish their facts.

This gives the great Sullivan County thunderbolt immense weight. 2 And they hurl it at no less a head than that which once evolved from its inner recesses the famous Leatherstocking Tales. The old storytellers of this district are continually shaking metaphorical fists at *The Last of the Mohicans* of J. Fenimore Cooper. Tell them that they are aiming their shafts at one of the standard novels of American literature and they scornfully sneer; endeavor to oppose them with the intricacies of Indian history and they shriek defiance. No consideration for the author, the literature or the readers can stay their hands, and they claim without reservation that the last of the Mohicans, the real and only authentic last of the Mohicans, was a demoralized, dilapidated inhabitant of Sullivan County.

The work in question is of course a visionary tale and the historical 3 value of the plot is not a question of importance. But when the two heroes of Sullivan County and J. Fenimore Cooper, respectively, are compared, the pathos lies in the contrast, and the lover of the noble and fictional Uncas is overcome with great sadness. Even as Cooper claims that his Uncas was the last of the children of the Turtle, so do the sages of Sullivan County roar from out their rockbound fastnesses that their nondescript Indian was the last of the children of the Turtle. The pathos lies in the contrast between the noble savage of fiction and the sworn-to-claimant of Sullivan County.

All know well the character of Cooper's hero, Uncas, that bronze 4 god in a North American wilderness, that warrior with the eye of the eagle, the ear of the fox, the tread of the catlike panther, and the tongue of the wise serpent of fable. Over his dead body a warrior cries:

"Why has thou left us, pride of the Wapanachki? Thy time has been 5 like that of the sun when in the trees; thy glory brighter than his light at noonday. Thou art gone, youthful warrior, but a hundred Wyandots are clearing the briers from thy path to the world of spirits. Who that saw thee in battle would believe that thou couldst die? Who before thee has ever shown Uttawa the way into the fight? Thy feet were like the wings of eagles; thine arm heavier than falling branches from the pine; and thy voice like the Manitto when he speaks in the clouds. The tongue of Uttawa is weak and his heart exceedingly heavy. Pride of the Wapanachki, why hast thou left us?"

The last of the Mohicans supported by Sullivan County is a totally 6 different character. They have forgotten his name. From their description of him he was no warrior who yearned after the blood of his enemies as the hart panteth for the water-brooks; on the contrary he developed a craving for the rum of the white men which rose superior to all other anxieties. He had the emblematic Turtle tattooed somewhere under his shirtfront. Arrayed in tattered, torn and ragged garments which some white man had thrown off, he wandered listlessly from village to village and from house to house, his only ambition being to beg, borrow or steal a drink. The settlers helped him because they knew his story. They knew of the long line of mighty sachems sleeping under the pines of the mountains. He was a veritable "poor Indian." He dragged through his wretched life in helpless misery. No one could be more alone in the world than he and when he died there was no one to call him pride of anything nor to inquire why he had left them.

Analysis of a Comparative Analysis

Crane's sketch, as you have no doubt noticed, works by comparison and contrast. Your assignment is to analyze how Crane's sketch is put together. You might begin by examining paragraphs 3 through 6, the most explicitly comparative part of the sketch. To see how this part works, consider writing down, in two columns, phrases from Crane's text that balance one another. For instance, the contrasting phrases that conclude the final two paragraphs could come at the bottom of your columns:

Noble Savage	*Poor Indian*
. . . .	. . . .
. . . .	. . . .
why has thou left us?	no one . . . to inquire why he had left them.

Next, you will want to consider how the phrases in these columns relate to Crane's statement that "the pathos lies in the contrast." To what extent do the formal features and language of paragraphs 3 through 6 support Crane's statement?

Finally, consider the relationship between the first two paragraphs and the rest of the sketch. What do these paragraphs do? To what extent do they prepare the way for the comparative analysis in paragraphs 3 through 6? To what extent do they complicate or change the point of the comparative analysis in paragraphs 3 through 6?

Fiction and Experience

Write an essay in which you compare and contrast two versions of a contemporary figure that you know something about, such as the doctor, the professor, the farmer, the cowboy, the cop, the rock musician, the immigrant, the corporate executive, the writer. How is this figure presented in popular culture (movies, magazines, television series, or novels)? How does this fictional representation compare with what you know from personal experience about such a figure?

To get started, you might make a list of the points to be compared for each version of the figure. After working through these points of comparison, you will need to select the points you will include and arrange them in order of importance. Will your essay be more effective if you start with the most significant points of similarity or difference, or if you end with them? In your introduction or conclusion you might want to consider why we construct fictions about this particular figure.

Two Poets and a Painting

As we have said, one of the basic tools of analytic writing is the method of comparison and contrast. Our minds work in terms of relationships. It is very hard—perhaps impossible—for us to consider a thing by itself. Inevitably, we make analogies or invent metaphors whenever we are forced to discuss a single thing in isolation.

The method of comparison and contrast simply formalizes what we all do when thinking. In using this method, we look separately for points of resemblance (comparison) between two objects and for points of difference (contrast). If there are no points of resemblance, then there is no reason to discuss the two things together. On the other hand, if two things are too similar, there is not much to say about them. The method of comparison and contrast is of most use when we wish to distinguish the specific differences between two things that are both members of the same category: like humans and monkeys (same genus, different species), or men and women (same species, different sex), or this shortstop and that shortstop (same function, different performance).

In this assignment, you are to compare and contrast two modern poems that were inspired by the same painting, Pieter Brueghel's *The Fall of Icarus*. The painting is based on the Greek legend of Icarus and his father, Daedalus, who tried to escape from imprisonment on the island of Crete. A master craftsman, Daedalus made wings for himself and his son out of birds' feathers held together with wax. He warned the boy not to fly too low or the water would wet the wings and weigh him down, nor too high or the heat of the sun would melt the wax. But Icarus was a high-spirited lad and ignored his father's advice. He flew too high, his wings came apart, and he fell into the sea and drowned.

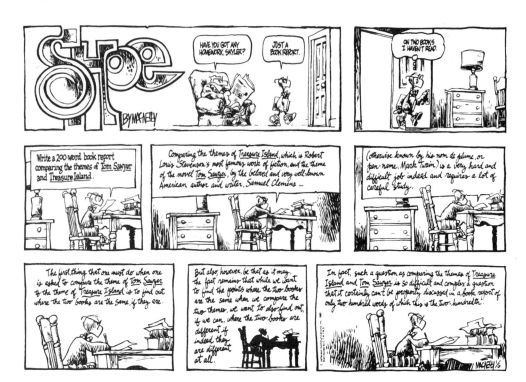

Your specific task is to discuss the similarities and differences between the two poems in terms of their ideas and the language in which the ideas are conveyed. You are not being asked to judge which is the better poem. The thesis of your paper should simply be a statement as to whether the *similarities* or *differences* seem to you most significant. For example, you might argue, "The most striking thing about these two poems is that they treat the same painting in such different ways," or "The interesting thing about these two poems is that, despite superficial differences in style, they treat the painting in essentially the same way."

Read the poems several times, take notes, and sort out your thoughts before you begin. For inspiration, we present above Jeff MacNelly's cartoon version of young Skyler Fishawk at work upon a similar project. Please do *not* follow his method of composition. He understands the theory of comparison and contrast very well, but he manages to avoid the practice completely.

The Fall of Icarus by Pieter Brueghel

Musée des Beaux Arts[1]

About suffering they were never wrong,   1
The Old Masters: how well they understood
Its human position; how it takes place
While someone else is eating or opening a window or just walking dully
    along;
How, when the aged are reverently, passionately waiting
For the miraculous birth, there always must be
Children who did not specially want it to happen, skating
On a pond at the edge of the wood:
They never forgot
That even the dreadful martyrdom must run its course
Anyhow in a corner, some untidy spot
Where dogs go on with their doggy life and the torturer's horse
Scratches its innocent behind on a tree.

In Brueghel's *Icarus*, for instance: how everything turns away   2
Quite leisurely from the disaster; the ploughman may
Have heard the splash, the forsaken cry,
But for him it was not an important failure; the sun shone
As it had to on the white legs disappearing into the green
Water; and the expensive delicate ship that must have seen
Something amazing, a boy falling out of the sky,
Had somewhere to get to and sailed calmly on.

—W. H. AUDEN

Landscape with the Fall of Icarus

According to Brueghel   1
when Icarus fell
it was spring

a farmer was ploughing   2
his field
the whole pageantry

of the year was   3
awake tingling
near

the edge of the sea   4
concerned
with itself

---

[1]Museum of Fine Arts.

---

sweating in the sun   5
that melted
the wings' wax

unsignificantly   6
off the coast
there was

a splash quite unnoticed   7
this was
Icarus drowning

    —WILLIAM CARLOS WILLIAMS

Analyzing an Advertisement

At this point we had planned to reproduce a recent advertisement and then demonstrate how one might analyze it to discover its persuasive appeals. But advertisers do not like their work to be analyzed critically—which suggests that critical analysis is indeed an effective way to defend ourselves against the power of advertising. Although we cannot get permission to reprint an ad in a context of criticism, we will compensate for that by describing one as fully as we can. For those of you who are willing to do some research, the particular ad we have selected first appeared as part of a ten-page insert in *Vanity Fair* magazine (February 1988), advertising Guess jeans by Georges Marciano. Although these ten pages of images do not tell a complete story, they make a sequence based on a single theme.

Most advertisements that go beyond the mere providing of information are organized around a theme. The rhetorical analysis of such ads involves putting a name to the theme and exploring the ways in which the various elements of the ad function to give a certain shape and direction to the viewer's response to the ad. We analyze ads in this way in order to free ourselves from manipulation by understanding how we are being manipulated. Advertising seeks to direct our attention and our emotions toward some product. The best way to free ourselves from such manipulation is to direct our attention to the ads themselves: to analyze them. The trick—and it is easier said than done—is to become fully conscious of the emotional logic embodied in the text (the words *and* the images) of each advertisement.

We can start by naming the elements that are present in any given ad and then go on to explore their connotations and how the ad emphasizes and connects them in a persuasive structure. In the particular ad we are describing the major elements are an attractive young woman, dressed in a certain way, whose pose and expression are open to interpretation. She stands against a background of wall posters, and just above her forehead she holds a pair of horns like those of a cow or bull. The photograph is in black and white, with only the name of the advertiser, Georges Marciano, scrawled across the page in bright red. We cannot miss the name, but its color separates it from the other images. The name is *on* the picture, not in it, like the signature of an artist on a painting, only much more prominent: It might be written in red lipstick. The posters on the wall in the background are just clear enough for us to make them out.

In the ten pages of ads we are describing, this young woman is the only person we see, except for a bullfighter, whose images dominate three of the ten pages, dressed in his splendid costume, which is technically called a "suit of lights." In the first of the ten pages the woman is part of a photo-montage in which several images are printed together, so that we cannot tell exactly where she is or what we are seeing. She is partly clothed, and her hair is disheveled. She appears to be standing, but the angle of the image also suggests that she might be lying in a bed. Behind her, in the upper half of the page, is a white background that might be interpreted as sheets or newspapers or posters. The lower half of the page is dominated by in-termingled images—what appears to be a wrought-iron balcony and part of a "suit of lights." The woman's eyes are open but lowered. Her arms are crossed over her breasts, perhaps protectively. In or near her hands is a string of beads, possibly a rosary.

The other pages carry out these motifs in various ways. In one two-page spread the woman, wearing a black blouse and shorts decorated on the sides to suggest the embroidery of a suit of lights, is bent over a low bench or stool, as if to be spanked. She gazes directly into the camera. On another page, with eyes closed and lips slightly parted, she seems to swoon against a tattered wall poster of the same bullfighter who appears on the other pages. A black shawl, or mantilla, hangs from her hand, which is pressed against the heart of the bullfighter on the poster. The other pages carry these motifs further, resulting in a strong dose of what the French semiotician Roland Barthes would have called "Latinicity"—that is, certain stereotypes or cultural codes that link things Hispanic with the erotic and the violent, as in the opera *Carmen* or in several works by Ernest Hemingway. The young woman—with black hair, thick, straight eyebrows, a mantilla, and (in two of the pages) a black sombrero—is presented to us as a Hispanic or Latin beauty, although a very well-scrubbed and well-depilated one, to be sure, as the audience for these ads is also presumed to be.

One ad combines all the motifs. The young woman is wearing a white blouse like a schoolgirl, a cummerbund like a bullfighter (who always wears one under the suit of lights), and a bullfighter's black tie, while holding up a pair of horns like a bull awaiting the sword of the matador—in submission. This female bull has a thing about bullfighters and is clearly waiting for one to come along and put her out of her misery. Her downcast eyes (carefully made up) proclaim her submission, and the dangerous points of those horns are outside the frame of the picture. She's only playing, after all, but you, too, can play if you join her and present your own dangerous attractions in some jeans by Guess. That is the message, and it is delivered through an extremely slick and sophisticated series of images. The way to avoid being unduly influenced by such clever visual persuasion is to understand clearly how it works, to question the cultural stereotypes on which it is based, and finally to ask whether you really want to go for this bull.

PRACTICE

Analyzing a Magazine Advertisement

Select an ad—preferably a full-page, color ad—from a current magazine. Then write a critical analysis of it. Remember, a lot depends on selecting an ad that will reward such analysis. Try to find something that is complex enough to be interesting. The best ads for this purpose make a powerful appeal but in subtle or complex ways. Your procedure should be to describe the purpose of the ad—what it is trying to accomplish, what it wants you to do or buy—and then to show by analysis how it is making its appeal to an audience. You may well wish to describe the audience to which the ad is directed, so that you can connect the ad's methods to the desired results.

Although you will have to describe the ad in order to analyze it, remember that analysis is your main goal: You want to show how the ad's words and images are related to its theme and purpose. Our discussion of the Guess jeans ad presents a general rhetorical framework for analyzing advertisements and then provides an example of such an analysis. To get started, you might want to examine your ad in terms of the general rhetorical framework we presented. However, you should feel free to change that framework as needed in order to account for the specific ways your advertisement works.

READING

A Critic Theorizes about Advertising

The following selection by the British art critic John Berger is taken from *Ways of Seeing*, a book on the language of images. In this excerpt, Berger offers his readers a general theory about how advertising works and what it works for. Please note that Berger uses the British term "publicity" for what we call "advertising."

John Berger, from *Ways of Seeing*

Publicity is usually explained and justified as a competitive medium 1
which ultimately benefits the public (the consumer) and the most
efficient manufacturers—and thus the national economy. It is closely
related to certain ideas about freedom: freedom of choice for the
purchaser; freedom of enterprise for the manufacturer. The great
hoardings and the publicity neons of the cities of capitalism are the
immediate visible sign of "The Free World."

For many in Eastern Europe such images in the West sum up what 2
they in the East lack. Publicity, it is thought, offers a free choice.

It is true that in publicity one brand of manufacture, one firm, 3
competes with another; but it is also true that every publicity image
confirms and enhances every other. Publicity is not merely an assem-
bly of competing messages: it is a language in itself which is always
being used to make the same general proposal. Within publicity,
choices are offered between this cream and that cream, that car and
this car, but publicity as a system only makes a single proposal.

It proposes to each of us that we transform ourselves, or our lives, 4
by buying something more.

This more, it proposes, will make us in some way richer—even 5
though we will be poorer by having spent our money.

Publicity persuades us of such a transformation by showing us 6
people who have apparently been transformed and are, as a result,
enviable. The state of being envied is what constitutes glamor. And
publicity is the process of manufacturing glamor.

It is important here not to confuse publicity with the pleasure or 7
benefits to be enjoyed from the things it advertises. Publicity is effective precisely because it feeds upon the real. Clothes, food, cars,
cosmetics, baths, sunshine are real things to be enjoyed in themselves.
Publicity begins by working on a natural appetite for pleasure. But it
cannot offer the real object of pleasure and there is no convincing
substitute for a pleasure in that pleasure's own terms. The more
convincingly publicity conveys the pleasure of bathing in a warm,
distant sea, the more the spectator-buyer will become aware that he is
hundreds of miles away from that sea and the more remote the chance
of bathing in it will seem to him. This is why publicity can never really
afford to be about the product or opportunity it is proposing to the
buyer who is not yet enjoying it. Publicity is never a celebration of a
pleasure-in-itself. Publicity is always about the future buyer. It offers
him an image of himself made glamorous by the product or opportunity
it is trying to sell. The image then makes him envious of himself as he
might be. Yet what makes this self-which-he-might-be enviable? The
envy of others. Publicity is about social relations, not objects. Its

promise is not of pleasure, but of happiness: happiness as judged from the outside by others. The happiness of being envied is glamor.

Being envied is a solitary form of reassurance. It depends precisely 8 upon not sharing your experience with those who envy you. You are observed with interest but you do not observe with interest—if you do, you will become less enviable. In this respect the envied are like bureaucrats; the more impersonal they are, the greater the illusion (for themselves and for others) of their power. The power of the glamorous resides in their supposed happiness: the power of the bureaucrat in his supposed authority. It is this which explains the absent, unfocused look of so many glamor images. They look out *over* the looks of envy which sustain them.

The spectator-buyer is meant to envy herself as she will become if 9 she buys the product. She is meant to imagine herself transformed by the product into an object of envy for others, an envy which will then justify her loving herself. One could put this another way: the publicity image steals her love of herself as she is, and offers it back to her for the price of the product.

Questions

1. How does Berger qualify the idea that publicity is a sign of freedom of choice and freedom of enterprise?
2. Why does he call publicity a "language in itself"?
3. What does Berger mean when he says, "Publicity is about social relations, not objects"?
4. Cite an example of a new product being advertised that would illustrate Berger's statement that "The state of being envied is what constitutes glamor."

PRACTICE

Analyzing Images of Women in Advertising

The following pages present a brief survey of images of women in advertising. Using Berger's terms, analyze each ad: What desirable transformations of self are being offered to the woman who reads these advertisements? How is glamor being defined in these ads? In what ways are these ads about social relations rather than objects?

Try reading these ads as a sort of historical narrative of advertising. Do you notice any significant differences in the image of woman created by advertising over the years? While it's obvious that clothing and hair styles have changed during the twentieth century, has there been any significant change in the way advertisements work and what they work for? How valid are Berger's generalizations about advertising? The more carefully you consider these specific advertisements, the richer your analysis will be.

If your instructor wishes to include some library research in this assignment so that you can consider the topic more thoroughly, you might concentrate on the image of women in a particular decade, such as the 1950s, by looking at the advertising in a number of popular magazines of that period. Or, if you wish to enlarge your historical survey, concentrate on advertising over a period of several decades in one or more magazines with fairly long publishing histories, such as *Ladies' Home Journal, Redbook, Cosmopolitan,* or *Good Housekeeping*.

Make that dream come true

W HAT woman lives who has not at some time enjoyed the vision of herself a bride. For many the dream has been fulfilled. Don't allow a bad complexion to place you among the others!

Your beauty of feature, becoming dress, graceful bearing, keen wit, can be completely overshadowed by a blotchy or otherwise unattractive skin. But there is no excuse for submission to such a condition, when to correct it is so easy.

Usually all that nature requires to make a clear pleasing complexion is right living—and—proper, regular cleansing of the skin. It is this knowledge that has made Resinol Soap a favorite in thousands of homes where it is now in daily use.

If you are neglected and humiliated because of a red, oily, or otherwise repellent skin, begin today the following treatment:

Gently work the profuse foamy lather of Resinol Soap well into the pores with the finger tips. It rinses easily and completely with a little clear warm water. A dash of cold water to close the pores completes the treatment. Now see how velvety your skin looks and feels—how invigorated it is—and what a delicate glow it has. These are only the first happy effects of this delightful toilet soap.

At all drug and toilet goods counters. May we send you a free trial? Write now. Dept. 5-A, Resinol, Baltimore, Md.

Resinol Soap

"Girls who know this secret always win out"

says Irene Dunne

1 YEARS AGO MY LOVELY SOUTHERN GRANDMOTHER FIRST TAUGHT ME THAT A GIRL WHO WANTS TO BREAK HEARTS SIMPLY <u>MUST</u> HAVE A TEAROSE COMPLEXION.

RKO-RADIO STAR

2 NOW THAT I'M ON THE SCREEN I REALIZE MORE THAN EVER THE FASCINATION THERE IS IN PEARLY-SMOOTH SKIN. I FOLLOW MY LUX TOILET SOAP BEAUTY TREATMENT REGULARLY EVERY DAY.

3 IT'S REALLY AMAZING HOW QUICKLY JUST THIS SIMPLE CARE BRINGS TEMPTING NEW BEAUTY TO THE SKIN. TRY IT-YOU GIRLS WHO WANT TO MAKE NEW CONQUESTS! YOU'RE <u>SURE</u> TO WIN OUT!

So MANY GIRLS have asked Irene Dunne how to make themselves more attractive . . . how to win admiration . . . romance.

Here this lovely star tells you! And her beauty method is so simple . . . so easy to try . . . regular, everyday care with exquisitely gentle Lux Toilet Soap.

Do follow her advice! See how much clearer, softer *your* skin becomes . . . how that extra-lovely complexion wins hearts—and *holds* them!

9 out of 10 glamorous Hollywood stars . . . countless girls the country over . . . have *proved* what this fragrant, white soap does for the skin. Is yours just an "average" complexion? Don't be content—start today—have the *added beauty* Lux Toilet Soap brings.

Precious Elements in this Soap—*Scientists say:* "Skin grows old-looking through the gradual loss of certain elements Nature puts in skin to keep it youthful. Gentle Lux Toilet Soap, so readily soluble, *actually* contains such precious elements—checks their loss from the skin."

LUX TOILET SOAP

For EVERY Type of Skin . . . *dry . . . oily . . . "in-between"*

NRA

<u>YOU</u> can have the *Charm* men can't resist

1934

169

Never Beyond This Shore

HERE at the sea's edge is as near to Jim as I can go.

Other women have gone farther than this. There were women on Corregidor; women have gone to Ireland and Australia and Iceland; women have been lost in the Battle of the Atlantic.

But I know I would be foolish to dream of serving as they have. For a woman to go farther than this shore demands a special skill, complete independence—and I have neither.

No, my task is here, here in the little storm-tight house that sits back from the cove, here with my son.

And if I become discontent with the seeming smallness of my task, Jim's words come back to steady me. "I'm leaving you a very important job, Mary. Until this war is won, there won't be any more evenings when we can sit by the fireside and plan our tomorrows together. It will be up to you to make the plans for the three of us.

"Mary," he said, "keep our dreams alive."

★ ★ ★

MAKE no little plans, you who build the dream castles here at home. When you try to imagine the future, after he returns, be sure your imaginings are full of bright and cheerful hues, for that world of tomorrow will be resplendent in things you don't know—never even imagined. Allow for wonderful new developments in such fields as television, fluorescent lighting, plastics. And leave a flexible horizon for the marvels that are sure to come from the new science of electronics. When you're dreaming of your better tomorrow, count on us. General Electric Company, Schenectady, N. Y.

★ ★ ★

THE VOLUME *of General Electric war production is so high and the degree of secrecy required is so great that we can tell you little about it now. When it can be told completely we believe that the story of industry's developments during the war years will make one of the most fascinating chapters in the history of industrial progress.*

852-340K- 1

GENERAL ELECTRIC

1942

170

Stay Sweet As You Are!

There are good times, good friends, and gaiety ahead if you do. And laughter and love . . . and marriage almost before you know it. But if you don't . . . you're headed for boredom and loneliness.

And it's so easy to stay sweet . . . stay adorable . . . if you let Listerine Antiseptic look after your breath. Every morning. Every night. And especially before every date when you want to be at your best. Listerine instantly stops bad breath, and keeps it stopped for hours, usually . . . *four times better than any tooth paste.*

No Tooth Paste Kills Odor Germs Like This . . . Instantly

Listerine Antiseptic does for you what no tooth paste does. Listerine instantly kills bacteria . . . by millions—stops bad breath instantly, and usually for hours on end.

You see, far and away the most common cause of offensive breath is the bacterial fermentation of proteins which are always present in the mouth. *And research shows that your breath stays sweeter longer, depending upon the degree to which you reduce germs in the mouth.*

Listerine Clinically Proved Four Times Better Than Tooth Paste

No tooth paste, of course, is antiseptic. Chlorophyll does not kill germs—but Listerine kills bacteria by millions, gives you lasting antiseptic protection against bad breath.

Is it any wonder Listerine Antiseptic in recent clinical tests averaged at least four times more effective in stopping bad breath odors than the chlorophyll products or tooth pastes it was tested against? With proof like this, it's easy to see why Listerine belongs in your home. Every morning . . . every night . . . before every date, make it a habit to always gargle Listerine, the most widely used antiseptic in the world.

LISTERINE ANTISEPTIC STOPS BAD BREATH
4 times better than any tooth paste

A Product of The Lambert Company

Every week 2 different shows, Radio & Television—"THE ADVENTURES OF OZZIE & HARRIET" See your paper for times and stations

1954

171

Beautiful but dumb...that's how pretty girls used to be referred to in the thirties and forties, and actually a lot of them were kind of dumb. If a girl looked like anything, she just sat there like a cup-cake and never opened her mouth. I guess some people still expect a pretty girl to be marshmallow-brained and doe-eyed but they're often in for a shock! Some of the best-looking girls I know are also the brightest...they work at it. My favorite magazine says, "If you have a brain, use it...it's the best gift nature ever gave a girl ...yes, even better than beauty!" I love that magazine. I guess you could say I'm That COSMOPOLITAN Girl.

Photographed by Jim Houghton

If you want to reach me you'll find me reading
COSMOPOLITAN

1966

"I have 23 people working for me...and 4 against me"

It takes a woman's touch.

Sometimes...to really know what's going on...it takes a woman's touch. It's as true in business as it is in the home.

The fact that almost half the women in the country work is no longer news. But the "why" still might be. Women work because they want to. Because they have to. For much the same reasons men do. It depends on the *individual.* Which is what women have been saying all along.

Over the past 20 years, Redbook has evolved, kept pace with the young women it serves. It has grown into one of the major women's magazines—from 308 advertising pages in 1956 to 1,415 last year. And 1977 started with the biggest first four months in Redbook's history.

Which shows that advertisers know what we know. Sometimes to get things done, it takes a woman's touch. Especially women 18–34.

It takes a woman's touch...especially 18-34

1977

1987

A kiss is *not* just a kiss.

Bisou Bisou
NOUVELLE COUTURE

AMERICAN RAG (LA)

PATRICIA FIELD (NYC)

RON HERMAN (LA)

MACY'S (USA)

LIGHT (PARIS)

1993

10. ARGUMENTATION

Presenting a Thesis

Where persuasion seeks to put the mind to sleep, so that its appeal to emotion will be effective, argumentation aims to awaken thought by appealing to reason. Persuasion is most at home in the rough and tumble worlds of advertising and politics. Argumentation is mainly an intellectual or academic use of language, requiring patience and moderation. In principle, an argument can always be reversed. New evidence or new reasoning can convince even the arguer that the matter under discussion should be seen in a different way. But you cannot convince an advertiser not to want your money or a politician to reject your vote.

For various reasons, persuasion and argumentation are often mixed in actual speech and writing, both in academic discourse and in the world of affairs. But for the purposes of study and practice, it is useful to treat them separately. The purest forms of argumentation appear in philosophy. Here, for instance, is Bertrand Russell reflecting (in *My Philosophical Development*, 1975) on one of his earlier books:

> In *The Analysis of Mind* I argued the thesis that the "stuff" of mental occurrences consists entirely of sensations and images. I do not know whether this thesis was sound. . . . (p. 111)

As Russell indicates, a "thesis" is essential to argumentation. Although he is not arguing in this passage, but reflecting upon his earlier argument, he summarizes the thesis he had argued in the past, adding the interesting comment that he is no longer certain that his thesis was sound. This kind of second thought is, as you know, typical of reflection, but it is also built into the processes of argumentation. The ultimate goal of argument is not persuasion but truth. Arguing a thesis is partly a way of testing it. A person writing advertising copy has a set goal: sell that product! The copywriter can revise to make the copy more persuasive, but cannot rethink the point of the writing. A person writing an argument, on the other hand, begins with a tentative thesis that may be rethought during the writing, or even, as Russell indicates, after its publication in a book.

A thesis, then, is the point or organizing principle of an argument: "I argued the thesis," Russell says. But there is always something tentative about a thesis. The writers of arguments often consider counterarguments against the theses they are supporting. Sometimes this is only a gesture, a persuasive trick, but in serious argumentation it is also a way of testing. If you do this scrupulously while writing, it may lead you to modify your thesis or qualify it in some important way.

Here is an example of a philosopher introducing a long and serious argument:

> Let me start with a confession.
>
> I wrote this paper in a fit of anger and self-righteousness caused by what I thought were certain disastrous developments in the sciences. The paper will therefore sound a little harsh, and it will perhaps also be a little unjust. Now while I think that self-righteousness has no positive function whatever and while I am convinced that it can only add to the fear and to the tensions that already exist, I also think that a little anger can on occasions be a good thing and can make us see our surroundings more clearly.
>
> I think very highly of science, but I think very little of experts, although experts form about 95 percent or more of science today. It is my belief that science was advanced, and is still being advanced, by *dilettantes* and that experts are liable to bring it to a standstill. I may be entirely wrong in this belief of mine, but the only way to find out is to tell you. Therefore, with my apologies, here is my paper. (Paul Feyerabend, "Experts in a Free Society," *The Critic* [November–December 1970])

This is unusually personal and informal for philosophical argument, but there are reasons for that. The author doesn't want to sound like an expert, so he makes a personal confession. He refers to his thesis as a "belief," but his attitude toward his belief is the attitude toward argumentation we have been describing. Even in his anger, his passionate concern, he does not want to carry the day by emotion. In fact, by confessing his own emotion he is putting the reader on guard against it. He has written in anger, but he will not appeal to anger in his readers. Above all, he does not want to bully readers into thinking that there are no alternatives to his own attitude. "I may be entirely wrong," he says, "but the only way to find out is to tell you." This is the true spirit of argumentation: make a case for your thesis as strongly as you can, but be prepared to rethink it on the basis of new evidence or an argument that you haven't foreseen.

Learning to argue well is a complex process, and there are no real short cuts. The study of formal logic may help, but this is a demanding discipline and gives no guarantee of effective writing. A little bit of it is likely to confuse more than it helps. It is our belief that the best way to learn every kind of writing is through close study of actual written texts and through disciplined practice, which is what we offer in the rest of this chapter.

The connection—and the gap—between the theory and practice of argument has been well described by the philosopher Gilbert Ryle, in his book *The Concept of Mind* (1949). Describing a man arguing a case before a court, Ryle says,

> He probably observes the rules of logic without thinking about them. He does not cite Aristotle's formulae to himself or to the court. He applies in his practice what Aristotle abstracted in his theory of such practices. He reasons with a correct method but without considering the prescriptions of a methodology. The rules that he observes have become his way of thinking, when he is taking care. (p. 48)

All kinds of writing, including argumentation, are finally kinds of practice, not kinds of theory. As Ryle says elsewhere, "knowing how" is different from "knowing that." And he adds, a "surgeon must indeed have learned from instruction, or by his own inductions and observations, a great number of truths; but he must also have learned by practice a great number of aptitudes" (p. 49).

Like surgery, writing must be learned by practice as well as by observation and instruction. There is no perfect method that will ensure the composition of a strong argument. But before you examine the practice of others and undertake some assignments of your own, we would like to offer you a brief list of the features that are found in most good arguments: at least, it is our thesis that these features will be found there. You can check for yourself and see if we are right.

1. The clear statement of a thesis or position to be argued
2. The orderly presentation of evidence to support this thesis
3. A reasoned connection of the evidence to the thesis
4. The fair consideration of evidence and arguments that run counter to the thesis
5. A conclusion that emphasizes the thesis

READING

A Scientist Argues about Means and Ends

In everyday speech, the term *argument* is often used to refer to a face-off between two people that involves shouting, name calling, personal attacks, emotional outbursts, slamming doors, and closed minds. In the domain of writing, however, argument means something else: the reasoned presentation and development of a thesis. Although there are many reasonable ways to argue a thesis, one way seems to resemble a personal face-off: the critique or refutation of someone else's argument.

In the following essay, the paleontologist Stephen Jay Gould critiques Jeremy Rifkin's *Algeny*, a book on biotechnology, science, and society that Gould believes to be nothing but "a cleverly constructed tract of anti-intellectual propaganda." While he admits to being "harsh," Gould nevertheless insists that his critique of Rifkin is not unreasonable. What do you think? As you read Gould's essay, consider the following questions: Is Gould's critique a personal attack on Rifkin? Is there some important intellectual and social issue at stake? Does Gould have a reasonable thesis to argue? Are his means—or ways—of arguing reasonable? What about his ends? What, if anything, differentiates Gould's essay from both an everyday "argument" between two angry people and a piece of devious persuasion or propaganda?

Stephen Jay Gould, "Integrity and Mr. Rifkin"

Evolution has a definite geometry well portrayed by our ancient 1 metaphor, the tree of life. Lineages split and diverge like the branches of a tree. A species, once distinct, is permanently on its own; the branches of life do not coalesce. Extinction is truly forever, persistence a personal odyssey. But art does not always imitate nature. Biotechnology, or genetic engineering, has aroused fear and opposition because it threatens to annul this fundamental property of life—to place genes of one species into the program of another, thereby combining what nature has kept separate from time immemorial. Two concerns—one immediate and practical, the other distant and deep—have motivated the opposition.

Some critics fear that certain conjunctions might have potent and 2 unanticipated effects—creating a resistant agent of disease or simply a new creature so hardy and fecund that, like Kurt Vonnegut's *ice-nine,* it spreads to engulf the earth in a geological millisecond. I am not persuaded by these excursions into science fiction, but the distant and deeper issue does merit discussion: What are the consequences, ethical, aesthetic, and practical, of altering life's fundamental geometry and permitting one species to design new creatures at will, combining bits and pieces of lineages distinct for billions of years?

Jeremy Rifkin has been our most vocal opponent of genetic 3 engineering. He has won court cases and aroused fury in the halls of science with his testimony about immediate dangers. However, his major statement, a book titled *Algeny* (for the modern alchemy of genes), concentrates almost entirely on the deep and distant issue. His activities based on immediate fears have been widely reported and rebutted. But *Algeny* has not been adequately analyzed or dissected. Its status as prophecy or pretension, philosophy or pamphleteering, must be assessed, for *Algeny* touts itself as the manifesto of a movement to save nature and simple decency from the hands of impatient and rapacious science.

I will state my conclusion—bald and harsh—at the outset. I regard   4 *Algeny* as a cleverly constructed tract of anti-intellectual propaganda masquerading as scholarship. Among books promoted as serious intellectual statements by important thinkers, I don't think I have ever read a shoddier work. Damned shame, too, because the deep issue is troubling and I do not disagree with Rifkin's basic plea for respecting the integrity of evolutionary lineages. But devious means compromise good ends, and we shall have to save Rifkin's humane conclusion from his own lamentable tactics.

The basic argument of *Algeny* rests upon a parody of an important   5 theme advanced by contemporary historians of science against the myth of objectivity and inexorable scientific progress: science is socially embedded; its theories are not simple deductions from observed facts of nature, but a complex mixture of social ideology (often unconsciously expressed) and empirical constraint. This theme is liberating for science; it embodies the human side of our enterprise and depicts us as passionate creatures struggling with limited tools to understand a complex reality, not as robots programmed to convert objective information into immutable truth. But in Rifkin's hands, this theme becomes a caricature. Rifkin ignores the complex interplay of social bias with *facts* of nature and promotes a crude socioeconomic determinism that views our historical succession of biological worldviews—from creationism to Darwinism to the new paradigm now supposedly under construction—as so many simple reflections of social ideology.

From the crudity of this socioeconomic determinism, Rifkin con-   6 structs his specific brief: Darwinian evolutionism, he asserts, was the creation of industrial capitalism, the age of pyrotechnology. Arising in this context as a reflection of social ideology, it never had any sound basis in reason or evidence. Darwinism is now dying because the age of pyrotechnology is yielding to an era of biotechnology—and biotech demands a new view of life. Darwinism translated the industrial machine into nature; biotech models nature as a computer and substitutes information for material parts.

Darwinism spawned (or reflected) evil in its support for exploitation   7 of man and nature, but at least Darwinism respected the integrity of species (while driving some to extinction) because it lacked the technology to change them by mixture and instant transmutation. But the new paradigm dissolves species into strings of information that can be reshuffled at will.

The new temporal theory of evolution replaces the idea of life as 8
mere machinery with the notion of life as mere information. All living things are drained of their aliveness and turned into abstract messages. We can no longer entertain any question of sacredness or inviolability. What could such concepts mean in a world with no recognizable boundaries to respect? In the age of biotechnology, separate species with separate names gradually give way to systems of information that can be reprogrammed into an infinite number of biological combinations.

But what can we do if we wish to save nature as it actually evolved— 9
a system divided into packages of porcupines and primroses, cabbages and kings? We can seek no help from science, Rifkin claims, for science is a monolith masquerading as objective knowledge, but really reflecting the dominant ideology of a new technological age. We can only make an ethical decision to "re-sacralize" nature by respecting the inviolability of its species. We must, for the first time in history, decide *not* to institute a possible technology, despite its immediately attractive benefits in such areas as medicine and agriculture.

I have devoted my own career to evolutionary biology, and I have 10
been among the strongest critics of strict Darwinism. Yet Rifkin's assertions bear no relationship to what I have observed and practiced for 25 years. Evolutionary theory has never been healthier or more exciting. We are experiencing a ferment of new ideas and theories, but they are revising and extending Darwin, not burying him. How can Rifkin construct a world so different from the one I inhabit and know so well? Either I am blind or he is wrong—and I think I can show, by analyzing his slipshod scholarship and basic misunderstanding of science, that his world is an invention constructed to validate his own private hopes. I shall summarize my critique in five charges:

1. Rifkin does not understand Darwinism, and his arguments refute 11
an absurd caricature, not the theory itself. He trots out all the standard mischaracterizations, usually confined nowadays to creationist tracts. Just three examples: "According to Darwin," Rifkin writes, "everything evolved by chance." Since the complexity of cellular life cannot arise by accident, Darwinism is absurd: "According to the odds, the one-cell organism is so complex that the likelihood of its coming together by sheer accident and chance is computed to be around $1/10^{78438}$." But Darwin himself, and Darwinians ever since, have always stressed, as a cardinal premise, that natural selection is not a theory of randomness. Chance may describe the origin of new variation by mutation, but

natural selection, the agent of change, is a conventional deterministic process that builds adaptation by preserving favorable variants.

Rifkin then dismisses Darwinism as a tautology; fitness is defined by 12 survival, and the catch phrase "survival of the fittest" reduces to "survival of those that survive"—and therefore has no meaning. Darwin resolved this issue by defining fitness as predictable advantage before the fact, not as recorded survival afterward (as we may predict the biomechanical improvements that might help zebras outrun or outmaneuver lions; survival then becomes a testable consequence of good design).

Rifkin regards Darwinism as absurd because "natural selection 13 makes no room for long-range considerations. Every new trait has to be immediately useful or it is discarded." How, therefore, can natural selection explain the origin of a bird's wing, since the intermediate forms cannot fly: What good is five per cent of a wing? The British biologist St. George Jackson Mivart developed this critique in 1871 as the argument about "incipient stages of useful structures." Darwin met the challenge by adding a chapter to the sixth edition of the *Origin of Species*. One need not agree with Darwin's resolution, but one does have a responsibility to acknowledge the argument's existence. Darwin proposed that intermediate stages performed different functions; feathers of an incipient wing may act as excellent organs of thermoregulation—a particular problem in the smallest of dinosaurs, the lineage that evolved into birds.

Rifkin displays equally little comprehension of basic arguments 14 about evolutionary geometry. He thinks that *Archaeopteryx* has been refuted as an intermediate link between reptiles and birds because some true birds have been found in rocks of the same age. But evolution is a branching bush, not a ladder. Ancestors survive after descendants branch off. Dogs evolved from wolves, but wolves (though threatened) are hanging tough. And a species of *Australopithecus* lived side by side with its descendant *Homo* for more than a million years in Africa.

Rifkin doesn't grasp the current critiques of strict Darwinism any 15 better. He caricatures my own theory of punctuated equilibrium as a sudden response to ecological catastrophe: "The idea is that these catastrophic events spawned monstrous genetic mutations within existing species, most of which were lethal. A few of the mutations, however, managed to survive and become the precursors of a new species." But punctuated equilibrium, as Niles Eldredge and I have always emphasized, is a theory about ordinary speciation (taking tens of thousands of years) and its abrupt appearance at low scales of geological resolution, not about ecological catastrophe and sudden genetic change.

Rifkin, it appears, understands neither the fundamentals of Darwin- 16
ism, its current critiques, nor even the basic topology of the evolutionary tree.

2. Rifkin shows no understanding of the norms and procedures of 17
science: he displays little comprehension of what science is and how
scientists work. He consistently misses the essential distinction between fact (claims about the world's empirical content) and theory
(ideas that explain and interpret facts)—using arguments from one
realm to refute the other. Against Darwinism (a theory of evolutionary
mechanisms) he cites the British physiologist Gerald Kerkut's *Implications of Evolution*, a book written to refute the factual claim that
all living creatures have a common ancestry, and to argue instead that
life may have arisen several times from chemical precursors—an issue
not addressed by Darwinism. (Creationist lawyers challenged me with
the same misunderstanding during my cross-examination at the Arkan-
sas "equal time" trial five years ago.) Rifkin then suggests that the
entire field of evolution may be pseudo science because the great
French zoologist Pierre-Paul Grassé is so critical of Darwinism (the
theory of natural selection might be wrong, but Grassé devoted his
entire life to studying the facts of evolution).

Science is a pluralistic enterprise, validly pursued in many modes. 18
But Rifkin ignores its richness by stating that direct manipulation by
repeatable experiment provides the only acceptable method for reaching a scientific conclusion. Since evolution treats historically unique
events that occurred millions of years ago, it cannot pass muster. Rifkin
doesn't seem to realize that he is throwing out half of science—nearly
all of geology and most of astronomy, for instance—with his evolutionary bath water. Historical science is a valid pursuit, but uses methods
different from the controlled experiment of Rifkin's all-encompassing
caricature—search for an underlying pattern among unique events,
and retrodiction (predicting the yet undiscovered results of past
events), for example.

3. Rifkin does not respect the procedures of fair argument. He uses 19
every debater's trick in the book to mischaracterize and trivialize his
opposition, and to place his own dubious claims in a rosy light. Just
four examples:

The synecdoche (trying to dismiss a general notion by citing a single 20
poor illustration). Rifkin suggests that science knows nothing about the
evolutionary tree of horses, and has sold the public a bill of goods
(the great horse caper, he calls it), because one exhibit, set up at the
American Museum of Natural History in 1905, arranged fossil horses in
order of size, not genealogy. Right, Jeremy, that was a lousy exhibit,
but you might read George Gaylord Simpson's book *Horses* to see what
we do know.

The half quote (stopping in the middle so that an opponent appears 21 to agree with you, or seems merely ridiculous). Rifkin quotes me on the argument about incipient stages of useful structures discussed a few paragraphs ago: "Harvard's Stephen Jay Gould posed the dilemma when he observed, 'What good is half a jaw or half a wing?' " Sure, I posed the dilemma, but then followed it with an entire essay supporting Darwin's resolution based on different function in intermediate stages. Rifkin might have mentioned the true subject and not cited me in his support. Rifkin then quotes a famous line from Darwin as if it represented the great man's admission of impotence: "Darwin himself couldn't believe it, even though it was his own theory that advanced the proposition. He wrote: 'To suppose that the eye, with all of its inimitable contrivances . . . could have been formed by natural selection, seems, I freely confess, absurd in the highest possible degree.' " But Rifkin might have mentioned that Darwin follows this statement with one of his most brilliant sections—a documentation of nature's graded intermediates between simple pinhole eyes and the complexity of our own, and an argument that the power of new theories resides largely in their ability to resolve previous absurdities.

Refuting what your opponents never claimed. In the 1950s, Stanley 22 Miller performed a famous experiment that synthesized amino acids from hypothetical components of the earth's original atmosphere. Rifkin describes Miller's experiment with glaring hype: "With great fanfare, the world was informed that scientists had finally succeeded in forming life from non-life, the dream of magicians, sorcerers, and alchemists from time immemorial." He then points out, quite correctly, that the experiment did no such thing, and that the distance from amino acid to life is immense. But Miller never claimed that he had made life. The experiment stands in all our textbooks as a demonstration that some simple components of living systems can be made from inorganic chemicals. I was taught this interpretation 25 years ago; I have lectured about this experiment for 15 years. I have never in all my professional life heard a scientist say that Miller or anyone else has made life from non-life.

Refuting what your opponents refuted long ago. Rifkin devotes a whole 23 section to ridiculing evolution because its supporters once advanced the "biogenetic law" that embryos repeat the adult stages of their ancestry— now conclusively refuted. But Darwinian evolutionists did the refuting more than 50 years ago (good science is self-correcting).

4. Rifkin ignores the most elementary procedures of fair scholar- 24 ship. His book, touted as a major conceptual statement about the nature of science and the history of biology, displays painful ignorance of its subject. His quotations are primarily from old and discredited secondary sources (including some creationist propaganda tracts). I see

no evidence that he has ever read Darwin in the original. He obviously knows nothing about (or chooses not to mention) all the major works of Darwinian scholarship written by modern historians. His endless misquotes and half quotes are, for the most part, taken directly from excerpts in hostile secondary sources.

His prose is often purple in the worst journalistic tradition. When 25 invented claims are buttressed by such breathless description, the effect can be highly amusing. He mentions T. H. Morgan's invocation of the tautology argument discussed previously in this essay: "Not until Morgan began to suspect that natural selection was a victim of circular reasoning did anyone in the scientific community even question what was regarded by all as a profound truth . . . Morgan's observation shocked the scientific establishment." Now, I ask, how does he know this? Rifkin cites no evidence of any shock, even of any contemporary comment. He quotes Morgan himself only from secondary sources. In fact, everything about Rifkin's statement is wrong, just plain wrong. The tautology argument dates from the 1870s. Morgan didn't invent it (and Darwin, in my opinion, presented an able refutation when Morgan was a baby). Morgan, moreover, was no noble knight sallying forth against a monolithic Darwinian establishment. When Morgan wrote his critique, natural selection was an unpopular minority theory among evolutionists (the tide didn't turn in Darwin's favor until the late 1930s). Morgan, if anything, *was* the establishment, and his critique, so far as I know, didn't shock a soul or elicit any extensive commentary.

5. *Algeny* is full of ludicrous, simple errors. I particularly enjoyed 26 Rifkin's account of Darwin in the Galapagos. After describing the "great masses" of vultures, condors, vampire bats, and jaguars, that Darwin saw on these islands, Rifkin writes: "It was a savage, primeval scene, menacing in every detail. Everywhere there was bloodletting, and the ferocious, unremittent battle for survival. The air was dank and foul, and the thick stench of volcanic ash veiled the islands with a kind of ghoulish drape." Well, I guess Rifkin has never been there; and he obviously didn't bother to read anything about these fascinating islands. None of those animals live on the Galapagos. In fact, the Galapagos house no terrestrial predators at all; as a result, the animals have no fear of humans and do not flee when approached. The Galapagos are unusual, as Darwin noted, precisely because they are *not* scenes of Hobbes's *bellum omnium contra omnes* (the war of all against all). And, by the way, no thick stench or ghoulish drape either; the volcanic terrains are beautiful, calm, and peaceful—not in eruption when Darwin visited, not now either.

Jeremy Rifkin, in short, has argued himself, inextricably, into a 27 corner. He has driven off his natural allies by silly, at times dishonest, argument and nasty caricature. He has saddled his legitimate concern with an extremism that would outlaw both humane and fascinating scientific research. His legitimate brief speaks for the integrity of organisms and species. Our world would become a bleak place if we treated living things as no more than separable sequences of information, available for disarticulation and recombination in any order that pleased human whim. But I do not see why we should reject all genetic engineering because its technology might, one day, permit such a perversion of decency in the hands of some latter-day Hitler—you may as well outlaw printing because the same machine that composes Shakespeare can also set *Mein Kampf*. The domino theory does not apply to all human achievements. If we could, by transplanting a bacterial gene, confer disease or cold resistance upon an important crop plant, should we not do so in a world where people suffer so terribly from malnutrition? Must such a benefit imply that, tomorrow, corn and wheat, sea horses and orchids will be thrown into a gigantic vat, torn apart into genetic units, and reassembled into rows of identical human servants? Eternal vigilance, to recombine some phrases, is the price of technological achievement.

The debate about genetic engineering has often been portrayed, 28 falsely, as one of many battles between the political left and right—leftists in opposition, rightists plowing ahead. The issues are not so simple; they rarely are. Used humanely for the benefit of ordinary people, not the profits of a few entrepreneurs, the left need not fear this technology. I, for one, would rather campaign for proper use, not abolition. If Rifkin's argument embodies any antithesis, it is not left versus right, but romanticism, in its most dangerous anti-intellectual form, versus respect for knowledge and its humane employment. In both its content and presentation, *Algeny* belongs in the sordid company of anti-science. Few campaigns are more dangerous than emotional calls for proscription rather than thought.

I have been so harsh because I believe that Rifkin has seriously 29 harmed a cause that is very dear to me and to nearly all my scientific colleagues. Rifkin has placed all of us beyond the pale of decency by arguing that scientific paradigms are simple expressions of socioeconomic bias, that biotech implies (and will impose) a new view of organisms as strings of separable information (not wholes of necessary integrity), and that all scientists will eventually go along with this heartless idea. Well, Mr. Rifkin, who then will be for you? Where will you find your allies in the good fight for respect of evolutionary lineages? You have rejected us, reviled us, but we are with you. We are taxonomists, ecologists, and evolutionists—most of us Darwinians. We have devoted our lives to the study of species in their natural habitats. We have struggled to understand—and we greatly admire—

the remarkable construction and operation of organisms, the product of complex evolutionary histories, cascades of astounding improbability stretching back for millions of years. We know these organisms, and we love them—as they are. We would not dissolve this handiwork of four billion years to satisfy the hubris of one species. We respect the integrity of nature, Mr. Rifkin. But your arguments lack integrity. This we deplore.

Reconstructing, Summarizing, and Evaluating Gould's Argument

This practice has three parts. First, try to reconstruct in a diagrammatic or outline form the argument of "Integrity and Mr. Rifkin." Your diagram or outline should identify the following: the controversial issue at stake in this essay; Gould's thesis or position on the issue; the argumentative strategy Gould chooses to use; the reasons he gives for his position; and the evidence he cites to support his reasons.

To produce your diagram or outline, you may want to consider the essay paragraph by paragraph, noting what each paragraph does as well as what it says. For example, you might note that paragraph 1 introduces a controversy by saying that some people fear and oppose genetic engineering, while paragraph 2 attempts to clarify the controversy by saying that the really important issue has to do with the consequences of allowing one species to alter the "fundamental geometry" of nature. There are twenty-nine paragraphs in Gould's essay; can you reduce each paragraph to one or two sentences that note what the paragraph does and says? If so, you should find it relatively easy to turn your notes into an outline that identifies the essay's issue, thesis, strategy, reasons, and evidence.

After you have reconstructed Gould's argument in outline form, write a one-paragraph summary of "Integrity and Mr. Rifkin" that would be suitable for inclusion in an informative report about the positions Stephen Jay Gould has taken on controversial issues. In writing your summary, you should assume that your readers have not read Gould's essay but are nevertheless interested in knowing its argument. One caution: Be careful not to plagiarize. Give Gould general credit for his argument and, if you borrow his phraseology, be sure to use quotation marks as we did when we included the phrase "fundamental geometry" in the preceding paragraph.

Finally, write an informal response to Gould's essay in which you evaluate its ends and means. Do you think the ultimate goal of Gould's argument is truth, persuasion, or something else? To what extent does his argument have the features we claimed most good arguments have (p. 178)? Does he respect what he calls the "procedures of fair argument" and the "procedures of fair scholarship"? What changes, if any, would make Gould's essay a better argument?

A Feminist Discusses Women and Names

The following selection from Dale Spender's book *Man Made Language* is a straightforward argument for changing certain practices in the use of names and titles for women. In reading this, you should attempt to produce a clear paraphrase of the argument, and you should notice how the evidence supporting the argument is introduced. This is the sort of topic that often produces more emotion than reason. How many emotional appeals can you find in Spender's argument?

Dale Spender, from *Man Made Language*

One of the features of English language practices which is in- 1 herently sexist is the use of names. In our society "only men have real names" in that their names are permanent and they have "accepted the permanency of their names as one of the rights of being male" (Miller and Swift, 1976:14). This has both practical and psychological ramifications for the construction—and maintenance—of male supremacy.

Practically it means that women's family names do not count and 2 that there is one more device for making women invisible. Fathers pass their names on to their sons and the existence of daughters can be denied when in the absence of a male heir it is said that a family "dies out." One other direct result of this practice of only taking cognizance of the male name has been to facilitate the development of history as the story of the male line, because it becomes almost impossible to trace the ancestry of women—particularly if they do not come into the male-defined categories of importance.

Very little is known about women, says Virginia Woolf (1972), for 3 "the history of England is the history of the male line" (p. 41); this point was brought home to Jill Liddington and Jill Norris (1978) when they undertook to document the story of women's suffrage in Lancashire for "this vital contribution had been largely neglected by historians" (p. 11). They had difficulty with sources, and one difficulty was not one which would be encountered in tracing men (1978:17):

> Sometimes we seemed to be forever chasing down blind alleys. For
> instance, one of the most active women, Helen Silcock, a weavers' union

leader from Wigan, seemed to disappear after 1902. We couldn't think why, until we came across a notice of "congratulations to Miss Silcock on her marriage to Mr. Fairhurst" in a little known labor journal, the *Women's Trade Union Review* . . . it was an object lesson for us in the difficulties of tracing women activists.

It is also an extremely useful device for eliminating women from history and for making it exceedingly difficult to perceive a continuum and develop a tradition.

When females have no right to "surnames," to family names of their 4 own, the concept of women as the property of men is subtly reinforced (and this is of course assisted by the title *Mrs*). Currently many women are changing their names and instead of taking the name of either their father or their husband they are coining new, autonomous names for themselves; for example, Cheris Kramer has become Cheris Kramarae, Julia Stanley has become Julia Penelope—there are almost countless examples of this change. A common practice has become that of taking the first name of a close female friend or relative—such as mother—as the new family name (for example, Janet Robyn, Elizabeth Sarah). When asked why she had legally dropped her surname and retained her first two given names, Margaret Sandra stated that a "surname" was intended as an indication of the "sire" and was so closely linked socially with the ownership of women that there was no "surname" that she found acceptable.

Although attempts have been made to trivialize these new naming 5 activities among women, such activities are serious and they do undermine patriarchal practices. At the very least they raise consciousness about the role men's names have played in the subordination of women, and at best they confound traditional patriarchal classification schemes which have not operated in women's interest. I have been told that it makes it very difficult to "pigeon-hole" women, to "place" them, if they persist with this neurotic practice of giving themselves new names. One male stated quite sincerely that it was becoming "jolly difficult to work out whether women were married these days because of the ridiculous practice of not taking their husband's names." In order to operate in the world, however, it has *never* been necessary to know from a name whether someone is married or single, as women can testify. Men have not thought that *not* changing their name upon marriage should present difficulties to women and once more the bias of language practices is revealed.

But many males are confused, and not without cause. The language 6 has helped to create the representation of females as sex objects; it has also helped to signal when a sex object is not available and is the property of another male. The patriarchal order has been maintained by such devices and when women consciously and intentionally abolish them men have reason to feel insecure; they do not however have reason to protest.

There are also other "by-products" of this process of permitting the permanency of names only to males. Miller and Swift (1976) ask whether it is because of the unenduring nature of female family names that much more emphasis is placed on their first names. Whatever the reason, it is clear that males are more frequently addressed by their family name (and title) and women by their first name. Psychologically this can also work to produce sexual asymmetry. 7

The use of first names can be evidence of intimacy or friendship but in such circumstances the practice, generally speaking, has to be reciprocal. When one party is referred to by the first name, and the other by the family name and title, it is usually evidence that one has more power than the other. So, for example, the employer may be Mr. Smith and the employees Bill and Mary. The practice of those "in power" referring to those "out of power" by their first names—while still retaining the use of their own title and family name—is widespread and applies to both sexes in a hierarchical society. But there are still instances where both sexes occupy comparable positions but where males are referred to by their family names and women referred to by their first names, indicating the operation of yet another hierarchy. 8

This is frequently illustrated in the media. Even where there are both male and female contestants on some "quiz" shows, the women are more likely to be addressed by their first names. Interviewers are also more inclined to use women's first names. News items are more likely to make reference to women by their first name (and of course their coloring, for example, blond or brunette, and their age and marital status) and the usually male presenter of "talk-back" shows indicates a decided disposition to discriminate between the callers in this way. 9

But it is not confined to the media. I have never heard a male complain that a medical practitioner addressed him (perhaps patronizingly) by his first name at the first consultation, yet this protest is often made by women. It would, however, break the social rules which govern subordination if women were to respond by addressing medical practitioners by their first names. This is precisely why I think they should do so. 10

Regardless of the reason for the development of this practice of calling women by their first names in formal situations, it assists in making "visible" the subordination of the female. 11

The practice of labelling women as married or single also serves supremely sexist ends. It conveniently signals who is "fair game" from the male point of view. There is tension between the representation of 12 women as sex objects and the male ownership rights over women and this has been resolved by an explicit and most visible device of designating the married status of women. As women do not "own" men, and as men have many dimensions apart from their sexual ones in a patriarchal order, it has not been necessary to make male marital status visible. On the contrary, it could hinder rather than help male operations in the world so it has never appeared as a "logical" proposition.

Contrary to the belief of many people, the current usage of *Miss* and *Mrs.* is relatively recent, for until the beginning of the nineteenth century the title *Miss* was usually reserved for young females while *Mrs.* designated mature women. Marital status played no role in the use of these terms. How and why this usage changed is a matter of some speculation,[1] but there is nothing speculative about the ends that it serves.   13

It labels women for the convenience of men. It also labels those whom men do not want. To be over thirty and *Miss* Jones in times but recently passed was an advertisement of failure and an invitation for ridicule.   14

The question arises as to why more women have not objected to this offensive labelling in the past. Why was there not greater protest when in the late nineteenth century women were required to surrender even more of themselves and their identity and to become not just Mrs. *Jane* Smith, but Mrs. *John* Smith? (Casey Miller and Kate Swift point out that there would have been bewilderment if a letter had ever arrived addressed to Mrs. *George* Washington.)   15

---

[1]Miller and Swift (1976) suggest that the use of *Miss* and *Mrs.* to designate marital status was a response to some of the pressures created by the industrial revolution, which disrupted the familiar patterns of small communities in which relationships were readily known. There was no need for this usage prior to the industrial revolution for a woman's marital status was already known in the community in which she lived, but with the migration of population that occurred at the onset of the revolution and with women's entry into the workforce outside the home or local community,

> a simple means of distinguishing married from unmarried women was needed [for men] and it served a double purpose: it supplied at least a modicum of information about women's sexual availability, and it applied not so subtle pressure toward marriage by lumping single women with the young and inexperienced. Attached to anyone over the age of eighteen, Miss came in time to suggest the unattractive or socially undesirable qualities associated with such labels as *old maid* and *spinster* or that dreadful word *barren*. So the needs of patriarchy were served when a woman's availability for her primary role as helper and sexual partner was made an integral part of her identity—in effect, a part of her name (p. 99).

It is I think a mark of the identity options open to women in a 16
partriarchal order that so many women voluntarily and even enthusiastically seek to be labelled as the property of a male. The title *Mrs.* and
the abandonment of their father's name (a name which required no
effort on their part and could not be construed as an achievement) for
their husband's name, appears to confirm their identity. In a patriarchal society it is not unrealistic to perceive that security lies in marriage—even if this is eventually revealed as a myth. That so many
women continue to choose to be Mrs. Jack Smart and to become
"invisible" is an indication of the success of patriarchal ideology.

This is why the refusal of some women to be designated *Mrs.* is 17
significant. To insist on the title *Ms.* (if titles are unavoidable) does
undermine some of the patriarchal practices. If the strength of the
resistance is proportionate to the danger posed by the strategy then it
is clear that some individuals are aware of the subversive influence of
the use of *Ms.*

Numerous arguments other than the fundamental one have been 18
advanced to substantiate the undesirability of the term *Ms.* and they
share the common features of being inadequate and illogical—and
even absurd. For example, one reason that has been given is that the
pronunciation of *Ms.* cannot be determined by its spelling. This is a
non-starter in English. If we were to find unacceptable all those words
which do not reveal their pronunciation from their spelling we would
have to dispense with a sizable number and we could begin with *Mr.*
and *Mrs.*

The (unstated) reason for the undesirability of *Ms.* is that it is of no 19
assistance in the maintenance of the patriarchal order and it can even
be problematic for males. Again, this is why I think it extremely
important that all women should make use of it as a title—if we are to
persist with titles.

References

Liddington, Jill and Jill Norris, *One Hand Tied Behind Us: The Rise of
the Women's Suffrage Movement*. Virago, 1978.

Miller, Casey and Kate Swift, *Words and Women: New Language in
New Times*. New York: Anchor/Doubleday, 1976.

Woolf, Virginia, "Women and Fiction," in *Collected Essays: Virginia
Woolf*, vol. 2 (ed. Leonard Woolf). Chatto & Windus, 1972.

Questions

1. What does Spender mean by saying in paragraph 1 that the English use of
names is "inherently sexist"? What does "sexist" mean?

2. What do you think of the attempts of women to change their names (paragraphs 4 and 5)?
3. At the end of paragraph 6, Spender says "men have reason to feel insecure; they do not have reason to protest." Do you agree or disagree?
4. In paragraph 9 Spender speaks of the treatment of men and women on quiz shows and in newspapers. Are her statements still accurate?
5. What would happen if you called your doctor by his first name? What if the doctor were a woman?
6. Spender mentions the "patriarchal ideology" and the "patriarchal order." What does she mean by these terms? What have they to do with names?
7. Are you convinced by Spender's argument? Are some parts more convincing than others?

PRACTICE

Arguing about Men and Women

The air is full of debates about the roles of men and women. Take some issue that is current and produce a reasonable argument on one side or the other of the debate.

For example, you may wish to argue against Spender, who opposes the use of male surnames and favors the use of *Ms.* by all women. Before doing so, consider what assumptions, definitions, classes, and categories you will need to support your argument. Spender relies on such notions as "sexism" and "patriarchy." To argue with her you will have to either change the value signs attached to these notions (patriarchy is good, not bad) or change the categories in some way.

You may wish to take up some other issue, such as sexual segregation in sports, gender bias in education, sexual harassment in the workplace, or affirmative action in hiring practices. The basic requirements are that you find a truly controversial issue in the area of male/female relationships and that you take a position on the issue without losing your head. Concentrate on finding appropriate evidence to support your argument.

READING

An Educator Considers Class Myths and Realities

The following selection is taken from a longer essay. We have excerpted those sections in which the writer presents statistical evidence to counter class myths with class realities.

Gregory Mantsios, from "Class in America: Myths and Realities"

People in the United States don't like to talk about class. Or so it 1 would seem. We don't speak about class privileges, or class oppression, or the class nature of society. These terms are not part of our everyday vocabulary, and in most circles they are associated with the language of the rhetorical fringe. Unlike people in most other parts of the world, we shrink from using words that classify along economic lines or that point to class distinctions: phrases like *working class*, *upper class*, and *ruling class* are rarely uttered by Americans.

For the most part, avoidance of class-laden vocabulary crosses class 2 boundaries. There are few among the poor who speak of themselves as lower class; they identify, rather, with their race, ethnic group, or geographic location. Workers are more likely to identify with their employer, industry, or occupational group than with other workers, or with the working class.[1]

Neither are those at the other end of the economic spectrum likely 3 to identify with the word *class*. In her study of 38 wealthy and socially prominent women, Susan Ostrander asked participants if they considered themselves members of the upper class. One participant responded,

> I hate to use the word 'class.' We are responsible, fortunate people, old families, the people who have something.

Another said,

> I hate [the term] upper class. It is so non–upper class to use it. I just call it 'all of us,' those who are wellborn.[2]

It is not that Americans, rich or poor, aren't keenly aware of class 4 differences—those quoted above obviously are—it is that class is not in the domain of public discourse. Class is not discussed or debated in public because class identity has been stripped from popular culture. The institutions that shape mass culture and define the parameters of public debate have avoided class issues. In politics, in primary and secondary education, and in the mass media, formulating issues in terms of class is unacceptable, perhaps even un-American.

There are, however, two notable exceptions to this phenomenon. 5 First, it is acceptable in the United States to talk about "the middle class." Interestingly enough, such references appear to be acceptable precisely because they mute class differences. References to the middle class by politicians, for example, are designed to encompass and attract the broadest possible constituency. Not only do references to the middle class gloss over differences, but also these references avoid any suggestion of conflict or exploitation.

This leads us to the second exception to the class avoidance phe- 6
nomenon. We are, on occasion, presented with glimpses of the upper
class and the lower class (the language used is "the wealthy" and "the
poor"). In the media, these presentations are designed to satisfy some
real or imagined voyeuristic need of "the ordinary person." As curiosi-
ties, the ground-level view of street life and the inside look at the rich
and the famous serve as unique models, one to avoid and one to aspire
to. In either case, the two models are presented without causal relation
to each other: One is not rich because the other is poor. Similarly,
when social commentators or liberal politicians draw attention to the
plight of the poor, they do so in a manner that obscures the class
structure and denies class exploitation. Wealth and poverty are viewed
as one of several natural and inevitable states of being: Differences are
only differences. One may even say differences are the American way,
a reflection of American social diversity.

We are left with one of two possibilities: Either talking about class 7
and recognizing class distinctions are not relevant to U.S. society, or
we mistakenly hold a set of beliefs that obscure the reality of class
differences and their impact on people's lives.

Let us look at four common, albeit contradictory, beliefs about the 8
United States.

Myth Number 1: The United States is fundamentally a classless 9
society. Class distinctions are largely irrelevant today, and whatever
differences do exist in economic standing are, for the most part,
insignificant. Rich or poor, we are all equal in the eyes of the law, and
such basic needs as health care and education are provided to all
regardless of economic standing.

Myth Number 2: We are, essentially, a middle-class nation. Despite 10
some variations in economic status, most Americans have achieved
relative affluence in what is widely recognized as a consumer society.

Myth Number 3: We are all getting richer. The American public as a 11
whole is steadily moving up the economic ladder, and each generation
propels itself to greater economic well-being. Despite some fluctua-
tions, the United States position in the global economy has brought
previously unknown prosperity to most, if not all, North Americans.

Myth Number 4: Everyone has an equal chance to succeed. Success 12
in the United States requires no more than hard work, sacrifice, and
perseverance: "In America, anyone can be president." And with a little
luck (a clever invention or a winning lottery ticket), there are opportunities for the easygoing as well. "In America, anyone can become a
millionaire; it's just a matter of being in the right place at the right
time."

In trying to assess the legitimacy of these beliefs, we want to ask 13
several important questions. Are there significant class differences

among Americans? If these differences do exist, are they getting bigger or smaller, and do these differences have a significant impact on the way we live? Finally, does everyone in the United States really have an equal opportunity to succeed?

The Economic Spectrum

We will begin by looking at differences. An examination of official 14 census material reveals that variations in economic well-being are in fact immense. Consider the following:

- The wealthiest 15 percent of the American population holds nearly 75 percent of the total household wealth in the country. That is, they own three-quarters of all the consumer durables (such as houses, cars, and stereos) and financial assets (such as stocks, bonds, property, and savings accounts).[3]
- Approximately 17,000 Americans declared more than $1 million of *annual* income on their 1985 tax returns; that is more money than most Americans expect to earn in an entire lifetime.[4]

Affluence and prosperity are clearly alive and well in certain segments of the United States population. However, this abundance is in contrast to the poverty and despair that is also prevalent in the United States. At the other end of the spectrum:

- A total of 15 percent of the American population—that is, one of every seven—live below the government's official poverty line (calculated in 1984 at $5,278 for an individual and $10,600 for a family of four).[5] These poor include a significant number of homeless people—approximately three million Americans.[6]
- Nearly a quarter of all the children in the United States under the age of six live in poverty.[7]

The contrast between rich and poor is sharp, and with nearly 15 one-third of the American population living at one extreme or the other, it is difficult to argue that we live in a classless society. The income gap between rich and poor in the United States (measured as the percentage of total income held by the wealthiest 20 percent of the population versus the poorest 20 percent is approximately 11 to 1, one of the highest ratios in the industrialized world.[8] (For example, the ratio in Great Britain is 7 to 1; in Japan, it is 4 to 1.)

Reality 1: There are enormous differences in the economic status of 16 American citizens. A sizable proportion of the United States population occupies opposite ends of the economic spectrum.

Nor can it be said that the majority of the American population fares 17 very well. In the middle range of the economic spectrum:

- 50 percent of the American population holds less than 3.5 percent of the nation's wealth.[9]

- The median household income (that is, half the American population made more and the other half made less) was $22,420 in 1984. This is a margin of approximately $225 per week above the poverty level.[10]

The level of inequality is sometimes difficult to comprehend fully 18 with dollar figures and percentages. To help his students visualize the distribution of income, the well-known economist Paul Samuelson asked them to picture an income pyramid made of children's blocks, with each layer of blocks representing $1000. If we were to construct Samuelson's pyramid today, the peak of the pyramid would be much higher than the Eiffel Tower, yet almost all of us would be within six feet of the ground.[11] In other words, the distribution of income is heavily skewed; a small minority of families take the lion's share of national income, and the remaining income is distributed among the vast majority of middle-income and low-income families. Keep in mind that Samuelson's pyramid represents the distribution of income, not wealth. The distribution of wealth is skewed even further.

Reality 2: The middle class in the United States holds a very small 19 share of the nation's wealth.

Lottery millionaires and Horatio Alger stories notwithstanding, evi- 20 dence suggests that the level of inequality in the United States is getting higher. Statistically, it is getting harder to make it big and more difficult to even stay in the middle-income level. Census data show the gap between the rich and the poor to be the widest since the government began collecting information in 1947. Furthermore, the percentage of households earning at a middle-income level (that is, between 75% and 125% of the median income) has been falling steadily since 1967.[12] Most of those who disappeared from the middle-income level moved downward, not upward. And economic polarization is expected to increase over the next several decades.[13]

Reality 3: The middle class is shrinking in size, and most of those 21 leaving the ranks of the middle class are falling to a lower economic standing. . . .

Class affects more than life-style and material well-being. It has a 22 significant impact on our physical and mental well-being as well.

Researchers have found an inverse relation between social class and 23 health. Lower-class standing is correlated to higher rates of infant mortality,[14] eye and ear disease, arthritis, physical disability, diabetes, nutritional deficiency,[15] respiratory disease,[16] mental illness,[17] and heart disease.[18] In all areas of health, poor people do not share the same life chances as those in the social class above them. Furthermore, lower-class standing is correlated to a lower quality of treatment for illness and disease. The results of poor health and poor treatment are born out in the life expectancy rates within each class. Aaron Antonovsky found that the higher your class standing, the higher your life expectancy.[19] Conversely, Lillian Guralnick studied the relationship between class and the death rate per 1000 in each of six age categories. Within each age group, she found that the lower one's class standing, the higher the death rate; in some age groups, the figures were as much as two and three times as high.[20]

Reality 4: From cradle to grave, class standing has a significant 24 impact on our chances for survival.

The lower one's class standing, the more difficult it is to secure 25 appropriate housing, the more time is spent on the routine tasks of everyday life, the greater is the percentage of income that goes to pay for food and other basic necessities,[21] and the greater is the likelihood of crime victimization.[22] Class can predict chances for both survival and success.

Notes

1. See Oscar Glantz, "Class Consciousness and Political Solidarity," *American Sociological Review*, vol. 23, August 1958, pp. 375–382; Robert Nisbet, "The Decline and Fall of Social Class," *Pacific Sociological Review*, vol. 2, Spring 1959, pp. 11–17; Charles W, Tucker, "A Comparative Analysis of Subjective Social Class: 1945–1963," *Social Forces*, no. 46, June 1968, pp. 508–514; and Ira Katznelson, *City Trenches: Urban Politics and Patterning of Class in the United States*, New York, Pantheon Books, 1981.

2. Susan Ostander, "Upper-Class Women: Class Consciousness as Conduct and Meaning," in *Power Structure Research*, by G. William Domhoff, Beverly Hills, California, Sage Productions, 1980, pp. 78–79.

3. Steven Rose, *The American Profile Poster*, New York, Pantheon Books, 1986, p. 31.

4. Barbara Kallen, "Getting By on $1 Million a Year," *Forbes*, October 27, 1986, p. 48.

5. "Characteristics of the Population Below the Poverty Level: 1984," from *Current Population Reports, Consumer Income Series P-60, No. 152*, Washington, D.C., U.S. Department of Commerce, Bureau of the Census, June 1986.

6. Constance Holden, "Homelessness: Experts Differ on Root Causes," *Science*, May 2, 1986, pp. 569–570.

7. "New Class of Children Is Poorer and the Prospects of Advancement Are Dim," *New York Times*, October 20, 1985, p. 56.

8. "United Nations National Accounts Statistics," *Statistical Papers, Series M no. 79*, New York, United Nations, 1985, pp. 1–11. See also Ira C. Magaziner and Robert B. Reich, *Minding America's Business: The Decline and Rise of the American Political Economy,"* New York, Vintage, 1983, p. 23.

9. Steven Rose, *The American Profile Poster*, p. 31.

10. "Money Income of Households, Families, and Persons in the United States: 1984," *Current Population Reports P-60, no. 151*, Washington D.C., Department of Commerce, Bureau of Census, 1986, p. 1.

11. Paul Samuelson, *Economics*, 10th ed., New York, McGraw-Hill, 1976, p. 84.

12. Chris Tilly, "U-Turn on Equality," *Dollars and Sense*, May 1986, p. 11.

13. Paul Blumberg, *Inequality in an Age of Decline*, Oxford University Press, 1980.

14. Kyriakos S. Markides and Connie McFarland, "A Note on Recent Trends in the Infant Mortality–Socioeconomic Status Relationship," *Social Forces*, 61:1, September 1982, pp. 268–276.

15. Stanley D. Eitzen, *In Conflict and Order: Understanding Society*, Boston, Allyn and Bacon, 1985, p. 265. Lucile Duberman, *Social Inequality: Class and Caste in America*, New York, J. B. Lippincott, 1976, p. 200.

16. *Statistical Abstracts of the U.S.*, 1986, p. 116.

17. August Hollingshead and Frederick Redlick, *Social Class and Mental Illness: A Community Study*, New York, John Wiley, 1958. Also Leo Srole, *Mental Health in the Metropolis: The Midtown Manhattan Study*, New York, McGraw-Hill, 1962.

18. U.S. Bureau of the Census, *Social Indicators III*, Washington D.C., U.S. Government Printing Office, 1980, p. 101.

19. Aaron Antonovsky, "Social Class, Life Expectancy and Overall Mortality," *The Impact of Social Class*, New York, Thomas Crowell, 1972, pp. 467–491.

20. Lillian Guralnick, "Socioeconomic Differences in Mortality by Cause of Death," in *International Population Conference, Ottawa, 1963*, Liège, International Union for the Scientific Study of Population, 1964, p. 298, quoted in Antonovsky, op. cit. See also Steven Caldwell and Theodore Diamond, "Income Differentials in Mortality" in Linda Del Bene and Fritz Scheuren, eds. *Statistical Uses of Administrative Records*, Washington, D.C., United States Social Security Administration, 1979, p. 58. Harriet Duleep, "Measuring the Effect of Income on Adult Mortality Using Longitudinal Administrative Record Data," *Journal of Human Resources*, vol. 21, no. 2, Spring 1986.

21. Paul Jacobs, "Keeping the Poor, Poor?" in Jerome H. Skolnick and Elliot Currie, *Crisis in American Institutions*, Boston, Little, Brown and Company, 1982, pp. 104–114.

22. Dennis W. Roncek, "Dangerous Places: Crime and Residential Environment," *Social Forces*, 60:1, September 1981, pp. 74–96.

Questions

1. Why don't Americans like to use the term *class?*
2. What is Mantsios's main argument against the myth of a classless society?
3. What are the realities? Do numbers always qualify as bearers of reality? What other statistics might Mantsios have used in his argument?

PRACTICE

Arguing from Statistics—The Education, Employment, and Income of Women

The following four tables give information on the education, employment, and income of women from 1970 to 1991. Your task is to use these materials as the basis for an argument. The thesis you present should involve the change or lack of change over this twenty-year period, and it should be supported by citations from the data provided.

First look at the data with some care, testing out possible theses as you check them through from table to table. The basic possibilities open to you with this relatively limited body of data are simple. The status of women has improved, deteriorated, or remained the same—these are the essential positions. A more complex thesis might argue yes and no; that is, the situation of women has changed with respect to one thing and remained the same with respect to another thing.

The more time you spend interpreting the statistics, the more complex and interesting your discussion will be. You should try to translate the statistics into human terms. For example, what advice would you give to a young woman about to graduate from high school who is interested in a clerical career, and is trying to decide whether to seek full-time clerical work or to enroll in a community college? Table 1 shows a continuing increase in the educational attainment of both men and women from 1970 to 1991. While a larger percentage of women (41.8%) completed high school than men (36.1%) in 1991, a larger percentage of men (25.4%) completed four years of college than women (19.3%). Table 2, which gives the educational attainment of men and women in various occupations, shows a larger number of male clerical workers with a college education. In Table 3, we can see that from 1970 to 1991, women dominated the clerical sector of the labor force; in 1991, 80% of all clerical workers were women. Table 4 shows a slow proportional gain in women's clerical salaries. Table 4a shows the 1991 percentage of female to male earnings at 75%, an increase from 68% in 1983.

To advise the high school student, you might conjecture that the men's higher educational attainment is the reason for the discrepancy in salaries, and that the young woman would be better off if she furthered her education. But what if she asked you if the same disparities in pay and education exist in other occupations? Would she be better off in an occupation where the numerical proportions of male and female workers were more equal? You consult your tables. . . .

Remember, this is not the place for emotional persuasion. Nor should you need to bring additional data to bear on the question unless specifically invited to do so by your instructor. The best papers will make the richest possible use of this limited body of material to make an argument that is not obvious, but is nonetheless justified by the data being used.

TABLE 1

Educational Attainment of the Population, 25 Years of Age and Over by Year and Sex (Percent)

Educational Attainment	1970		1979		1991	
	M	F	M	F	M	F
No School	1.6	1.6	—	—	—	—
Elementary:						
1–4 years	4.4	3.4	1.6	0.9	2.2	1.8
5–7 years	10.5	9.5	3.5	2.3	3.6	3.3
8 years	12.9	12.6	5.1	3.4	4.5	4.5
High School:						
1–3 years	18.6	20.0	14.9	14.8	9.9	10.5
4 years	27.8	34.1	36.8	44.8	36.1	41.8
College:						
1–3 years	10.6	10.7	17.6	18.2	18.4	18.8
4 years	13.5	8.1	20.5	15.5	25.4	19.3
Median Years Completed	12.1	12.1	12.7	12.6	12.8	12.7

Source: U.S. Bureau of the Census, 1970 Census, Subject Reports, *Educational Attainment,* Table 1, pp. 3, 6. For 1979: Bureau of Labor Statistics, Special Report 240. For 1991, *Current Population Reports,* Series P-20, No. 462.

TABLE 2
Occupation of Employed Civilians, by Sex, Race, and Educational Attainment: 1991 (in thousands)

Sex, Race, and Years of School	Total employed	Managerial/ professional	Tech./sales/ administrative	Service[1]	Precision production[2]	Operators/ fabricators[3]	Farming, forestry, fishing
Male, total[4]	**54,293**	**15,849**	**10,649**	**4,508**	**10,696**	**10,249**	**2,341**
Less than 4 years of high school	7,676	413	595	986	2,038	2,827	816
4 years of high school only	19,831	2,313	3,453	1,974	5,674	5,435	980
1 to 3 years of college	11,007	2,744	3,113	1,067	2,267	1,499	317
4 years of college or more	15,779	10,378	3,489	480	716	488	228
White	47,483	14,464	9,425	3,449	9,640	8,396	2,109
Less than 4 years of high school	6,420	367	511	729	1,818	2,302	693
4 years of high school only	17,248	2,130	3,082	1,479	5,151	4,507	898
1 to 3 years of college	9,648	2,513	2,735	856	2,045	1,203	296
4 years of college or more	14,168	9,453	3,096	385	627	384	222
Black	4,957	758	819	832	810	1,566	173
Less than 4 years of high school	1,014	30	59	202	180	447	96
4 years of high school only	2,101	127	298	396	413	808	60
1 to 3 years of college	1,051	167	287	173	164	246	13
4 years of college or more	791	435	175	60	53	65	3

Female, total[4]	**44,723**	**13,300**	**18,856**	**7,321**	**1,030**	**3,739**	**476**
Less than 4 years of high school	4,729	244	1,016	1,905	220	1,238	105
4 years of high school only	18,628	2,486	9,583	3,758	549	2,013	239
1 to 3 years of college	10,032	2,831	5,336	1,238	176	370	81
4 years of college or more	11,335	7,739	2,921	419	85	119	52
White	38,055	11,799	16,455	5,591	854	2,909	447
Less than 4 years of high school	3,709	214	903	1,346	186	968	92
4 years of high school only	15,960	2,249	8,537	2,912	459	1,576	227
1 to 3 years of college	8,541	2,523	4,530	992	139	280	78
4 years of college or more	9,844	6,813	2,485	341	70	85	51
Black	5,121	1,061	1,845	1,431	119	647	17
Less than 4 years of high school	825	22	85	486	22	203	8
4 years of high school only	2,176	183	854	710	63	358	8
1 to 3 years of college	1,211	240	672	197	27	74	2
4 years of college or more	909	617	234	38	7	13	*

*Represents or rounds to zero.
[1]Includes private household workers.
[2]Includes craft and repair.
[3]Includes laborers.
[4]Includes other races, not shown separately.
Source: U.S. Bureau of Labor Statistics, unpublished data.

203

TABLE 3

Women as Percent of Experienced Civilian Labor Force, 16 Years of Age and Over by Occupational Categories, 1991, 1983, and 1970

Occupational Category	Percent of Experienced Labor Force		
	1991	1983	1970
Professional, technical, and kindred workers	51.6	48.1	40.1
Managers and administrators, except farm	40.6	32.4	16.7
Sales workers	48.8	47.5	48.9
Clerical and kindred workers	80.0	79.9	73.8
Craftsmen and kindred workers	8.6	8.1	4.9
Laborers, except construction	19.1	19.4	n.a.
Machine operators, assemblers, inspectors	40.1	42.1	n.a.
Farmers and farm managers	16.5	12.1	5.1
Farm laborers and farm foremen	21.4	24.8	17.6
Service workers, except private household	64.6	64.0	55.8
Private household workers	96.0	96.1	97.0
Total number	116,877,000	100,834,000	n.a.
Percent of total experienced labor force	45.6	43.7	38.1

Source: U.S. Bureau of Labor Statistics, *Employment and Earnings,* Monthly, January issues; 1970 Census, Subject Reports, *Occupational Characteristics*.

TABLE 4

Full-Time Wage and Salary Workers—Number and Median Weekly Earnings, by Selected Characteristics: 1983 to 1991 (In current dollars of usual weekly earnings)

Characteristic	No. workers (1,000)				Median weekly earnings ($)			
	1983	1985	1990	1991	1983	1985	1990	1991
All workers[1]	70,976	77,002	85,082	83,525	313	343	415	430
Male	42,309	45,589	49,015	47,910	373	406	485	497
16 to 24 years old	6,702	6,956	6,313	5,714	223	240	283	286
25 years old and over	35,607	38,632	42,702	42,197	406	442	514	525
Female	28,667	31,414	36,068	35,615	252	277	348	368
16 to 24 years old	5,345	5,621	5,001	4,488	197	210	254	267
25 years old and over	23,322	25,793	31,066	31,127	267	296	370	388
White	61,739	66,481	72,637	71,176	319	355	427	446
Male	37,378	40,030	42,563	41,482	387	417	497	509
Female	24,361	26,452	30,075	29,694	254	281	355	374
Black	7,373	8,393	9,642	9,498	261	277	329	348
Male	3,883	4,367	4,909	4,832	293	304	360	374
Female	3,490	4,026	4,733	4,665	231	252	308	323
Hispanic origin[2]	(NA)	(NA)	6,993	6,887	(NA)	(NA)	307	315
Male	(NA)	(NA)	4,410	4,332	(NA)	(NA)	322	328
Female	(NA)	(NA)	2,583	2,554	(NA)	(NA)	280	293
Family relationship:								
Husbands	28,720	30,260	31,326	30,793	410	455	532	558
Wives	14,884	16,270	18,666	18,726	257	285	363	381
Women who maintain families	3,948	4,333	5,007	5,062	256	278	339	362

TABLE 4
Continued

Characteristic	No. workers (1,000)				Median weekly earnings ($)			
	1983	1985	1990	1991	1983	1985	1990	1991
Men who maintain families	1,331	1,313	1,786	1,694	377	396	444	448
Other persons in families:								
Men	5,518	6,173	6,434	6,008	219	238	296	299
Women	4,032	4,309	4,475	4,110	201	213	271	285
All other men[3]	6,740	7,841	9,468	9,416	350	380	442	458
All other women[3]	5,803	6,503	7,920	7,716	274	305	376	395
Occupation, male:								
Managerial and professional	10,312	11,078	12,263	12,254	516	583	731	753
Executive, administrative, managerial	5,344	5,835	6,401	6,402	530	593	742	758
Professional specialty	4,967	5,243	5,863	5,853	506	571	720	748
Technical, sales, and administrative support	8,125	8,803	9,596	9,363	385	420	496	509
Technical and related support	1,428	1,563	1,747	1,719	424	472	570	576
Sales	3,853	4,227	4,666	4,556	389	431	505	518
Administrative support, including clerical	2,844	3,013	3,183	3,088	362	391	440	459
Service	3,723	3,947	4,476	4,492	255	272	320	330
Private household	11	13	12	14	*	*	*	*
Protective	1,314	1,327	1,523	1,587	355	391	477	502
Other service	2,398	2,607	2,942	2,892	217	230	273	283

Precision production[4]	9,180	10,026	10,169	9,762	387	408	488	494
Mechanics and repairers	3,418	3,752	3,669	3,604	377	400	477	489
Construction trades	2,966	3,308	3,603	3,323	375	394	480	484
Other	2,796	2,966	2,897	2,835	408	433	510	512
Operators, fabricators and laborers	9,833	10,585	11,257	10,801	308	325	378	387
Machine operators, assemblers, and inspectors	4,138	4,403	4,510	4,272	319	341	391	396
Transportation and material moving	3,199	3,459	3,721	3,703	335	369	418	423
Handlers, equipment cleaners, helpers, and laborers	2,496	2,724	3,027	2,826	251	261	308	315
Farming, forestry, fishing	1,137	1,150	1,253	1,238	200	216	263	269
Occupation, female:								
Managerial and professional	7,139	8,302	10,595	10,854	357	399	511	527
Executive, administrative, managerial	2,772	3,492	4,764	4,918	339	383	485	504
Professional specialty	4,367	4,810	5,831	5,936	367	408	534	559
Technical, sales, and administrative support	13,517	14,622	16,202	15,779	247	269	332	350
Technical and related support	1,146	1,200	1,470	1,453	299	331	417	445
Sales	2,460	2,929	3,531	3,317	204	226	292	308
Administrative support, including clerical	9,911	10,494	11,202	11,009	248	270	332	348
Service	3,598	3,963	4,531	4,416	173	185	230	244
Private household	267	330	298	292	116	130	171	163
Protective	139	156	216	232	250	278	405	421
Other service	3,193	3,477	4,017	3,892	176	188	231	245

TABLE 4
Continued

Characteristic	No. workers (1,000)				Median weekly earnings ($)			
	1983	1985	1990	1991	1983	1985	1990	1991
Precision production[4]	784	906	893	880	256	268	316	341
Mechanics and repairers	120	144	139	144	337	392	459	506
Construction trades	45	53	50	42	*	265	394	*
Other	619	709	704	694	244	253	300	318
Operators, fabricators, and laborers	3,486	3,482	3,675	3,528	204	216	262	273
Machine operators, assemblers, and inspectors	2,853	2,778	2,840	2,731	202	216	260	270
Transportation and material moving	159	189	227	240	253	252	314	339
Handlers, equipment cleaners, helpers and laborers	474	514	608	556	211	209	250	261
Farming, forestry, fishing	143	138	171	159	169	185	216	224

*Data not shown where base is less than 50,000.
NA = Not available.
[1]Includes other races, not shown separately.
[2]Persons of Hispanic origin may be of any race.
[3]The majority of these persons are living alone or with nonrelatives. Also included are persons in families where the husband, wife, or other person maintaining the family is in the Armed Forces, and persons in unrelated subfamilies.
[4]Includes craft and repair.
Source: U.S. Bureau of Labor Statistics, Bulletin 2307, and *Employment and Earnings*, monthly, January issues.

TABLE 4a
Female Earnings as Percentage of Male Earnings, 1991[1]

Occupation	Percentage
Managerial and professional	69%
Executive, administrative, managerial	66%
Professional specialty	75%
Technical, sales, administrative	69%
Technical and related support	77%
Sales	59%
Administrative support, including clerical	75%
Service	74%
Private household[2]	n.a.
Protective	84%
Other service	86%
Precision production	69%
Mechanics and repairers	100+%
Construction[3]	n.a.
Other	100+%
Operators, fabricators, and laborers	70%
Machine operators, assemblers, and inspectors	68%
Transportation and material moving	80%
Handlers, equipment cleaners, helpers and laborers	83%
Farming, forestry, fishing	83%

[1]This chart is drawn from figures in Table 3, "Full-Time Wage and Salary Workers."
[2]Data not shown where database is less than 50,000 males.
[3]Data not shown where database is less than 50,000 females.

Two Positions on Bilingual Education

The following two position papers take opposing views on an important issue in contemporary education. Both papers were written in the 1980s. The first is from a chapter in a book about schooling. The second appeared as an editorial in the *New York Times*. The issue they both take up is bilingual education—whether elementary and secondary schools should be compelled to offer education in languages other than English for students who are not native speakers of English. We would like you to read these two arguments, paying special attention to the questions listed below. Then, we will propose a specific situation for you to argue your own position on bilingual education. As you read, try to keep the following points in mind:

1. What, specifically, is each person proposing with respect to bilingualism? Restate each of their final positions in your own words.
2. To what principles does each writer appeal on behalf of his or her position? In other words, what values do they assume that they share with their readers? How explicit are they about these shared values? Do you accept the principles proposed by each writer? If not, where do you disagree?
3. In your own words, explain the difference between the positions of the two writers on bilingual education. Is their disagreement about principles or about methods of achieving goals that both would accept?
4. What roles do "definition" and argument by "cause and effect" play in each argument?
5. Do you think one argument better than the other? Has either changed your mind? If so, how?

Diane Ravitch, from "Politicization of the Schools: The Case of Bilingual Education"

Demands for bilingual education arose as an outgrowth of the civil rights movement. As it evolved, that movement contained complex, and occasionally contradictory, elements. One facet of the movement appealed for racial integration and assimilation, which led to court orders for busing and racial balance; but the dynamics of the movement also inspired appeals to racial solidarity, which led to demands for black studies, black control of black schools, and other race-conscious policies. Whether the plea was for integration or for separatism, advocates could always point to a body of social science as evidence for their goals.

Race consciousness became a necessary part of the remedies that courts fashioned, but its presence legitimized ethnocentrism as a force in American politics. In the late 1960s, the courts, Congress, and policymakers—having been told for years by spokesmen for the civil rights movement that all children should be treated equally without regard to their race or ancestry—frequently heard compelling testimony by political activists and social scientists about the value of ethnic particularism in the curriculum.

Congress first endorsed funding for bilingual education in 1968, at a time when ethnocentrism had become a powerful political current. In hearings on this legislation, proponents of bilingual education argued that non–English-speaking children did poorly in school because they had low self-esteem, and that this low self-esteem was caused by the absence of their native language from the classroom. They claimed that if the children were taught in their native tongue and about their native culture, they would have higher self-esteem, better attitudes toward school, and higher educational achievement. Bilingual educators also insisted that children would learn English more readily if they already knew another language. 2

In the congressional hearings, both advocates and congressmen seemed to agree that the purpose of bilingual education was to help non–English speakers succeed in school and in society. But the differences between them were not then obvious. The congressmen believed that bilingual education would serve as a temporary transition into the regular English language program. But the bilingual educators saw the program as an opportunity to maintain the language and culture of the non–English-speaking student, while he was learning English.[1] 3

What was extraordinary about the Bilingual Education Act of 1968, which has since been renewed several times, is that it was the first time that the Congress had ever legislated a given pedagogical method. In practice, bilingual education means a program in which children study the major school subjects in a language other than English. Funding of the program, although small within the context of the federal education budget, created strong constituencies for its continuation, both within the federal government and among recipient agencies. No different from other interest groups, these constituencies pressed for expansion and strengthening of their program. Just as lifelong vocational educators are unlikely to ask whether their program works, so career bilingual educators are committed to their method as a philosophy, not as a technique for language instruction. The difference is this: Techniques are subject to evaluation, which may cause them to be revised or discarded; philosophies are not. 4

[1]U.S. Congress, Senate, Committee on Labor and Public Welfare, Special Subcommittee on Bilingual Education, 90th Cong., 1st sess., 1967.

In 1974, the Supreme Court's *Lau v. Nichols* decision reinforced 5 demands for bilingual education. The Court ruled against the San Francisco public schools for their failure to provide English language instruction for 1,800 non–English-speaking Chinese students. The Court's decision was reasonable and appropriate. The Court said, "There is no equality of treatment merely by providing students with the same facilities, textbooks, teachers, and curriculum; for students who do not understand English are effectively foreclosed from any meaningful education." The decision did not endorse any particular remedy. It said, "Teaching English to the students of Chinese ancestry who do not speak the language is one choice. Giving instruction to the group in Chinese is another. There may be others."[2]

Despite the Court's prudent refusal to endorse any particular 6 method of instruction, the bilingual educators interpreted the *Lau* decision as a mandate for bilingual programs. In the year after the decision, the United States Office of Education established a task force to fashion guidelines for the implementation of the *Lau* decision; the task force was composed of bilingual educators and representatives of language minority groups. The task force fashioned regulations that prescribed in exhaustive detail how school districts should prepare and carry out bilingual programs for non–English-speaking students. The districts were directed to identify the student's primary language, not by his proficiency in English, but by determining which language was most often spoken in the student's home, which language he had learned first, and which language he used most often. Thus a student would be eligible for a bilingual program even if he was entirely fluent in English.[3]

Furthermore, while the Supreme Court refused to endorse any 7 given method, the task force directed that non–English-speaking students should receive bilingual education that emphasized instruction in their native language and culture. Districts were discouraged from using the "English as a Second Language" approach, which consists of intensive, supplemental English-only instruction, or immersion techniques, in which students are instructed in English within an English-only context.

Since the establishment of the bilingual education program, many 8 millions of dollars have been spent to support bilingual programs in more than sixty different languages. Among those receiving funding to

---

[2]*Lau v. Nichols,* 414 U.S. 563 (1974).
[3]U.S. Department of Health, Education, and Welfare, "Task Force Findings Specifying Remedies Available for Eliminating Past Educational Practices Ruled Unlawful under *Lau v. Nichols*" (Washington, D.C., Summer 1975).

---

administer and staff such programs, bilingual education is obviously popular, but there are critics who think that it is educationally unsound. Proponents of desegregation have complained that bilingual education needlessly segregates non–English-speakers from others of their age. At a congressional hearing in 1977, one desegregation specialist complained that bilingual programs had been funded "without any significant proof that they would work. . . . There is nothing in the research to suggest that children can effectively learn English without continuous interaction with other children who are native English speakers."[4]

The research on bilingual education has been contradictory, and [9] studies that favor or criticize the bilingual approach have been attacked as biased. Researchers connected to bilingual institutes claim that their programs resulted in significant gains for non–English-speaking children. But a four-year study commissioned by the United States Office of Education concluded that students who learned bilingually did not achieve at a higher level than those in regular classes, nor were their attitudes towards school significantly different. What they seemed to learn best, the study found, was the language in which they were instructed.[5]

One of the few evidently unbiased, nonpolitical assessments of [10] bilingual research was published in 1982 in the *Harvard Educational Review*. A survey of international findings, it concluded that "bilingual programs are neither better nor worse than other instructional methods." The author found that in the absence of compelling experimental support for this method, there was "no legal necessity or research bias for the federal government to advocate or require a specific educational approach."[6]

If the research is in fact inconclusive, then there is no justification [11] for mandating the use of bilingual education or any other single pedagogy. The bilingual method may or may not be the best way to learn English. Language instruction programs that are generally regarded as outstanding, such as those provided for Foreign Service officers or by

---

[4]U.S. Congress, House, Subcommittee on Elementary, Secondary, and Vocational Education of the Committee on Education and Labor, Bilingual Education, 95th Cong., 1st sess., 1977, pp. 335–336. The speaker was Gary Orfield.

[5]Malcolm N. Danoff, "Evaluation of the Impact of ESEA Title VII Spanish/English Bilingual Education Programs" (Palo Alto, Calif.: American Institutes for Research, 1978).

[6]Iris Rotberg, "Some Legal and Research Considerations in Establishing Federal Policy in Bilingual Education," *Harvard Educational Review*, vol. 52, May 1982, pp. 148–168.

the nationally acclaimed center at Middlebury College, are immersion programs, in which students embark on a systematic program of intensive language learning without depending on their native tongue. Immersion programs may not be appropriate for all children, but then neither is any single pedagogical method. The method to be used should be determined by the school authorities and the professional staff, based on their resources and competence.

Despite the fact that the Supreme Court did not endorse bilingual 12 education, the lower federal courts have tended to treat this pedagogy as a civil right, and more than a dozen states have mandated its use in their public schools. The path by which bilingual education came to be viewed as a civil right, rather than as one method of teaching language, demonstrates the politicization of the language issue in American education. The United States Commission on Civil Rights endorsed bilingual education as a civil right nearly a decade ago. Public interest lawyers and civil rights lawyers have also regarded bilingual education as a basic civil right. An article in 1983 in the *Columbia Journal of Law and Social Problems* contended that bilingual education "may be the most effective method of compensatory language instruction currently used to educate language-minority students." It based this conclusion not on a review of educational research but on statements made by various political agencies.[7]

The article states, for example, as a matter of fact rather than 13 opinion: ". . . by offering subject matter instruction in a language understood by language-minority students, the bilingual-bicultural method maximizes achievement, and thus minimizes feelings of inferiority that might accompany a poor academic performance. By ridding the school environment of those features which may damage a language-minority child's self-image and thereby interfere with the educative process, bilingual-bicultural education creates the atmosphere most conducive to successful learning."[8]

If there were indeed conclusive evidence for these statements, then 14 bilingual-bicultural education *should* be imposed on school districts throughout the country. However, the picture is complicated; there are good bilingual programs, and there are ineffective bilingual programs. In and of itself, bilingualism is one pedagogical method, as subject to variation and misuse as any other single method. To date, no school district has claimed that the bilingual method succeeded in

---

[7]Jonathan D. Haft, "Assuring Equal Educational Opportunity for Language-Minority Students: Bilingual Education and the Equal Educational Opportunity Act of 1974," *Columbia Journal of Law and Social Problems*, vol. 18, no. 2, 1983, pp. 209–293.
[8]Ibid., p. 253.

sharply decreasing the dropout rate of Hispanic children or markedly raising their achievement scores in English and other subjects. The bilingual method is not necessarily inferior to other methods; its use should not be barred. There simply is no conclusive evidence that bilingualism should be preferred to all other ways of instructing non–English-speaking students. This being the case, there are no valid reasons for courts or federal agencies to impose this method on school districts for all non–English speakers, to the exclusion of other methods of language instruction.

Bilingual education exemplifies politicization because its advocates 15 press its adoption regardless of its educational effectiveness, and they insist that it must be made mandatory regardless of the wishes of the parents and children who are its presumed beneficiaries. It is a political program whose goals are implicit in the term "biculturalism." The aim is to use the public schools to promote the maintenance of distinct ethnic communities, each with its own cultural heritage and language. This in itself is a valid goal for a democratic nation as diverse and pluralistic as ours, but it is questionable whether this goal is appropriately pursued by the public schools, rather than by the freely chosen activities of individuals and groups.

Then there is the larger question of whether bilingual education 16 actually promotes equality of educational opportunity. Unless it enables non–English-speaking children to learn English and to enter into the mainstream of American society, it may hinder equality of educational opportunity. The child who spends most of his instructional time learning in Croatian or Greek or Spanish is likely to learn Croatian, Greek, or Spanish. Fluency in these languages will be of little help to those who want to apply to American colleges, universities, graduate schools, or employers, unless they are also fluent in English.

Of course, our nation needs much more foreign language instruc- 17 tion. But we should not confuse our desire to promote foreign languages in general with the special educational needs of children who do not know how to speak and read English in an English-language society.

Will our educational institutions ever be insulated from the ex- 18 tremes of politicization? It seems highly unlikely, in view of the fact that our schools and colleges are deeply embedded in the social and political mainstream. What is notably different today is the vastly increased power of the federal government and the courts to intervene in educational institutions, because of the expansion of the laws and the dependence of almost all educational institutions on public funding. To avoid unwise and dangerous politicization, government agencies should strive to distinguish between their proper role as protectors of fundamental constitutional rights and inappropriate intrusion into complex issues of curriculum and pedagogy.

This kind of institutional restraint would be strongly abetted if 19 judges and policymakers exercised caution and skepticism in their use of social science testimony. Before making social research the basis for constitutional edicts, judges and policymakers should understand that social science findings are usually divergent, limited, tentative, and partial.

We need the courts as vigilant guardians of our rights; we need 20 federal agencies that respond promptly to any violations of those rights. But we also need educational institutions that are free to exercise their responsibilities without fear of pressure groups and political lobbies. Decisions about which textbooks to use, which theories to teach, which books to place in the school library, how to teach, and what to teach are educational issues. They should be made by appropriate lay and professional authorities on educational grounds. In a democratic society, all of us share the responsibility to protect schools, colleges, and universities against unwarranted political intrusion into educational affairs.

Angelo Gonzalez, "Bilingualism Pro: The Key to Basic Skills"

If we accept that a child cannot learn unless taught through the 1 language he speaks and understands; that a child who does not speak or understand English must fall behind when English is the dominant medium of instruction; that one needs to learn English so as to be able to participate in an English-speaking society; that self-esteem and motivation are necessary for effective learning; that rejection of a child's native language and culture is detrimental to the learning process; then any necessary effective educational program for limited or no English-speaking ability must incorporate the following:

Language arts and comprehensive reading programs taught in the 2 child's native language.

Curriculum content areas taught in the native language to further 3 comprehension and academic achievement.

Intensive instruction in English. 4

Use of materials sensitive to and reflecting the culture of children 5 within the program.

Most Important Goal

The mastery of basic reading skills is the most important goal in 6 primary education since reading is the basis for much of all subsequent learning. Ordinarily, these skills are learned at home. But where beginning reading is taught in English, only the English-speaking child profits from these early acquired skills that are prerequisites to successful reading development. Reading programs taught in English to children with Spanish as a first language waste their acquired linguistic attributes and also impede learning by forcing them to absorb skills of reading simultaneously with a new language.

Both local and national research data provide ample evidence for 7 the efficacy of well-implemented programs. The New York City Board of Education Report on Bilingual Pupil Services for 1982–83 indicated that in all areas of the curriculum—English, Spanish and mathematics—and at all grade levels, students demonstrated statistically significant gains in tests of reading in English and Spanish and in math. In all but two of the programs reviewed, the attendance rates of students in the program, ranging from 86 to 94 percent, were higher than those of the general school population. Similar higher attendance rates were found among students in high school bilingual programs.

At Yale University, Kenji Hakuta, a linguist, reported recently on a 8 study of working-class Hispanic students in the New Haven bilingual program. He found that children who were the most bilingual, that is, who developed English without the loss of Spanish, were brighter in both verbal and nonverbal tests. Over time, there was an increasing correlation between English and Spanish—a finding that clearly contradicts the charge that teaching in the home language is detrimental to English. Rather the two languages are interdependent within the bilingual child, reinforcing each other.

Essential Contribution

As Jim Cummins of the Ontario Institute for Studies in Education 9 has argued, the use and development of the native language makes an essential contribution to the development of minority children's subject-matter knowledge and academic learning potential. In fact, at least three national data bases—the National Assessment of Educational Progress, National Center for Educational Statistics High School and Beyond Studies, and the Survey of Income and Education—suggest that there are long-term positive effects among high school students who have participated in bilingual-education programs. These students are achieving higher scores on tests of verbal and mathematics skills.

These and similar findings buttress the argument stated per- 10 suasively in the recent joint recommendation of the Academy for Educational Development and the Hazen Foundation, namely, that America needs to become a more multilingual nation and children who speak a non-English language are a national resource to be nurtured in school.

Unfortunately, the [Reagan] Administration's educational policies 11 would seem to be leading us in the opposite direction. Under the guise of protecting the common language of public life in the United States, William J. Bennett, the Secretary of Education, unleashed a frontal attack on bilingual education. In a major policy address, he engaged in rhetorical distortions about the nature and effectiveness of bilingual programs, pointing only to unnamed negative research findings to justify the Administration's retrenchment efforts.

Arguing for the need to give local school districts greater flexibility 12 in determining appropriate methodologies in serving limited-English-proficient students, Mr. Bennett fails to realize that, in fact, districts serving large numbers of language-minority students, as is the case in New York City, do have that flexibility. Left to their own devices in implementing legal mandates, many school districts have performed poorly at providing services to all entitled language-minority students.

A Harsh Reality

The harsh reality in New York City for language-minority students 13 was documented comprehensively last month by the Educational Priorities Panel. The panel's findings revealed that of the 113,831 students identified as being limited in English proficiency, as many as 44,000 entitled students are not receiving any bilingual services. The issue at hand is, therefore, not one of choice but rather violation of the rights of almost 40 percent of language-minority children to equal educational opportunity. In light of these findings the Reagan Administration's recent statements only serve to exacerbate existing inequities in the American educational system for linguistic-minority children. Rather than adding fuel to a misguided debate, the Administration would serve these children best by insuring the full funding of the 1984 Bilingual Education Reauthorization Act as passed by the Congress.

PRACTICE

Arguing a Hypothetical Case of Bilingualism

Assume that you are a parent of one or more children in public schools. Your community consists of two main ethnic groups. The smaller of the two groups speaks English in the home and at school. The slightly larger group is mainly Latin American in heritage; Spanish is the language used in most homes of members of this group. You yourself were born in Puerto Rico and learned Spanish as your first language, although you now speak and write English reasonably well. Both languages are used in your home.

Your school district has been offered federal funds to implement a bilingual education program that would extend from kindergarten to twelfth grade. To receive this money your board of education would have to hire additional teachers and make other changes in the school curriculum, but federal funds would cover most of the expenses of the program. A meeting of citizens of your school district has been called to decide whether or not to institute bilingual education. You have been asked to speak.

Before writing your speech, you will have to decide what would be the best thing for your own children, for the children of your Spanish-speaking friends, and for all the students and all the families in the district. In other words, you will have to decide whether or not bilingual education is a good idea in itself, and especially whether or not it would be good for your children and those of your friends. Given everything you know about what it takes to function well in American life, would bilingual education be more or less likely to give the children a better chance? If you need to do some research to make up your mind, go ahead and do it. But try to see the picture as fully as possible before you write.

You know that some speakers at this meeting will be arguing for one side or another in the most emotional way possible. You do not wish to join in this kind of persuasion. You want to make the most reasonable case you can for the position you finally adopt. This means that in your speech you must look at the arguments on both sides and explain to your audience why some of these arguments are more reasonable than others, and why your way will be best for all concerned. Do your thinking, and write your speech.

Two Essays on Punishment of Crimes

The following two essays take opposite sides on one of the important issues of our time: the proper treatment of people convicted of crimes. In reading them, you are asked to consider the following questions:

1. How does each author define crime? How does he categorize the relationship between the convicted person, what that person has done, and what should be done to or for that person?
2. What parts of each argument seem most convincing? Why?
3. How would you paraphrase or summarize each argument? What roles do "definition" and "cause-and-effect" reasoning play in each?
4. Do you think one argument better than the other? Why?
5. Has either changed your mind? If so, how?

Karl Menninger, "The Crime of Punishment"

Few words in our language arrest our attention as do "crime," 1
"violence," "revenge," and "injustice." We abhor crime; we adore
justice; we boast that we live by the rule of law. Violence and vengeful-
ness we repudiate as unworthy of our civilization, and we assume this
sentiment to be unanimous among all human beings.

Yet crime continues to be a national disgrace and a world-wide 2
problem. It is threatening, alarming, wasteful, expensive, abundant,
and apparently increasing! In actuality it is decreasing in frequency of
occurrence, but it is certainly increasing in visibility and the reactions
of the public to it.

Our system for controlling crime is ineffective, unjust, expensive. 3
Prisons seem to operate with revolving doors—the same people going
in and out and in and out. *Who cares?*

Our city jails and inhuman reformatories and wretched prisons are 4
jammed. They are known to be unhealthy, dangerous, immoral, indecent, crime-breeding dens of iniquity. Not everyone has smelled
them, as some of us have. Not many have heard the groans and the
curses. Not everyone has seen the hate and despair in a thousand
blank, hollow faces. But, in a way, we all know how miserable prisons
are. *We want them to be that way*. And they are. *Who cares?*

Professional and big-time criminals prosper as never before. Gambling 5
syndicates flourish. White-collar crime may even exceed all others, but
goes undetected in the majority of cases. We are all being robbed and we
know who the robbers are. They live nearby. *Who cares?*

The public filches millions of dollars worth of food and clothing from 6
stores, towels and sheets from hotels, jewelry and knick-knacks from
shops. The public steals, and the same public pays it back in higher
prices. *Who cares?*

Time and time again somebody shouts about this state of affairs, just 7
as I am shouting now. The magazines shout. The newspapers shout.
The television and radio commentators shout (or at least they "deplore"). Psychologists, sociologists, leading jurists, wardens, and in-
telligent police chiefs join the chorus. Governors and mayors and
Congressmen are sometimes heard. They shout that the situation is
bad, bad, bad, and getting worse. Some suggested that we immediately replace obsolete procedures with scientific methods. A few
shout contrary sentiments. Do the clear indications derived from
scientific discovery for appropriate changes continue to fall on deaf
ears? Why is the public so long-suffering, so apathetic, and thereby so
continuingly self-destructive? How many Presidents (and other
citizens) do we have to lose before we do something?

The public behaves as a sick patient does when a dreaded treatment 8 is proposed for his ailment. We all know how the aching tooth may suddenly quiet down in the dentist's office, or the abdominal pain disappear in the surgeon's examining room. Why should a sufferer seek relief and shun it? Is it merely the fear of the pain of the treatment? Is it the fear of unknown complications? Is it distrust of the doctor's ability? All of these, no doubt.

But, as Freud made so incontestably clear, the sufferer is always 9 somewhat deterred by a kind of subversive, internal opposition to the work of cure. He suffers on the one hand from the pains of his affliction and yearns to get well. But he suffers at the same time from traitorous impulses that fight against the accomplishment of any change in himself, even recovery! Like Hamlet, he wonders whether it may be better after all to suffer the familiar pains and aches associated with the old method than to face the complications of a new and strange, even though possibly better, way of handling things.

The inescapable conclusion is that society *wants* crime, *needs* 10 crime, and gains definite satisfactions from the present mishandling of it! We condemn crime; we punish offenders for it; but we need it. The crime and punishment ritual is a part of our lives. We need crimes to wonder at, to enjoy vicariously, to discuss and speculate about, and to publicly deplore. We need criminals to identify ourselves with, to envy secretly, and to punish stoutly. They do for us the forbidden, illegal things we *wish* to do, and, like scapegoats of old, they bear the burdens of our displaced guilt and punishment—"the iniquities of us all." . . .

Fifty years ago, Winston Churchill declared that the mood and 11 temper of the public in regard to crime and criminals is one of the unfailing tests of the civilization of any country. Judged by this standard, how civilized are we?

[President Nixon's] National Crime Commission . . . declared re- 12 cently that organized crime flourishes in America because enough of the public wants its services, and most citizens are apathetic about its impact. It will continue uncurbed as long as Americans accept it as inevitable and, in some instances, desirable.

Are there steps that we can take which will reduce the aggressive 13 stabs and self-destructive lurches of our less well-managing fellow men? Are there ways to prevent and control the grosser violations, other than the clumsy traditional maneuvers which we have inherited? These depend basically upon intimidation and slow-motion torture. We call it punishment, and justify it with our "feeling." We know it doesn't work.

Yes, there *are* better ways. There are steps that could be taken; 14 some *are* taken. But we move too slowly. Much better use, it seems to me, could be made of the members of my profession and other behavioral scientists than having them deliver courtroom pronunciamentos. The consistent use of a diagnostic clinic would enable trained workers to lay what they can learn about an offender before the judge who would know best how to implement the recommendation.

This would no doubt lead to a transformation of prisons, if not to 15 their total disappearance in their present form and function. Temporary and permanent detention will perhaps always be necessary for a few, especially the professionals, but this could be more effectively and economically performed with new types of "facility" (that strange, awkward word for institution).

I assume it to be a matter of common and general agreement that 16 our object in all this is to protect the community from a repetition of the offense by the most economical method consonant with our other purposes. Our "other purposes" include the desire to prevent these offenses from occurring, to reclaim offenders for social usefulness, if possible, and to detain them in protective custody, if reclamation is *not* possible. But how?

The treatment of human failure or dereliction by the infliction of 17 pain is still used and believed in by many nonmedical people. "Spare the rod and spoil the child" is still considered wise counsel by many.

Whipping is still used by many secondary schoolmasters in Eng- 18 land, I am informed, to stimulate study, attention, and the love of learning. Whipping was long a traditional treatment for the "crime" of disobedience on the part of children, pupils, servants, apprentices, employees. And slaves were treated for centuries by flogging for such offenses as weariness, confusion, stupidity, exhaustion, fear, grief, and even overcheerfulness. It was assumed and stoutly defended that these "treatments" cured conditions for which they were administered.

Meanwhile, scientific medicine was acquiring many new healing 19 methods and devices. Doctors can now transplant organs and limbs; they can remove brain tumors and cure incipient cancers; they can halt pneumonia, meningitis, and other infections; they can correct deformities and repair breaks and tears and scars. But these wonderful achievements are accomplished on *willing* subjects, people who voluntarily ask for help by even heroic measures. And the reader will be wondering, no doubt, whether doctors can do anything with or for people who *do not want* to be treated at all, in any way! Can doctors cure willful aberrant behavior? Are we to believe that crime is a *disease* that can be reached by scientific measures? Isn't it merely "natural meanness" that makes all of us do wrong things at times even when we "know better"? And are not self-control, moral stamina, and will power the things needed? Surely there is no medical treatment for the lack of those!

Let me answer this carefully, for much misunderstanding accumu- 20 lates here. I would say that according to the prevalent understanding of the words, crime is *not* a disease. Neither is it an illness, although I think it *should* be! It *should* be treated, and it could be; but it mostly isn't.

These enigmatic statements are simply explained. Diseases are 21 undesired states of being which have been described and defined by doctors, usually given Greek or Latin appellations, and treated by long-established physical and pharmacological formulae. Illness, on the other hand, is best defined as a state of impaired functioning of such a nature that the public expects the sufferer to repair to the physician for help. The illness may prove to be a disease; more often it is only vague and nameless misery, but something which doctors, not lawyers, teachers, or preachers, are supposed to be able and willing to help.

When the community begins to look upon the expression of aggres- 22 sive violence as the symptom of an illness or as indicative of illness, it will be because it believes doctors can do something to correct such a condition. At present, some better-informed individuals do believe and expect this. However angry at or sorry for the offender, they want him "treated" in an effective way so that he will cease to be a danger to them. And they know that traditional punishment, "treatment-punishment," will not effect this.

What *will?* What effective treatment is there for such violence? It 23 will surely have to begin with motivating or stimulating or arousing in a cornered individual the wish and hope and intention to change his methods of dealing with the realities of life. Can this be done by education, medication, counseling, training? I would answer *yes*. It can be done successfully in a majority of cases, if undertaken in time.

The present penal system and the existing legal philosophy do not 24 stimulate or even expect such a change to take place in the criminal. Yet change is what medical science always aims for. The prisoner, like the doctor's other patients, should emerge from his treatment experi-ence a different person, differently equipped, differently functioning, and headed in a different direction than when he began the treatment.

It is natural for the public to doubt that this can be accomplished 25 with criminals. But remember that the public *used* to doubt that change could be effected in the mentally ill. No one a hundred years ago believed mental illness to be curable. Today *all* people know (or should know) that *mental illness is curable* in the great majority of instances and that the prospects and rapidity of cure are directly related to the availability and intensity of proper treatment.

The forms and techniques of psychiatric treatment used today num- 26 ber in the hundreds. No one patient requires or receives all forms, but each patient is studied with respect to his particular needs, his basic assets, his interests, and his special difficulties. A therapeutic team may embrace a dozen workers—as in a hospital setting—or it may narrow down to the doctor and the spouse. Clergymen, teachers, relatives, friends, and even fellow patients often participate informally but helpfully in the process of readaptation.

All of the participants in this effort to bring about a favorable change 27 in the patient—i.e., in his vital balance and life program—are imbued with what we may call a *therapeutic attitude*. This is one in direct antithesis to attitudes of avoidance, ridicule, scorn, or punitiveness. Hostile feelings toward the subject, however justified by his unpleasant and even destructive behavior, are not in the curriculum of therapy or in the therapist. This does not mean that therapists approve of the offensive and obnoxious behavior of the patient; they distinctly disapprove of it. But they recognize it as symptomatic of continued imbalance and disorganization, which is what they are seeking to change. They distinguish between disapproval, penalty, price, and punishment.

Doctors charge fees; they impose certain "penalties" or prices, but 28 they have long since put aside primitive attitudes of retaliation toward offensive patients. A patient may cough in the doctor's face or may vomit on the office rug; a patient may curse or scream or even struggle in the extremity of his pain. But these acts are not "punished." Doctors and nurses have no time or thought for inflicting unnecessary pain even upon patients who may be difficult, disagreeable, provocative, and even dangerous. It is their duty to care for them, to try to make them well, and to prevent them from doing themselves or others harm. This requires love, not hate. This is the deepest meaning of the therapeutic attitude. Every doctor knows this; every worker in a hospital or clinic knows it (or should).

There is another element in the therapeutic attitude. It is the 29 quality of hopefulness. If no one believes that the patient can get well, if no one—not even the doctor—has any hope, there probably won't be any recovery. Hope is just as important as love in the therapeutic attitude.

"But you were talking about the mentally ill," readers may interject, 30 "those poor, confused, bereft, frightened individuals who yearn for help from you doctors and nurses. Do you mean to imply that willfully perverse individuals, our criminals, can be similarly reached and rehabilitated? Do you really believe that effective treatment of the sort you visualize can be applied to people *who do not want any help*, who are so willfully vicious, so well aware of the wrongs they are doing, so lacking in penitence or even common decency that punishment seems to be the only thing left?"

Do I believe there is effective treatment for offenders, and that they 31 *can* be changed? *Most certainly and definitely I do*. Not all cases, to be sure; there are also some physical afflictions which we cannot cure at the moment. Some provision has to be made for incurables—pending new knowledge—and these will include some offenders. But I believe the majority of them would prove to be curable. The willfulness and the viciousness of offenders are part of the thing for which they have to be treated. These must not thwart the therapeutic attitude.

It is simply not true that most of them are "fully aware" of what they 32 are doing, nor is it true that they want no help from anyone, although some of them say so. Prisoners are individuals: Some want treatment, some do not. Some don't know what treatment is. Many are utterly despairing and hopeless. Where treatment is made available in institutions, many prisoners seek it even with the full knowledge that doing so will not lessen their sentences. In some prisons, seeking treatment by prisoners is frowned upon by the officials.

Various forms of treatment are even now being tried in some 33 progressive courts and prisons over the country—educational, social, industrial, religious, recreational, and psychological treatment. Socially acceptable behavior, new work-play opportunities, new identity and companion patterns all help toward community reacceptance. Some parole officers and some wardens have been extremely ingenious in developing these modalities of rehabilitation and reconstruction— more than I could list here even if I knew them all. But some are trying. The secret of success in all programs, however, is the replacement of the punitive attitude with a therapeutic attitude.

Offenders with propensities for impulsive and predatory aggression 34 should not be permitted to live among us unrestrained by some kind of social control. *But the great majority of offenders, even "criminals," should never become prisoners if we want to "cure" them.*

There are now throughout the country many citizens' action groups 35 and programs for the prevention and control of crime and delinquency. With such attitudes of inquiry and concern, the public could acquire information (and incentive) leading to a change of feeling about crime and criminals. It will discover how unjust is much so-called "justice," how baffled and frustrated many judges are by the ossified rigidity of old-fashioned, obsolete laws and state constitutions which effectively prevent the introduction of sensible procedures to replace useless, harmful ones.

I want to proclaim to the public that things are not what it wishes 36 them to be, and will only become so if it will take an interest in the matter and assume some responsibility for its own self-protection.

Will the public listen? 37

If the public does become interested, it will realize that we must 38 have more facts, more trial projects, more checked results. It will share the dismay of the President's Commission in finding that no one knows much about even the incidence of crime with any definiteness or statistical accuracy.

The average citizen finds it difficult to see how any research would 39 in any way change his mind about a man who brutally murders his children. But just such inconceivably awful acts most dramatically point up the need for research. Why should—how can—a man become so dreadful as that in our culture? How is such a man made? Is it comprehensible that he can be born to become so depraved?

There are thousands of questions regarding crime and public pro- 40 tection which deserve scientific study. What makes some individuals maintain their interior equilibrium by one kind of disturbance of the social structure rather than by another kind, one that would have landed him in a hospital? Why do some individuals specialize in certain types of crime? Why do so many young people reared in areas of delinquency and poverty and bad example never become habitual delinquents? (Perhaps this is a more important question than why some of them do.)

The public has a fascination for violence, and clings tenaciously to its 41 yen for vengeance, blind and deaf to the expense, futility, and dangerousness of the resulting penal system. But we are bound to hope that this will yield in time to the persistent, penetrating light of intelligence and accumulating scientific knowledge. The public will grow increasingly ashamed of its cry for retaliation, its persistent demand to punish. This is its crime, *our* crime against criminals—and, incidentally, our crime against ourselves. For before we can diminish our sufferings from the ill-controlled aggressive assaults of fellow citizens, we must renounce the philosophy of punishment, the obsolete, vengeful penal attitude. In its place we would seek a comprehensive constructive social attitude—therapeutic in some instances, restraining in some instances, but preventive in its total social impact.

In the last analysis this becomes a question of personal morals and 42 values. No matter how glorified or how piously disguised, vengeance as a human motive must be personally repudiated by each and every one of us. This is the message of old religions and new psychiatries. Unless this message is heard, unless we, the people—the man on the street, the housewife in the home—can give up our delicious satisfactions in opportunities for vengeful retaliation on scapegoats, we cannot expect to preserve our peace, our public safety, or our mental health.

C. S. Lewis, "The Humanitarian Theory of Punishment"

In England we have lately had a controversy about Capital Punish- 1 ment. I do not know whether a murderer is more likely to repent and make a good end on the gallows a few weeks after his trial or in the prison infirmary thirty years later. I do not know whether the fear of death is an indispensable deterrent. I need not, for the purpose of this article, decide whether it is a morally permissible deterrent. Those are questions which I propose to leave untouched. My subject is not Capital Punishment in particular, but that theory of punishment in general which the controversy showed to be almost universal among my fellow-countrymen. It may be called the Humanitarian theory. Those who hold it think that it is mild and merciful. In this I believe that they are seriously mistaken. I believe that the "Humanity" which it claims is a dangerous illusion and disguises the possibility of cruelty and injustice without end. I urge a return to the traditional or Retributive theory not solely, not even primarily, in the interests of society, but in the interests of the criminal.

According to the Humanitarian theory, to punish a man because he 2 deserves it, and as much as he deserves, is mere revenge and, therefore, barbarous and immoral. It is maintained that the only legitimate motives for punishing are the desire to deter others by example or to mend the criminal. When this theory is combined, as frequently happens, with the belief that all crime is more or less pathological, the idea of mending tails off into that of healing or curing, and punishment becomes therapeutic. Thus it appears at first sight that we have passed from the harsh and self-righteous notion of giving the wicked their deserts to the charitable and enlightened one of tending the psychologically sick. What could be more amiable? One little point which is taken for granted in this theory needs, however, to be made explicit. The things done to the criminal, even if they are called cures, will be just as compulsory as they were in the old days when we called them punishments. If a tendency to steal can be cured by psychotherapy, the thief will no doubt be forced to undergo the treatment. Otherwise, society cannot continue.

My contention is that this doctrine, merciful though it appears, 3 really means that each one of us, from the moment he breaks the law, is deprived of the rights of a human being.

The reason is this. The Humanitarian theory removes from Punish- 4 ment the concept of Desert. But the concept of Desert is the only connecting link between punishment and justice. It is only as deserved or undeserved that a sentence can be just or unjust. I do not here contend that the question "Is it deserved?" is the only one we can reasonably ask about a punishment. We may very properly ask whether it is likely to deter others and to reform the criminal. But neither of these two last questions is a question about justice. There is no sense in talking about a "just deterrent" or a "just cure." We demand of a deterrent not whether it is just but whether it succeeds.

Thus when we cease to consider what the criminal deserves and consider only what will cure him or deter others, we have tacitly removed him from the sphere of justice altogether; instead of a person, a subject of rights, we now have a mere object, a patient, a "case."

The distinction will become clearer if we ask who will be qualified to 5 determine sentences when sentences are no longer held to derive their propriety from the criminal's deservings. On the old view the problem of fixing the right sentence was a moral problem. Accordingly, the judge who did it was a person trained in jurisprudence; trained, that is, in a science which deals with rights and duties, and which, in origin at least, was consciously accepting guidance from the Law of Nature and from Scripture. We must admit that in the actual penal code of most countries at most times these high originals were so much modified by local custom, class interests, and utilitarian concessions as to be very imperfectly recognizable. But the code was never in principle, and not always in fact, beyond the control of the conscience of the society. And when (say, in eighteenth-century England) actual punishments conflicted too violently with the moral sense of the community, juries refused to convict and reform was finally brought about. This was possible because, so long as we are thinking in terms of Desert, the propriety of the penal code, being a moral queston, is a question on which every man has the right to an opinion, not because he follows this or that profession, but because he is simply a man, a rational animal enjoying the Natural Light. But all this is changed when we drop the concept of Desert. The only two questions we may now ask about a punishment are whether it deters and whether it cures. But these are not questions on which anyone is entitled to have an opinion simply because he is a man. He is not entitled to an opinon even if, in addition to being a man, he should happen also to be a jurist, a Christian, and a moral theologian. For they are not questions about principle but about matter of fact; and for such *cuiquam in sua arte credendum*.[1] Only the expert "penologist" (let barbarous things have barbarous names), in the light of previous experiment, can tell us what is likely to deter: Only the psychotherapist can tell us what is likely to cure. It will be in vain for the rest of us, speaking simply as men, to say, "But this punishment is hideously unjust, hideously disproportionate to the criminal's deserts." The experts with perfect logic will reply, "But nobody was talking about deserts. No one was talking about *punishment* in your archaic, vindictive sense of the word. Here are the statistics proving that this treatment deters. Here are the statistics proving that this other treatment cures. What is your trouble?"

---

[1] "We must believe the expert in his own field."

The Humanitarian theory, then, removes sentences from the hands 6 of jurists whom the public conscience is entitled to criticize and places them in the hands of technical experts whose special sciences do not even employ such categories as rights or justice. It might be argued that since this transference results from an abandonment of the old idea of punishment, and, therefore, of all vindictive motives, it will be safe to leave our criminals in such hands. I will not pause to comment on the simple-minded view of fallen human nature which such a belief implies. Let us rather remember that the "cure" of criminals is to be compulsory; and let us then watch how the theory actually works in the mind of the Humanitarian. The immediate starting point of this article was a letter I read in one of our Leftist weeklies. The author was pleading that a certain sin, now treated by our laws as a crime, should henceforward be treated as a disease. And he complained that under the present system the offender, after a term in jail, was simply let out to return to his original environment, where he would probably re-lapse. What he complained of was not the shutting up but the letting out. On his remedial view of punishment the offender should, of course, be detained until he was cured. And of course the official straighteners are the only people who can say when that is. The first result of the Humanitarian theory is, therefore, to substitute for a definite sentence (reflecting to some extent the community's moral judgment on the degree of ill-desert involved) an indefinite sentence terminable only by the word of those experts—and they are not experts in moral theology nor even in the Law of Nature—who inflict it. Which of us, if he stood in the dock, would not prefer to be tried by the old system?

It may be said that by the continued use of the word "punishment" 7 and the use of the verb "inflict" I am misrepresenting Humanitarians. They are not punishing, not inflicting, only healing. But do not let us be deceived by a name. To be taken without consent from my home and friends; to lose my liberty; to undergo all those assaults on my personality which modern psychotherapy knows how to deliver; to be re-made after some pattern of "normality" hatched in a Viennese laboratory to which I never professed allegiance; to know that this process will never end until either my captors have succeeded or I have grown wise enough to cheat them with apparent success—who cares whether this is called Punishment or not? That it includes most of the elements for which any punishment is feared—shame, exile, bondage, and years eaten by the locust—is obvious. Only enormous ill-desert could justify it; but ill-desert is the very conception which the Humanitarian theory has thrown overboard.

If we turn from the curative to the deterrent justification of punish- 9 ment we shall find the new theory even more alarming. When you punish a man *in terrorem*,[2] make of him an "example" to others, you are admittedly using him as a means to an end; someone else's end. This, in itself, would be a very wicked thing to do. On the classical theory of Punishment it was of course justified on the ground that the man deserved it. That was assumed to be established before any question of "making him an example" arose. You then, as the saying is, killed two birds with one stone; in the process of giving him what he deserved you set an example to others. But take away desert and the whole morality of the punishment disappears. Why, in Heaven's name, am I to be sacrificed to the good of society in this way?—unless, of course, I deserve it.

But that is not the worst. If the justification of exemplary punish- 9 ment is not to be based on desert but solely on its efficacy as a deterrent, it is not absolutely necessary that the man we punish should even have committed the crime. The deterrent effect demands that the public should draw the moral, "If we do such an act we shall suffer like that man." The punishment of a man actually guilty whom the public think innocent will not have the desired effect; the punishment of a man actually innocent will, provided the public think him guilty. But every modern State has powers which make it easy to fake a trial. When a victim is urgently needed for exemplary purposes and a guilty victim cannot be found, all the purposes of deterrence will be equally served by the punishment (call it "cure" if you prefer) of an innocent victim, provided that the public can be cheated into thinking him guilty. It is no use to ask me why I assume that our rulers will be so wicked. The punishment of an innocent, that is, an undeserving, man is wicked only if we grant the traditional view that righteous punishment means deserved punishment. Once we have abandoned that criterion, all punishments have to be justified, if at all, on other grounds that have nothing to do with desert. Where the punishment of the innocent can be justified on those grounds (and it could in some cases be justified as a deterrent) it will be no less moral than any other punishment. Any distaste for it on the part of a Humanitarian will be merely a hang-over from the Retributive theory.

It is, indeed, important to notice that my argument so far supposes 10 no evil intentions on the part of the Humanitarian and considers only what is involved in the logic of his position. My contention is that good men (not bad men) consistently acting upon that position would act as cruelly and unjustly as the greatest tyrants. They might in some respects act even worse. Of all tyrannies a tyranny sincerely exercised for the good of its victims may be the most oppressive. It may be better

---

[2]"To frighten."

---

to live under robber barons than under omnipotent moral busybodies. The robber baron's cruelty may sometimes sleep, his cupidity may at some point be satiated; but those who torment us for our own good will torment us without end, for they do so with the approval of their own conscience. They may be more likely to go to Heaven yet at the same time likelier to make a Hell of earth. Their very kindness stings with intolerable insult. To be "cured" against one's will and cured of states which we may not regard as disease is to be put on a level with those who have not yet reached the age of reason or those who never will; to be classed with infants, imbeciles, and domestic animals. But to be punished, however severely, because we have deserved it, because we "ought to have known better," is to be treated as a human person made in God's image.

In reality, however, we must face the possibility of bad rulers armed 11 with a Humanitarian theory of punishment. A great many popular blueprints for a Christian society are merely what the Elizabethans called "eggs in moonshine" because they assume that the whole society is Christian or that the Christians are in control. This is not so in most contemporary States. Even if it were, our rulers would still be fallen men and, therefore, neither very wise nor very good. As it is, they will usually be unbelievers. And since wisdom and virtue are not the only or the commonest qualifications for a place in the government, they will not often be even the best unbelievers.

The practical problem of Christian politics is not that of drawing up 12 schemes for a Christian society, but that of living as innocently as we can with unbelieving fellow-subjects under unbelieving rulers who will never be perfectly wise and good and who will sometimes be very wicked and very foolish. And when they are wicked the Humanitarian theory of punishment will put in their hands a finer instrument of tyranny than wickedness ever had before. For if crime and disease are to be regarded as the same thing, it follows that any state of mind which our masters choose to call disease can be treated as crime and compulsorily cured. It will be vain to plead that states of mind which displease government need not always involve moral turpitude and do not therefore always deserve forfeiture of liberty. For our masters will not be using the concepts of Desert and Punishment but those of disease and cure. We know that one school of psychology already regards religion as a neurosis. When this particular neurosis becomes inconvenient to government, what is to hinder government from pro-ceeding to "cure" it? Such "cure" will, of course, be compulsory; but under the Humanitarian theory it will not be called by the shocking name of Persecution. No one will blame us for being Christians, no one will hate us, no one will revile us. The new Nero will approach us with the silky manners of a doctor, and though all will be in fact as compulsory as the *tunica molesta*[3] or Smithfield or Tyburn,[4] all will go on within the unemotional therapeutic sphere, where words like "right" and "wrong" or "freedom" and "slavery" are never heard. And thus when the command is given, every prominent Christian in the land may vanish overnight into Institutions for the Treatment of the Ideologically Unsound, and it will rest with the expert jailers to say when (if ever) they are to re-emerge. But it will not be persecution. Even if the treatment is painful, even if it is lifelong, even if it is fatal, that will be only a regrettable accident; the intention was purely therapeutic. In ordinary medicine there were painful operations and fatal operations; so in this. But because they are "treatment," not punishment, they can be criticized only by fellow-experts and on technical grounds, never by men as men and on grounds of justice.

This is why I think it essential to oppose the Humanitarian theory of punishment, root and branch, wherever we encounter it. It carries on its front a semblance of mercy which is wholly false. That is how it can deceive men of good will. The error began, perhaps, with Shelley's statement that the distinction between mercy and justice was invented in the courts of tyrants. It sounds noble, and was indeed the error of a noble mind. But the distinction is essential. The older view was that mercy "tempered" justice, or (on the highest level of all) that mercy and justice had met and kissed. The essential act of mercy was to pardon; and pardon in its very essence involves the recognition of guilt and ill-desert in the recipient. If crime is only a disease which needs cure, not a sin which deserves punishment, it cannot be pardoned. How can you pardon a man for having a gumboil or a club foot? But the Humanitarian theory wants simply to abolish Justice and substitute Mercy for it. This means that you start being "kind" to people before you have considered their rights, and then force upon them supposed kindnesses which no one but you will recognize as kindnesses and which the recipient will feel as abominable cruelties. You have overshot the mark. Mercy, detached from Justice, grows unmerciful. That is the important paradox. As there are plants which will flourish only in mountain soil, so it appears that Mercy will flower only when it grows in the crannies of the rock of Justice: Transplanted to the marsh-lands of mere Humanitarianism, it becomes a man-eating weed, all the more dangerous because it is still called by the same name as the mountain variety. But we ought long ago to have learned our lesson. We should be too old now to be deceived by those humane pretensions which have served to usher in every cruelty of the revolutionary period in

13

---

[3]An uncomfortable tunic worn as a punishment.
[4]Two places of execution in England.

---

which we live. These are the "precious balms" which will "break our heads."[5]

There is a fine sentence in Bunyan: "It came burning hot into my mind, whatever he said, and however he flattered, when he got me home to his House, he would sell me for a Slave."[6] There is a fine couplet, too, in John Ball:

Be war or ye be wo;
Knoweth your frend from your foo.[7]

PRACTICE

Arguing a Hypothetical Case of Punishment or Treatment for a Convicted Criminal

You have read what a social scientist and a theologian have to say about dealing properly with criminals. You may feel that one is right and the other wrong or that the truth is somewhere in between. In any case, here is a chance for you to argue for your own solution to the problem.

To make your argument sufficiently different from the other two so that you can avoid repeating what they have said, make your own argument in terms of a specific but hypothetical criminal. That is, invent a crime of some serious but not hideous sort, imagine the history of the criminal (especially age, family background, previous criminal record) and argue the case for proper treatment of this particular person, convicted of this particular crime.

Assume the availability of a full range of responses, ranging from what Menninger would approve to what Lewis would recommend. Take into account the probable result of your recommendation, both for the person who has been convicted and for society.

You may quote Lewis and Menninger if you wish, either for support or in order to dispute with them. However, this should not be the main purpose of your argument. You should be trying to convince a group of reasonable people (us, your teacher, your classmates) that your recommendation is the proper one.

You must *not* deal with a case like a parent stealing food for a starving baby, or a serial killer of innocent youngsters who tortures and mutilates the victims. Stick to the middle range of crime, to deeds that are clearly wrong

---

[5]Psalm cxli. 6.

[6]*The Pilgrim's Progress*, ed. James Blanton Wharey, 2nd ed. (rev. Roger Sharrock), Oxford English Texts (Oxford, 1960), part 1, p. 70.

[7]"John Ball's Letter to the Peasants of Essex, 1381," lines 11–12, found in *Fourteenth Century Verse and Prose*, ed. Kenneth Sisam (Oxford, 1921), p. 161.

but not monstrous. Suppose, for instance, an idealistic but angry college student decides to rob a grasping slumlord who has once again raised the rent that he and other poor tenants must pay on their run-down apartments. The student intends to share the fruits of the robbery with the other needy tenants. In committing the crime, the student is surprised by the landlord and picks up a kitchen knife, stabs the landlord three times, and runs out of the apartment abandoning the goods.

There is no question about the student's guilt. He was seen entering and leaving the victim's home and has confessed to the attempted robbery and the stabbing that has disabled the landlord for life. He has no previous criminal record except for traffic violations. Assume that he is a person like yourself, except that he has been transformed into a criminal by violent actions against life and property. Assume that the victim is not an entirely nice person, but has a family and other relatives who depend upon him. In other words, we have a real crime here, of an important sort, that society cannot ignore. Whatever crime you invent, the question for you to decide is essentially whether "punishment" or "treatment" is the better response, from the point of view of society; that is, whether Lewis or Menninger is right. You might consider how you would wish to be dealt with yourself if you were the criminal—or how you would wish the criminal treated if you were the child of the victim. But the real question cannot be solved on a personal level. You must try to formulate an argument for the proper response to serious crime *in general*, using your hypothetical case as your main example, and the arguments of Lewis or Menninger as your main source of positions on the issue at hand.

Remember, this is not a detective story, but an argument. Give yourself a problem that your argument will attempt to resolve, not a mystery that must be solved. Above all, try to be balanced, reasonable, and thoughtful, rather than getting carried away by emotion.

READING

A Critic Reflects on the Violence of Western Reason

How are Westerns and academic discourse alike? Although this may sound like a joke question or riddle, the answer is no laughing matter to Jane Tompkins. In reflecting on the reason for violence in Westerns and the violence of reason in academic argumentation, Tompkins discovers a disconcerting yet all-too-pervasive "moral universe"—a universe composed of good guys and bad guys, pro and con, in which murderousness is not merely accepted but applauded. She wonders if it has to be this way. As important as this question is, we'd like you to consider another question as you read Tompkins's essay: Is it really the way she says it is? Are Westerns really structured to justify violence? In academia, is argumentative reason really as adversarial and violent as Tompkins says it is?

Jane Tompkins, "Fighting Words: Unlearning to Write the Critical Essay"

The work I've been doing recently has circled around the subject of 1 violence. I've been trying to figure out what constitutes violence, and whether one can ever avoid it, really. Can thoughts be violent? And if so, do they have the same moral weight as violent acts? Are we, by virtue of our bodily existence, violent by definition, killing with every breath we take? (This was the position Thoreau arrived at in *Walden*, where, in the chapter on meat-eating called "Higher Laws," he exclaims: "Our very life is our disgrace!" It is also the conclusion Jacques Derrida reaches, by another route, in the chapter called "The Violence of the Letter" from *Grammatology*.) Or is violence, in any meaningful sense, circumscribable, and hence avoidable? The question comes up for me because I've been working on westerns—popular novels and movies produced between 1900 and, roughly, 1975.

When it shows up in westerns, we think we know what violence is: 2 It's the shootout on main street at the end of the movie, and the fistfight or two that precede it. It's what Amy, played by Grace Kelly in *High Noon*, is protesting against when she says, just before Gary Cooper has his duel with Frank Miller's gang: "I don't care who's right or who's wrong. There has to be some better way to live!" The definition of violence most of us carry around in our heads differs very little from the one the western offers: violence is killing or beating up on other people, deliberately inflicting pain. The rifle that misfires can kill violently, but that's not the kind of thing we're concerned with when we think about violence as a moral issue. Intention has to be involved.

Working on westerns has made me aware of the extent to which the 3 genre exists in order to provide a justification for violence. Violence needs justification because our society puts it under interdict—morally and legally, at any rate. In *Shane*, for example, when Shane first appears at Grafton's store, he goes into the saloon section and buys a bottle of soda pop. One of the Riker gang (the villains in this movie) starts insulting him, first saying he smells pigs (Shane is working for a farmer), then ridiculing him for drinking soda pop, then splashing a shot of whiskey on his brand new shirt with the words "smell like a man," and finally ordering him out of the saloon. Shane goes quietly. But the next time, when he returns the empty soda bottle and the insults start again, he's had enough. When Shane is told he can't "drink with the men," he splashes whiskey in the other guy's face, hauls off and socks him one, and the fight is on.

The structure of this sequence reproduces itself in a thousand 4 western novels and movies. Its pattern never varies. The hero, provoked by insults, first verbal, then physical, resists the urge to retaliate, proving his moral superiority to those who are taunting him. It is never the hero who taunts his adversary; if he does, it's only after he's been pushed "too far." And this, of course, is what always happens. The villians, whoever they may be, finally commit an act so atrocious that the hero *must* retaliate in kind. He wants to, and we want him to, and, if there's a crowd of innocent bystanders, they want him to, too. At this juncture, the point where provocation has gone too far, retaliatory violence becomes not simply justifiable but imperative: now, we are made to feel, *not* to transgress the interdict against violence would be the transgression.

Why does the western tell this story over and over? This is not a 5 question I am prepared to answer now, but one or two things can be said. There's no denying the satisfying sense of release the plot's culmination in violence affords. The entire purpose of the pattern I've described is to get the audience to the point where it can't wait till the hero lets loose with his six-shooters. (In fact, the culminating moment is not always—or perhaps even usually—one of letting go: the actual movements involved, the facial expressions, the bodily positions, are not those of all-out effort or abandon but of taut control.) Still, there's a tremendous feeling of relief at the moment of discharge, relief from the tension that holding back the urge to strike has built up. Vengeance, by the time it arrives, feels biologically necessary. It's as if the hero had been dying of thirst, and suddenly he's given the chance to take a drink of water; it's as if he's been waiting eight-and-a-half innings to come up to bat. Whatever the appropriate analogy is (the most common one is sexual) the violence, by the time it arrives, fills a visceral need.

Mixed with the pleasure of this moment is another, less noted, for it 6 tends to become submerged in the fury of physical appeasement. The story can climax, and desire be sated, only if the moral applause meter reads way off the scale in the hero's favor. What justifies his violence is that he is in the right, which is to say that he has been unduly victimized and can now be permitted to do things which a short while ago only the villains did. At this moment, a flip-flop occurs. Virtue, which up till then had shown itself in long-suffering and restraint, is suddenly transformed and now consists of all-out aggression. This is the moment of moral ecstasy. The hero is *so right* (that is, so wronged) that he can kill with impunity. And we are with him one hundred percent. The feeling of supreme righteousness in this instant is delicious and hardly to be distinguished from murderousness. I would almost say they are the same thing.

I want to switch now to a different *mise en scène:* an academic 7 conference, where a woman is giving a paper. It is an attack on another woman's recent book; the entire paper is devoted to demolishing it, and the speaker is doing a superb job. The audience has begun to catch the spirit of the paper, which is witty, elegant, pellucid, and razor sharp; they appreciate the deftness, the brilliance, the grace, with which the assassination is being conducted; the speaker's intelligence flatters their intelligence, her taste becomes their taste, her principles their principles. They start to laugh at the jokes. They are inside the paper now, pulling with the speaker, seeing her victim in the same way she does, as the enemy, as someone whose example should be held up to scorn because her work is pernicious and damaging to the cause. (For my purposes here, it doesn't matter what the cause is, what the speaker was right about, or what sins the victim was guilty of.)

Listening to the paper, which I admired very much for the perfor- 8 mance values I've mentioned, I began to feel more and more uncomfortable. The more the audience pulled with the speaker, the more I shrank away. The sensation I felt was fear. I was afraid that this woman might someday turn her attack on me—indeed, in one of her devastating sideswipes, I thought I had already been anonymously grazed by her dagger—and I imagined the audience, which only the day before had enthusiastically applauded my own presentation, turning on me like a pack of dogs. By the time the paper was over, I felt as if I had been present at a ritual execution of some sort, something halfway between a bullfight, where the crowd admires the skill of the matador and enjoys his triumph over the bull, and a public burning, where the crowd witnesses the just punishment of a criminal. For the academic experience combined the elements of admiration, bloodlust, and moral self-congratulation.

Afterwards, I began to recall in a kind of phantasmagoria all the 9 essays I had read where similar executions had occurred. It wasn't the essays themselves that came to mind as much as the moves they characteristically made. The audience, a moment ago, had laughed loudest when the victim's stylistic gaffes were held up to scorn, and I remembered the times I had seen someone's diction ridiculed, or their unhappy choice of metaphor derided. I remembered the shapes of dismemberment: occasions when the absurd consequences of the victim's arguments were displayed for all to see, the innumerable times people had been garrotted by their own self-contradictions. But most vivid of all were the moments when the characterological defects implicit in someone's style or point of view were indignantly paraded

by. Following traditional lines of thought was translated into cowardice; dependence on another scholar's work into toadyism; failing to
mention another critic's work into lack of generosity, and so on. The
list is practically endless. In veiled language, I realized, we accuse one
another of stupidity, ignorance, fear, envy, pride, malice, and hypoc-
risy; we picture those with whom we disagree as monsters of inhuman-
ity and manage to insinuate that they lack social graces as well as social
conscience and moral virtue; we hint that they are insensitive,
pompous, narrow, affected, shrill, exhibitionistic, and boring. We feel
justified in exposing these errors to view, that they may be scourged
not in the sight of God, since no god presides over modern warfare, but
in the sight of our professional peers and superiors. We feel justified in
this because we are right, so right, and they, like the villains in the
western, are wrong, so wrong.

Lost thus in amazement at the venality of my fellow human beings, I 10
remembered something else, an essay I had published in 1981 that,
twice anthologized since then, had been in many ways the making of
my career. Strange that such an essay should pop into mind. And then
I realized: the essay began with a frontal assault on another woman
scholar. When I wrote it I felt the way the hero does in a western. Not
only had this critic argued *a*, *b*, and *c*, she had held *x*, *y*, and *z!* It was a
clear case of outrageous provocation. Moreover, she was famous and I
was not. She was teaching at a prestigious university and I was not. She
had published a major book and I had not. In this David and Goliath
situation—my slingshot against her ca(n)non—surely I was justified in
hitting her with everything I had. And so, casting myself as champion
of the oppressed, and wielding scare quotes and withering sarcasm, I
showed the world the evil of her ways and out of the shambles of her
position went on to build the temple of my own. The actual onslaught
only lasted a page and a half, but the sense of outrage that produced it
fueled me as I wrote the entire essay; sometimes, I would even reopen
her book to get back my sense of passionate conviction.

The showdown on main street isn't the prerogative of the western; 11
it's not the special province of men (as opposed to women); or of
popular culture as opposed to literary criticism. TV cop shows, Rambo
and Dirty Harry, and their fans do not occupy a different moral
universe from the one populated by academicians. Violence takes place
in the conference rooms at scholarly meetings and in the pages of
professional journals; and although it's not the same thing to savage a
person's book as it is to kill them with a machine gun, I suspect that the
nature of the feelings that motivate both acts is qualitatively the same.
This bloodless kind of violence that takes place in our profession is not
committed by other people; it's practiced at some time or other by

virtually everyone. *Have gun, will travel* is just as fitting a theme for academic achievers as it was for Paladin.

These remarks could be expanded considerably and their im- 12 plications variously drawn out. It would be possible, for instance, to look at what I've said within the context of entrepreneurial capitalism, which presumably creates an incentive and framework for both the sorts of confrontational behavior I've been describing. Or, the scenario could be contextualized institutionally, where the competitive nature of academic professionalism could be blamed for the patterns of conduct chronicled here. But although I think it would be fruitful to examine such circumstantial constraints, I find myself focusing inward, drawn back to the moment when I returned to my adversary's text for replenishment. I did so instinctively because I knew subconsciously that it would sharpen my mind, energize my body, strengthen my will—in short, that it would restore vigor and momentum to my argument. In order to go on, I needed to feel again the moment when the villains go too far, the moment of righteous wrath which sweeps everything else away. At that precise instant, something inside says "charge." It is an experience of tremendous empowerment. You feel, temporarily, invincible. All the faculties are galvanized, perfectly aligned, ready to do to your will. It's the moment to look out for, the moment whose content and whose consequences need to be examined.

These remarks have a moralistic tendency, to say the least, and at 13 this juncture, it would seem I ought to say something like, "and so the cowboys and the farmers should be friends," or "do unto other critics as you would have other critics do unto you." I believe in peace and I believe in the Golden Rule, but I don't believe I've earned the right to such pronouncements. At least not yet. It's difficult to unlearn the habits of a lifetime, and this very essay has been fueled by a good deal of the righteousness it is in the business of questioning. So instead of offering you a moral, I call your attention to a moment: the moment of righteous ecstasy, the moment when you know you have the moral advantage of your adversary, the moment of murderousness. It's a moment when there's still time to stop, there's still time to reflect, there's still time to recall what happened in *High Noon*, there's still time to say: "I don't care who's right or who's wrong. There has to be some better way to live."

Questions

1. As you see it, what is the main point of Tompkins's essay? What does Tompkins aim to do to and for her readers by making this point?
2. Tompkins posits an analogy between Westerns and the critical or argumenta-

tive essay. What is the basis for the analogy she posits? Is she explicit about the basis for her analogy? Does she note differences as well as resemblances between Westerns and critical arguments? Although writers are often advised to use analogies, they are also told to beware of committing the logical fallacy known as "false analogy." A false analogy occurs when a writer assumes that because one thing resembles another thing, conclusions based on a consideration of one thing automatically apply to the other thing. Do you think that Tompkins's essay commits the logical fallacy known as false analogy?

3. To what extent is Tompkins's essay an argument? In answering this question, consider both the essay's means and its ends. Are its formal features those we identified as characteristic of good arguments (p. 178)? Is the essay primarily a topic-oriented piece of writing that aims at truth? Or is it more a writer-oriented piece that works through reflection towards a better understanding of the past and present? Or is it primarily a reader-oriented work that appeals to the emotions instead of the mind?

4. In the beginning and end of her essay, Tompkins uses the same quote from *High Noon:* "I don't care who's right or who's wrong. There has to be some better way to live." Do you think this quote is an accurate description of Tompkins's attitude and conduct in her essay? What, if anything, differentiates the value judgments she makes from those promoted in and by the moral universe of Western reason? In short, are ethics and moralism the same thing? What about values and morals?

PRACTICE

Is There a Better Way?

In "Fighting Words," Jane Tompkins doesn't just say that there must be a better way to live and write. She also experiments with the form of argumentation, as if she were intent on inventing or discovering some other, nonadversarial way of presenting and supporting a thesis. This practice invites you to do something similar: to experiment with the form of argumentation by trying out another way of presenting a thesis.

At issue are the means and ends of argumentation. What do you find to be true about argumentation? What do you believe makes an argument good? What do you think it is possible to achieve in and through argument? To answer these questions, reflect on the reading and writing you've done while working through this chapter on argumentation. Then, put your answers in the form of a tentative thesis or hypothesis about the means and ends of argumentation.

Keeping your hypothesis in mind, try arguing it in a nonadversarial way. For example, you might stage a dialogue between the Jane Tompkins of "Fighting Words" and the Stephen Jay Gould of "Integrity and Mr. Rifkin." In writing such a dialogue, you can implicitly present and explore *your* ideas by allowing Tompkins and Gould to argue the issues with one another until one or both of them either takes up or refuses to take up your position. If you think that something dialogical but less explicitly dramatic would be better, then you might try writing an essay in which you work through your reflections on Gould's and Tompkins's arguments until you reach a thesis or position on the means and ends of argumentation that you can live with. If neither of these options appeals to you, then you might want to experiment with presenting and supporting your thesis in some other form of writing such as direction, narration, or analysis. But remember that the purpose of this practice is to try out some nonadversarial way of making an argument about arguments. And the question is, "Is the way you tried really a better way?"

11. SYNTHESIS

Putting Things Together

The production of a synthetic text calls upon all of an individual's writing skills. Ideally, a synthesis is not just an argument, for it seeks to make sense of a complex body of material rather than to argue for one point of view over another. A synthesis may even conclude that two opposing views are both partly right. Still less is synthesis an explicit act of persuasion, since its appeal is more to reason than to emotion. Nevertheless, a strong synthetic text has some of the cohesive qualities of an argument and some of the liveliness of persuasion. Moreover, it displays the kind of personal engagement associated with reflective writing, even though it focuses on ideas rather than experiential events.

In constructing a synthesis, the writer must examine a body of material and apply the processes of analysis and classification in such a way that he or she can develop a hypothesis about this material. In a synthetic text, the thesis is always a hypothesis, a provisional idea to be explored, explained, supported, and qualified by reference to the material at issue. Although a synthetic text may be organized like an argument, it is usually as concerned to raise questions as it is to provide answers. A major fault in this kind of writing can be claiming to have proved the hypothesis once and for all.

In order to generate a hypothesis, you need to understand a body of material. But in order to understand a body of material, you need some hypothesis or organizing principle. This seems to present a problem so circular that it cannot be solved. But in practice, you begin to work through your materials with one or more possible ideas already in mind. You try classification and analysis to see if they can help you to shape the material in a way that leads you to formulate a clearer, working hypothesis. Sometimes you'll find that more material must be gathered before you can develop and support a certain hypothesis. In doing this, you may discover new questions and new directions to explore. The hypothesis you eventually settle on will be limited by the data you're working with and you must acknowledge this limitation in two ways: by not claiming more than your data will support and by not ignoring significant material in your data base.

Writing a synthesis paper involves a process of moving back and forth from your material to your writing. It may well involve starting to write, stopping, returning to the material, discarding some of what you have done, beginning over again. For some people, written outlines are extremely helpful. For others, sketchy notes, diagrams, and mental outlines will be more important. Each individual must find the appropriate way. Practice helps. But as every writer of synthetic essays discovers, you can't simply gather material aimlessly and then sit down and write. You must think about the text you will write as you work through the material you've gathered.

READING AND PRACTICE

How Should Photographs Be "Read"?

The special nature of the photographic image has led to a wide difference of opinion about how photographs should be interpreted, or "read." In this synthesis project we aim to involve you in that controversy. Before presenting you with some pictures, and words about pictures, however, we want to offer a brief sketch of the nature of the controversy about photography. Later on, you may find this sketch too neat and simple; but it should serve you—and us—as a place to start.

A photograph can be seen as a document—a record of a moment snatched from history—or as a work of art—a text free of simple connections to its origin and open to multiple interpretations. Knowing this, you might consider it a simple matter to divide all photographs into one category or the other, with documents here and art works there. But such division would lead to many problems if you tried it; some photographs would refuse to rest nicely in one category or the other. Some could be seen either as documents or as works of art and, in fact, would seem most properly described as belonging to both categories at the same time.

Another way to regard this problem is to see it not as a matter of categorizing individual photographs but as a matter of interpretation. How should a given photograph be interpreted? Must it be connected to its time and place of origin? Do we need to know where and when it was taken? Do we need to know what was "really" going on in front of the camera? Or can we use the image for our own purposes? Can we simply go where the photograph stimulates us to go, using it as a key to our own thoughts, feelings, and dreams?

The material in this section should make the issues involved in "reading" photographs more concrete and more complicated for you. We ask you to consider and discuss these materials as the basis for an essay on the interpretation of photographic images. Later we will offer some advice about how to proceed in writing. For the moment, however, you need only read and consider. Take your time. Stop and think about the words and images that follow.

Jean Mohr, "A Photo and Some Reactions," from *Another Way of Telling*

On one occasion, the photographer and teacher Jean Mohr showed a group of people a particular photograph and asked them to interpret it. He gives us their reactions and then tells us what was actually happening. Before you read any of the responses, jot down what comes into your mind when you look at the picture on page 245.

Market-gardener: (Laughs) This one makes me think of a little girl   1
who already has a maternal capacity, and who's treating her doll like it was her own baby. All right, the doll is not pretty and is undressed, but it's hers!

Clergyman: An odd photo. Should one protect children from seeing   2
the cruelty of the world? Should one hide certain aspects of reality from them? Her hands over the doll's eyes shouldn't be there. One ought to be able to show everything, to see all.

Schoolgirl: She's crying because her doll hasn't any clothes.   3

Banker: Well-fed, well-dressed, such a child is probably spoilt.   4
Given the luxury of no material worries, people can give in to any whim or fancy.

Actress: "My baby is crying but doesn't want to show it." What   5
surprises me is how she hides the doll's face. There's a strong sense of identification between the doll and the child. The girl is playing out what is happening to the doll and what the doll feels. The vine in the background is strange. . . .

Dance-teacher: She has everything, yet she doesn't realize it, she is 6
crying with her eyes shut. And the tree behind. The doll is as big as she
is.

Psychiatrist: It puzzles me. She's crying as if she has a pain, and yet 7
she's well. She's crying on behalf of her doll, and she covers the eyes as
if there was a sight which shouldn't be seen.

Hairdresser: It's a child and somebody has tried to take her doll, 8
which is precious to her. She's going to hold on to it. Perhaps she's
German, she's blonde. It makes me think of myself when I was that
age.

Factory worker: It's sweet. It reminds me of my niece when her 9
sister tries to take her doll away from her. She's crying, screaming,
because someone wants to take her doll away.

What was happening: Great Britain, in the country. A small girl was 10
playing with her doll. Sometimes sweetly, sometimes brutally. At one
moment she even pretended to eat her doll.

Questions

1. Compare your written response to the picture with those of Mohr's respon-
dents and with your classmates' responses. Which responses do you find most
interesting? Why?
2. What makes a "good" response good? Is it a matter of "correctness" or "imagination" or what?

Allan Sekula, from "On the Invention of Photographic Meaning"

I would like to conclude with a rather schematic summary. All
photographic communication seems to take place within the conditions
of a kind of binary folklore. That is, there is a "symbolist" folk-myth and
a "realist" folk-myth. The misleading but popular form of this opposition is "art photography" vs. "documentary photography." Every
photograph tends, at any given moment of reading in any given context, toward one of these two poles of meaning. The oppositions
between these two poles are as follows: photographer as seer vs.
photographer as witness, photography as expression vs. photography
as reportage, theories of imagination (and inner truth) vs. theories of
empirical truth, affective value vs. informative value. . . .

Questions

1. Summarize in your own words the differences between the two notions of photography that Sekula describes.
2. Is Sekula talking about two kinds of photograph or two ways of seeing photographs?
3. Can photographs be described in any other way than those Sekula defines? Can these two opposed descriptions be combined or surpassed? What is a photograph?

John Berger Reads a Photograph (from *Another Way of Telling*)

A mother with her child is staring intently at a soldier. Perhaps they 1 are speaking. We cannot hear their words. Perhaps they are saying nothing and everything is being said by the way they are looking at each other. Certainly a drama is being enacted between them.

The caption reads: "A Red Hussar leaving, June 1919, Budapest." 2 The photograph is by André Kertész.

So, the woman has just walked out of their home and will shortly go 3 back alone with the child. The drama of the moment is expressed in the difference between the clothes they are wearing. His for travelling, for sleeping out, for fighting; hers for staying at home.

The caption can also entail other thoughts. The Hapsburg monarchy 4
had fallen the previous autumn. The winter had been one of extreme
shortages (especially of fuel in Budapest) and economic disintegration.
Two months before, in March, the socialist Republic of Councils had
been declared. The Western allies in Paris, fearful lest the Russian and
now the Hungarian example of revolution should spread throughout
Eastern Europe and the Balkans, were planning to dismantle the new
republic. A blockade was already imposed. General Foch himself was
planning the military invasion being carried out by Rumanian and
Czech troops. On June 8th Clemenceau telegraphed an ultimatum to
Béla Kun demanding a Hungarian military withdrawal which would
have left the Rumanians occupying the eastern third of their country.
For another six weeks the Hungarian Red Army fought on, but it was
finally overwhelmed. By August, Budapest was occupied and very
soon after, the first European fascist regime under Horthy was established.

If we are looking at an image from the past and we want to relate it 5
to ourselves, we need to know something of the history of that past.
And so the foregoing paragraph—and much more than that might be
said—is relevant to the reading of Kertész's photograph. Which is
presumably why he gave it the caption he did and not just the title
"Parting." Yet the photograph—or rather, the way this photograph
demands to be read—cannot be limited to the historical.

Everything in it is historical: the uniforms, the rifles, the corner by 6
the Budapest railway station, the identity and biographies of all the
people who are (or were) recognizable—even the size of the trees on
the other side of the fence. And yet it also concerns a resistance to
history: an opposition.

This opposition is not the consequence of the photographer having 7
said Stop! It is not that the resultant static image is like a fixed post in a
flowing river. We know that in a moment the soldier will turn his back
and leave; we presume that he is the father of the child in the woman's
arms. The significance of the instant photographed is already claiming
minutes, weeks, years.

The opposition exists in the parting look between the man and the 8
woman. This look is not directed towards the viewer. We witness it as
the older soldier with the moustache and the woman with the shawl
(perhaps a sister) do. The exclusivity of this look is further emphasized
by the boy in the mother's arms; he is watching his father, and yet he is
excluded from their look.

This look, which crosses before our eyes, is holding in place what *is*, 9
not specifically what is there around them outside the station, but what
is their life, what *are* their lives. The woman and the soldier are
looking at each other so that the image of what *is* now shall remain for

them. In this look their being *is* opposed to their history, even if we assume that this history is one they accept or have chosen.

Questions

1. Using Sekula's terminology, describe Berger's way of reading the photograph. Now, describe it in your own words.
2. What do you like and dislike in Berger's way of reading? How important do you think it is to know the historical context of a photograph?

John Berger on the Use of Photography (from *About Looking*)

We need to return to the distinction I made between the private   1
and public uses of photography. In the private use of photography, the context of the instant recorded is preserved so that the photograph lives in an ongoing continuity. (If you have a photograph of Peter on your wall, you are not likely to forget what Peter means to you.) The public photograph, by contrast, is torn from its context, and becomes a dead object which, exactly because it is dead, lends itself to any arbitrary use.

In the most famous photographic exhibition ever organized, *The*   2
Family of Man (put together by Edward Steichen in 1955), photographs from all over the world were presented as though they formed a universal family album. Steichen's intuition was absolutely correct: the private use of photographs can be exemplary for their public use. Unfortunately the shortcut he took in treating the existing class-divided world as if it were a family, inevitably made the whole exhibition, not necessarily each picture, sentimental and complacent. The truth is that most photographs taken of people are about suffering, and most of that suffering is man-made.

"One's first encounter," writes Susan Sontag, "with the photograph-   3
ic inventory of ultimate horror is a kind of revelation, the prototypically modern revelation: a negative epiphany. For me, it was photographs of Bergen-Belsen and Dachau which I came across by chance in a bookstore in Santa Monica in July 1945. Nothing I have seen—in photographs or in real life—ever cut me as sharply, deeply, instantaneously. Indeed, it seems plausible to me to divide my life into two parts, before I saw those photographs (I was twelve) and after, though it was several years before I understood fully what they were about."

Photographs are relics of the past, traces of what has happened. If   4
the living take that past upon themselves, if the past becomes an integral part of the process of people making their own history, then all photographs would reacquire a living context, they would continue to exist in time, instead of being arrested moments. It is just possible that

photography is the prophecy of a human memory yet to be socially and politically achieved. Such a memory would encompass any image of the past, however tragic, however guilty, within its own continuity. The distinction between the private and public uses of photography would be transcended. The Family of Man would exist.

Questions

1. What do you think Berger means about *The Family of Man* exhibition being "sentimental and complacent"? Have you seen that exhibit or the book made from it? If so, what is your own view of the matter?
2. Berger makes a distinction between the private and public uses of photography. Do you understand what he means by these two kinds of use? Can you put his definitions in your own words? Does it make sense to you? Is this the same as the distinction described by Sekula between the photograph as document and as symbol?

READING

Three Photographs in Context

Gisèle Freund on Doisneau's Photograph (from *Photography & Society*)

The photographer Robert Doisneau saw one of his photographs used in a different context from his intention. For him, Parisians had always been the most fascinating of subjects. He loved to wander the streets and stop at cafés. One day, in a small café on the rue de Seine where he was accustomed to meeting his friends, he noticed a delightful young woman at the bar drinking a glass of wine. She was seated next to a middle-aged gentleman who was looking at her with a smile that was both amused and greedy. Doisneau asked and received permission to photograph them. The photograph appeared in the magazine *le Point*, in an issue devoted to cafés illustrated with Doisneau's photographs. He handed this photograph, among others, to his agency.

All sorts of publications call on agencies when they need pictures to illustrate an article. Sometime later, Doisneau's photograph appeared in a small magazine published by the temperance league to illustrate an article on the evils of alcohol. The gentleman in the photograph, who was a drawing instructor, was not pleased. "I shall be taken for a boozer," he complained to the apologetic photographer who had no control over how his photographs were used. Things went from bad to worse when the same photograph appeared in a scandal sheet which had reproduced it from *le Point* without the permission of either the agency or the photographer. The caption accompanying the photograph read: *"Prostitution in the Champs-Elysées."* This time the drawing teacher was furious and sued the magazine, the agency, and the photographer. The court fined the scandal magazine a large sum of money for fraud, and the agency, which had not released the photograph, was also found guilty. But the court acquitted the photographer, ruling that he was an "innocent artist."

[Doisneau's photograph is reproduced on page 252.]

From an Interview with Robert Doisneau (in *Dialogue with Photography*)

Don't you think that there is a certain historical value in your 1
picture?

Well, if this is correct, it is despite me, it wasn't a conscious aim of 2
mine. But if my work is of historical interest, so much the better. My
idea was much more egotistic, it was to hold the world that I loved! . . .

You just said that your photographic purpose was egotistic. Was 3
that a conscious intent?

"Intent" is often unconscious. It is the game of seizing and delaying! 4
There is something in Prévert that is wonderful—the "small second of
eternity." Nothing is more beautiful than this expression for me. It
appears in a poem called "Jardin" in *Parc Montsouris:*

> The bench of the Montsouris park 5
> Where you kissed me and I kissed you
> In the Montsouris park in Paris
> On the earth that is astral and that is all
> And this small second of eternity.

And this is it! This "small second of eternity" that we are lucky 6
enough to be able to find! The understanding of this is not yet visible
for all people. But when a tiny bit of this "small second" is captured by
photography, when it is put in a rectangle that has a form accepted by
culture or scholastic training, then people look and say, "Oh, yes!"
Maybe it would be ideal to think that, afterward, these same people
would want to go out and see for themselves. That would really be
success! But I don't think it will happen. I believe that the more time
goes by, the more people will use substitute experts. People will
delegate their eyes to the eye specialists! It is easier and more comfortable to let specialists be accountable for filtering our responses to life
than to face them ourselves. Already, people seem willing to delegate
all their senses to specialists.

Robert Doisneau, A Parisian Café

You were suggesting a while ago that you would like people to take 7
photographs and photographers more seriously.

I hate collectors, the ones who take something just for themselves. 8
Me, I like to give. I like to discover something and show it. I'm the
village idiot who goes off to the forest and comes back with a bird in his
hat and walks around everywhere saying, "Look and see what I've
unearthed!" And this bird of an unknown species immediately bothers
notable people simply because they don't know how to categorize it.
They never saw that kind of bird before, so they say: "Yes, it's amusing.
Now go play elsewhere and let us be, because we're talking about
serious things." This is a bit like the photographer's role now.

I do pictures as gifts for my friends. They are people who are my 9
accomplices, and I am very happy to tell them: "Here, just look at what
I've unearthed!" I am happy that it might make them chuckle a little
bit, like the way I chuckled inside when I took the picture. Or maybe
it's an emotion more delicate than chuckling. I want to give, *always* to
give.

There are certain things that you seek, situations that you wait for? 10

I am not interested in refined culture, but rather in instinctive 11
things. I wait for surprise, to be surprised, I do not ever want to have a
preconceived idea, or to bring back mere pictorial souvenirs.

Often, you find a scene, a scene that already is evoking something— 12
either stupidity, or pretentiousness, or, perhaps, charm. So you have a
little theater. Well, all you have to do is wait there in front of this little
theater for the actors to present themselves. I often operate in this
way. Here I have my setting and I wait. What I am waiting for, I don't
know exactly. I can stay half a day in the same place. And it's very rare
that I come home with a completely empty bag.

Photography is very subjective. Photography is not a document on 13
which a report can be made. It is a *subjective* document. Photography
is a false witness, a lie. People want to prove the universe is there. It is
a physical image that contains a certain amount of documentation,
which is fine, but it isn't evidence, a testimony upon which a general
philosophy can be based. People can say, "Here is a fellow who has
seen such and such facets of life, but not the whole."

If it is not about reality, what does photography mean to you? 14

It might involve the principle of the committed photographer who 15
thinks of himself as socially responsible. There may be something there
that is important. You may chose to report on a socially deprived area.
Most people would not take their cameras to these places. But the
committed photographer may reveal a certain aspect of the condition of
people's lives there. Photographers have done this, and I find that this

is one of the great merits of photography. Beforehand, apart from the few paintings, there were no documents of the actual social environment. The people of Viva who took pictures of low-income-housing projects did work that was very interesting. Whether it is reality or not, it is, nevertheless, the penetration of an environment that had never been seen in a picture before. The fact that the photographer may have this social responsibility is very important because he will be showing something that most people may hold in contempt, that they may want to hide.

You take a certain type of picture—how do you relate this to your 16
political ideology?

I am not militant. The photography profession doesn't permit me to 17
be militant. When you're militant you really have to spend a lot of time
at it. You really have to found your life on it. Whereas my militancy is
photographic and *all* my life, if I can, if I have enough will, if I am not
overwhelmed by paperwork and red tape, I spend taking pictures.
Thus, I do have convictions that are, if you like, political. My photos
are not pictures that say, "Here is good and evil, right and wrong." If
my work speaks, it does so by being a little less serious, a little less
solemn, and by its lightness it helps people to live. I think that this is a
social role that isn't negligible. I don't say that it is important, but just
that it isn't negligible. I would rather *help* people through photography
than produce "symbolic images" for propaganda purposes. I work more
in everyday chronicles and with "smallness." I would not be at ease
doing violent or "heavy" things.

From an Interview with Gordon Parks (in *The Photographs of Gordon Parks*)

Bush: Your work at the [Chicago] South Side Community Art Cen- 1
ter won you a Julius Rosenwald Fellowship in 1941. It was $200 a
month, and you chose to go to Washington in January 1942 to work
with Roy Stryker at the Farm Security Administration.

Parks: Yes, those were the photographers whose work I had seen 2
while I was working on the railroad. I went to work for Roy Stryker
at the Farm Security Administration. That's where I met Ben
Shahn, Russell Lee, Dorothea Lange and a number of others. Walker
Evans had gone by then. That was a great time in my life. And Stryker
taught me the importance of the camera in terms of being a documentary tool.

Bush: You also learned that Washington was a southern city, didn't 3
you?

Parks: I found out what prejudice was really like. I expected Wash- 4
ington, D.C., as the seat of our government, to be the one place where
I could find democracy. And that was the one place I didn't find
democracy. I found that discrimination and bigotry were worse there
than any place I had yet seen.

Bush: This was the time when you took the picture of the woman in 5
front of the American flag.

Parks: Yes, Stryker had taken my camera away from me when I got 6
to D.C. and told me to go out and get to know Washington. I went to
the motion pictures and was refused; I went to a place called Julius
Garfinkel, a big department store, and the clerk wouldn't sell me a
coat. They wouldn't feed me at several restaurants. I was furious. I
wanted to photograph discrimination. Roy said, "You just don't go out
and photograph discrimination. How do you do it? This is what you
have to learn. I want you to sit down and write me a long set of plans
about how you would attempt to do it." Of course, it was very difficult
for me. I didn't know how to do it. Finally, he sent me to talk with a
black charwoman who worked in the building. "You will find out a lot
from the lady," he said. And I did. I found out that she had been a
charwoman there for many years. Yet, she had been to high school,
and she deserved a much better job. I took her into a room where
there was an American flag draped on a wall. I posed her against
it—Grant Wood style—with a mop in one hand and a broom in the
other. When Roy saw that photograph, he said, "You're going to get us
all fired." I thought the photograph had been destroyed, but I found it
in the Library of Congress. I realize now that it is possibly the most
popular photograph of that whole series. I thought that it had long
since been destroyed.

Bush: You have often said since then: "I had learned how to fight 7
the evil of poverty—along with the evil of racism—with a camera."
How did you learn to do this? How have your feelings changed over
the years, if indeed they have, since you first became a photographer?

Parks: The photograph of the black cleaning woman standing in 8
front of the American flag with a broom and a mop expresses that more
than any other photograph I have taken. It was the first one I took in
Washington, D.C. I thought then, and Roy Stryker eventually proved
it to me, that you could not photograph a person who turns you away
from the motion picture ticket window, or someone who refuses to
feed you, or someone who refuses to wait on you in a store. You could
not photograph him and say, "This is a bigot," because bigots have a
way of looking just like everybody else. What the camera had to do was
expose the evils of racism, the evils of poverty, the discrimination and
the bigotry, by showing the people who suffered most under it. That
was the way it had to be done. . . .

Gordon Parks, American Gothic (Washington, D.C., 1942)

Bush: What were your basic assignments [when you joined the 9 Farm Security Administration]?

Parks: I was a documentary man. Roy wanted me to show the "face 10 of America." He wasn't just interested in showing the poverty-stricken. He wanted to capture on film the character of the New England farmer, the upstate New York businessman—whatever. There were other things to photograph besides poverty-stricken people. . . .

Bush: When you met Alexander Lieberman and people in the 11 fashion business, you must admit, in retrospect, that you really were not yet an experienced fashion photographer. But, when you free-lanced for Vogue and Glamour, you were really in the "big time." Was it just nerve, confidence, or had you just learned that fast? You learn things very fast.

Parks: I learned very fast, Martin. I had to learn fast. After my 12 mother died, it was a matter of survival. I had to learn fast. I didn't have a formal education. I had to do it on plain dreams, guts and hope. That's what it was. The determination that, by God, I'm going to do it. I wanted to be somebody. For some reason or other, I don't know why, even today—I sometimes attribute it to my mother—I never thought of my blackness when I did anything. Even today, I don't think of my blackness. I work as an artist who happens to be black. And I tell the kids that this is the only way. . . .

Bush: When did you begin writing as well as photographing Life 13 magazine articles?

Parks: I did my own research sometimes. I did my research in 14 Chicago while I was doing a story called, "The Modern Shouting Baptist." The white lad who was with me offended people there by not taking off his hat. The kid was very nice. He didn't mean any offense. But the members of the church were very uptight about it. So he told me that he had better not go back. I had better do it all; and I did. That's how I happened to start writing. . . .

Bush: You took an extraordinary photograph of an old woman five 15 minutes before she died. Was that an invasion of her privacy?

Parks: Oh, yes, but she had been conscious enough to know it. She 16 knew I was there. There were situations that I feel were more private, incidents while I was with Roberto Rosellini and Ingrid Bergman on Stromboli and while I was with Muhammad Ali. Ali had a busted jaw. He had invited me to his room, but I would not take the picture. George Plimpton (in his book) wondered why I never took that picture because he was sitting there with me. But, at the moment, I thought more of my friendship with Ali than I did about being a reporter, and my responsibilities as a reporter. This was a guy who had befriended me over the years. I would not photograph him that way.

Martin Bush on Gordon Parks (from *The Photographs of Gordon Parks*)

People are Gordon Parks' passion, all kinds of people: hungry 1
people, fashionable people, famous people. . . . They speak to us about
ourselves and about the world around us, and the viewer is constantly
reminded that poverty, hunger and intolerance are still three of the
most awful things that mankind has to endure.

Parks is no stranger to frustration and despair. He witnessed first- 2
hand how easily crime, drugs, prostitution and apathy claimed their
victims as he fought his way through the violent streets of urban
ghettos to emerge in places where few blacks dared to go—or even
aspired to go. But Parks freed himself from the past and turned his
own bitterness and violence into something positive. "When I felt I
couldn't say what was in me, I turned to photography," he said. "I
learned that it would enable me to show what was right and wrong
about America, the world and life. I wanted my children and my
children's children to be able to look at my pictures and know what my
world was like. My purpose has been to communicate, to somehow
evoke the same response from a seamstress in Paris or a housewife in
Harlem." . . .

Parks' big breakthrough came . . . later when Life magazine offered 3
him a full-time staff position as a photographer. "When I first went to
Life in 1949, I was the worst photographer they had," said Parks. "I
asked for and accepted help whenever I needed it, knowing that I
walked a tightrope; feeling the pressure of succeeding for blacks,
because I was black, and proving myself to certain whites who resented
my presence."

Later on, Parks could look back with pride on what he had achieved, 4
secure in the knowledge that he had become one of the magazine's
most versatile and talented photographers, a man who was at home in
the raw and often dangerous arena of photojournalism, or in the lush
world of high fashion.

But Life was only a step toward more significant things. What 5
things? Parks had no idea at the time. Still, that did not seem to
matter. "I felt," he said, "that I was working on a larger canvas. . . ."
That larger canvas would soon include a three-volume autobiography,
three books of poetry that were illustrated with his own photographs,
a novel, a ballet, several sonatas and symphonies, and musical scores
for two films. Parks eventually left Life to pursue an entirely new
form of expression—the motion pictures—and successfully directed
five major films. In recent years he has continued to seek an even
wider artistic expression by combining painting with his photography.

Eve Arnold on Her Work (from *The Unretouched Woman*)

Twenty-five years ago, when I became a photojournalist, I was 1
looked on as someone apart—a "career lady," a "woman photographer." My colleagues were not spoken of in inverted commas; they were
not "career men" or "men photographers." I was not happy about it,
but realized as have women before me that it was a fundamental part of
female survival to play the assigned rôle. I could not fight against those
attitudes. I needed to know more about other women to try to understand what made me acquiesce in this situation.

It was then that I started my project, photographing and talking to 2
women. I became both observer and participant. I photographed girl
children and women; the rich and the poor; the migratory potato
picker on Long Island and the Queen of England; the nomad bride in
the Hindu Kush waiting for a husband she had never seen, and the
Hollywood Queen Bee whose life was devoted to a regimen of beauty
care. There was the Zulu woman whose child was dying of hunger and
women mourning their dead in Hoboken, New Jersey. I filmed in
harems in Abu Dhabi, in bars in Cuba, and in the Vatican in Rome.
There was birth in London and betrothal in the Caucasus, divorce in
Moscow and protest marches of black women in Virginia. There were
the known and the unknown—and always those marvelous faces.

I am not a radical feminist, because I don't believe that siege 3
mentality works. But I know something of the problems and the
inequities of being a woman, and over the years the women I photographed talked to me about themselves and their lives. Each had her
own story to tell—uniquely female but also uniquely human.

Themes recur again and again in my work. I have been poor and I 4
wanted to document poverty; I had lost a child and I was obsessed with
birth; I was interested in politics and I wanted to know how it affected
our lives; I am a woman and I wanted to know about women.

I realize now that through my work these past twenty-five years I 5
have been searching for myself, my time, and the world I live in. . . .

I was anxious not to take just pretty pictures. I wanted my work to 6
have a purpose, to make a social comment, no matter how slight; to say
something about the world I lived in. . . .

When Bob Capa saw my photographs for the first time he said that 7
for him—metaphorically, of course—my work fell between Marlene
Dietrich's legs and the bitter lives of migrant potato pickers. I wonder
if he knew how close to the mark he was about me.

I want to deal with the "migrants" part first. As a second-generation 8
American, daughter of Russian immigrants, growing up during the
Depression, the reality I knew well was poverty and deprivation. So I
could identify easily with laborers who followed the potato crop north

along the Eastern seaboard, settling in each new area as the harvest was ready for them.

Now, about Marlene's legs—metaphorically, of course. I also grew 9 up with Hollywood movies. Although I was a reluctant host to their imagery, I could not deny their impact on me and on other women. They affected the way we saw ourselves and the way men saw us. The traditional still photograph was an idealized portrait. The subject was posed in the most flattering position, and the features were lit—eyes, lips, teeth, cheekbones, breasts, and in Dietrich's case, legs—like so many commodities. Wrinkles and blemishes were removed by the retoucher. Everything that life had deposited was penciled out.

When I photographed Marlene recording the songs she had sung to 10 the soldiers during World War II—"Lilli Marlene," "Miss Otis Regrets," etc.—I wanted the working woman, the unretouched woman.

From an Interview with Eve Arnold (in *Master Photographers*)

Eve Arnold's photographs demonstrate her passionate interest in 1 people, in the human and particularly the female predicament. She brings to her observations the sharply inquisitive, but at the same time uncensoring, eye of the journalist. She seeks to reveal inner meanings and truths by drawing attention to the unguarded moment when the subject has all but forgotten the presence of the camera, and she produces her vignettes unretouched, unposed, un-selfconscious. . . .

Would you call yourself a feminist? 2

I suppose I *am* a sort of half-baked feminist, and I do believe in the 3 feminist movement, but I have to say that it's been an enormous help to me to be a woman. You see, men like to be photographed by women, and women don't feel that they have to carry on a flirtation, which they often do with a male photographer.

Do you like commercial assignments? 4

I love the discipline that they demand. It teaches you great control, 5 and you have to draw on all your technical knowledge. Working with art directors isn't always easy, and sometimes you seem to be just clicking a shutter, but the organization that must precede the shoot is very comprehensive. I tend to be a very organized photographer, even when doing editorial work. I like to organize everything first, so that during the actual shoot I can loosen up and "play."

For example, when I first went to China in 1979 I had to rely on the Chinese to show me things, but I'd done my homework and I knew exactly what I wanted to see. So I asked them about religion and their art schools and their millionaires, because I knew that some capitalistic

Eve Arnold, Marlene Dietrich (United States, 1942)

principles had been reestablished. They hadn't been asked those sorts of questions before, and having been asked, they were quite happy to oblige. If I hadn't known what to ask for I would have seen all the usual sights that they had come to believe foreign journalists were interested in being shown. Preparation is the most important aspect of photojournalism—if you know what you want, most people will help you.

China is about as far removed from your photographs of the glam- 6
our and superficiality of Hollywood as anyone could imagine. Marlene Dietrich is perhaps the epitome of the glamorous woman and yet in these pictures you appear deliberately to have deglamorized her—why did you want to do that?

In this series of pictures I wanted to show her as she really was—a 7
working woman, quite different from the idealized version. Robert Capa got it right when he said, metaphorically, that my work fell between Marlene Dietrich's legs and the lives of migratory potato pickers!

Are you a technically minded person? 8
Not at all. I'm much more intuitive. For instance I never remember 9
what exposure I have given a picture—I just don't care. I bracket a lot, taking different exposures of the same subject, and I take pictures in situations and light conditions in which people say it can't be done. Often it works.

I remember one time when I took a photograph of a black girl in a dark hallway lit only by a 60 watt bulb. It shouldn't have come out, but it did, and I was happy with the result which was used as a double-page spread. If I had gone by the book and strobed it I wouldn't have got the picture I wanted.

I play these games because it's fun to play. After all, it's only film, and when it works it can be wonderful. I like to work on the edges of the film. With very little light and very slow film you can get some great images. It's dicey, and it doesn't always work, but when it does the rewards are enormous. I would far rather do anything than play it safe. I'm a gambler by nature and I think it has paid off. Of course I lose a lot of images, and I use up a lot more film, but it's vital to get something that is entirely my own.

How do you feel that magic working for you, when you are taking 10
pictures?
Even now when I work I may think that I've got something really 11
great, only to find that I haven't. It's not something I can explain. Perhaps it's best to let the images speak for themselves—at the end of the day they are the only things that matter.

I love photography. Maybe mystery is too big a word, but it has that unknown quantity about it. One thing I find interesting, and have only recently started to think about, is that in that split second when I actually press the shutter absolutely anything can happen. Other images are forming that perhaps I hadn't noticed. In that moment in time a new figure might appear—one that I hadn't anticipated. So I always get what I see, but often something else as well. Sometimes colour foxes me, too. There can be marvellous surprises, and disappointments, but it's the element of the unknown that keeps up my interest in photography.

Photography is now a recognized form of art, and prints sell for 12 *large sums. What do you feel about that?*

It's sad that a few elitist art pundits have made photography "es- 13 tablishment," and I think that its commercialization in terms of collecting limited editions and signed photographs is pretentious. I would prefer photographs to be cheap and available to everyone—students should be able to buy them to stick on their walls. I once asked a dear friend of mine—a gifted photographer—what the difference was between the photography of the fifties and that of today. He replied "That's easy. Photography in the fifties was about people. Now it's about photography."

Questions

1. Consider the titles or captions to the photographs by Doisneau, Parks, and Arnold. In what ways are the captions similar? In what ways are they different? Does each caption fit its photograph well? If it were up to you, how would you title each photograph?
2. Do these three pictures represent different approaches to photography? Can you relate them to the distinctions made earlier in this section by Sekula and Berger?
3. How does knowing something about the methods and purposes of each photographer affect the way you see and understand the pictures?
4. Do you prefer one of the three pictures? Why or why not?
5. What are your thoughts about photography after working through the materials presented here?

PRACTICE

Writing about Photographs

We would like you to write a synthesis paper about the reading or interpreting of photographs. In this paper, you should consider the various ways in which photographs can be read, and you should present your own theory about the best way to approach the interpretation of photographs. Your discussion should be based upon specific pictures. You may restrict yourself to those presented in this book, or you may introduce others, provided you supply copies of them with your finished paper. To help you get started, the following pages present a few additional photographs and some basic information about them.

In writing your paper, you need not discuss every picture that we present. Above all, you should not feel obliged to plod through discussions of each one in the order in which you find them here. Let your thoughts organize your whole essay, and let your discussions of individual photographs come where they are most appropriate to support your theory of interpretation. You should feel free to discuss more than one picture at a time, for the sake of comparison and contrast, or to discuss a number of works together to illustrate a point. If you wish, you may take up the question of an individual photographer's style, since you will have more than one picture by several well-known photographers to consider.

You need not confine yourself to the pictures immediately following, but may refer to others already presented in this book. For purposes of comparison and contrast, you may also refer to other kinds of visual images presented in the book, including images drawn from the worlds of art and advertising; but remember to emphasize photography. For many reasons, we have concentrated on black-and-white photography here, leaving the issue of color aside. We strongly suggest that you, too, accept this limitation. Remember that your task is to propose and demonstrate a theory about how photographs should be regarded, interpreted, or read, paying some attention to both their social and personal dimensions. You may, of course, cite statements about photography from material presented in this book or from other sources, provided you document such material according to whatever form your instructor recommends. The basic questions you should answer are, "What are photographs for?" "How should we look at them?" and "Why should we look at them in that way?"

Three More Photographs by Doisneau, Parks, and Arnold

Robert Doisneau, Sidelong Glance (Paris, 1948)

Gordon Parks, Muslim School Children (1963)

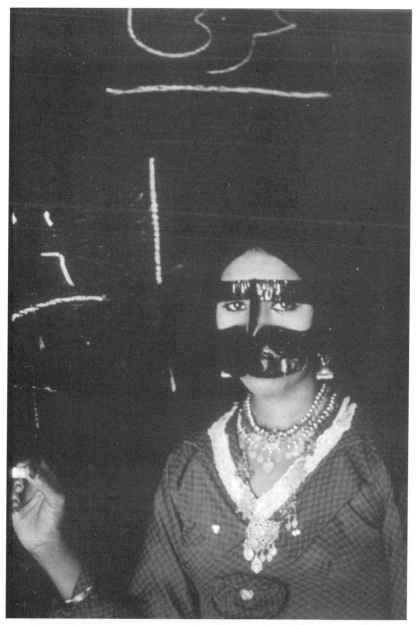

Eve Arnold, A Literacy Teacher in Abu Dhabi (1976)

Three Pictures from the Vietnam War Period

Associated Press, A Paratrooper Works to Save the Life of a Buddy

John Paul Filo, Student Killed by National Guardsmen, Kent State University, May 4, 1970

Huynh Cong (Nick) Ut, Children Fleeing a Napalm Strike, June 8, 1972

A Picture Album

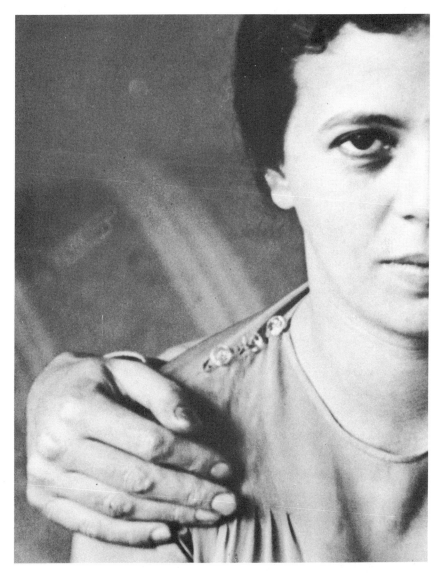

André Kertész, Elizabeth and I (Paris, 1931)

Dorothea Lange, Drought Refugees Hoping for Cotton Work (Blythe, California, 1936)

Russian and American troops meet at Torgau on the Elbe, April 27, 1945

Henri Cartier-Bresson, Athens (1953)

Automatic Reconnaissance Camera, Mirage Jet (July 1967)

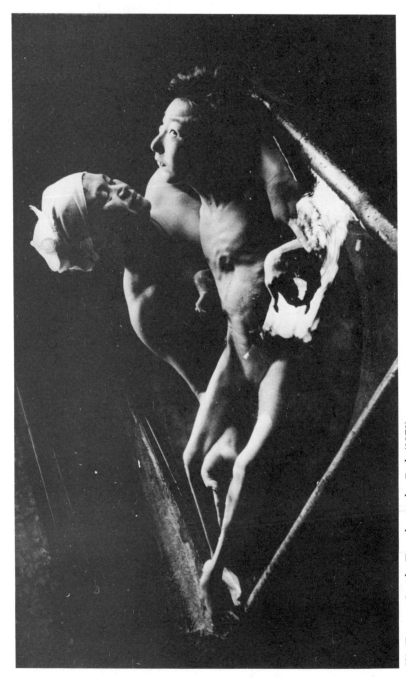

W. Eugene Smith, Tomoko in the Bath (1972)

(This is one of a series Smith made for his book *Minimata*, in which he recorded the victims of industrial pollution in a Japanese community. In this picture, a mother bathes her deformed child.)

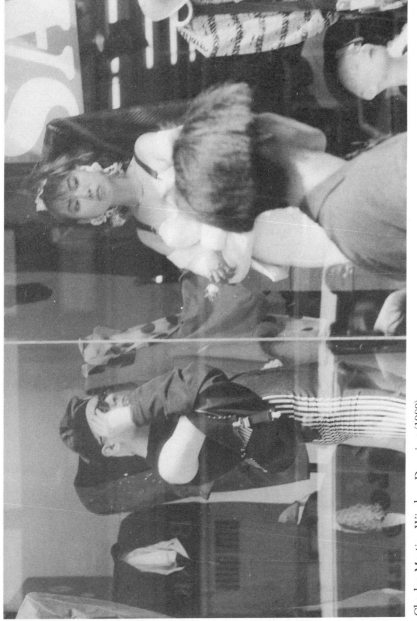

Charles Martin, Window Dressing (1989)

Working People

Here are a number of statements by working people, taken from various sources. Read the statements carefully, and then write a synthesis paper in which you present some hypothesis of your own about work and working that you can explore, support, or explain by referring to or quoting from the statements. Your instructor will indicate what form your documentation should take, such as footnotes or parenthetical citations.

Look for common themes or issues that appear in all or most of the source material. For instance, the issue of the worker's attitude toward work arises regularly in the statements, so a hypothesis about attitude might be possible, such as "X makes for happiness in work" or "Y makes for unhappiness."

Research: The Interview

Your instructor might want you to expand upon the data given in the next few pages by conducting your own interview and writing it up. Here are some suggestions.

1. A tape recorder is a great help in an interview, but if you don't have access to one, try to capture the voice of the person you interview by using direct quotation in your notes.
2. Begin your written account of the interview with a paragraph describing the person's work place and job responsibilities. You should observe the person at work to get a sense of the physical and intellectual demands of the job and to see how the person reacts to the job. (Does he or she look tired, bored, confident, or happy?)
3. When you start your interview, a question as simple as "Do you like your job?" may be the only one you have to ask. Perhaps the advice of Studs Terkel, whose books *Division Street: America, Hard Times,* and *Working* are based on interviews, might be most helpful: "I realized quite early in this adventure that interviews, conventionally conducted, were meaningless. Conditioned clichés were certain to come. The question-and-answer technique may be of some value in determining favored detergents, toothpaste and deodorants, but not in the discovery of men and women." Terkel suggests having a *conversation* with the person. If you are friendly and relaxed, responding with interest to the person's remarks, you'll learn a lot more than if you approach someone coldly and humorlessly, probing with a set of rigid questions.

4. Certainly it helps to have some questions in mind to get your conversation started and to keep it going if it lags, so here are some suggestions.

   a. What are the most rewarding things about your job?

   b. What are the worst aspects of your job?

   c. If you were starting over, would you choose the same job?

   d. When you were eighteen, what did you want to do with your life?

Note that some of the following interviews were obtained by students at the University of Oklahoma and that these interviews started off with that simple question, "Do you like your job?"

Studs Terkel, from *Working*

Mike Lefevre, steelworker, Cicero, Illinois

It is a two-flat dwelling, somewhere in Cicero, on the outskirts of Chicago. He is thirty-seven. He works in a steel mill. On occasion, his wife Carol works as a waitress in a neighborhood restaurant; otherwise, she is at home, caring for their small children, a girl and a boy.

At the time of my first visit, a sculpted statuette of Mother and Child was on the floor, head severed from body. He laughed softly as he indicated his three-year-old daughter: "She Doctor Spock'd it."

"I'm a dying breed. A laborer. Strictly muscle work . . . pick it up, 1 put it down, pick it up, put it down. We handle between forty and fifty thousand pounds of steel a day. (Laughs) I know this is hard to believe—from four hundred pounds to three and four-pound pieces. It's dying.

"You can't take pride any more. You remember when a guy could 2 point to a house he built, how many logs he stacked. He built it and he was proud of it. I don't really think I could be proud if a contractor built a home for me. I would be tempted to get in there and kick the carpenter in the ass (laughs), and take the saw away from him. 'Cause I would have to be part of it, you know.

"It's hard to take pride in a bridge you're never gonna cross, in a 3 door you're never gonna open. You're mass-producing things and you never see the end result of it. (Muses) I worked for a trucker one time. And I got this tiny satisfaction when I loaded a truck. At least I could see the truck depart loaded. In a steel mill, forget it. You don't see where nothing goes.

"I got chewed out by my foreman once. He said, 'Mike, you're a 4 good worker but you have a bad attitude.' My attitude is that I don't get excited about my job. I do my work but I don't say whoopee-doo. The day I get excited about my job is the day I go to a head shrinker. How are you gonna get excited about pullin' steel? How are you gonna get excited when you're tired and want to sit down?

"It's not just the work. Somebody built the pyramids. Somebody's 5 going to build something. Pyramids, Empire State Building—these things just don't happen. There's hard work behind it. I would like to see a building, say, the Empire State, I would like to see on one side of it a foot-wide strip from top to bottom with the name of every brick-layer, the name of every electrician, with all the names. So when a guy walked by, he could take his son and say, 'See, that's me over there on the forty-fifth floor. I put the steel beam in.' Picasso can point to a painting. What can I point to? A writer can point to a book. Everybody should have something to point to.

"It's the not-recognition by other people. To say a woman is *just* a 6 housewife is degrading, right? Okay. *Just* a housewife. It's also degrad-ing to say *just* a laborer. The difference is that a man goes out and maybe gets smashed.

"When I was single, I could quit, just split. I wandered all over the 7 country. You worked just enough to get a poke, money in your pocket. Now I'm married and I got two kids . . . (trails off). I worked on a truck dock one time and I was single. The foreman came over and he grabbed my shoulder, kind of gave me a shove. I punched him and knocked him off the dock. I said, 'Leave me alone. I'm doing my work, just stay away from me, just don't give me the with-the-hands busi-ness.'

"Hell, if you whip a damn mule he might kick you. Stay out of my 8 way, that's all. Working is bad enough, don't bug me. I would rather work my ass off for eight hours a day with nobody watching me than five minutes with a guy watching me. Who you gonna sock? You can't sock General Motors, you can't sock anybody in Washington, you can't sock a system.

"A mule, an old mule, that's the way I feel. Oh yeah. See. (Shows 9 black and blue marks on arms and legs, burns.) You know what I heard from more than one guy at work? 'If my kid wants to work in a factory, I am going to kick the hell out of him.' I want my kid to be an effete snob. Yeah, mm-hmm. (Laughs) I want him to be able to quote Walt Whitman, to be proud of it.

"If you can't improve yourself, you improve your posterity. Other- 10 wise life isn't worth nothing. You might as well go back to the cave and stay there. I'm sure the first caveman who went over the hill to see what was on the other side—I don't think he went there wholly out of curiosity. He went there because he wanted to get his son out of the cave. Just the same way I want to send my kid to college."

Babe Secoli, checker at a supermarket for 30 years

"I don't have to look at the keys on my register. I'm like the 1 secretary that knows her typewriter. The touch. My hand fits. The number 9 is my big middle finger. The thumb is number one, 2 and 3 and up. The side of my hand uses the bar for the total and all that.

"I use my 3 fingers—my thumb, my index finger, and my middle 2 finger. The right hand. And my left hand is on the groceries. They put down their groceries. I got my hips pushin' on the button and it rolls around on the counter. When I feel I have enough groceries in front of me, I let go of my hip. I'm just movin' the hips, the hand, and the register, the hips, the hand, and the register. . . . (As she demonstrates, her hands and hips move in the manner of an Oriental dancer.) You just keep goin' one, 2, one 2. If you've got that rhythm, you're a fast checker. . . .

"I'm a checker and I'm very proud of it. There's some, they say, 'A 3 checker—ugh!' To me, it's like somebody being a teacher or a lawyer. I'm not ashamed that I wear a uniform and nurse's shoes and that I got varicose veins. I'm makin' an honest living. Whoever looks down on me, they're lower than I am."

Barbara Herrick, advertising writer/producer

On first meeting, I'm frequently taken for the secretary, you know, 1 traveling with the boss. I'm here to keep somebody happy. Then I'm introduced as the writer. One said to me after the meeting was over and the drinking had started, "When I first saw you, I figured you were a—you know. I never knew you were the person *writing* this all the time." (Laughs.) Is it a married woman working for extra money? Is it a lesbian? Is it some higher-up's mistress? . . .

Now I'm definitely the token woman. In the current economic 2 climate, I'm one of the few writers at my salary level getting job offers. Unemployment is high right now among people who do what I do. Yet I get calls: "Will you come and write on feminine hygiene products?" Another, involving a food account: "We need you, we'll pay you thirty grand and a contract. Be the answer for Such-an-such Foods." I'm ideal because I'm young enough to have four or five solid years of experience behind me. I know how to handle myself or I wouldn't be where I am.

I'm very secure right now. But when someone says to me, "You 3 don't have to worry," he's wrong. In a profession where I absolutely cannot age, I cannot be doing this at thirty-eight. For the next years, until I get too old, my future's secure in a very insecure business. It's like a race horse or a show horse. Although I'm holding the job on talent and responsibility, I got here partly because I'm attractive and it's a big kick for a client to know that for three days in Montreal there's going to be this young brunette, who's very good, mind you. I don't know how they talk about me, but I'd guess: "She's very good, but to look at her you'd never know it. She's a knockout." . . .

I've never pretended this is the best writing I can do. Every 4 advertising writer has a novel in his drawer. Few of them ever do it.

I don't think what I do is necessary or that it performs a service. If 5 it's a very fine product—and I've worked on some of those—I love it. It's when you get into that awful area of hope, cosmetics—you're just selling image and a hope. It's like the arthritis cure or cancer—quackery. You're saying to a lady, "Because this oil comes from the algae at the bottom of the sea, you're going to have a timeless face." It's a crock of shit! I know it's part of my job, I do it. If I made the big stand my friend made, I'd lose my job. Can't do it. I'm expected to write whatever assignment I'm given. It's whorish. I haven't written enough to know what kind of writer I am. I suspect, rather than a writer, I'm a good reader. I think I'd make a good editor. I have read so many short stories that I bet you I could turn out a better anthology than anybody's done yet, in certain categories.

Fred Roman, accountant, auditor

The company I work for doesn't make a product. We provide a 1 service. Our service is auditing. We are usually hired by stockholders or the board of directors. We will certify whether a company's financial statement is correct. They'll say, "This is what we did last year. We made X amount of dollars." We will come in to examine the books and say, "Yes, they did."

We're looking for things that didn't go out the door the wrong way. 2 Our clients could say, "We have a million dollars in accounts receivable." We make sure that they do, in fact, have a million dollars and not a thousand. We ask the people who owe the money, "Do you, in fact, owe our client two thousand dollars as of this date?" We do it on a spot check basis. Some companies have five thousand individual accounts receivable. We'll maybe test a hundred. . . .

People look at you with fear and suspicion. The girl who does 3 accounts receivable never saw an auditor before. The comptroller knows why you're there and he'll cooperate. But it's the guy down the line who is not sure and worries. You ask him a lot of questions. What does he do? How does he do it? Are you after his job? Are you trying to get him fired? He's not very friendly.

We're supposed to be independent. We're supposed to certify their 4 books are correct. We'll certify this to the Securities Exchange Commission, to the stockholders, to the banks. They'll all use our financial statements. But if we slight the company—if I find something that's going to take away five hundred thousand dollars of income this year—they may not hire us back next year. . . .

Our firm has a philosophy of progress, up or out. I started three 5 years ago. If that second year I didn't move from SA–3, staff assistant, to SA–4, I'd be out. Last June I was SA–4. If I hadn't moved to SA–5, I'd be out. Next year if I don't move to senior, I'll be out. When I make senior I'll be Senior–1. The following year, Senior–2. Then Senior–3. Then manager—or out. By the time I'm thirty-four or so, I'm a partner or I'm out. . . .

I'd like to go back to college and get a master's or Ph. D. and become 6 a college teacher. The only problem is I don't think I have the smarts for it. When I was in high school I thought I'd be an engineer. So I took math, chemistry, physics, and got my D's. I thought of being a history major. Then I said, "What will I do with a degree in history?" I thought of poli sci. I thought most about going into law. I still think about that. I chose accounting for a very poor reason. I eliminated everything else. Even after I passed my test as a CPA I was saying all along, "I don't want to be an accountant." (Laughs.) I'm young enough. After June I can look around. As for salary, I'm well ahead of my contemporaries. I'm well ahead of those in teaching and slightly ahead of those in engineering. But that isn't it . . .

Suzanne Seed, from *Saturday's Child*
Ruth Nelson, systems analyst

"I enjoy working in the field of data processing for many reasons; 1 one is that the work is done by individuals. I've heard many programmers express the feeling of satisfaction they get from doing a job entirely by themselves rather than with a committee. They identify with the system they use in working with their particular type of computer.

"Another thing I like about programming is that you always know 2 when you've made a mistake, because when you do, the system won't come out right. Then you're able to keep on trying until you finally get it perfect. There are no maybes, only wrong or right. There may be many different ways of approaching a problem, but only one that will come out exactly right. I get great satisfaction from having done something correctly."

Colin Henfrey, from *Manscapes*
Jacob Slotnik, tailor, age 81, Worcester, Massachusetts

"That's how my life is. Sometimes—lonesome in the house—during the week I don't mind, I go to the store. But Sunday—and now I can't work how I used to—arthritis, sometimes I can't keep the thimble there—but I can't stay home, you know. I get crazy. Lots of people, they get 65, they give up—walk about like dead people—thank God I got a trade. I don't have to go to my children and ask them for a few dollars. That's lucky. And down in the store the customers come, we talk a little, this one comes and that one. I see people, the day goes by. . . ."

Barbara Ehrenreich, from "Is Success Dangerous to Your Health?" (*Ms.* Magazine, May 1979)

Susan Johnson, secretary, Washington, D.C.

"Socially, if you say you're a secretary, you're immediately assumed   1
to be a drone. People turn off, especially in Washington where there's an obsession with status. . . . The lack of respect from the outside world sometimes keeps you from doing your job well. For instance, people won't tell me why they're calling even though my boss has given me that responsibility—but if I said I were an assistant or a paralegal, they would be more likely to trust my judgment. . . .

"And there's a frustration of never being able to do enough research   2
or see a whole process through because you're constantly being in-terrupted by the phone, small tasks, dictating equipment. . . . I'm not married and I don't have kids, so I don't have home stress. . . . I feel valuable, but the most constant frustration is how people perceive what I do."

Ann Follis, homemaker, Urbana, Illinois

"I strongly believe that homemakers suffer from stress less because   1
of the work we are doing than because we're not rewarded and recog-nized for it. . . . For me, the only way I can overcome that stress is to be assertive. No one, but no one, ever uses the term 'working woman' without my correcting them. Say 'salaried work' or 'work outside the home,' but don't imply that homemakers aren't 'working women' too. . . .

"We're discounted as people who don't work by the tax system, we   2
don't get equal treatment in the Social Security system, and we can't get disability payments—even though a husband may be much more easily replaced when he's sick than we are. . . . Under the Equal Rights Amendment, there would be much more legal protection for women—and it would help to make homemaking a choice, not just something that women are forced into because they have no alter-natives."

From Interviews by Students at the University of Oklahoma
Joan Carter, police officer

Job responsibilities: regular duties as other officers (give speeding 1
tickets, investigate burglaries, etc.).

She likes her job because it gives her "a feeling of satisfaction 2
because of the challenge it takes to be a police officer, but it's even
more of a challenge when you're a woman. Another good note of being
a police officer is that you're in the spotlight. People always come up to
me and ask what has been happening around town. They want to know
what crimes have been going on around town but more importantly
they want to know who has been committing them. . . .

"People are very friendly to me—that is, when I'm out of uniform. 3
People, I think, try to take advantage of me sometimes [when she is on
patrol], because they think since I'm a woman they can talk me out of a
ticket. Usually I'm a little bit tougher than the men officers, but I'm
still a woman and have a soft heart, sometimes, depending on the
situation. . . . The person that really tries to take advantage of me, and
I hate to handle them, are the drunk men who come out of bars. They
always want you to let them drive home, but while they're trying to
talk you into it, they're throwing out words like 'honey, please,' 'come
on, baby,' and some even take it a little far."

At first, she ran into some difficulty getting the job. She had to apply 4
three different times, and each time they told her she didn't have
enough education. By the third application, she had more schooling in
law enforcement than any other officer working on the police force. "At
first, there was a lot of respect lacking toward me. They [the male
officers] thought I couldn't handle it. They even put me on the midnight or night shift for over two months; then they knew I could take
it and I started working days. Now we all switch working shifts
every week. There's more respect for me now, but it took a while to
get it.

"This job is different than any other job I've ever had. It brings me 5
happiness, even though I go through some of them rough days, full of
frustrations. It makes me happy because of the challenge it has. When
I get home from it, I get a sense of accomplishment which makes me
happy. If it didn't make me happy I would have quit when it was
tough. It also makes me happy because I am a woman and have a job
like this, I mean it's a job that carries responsibility and gives you that
feeling of power. But I try not to let that power feeling get in the way of
my own self and treat people differently than when I'm not working. I
only use it (the power feeling) when I have to.

"I guess when I was a teenager I wanted to do something out of the 6
ordinary. It [being a police officer] might have crossed my mind when I

285

was young, but it really didn't stick till I was turned down the first time" (she was turned down by the chief of police when the only reason he had for not hiring her was that she was a woman).

—ROBERT KLEIN

Dave Hundley, warehouse foreman, Houston, Texas

Job responsibilities: checks stock, assigns jobs, rebuilds and repairs 1 machinery.

"What I have enjoyed most would have to be the fact that I achieved 2 my position through hard work. I started out a laborer just like you were last summer and worked my way up to warehouse foreman. Right now, I'm taking a few lessons from Limpy on how to drive an 18-wheeler so that soon, maybe by Christmas, I can be driving hydrils and joints of pipe around. When I started work here [a rental tool company], I only made $3.00 an hour, but that was 5 years ago. Now I make $5.14 and if I start driving a rig I will pull about $8.00 plus bread and gravy overtime. So I feel like I have achieved something on my own. Hard work does pay off.

"I guess some disadvantages to the job would have to be the starting 3 pay. Unskilled people like you start at only $3.50 and a lot of guys like Jeff are trying to support a family on that. You have to put in a lot of overtime to do that. I've seen a lot of drifters come and go. They go from job to job and never make much money, but I decided to stick it out when I came, and now it's starting to pay off. I guess that is an advantage too, because you can better yourself with hard work.

"I would do it again if I had to do over because I hated my 2 years of 4 college. I went to college with the expectation of becoming an accountant, but I couldn't get into going to work in a suit and sitting in an office every day. I love working outdoors and doing physical labor and I wouldn't trade it for anything. A lot of people don't like it, but I do. People who look down on me can —— off because this is what I like."

—RICHARD HOWELL

Linda Potter, secretary for a petroleum company, Oklahoma City, Oklahoma

Job responsibilities: she serves as secretary to seven men. She 1 receives and reads mail, answers telephones, makes travel arrangements, prepares training manuals for refinery workers, takes dictation, composes letters.

"Yes, I like my job, but I would like to have more responsibilities. I 2 feel I am capable of more than what I am allowed to do. If I was 18 again with all the opportunities women have today and was able to, I would go to college and get a degree in business in either accounting or marketing. I would try for the executive type jobs where I am more the boss than the employee. I would choose that type of job because it is interesting, exciting, challenging, and you can work with and meet a lot of different kinds of people. . . . I am frustrated part of the time, because during all the time I didn't work I did a lot of volunteer work that was challenging and that made me do some creative thinking. With the job I have now, there is not much creative thinking I can do and it is not very challenging.

"I also feel that my first and foremost career is being a good wife and 3 mother. When my children were at home, I did not have a paying job, because I felt my place was to be at home, so I did a lot of volunteer work. When my children grew up, I felt I needed to get a job, but I still feel my family is the most important thing in my life. I felt it was a real accomplishment just to get a job at my age and with the skill I had not used in 20 years, without even a brush-up course, and still be able to compete and do better than those just out of school."

—JANE POTTER

Marc Rogers, photographer, Norman, Oklahoma

"I've worked in the darkroom now for over three years and I can't 1 think of anything I'd rather do. But, then again my job isn't just another photography job. Let me start out by saying that working in News Services at the University isn't like a newspaper job, although the hours are sometimes just as bad. But it's also not like working at a commercial studio. It's really the best of both worlds. Working for News Services, I get to meet and see a lot of real interesting people like President Carter and Ted Kennedy on their campaigns; I even got to shake Henry Kissinger's hand when he was here last year. But I also get to shoot portraits and studio still lifes—in fact, I went out last spring and shot an 'on location' assignment for a poster you might've seen around campus this year.

"Do I like my job? I couldn't have it any better if I'd ordered it out of 2 a catalog. I don't know what I'd do if I could start all over again. I'm pretty much of a fatalist at heart and I figure that fate rules many of our actions. In that respect, I'm not sure I'd change much in my past. Being a photographer has given me a lot of freedom other jobs haven't. I worked four years in a stereo repair shop and it really affected my thinking. Being cooped up in an office is not the way to live. Being in photography gets me out among people at the University, people I really enjoy meeting.

"The best part I guess is the people I work with. You couldn't ask for 3 nicer people. If you get in a bind, there's always someone to listen, and better yet, if you shoot a really terrific picture, they let you know. It's weird but a photographer is just like any other artist—he needs praise when it's deserved and criticism when it's needed. I've learned more in my office about my own work, and it's nice to have people around that'll pat you on the back when you've done a good job.

"It's funny you should ask about pay because I just got a raise. I 4 worked here for over two years at student's pay. Needless to say it was kind of hard to make ends meet at $2.85 an hour. I just got my staff appointment this summer and got about a 125% increase. But I've gotten other responsibilities with the raise. It's not that I don't like the money, of course, nobody ever seems to have enough money and it sure was hard to get along with less.

"It's funny how our attitude is tied into the economics of our lives. 5 When I was making student's pay I felt like I was really being taken advantage of. Maybe I've succumbed to the bureaucratic brainwashing, but since I got that raise, I really feel like I'm being more adequately compensated for my talents, and my attitude about just going to work has really improved. Call me a capitalist, but if I don't have to worry so much about my finances, I sure enjoy my job more."

—DONNA SHAW

READING

The Western: Theory and Practice

The material presented here is designed to support a serious piece of synthetic writing without additional research. The first selection is taken from the scholar John Cawelti's book, *Six-Gun Mystique*. In the parts of his book reprinted here, Cawelti tries to define the elements that came to constitute the formula used in hundreds of Western stories, novels, plays, and movies. We suggest that you use Cawelti's discussion as a kind of working hypothesis, to be tested against the two stories by Stephen Crane that follow, which were written while the formula described by Cawelti was still being developed. You might also want to compare Cawelti's analysis with the structure of the Western described by Jane Tompkins in "Fighting Words: Unlearning to Write the Critical Essay," pp. 235–239. You may wish to look over the essay and the stories before turning to the two Practice assignments at the end of the second story, but you should probably turn to the Practices before you begin a careful study of this material.

John Cawelti, from *The Six-Gun Mystique*

The Western was created in the early nineteenth century by James 1 Fenimore Cooper. Cooper's initial invention of the Leatherstocking (*The Pioneers*, 1823) paved the way for many fictional treatments of the

West which strongly resembled his patterns of plot, character, and theme (e.g. R. M. Bird's *Nick of the Woods* and W. G. Simms, *The Yemassee*). By 1860 these patterns had become sufficiently stereotyped that they could serve Edward Ellis as the basis of his *Seth Jones; or The Captives of the Frontier,* one of the most successful early dime novels. In the later nineteenth century, the Western formula continued to flourish in the dime novel and in popular drama. Even the auto-biographical narratives of Western experiences and popular biographies of Western heroes like Kit Carson, Buffalo Bill, and General Custer, increasingly reflected the main elements of the formula, which was finally enshrined in the great spectacle of the Wild West Show. Gradually the cowboy replaced the frontier scout as the archetypal Western hero. Finally, in a number of works published around the turn of the century, the most important of which was Owen Wister's best-seller *The Virginian*, the Western formula arrived at most of the characteristics it has held through innumerable novels, stories, films and TV shows in the twentieth century.

In one sense the Western formula is far easier to define than that of 2 the detective story, for when we see a couple of characters dressed in ten-gallon hats and riding horses, we know we are in a Western. On the other hand, the Western formula contains a greater variety of plot patterns than the detective story with its single line of criminal in-vestigation. Frank Gruber, a veteran writer of pulp Westerns, suggests that there are seven basic Western plots which he lists as: (1) The Union Pacific Story centering around the construction of a railroad, telegraph or stagecoach line or around the adventures of a wagon train; (2) The Ranch Story with its focus on conflicts between ranchers and rustlers or cattlemen and sheepmen; (3) The Empire Story, which is an epic version of the Ranch Story; (4) The Revenge Story; (5) Custer's Last Stand, or the Cavalry and Indian Story; (6) the Outlaw Story; and (7) The Marshal Story. One could doubtless construct other lists of plots that have been used in Westerns, though Gruber's seems quite adequate. Later, I will suggest that there is a kind of action pattern that the Western tends to follow whether it be about ranchers, cavalrymen, outlaws, or marshals, but the possibility of such diversity of plot patterns suggests that we know a Western primarily by the presence of ten-gallon hats and horses. In other words, the Western formula is initially defined by its setting. Therefore in analyzing the components of the Western formula I will deal initially with the setting.

Setting

Tentatively, we might say that the western setting is a matter of 3 geography and costume; that is, a Western is a story that takes place somewhere in the western United States in which the characters wear certain distinctive styles of clothing. However, this formulation is clearly inadequate since there are many stories set in the American West which we would not call Westerns under any circumstances, for example the novels and stories of Hamlin Garland, or Ole Rolvaag. Moreover, there are novels set in the eastern United States which are really Westerns, for example, the Leatherstocking Tales of James Fenimore Cooper. Our geographical definition must immediately be qualified by a social and historical definition of setting: the Western is a story which takes place on or near a frontier, and consequently, the Western is generally set at a particular moment in the past.

The portrayal of the frontier in the Western formula differs signifi- 4
cantly from Frederick Jackson Turner's frontier thesis. For Turner, the frontier was less important as "the meeting point between savagery and civilization" than as a social and economic factor in American history. His well-known frontier thesis consisted of two central propositions: first, because the American frontier lay "at the hither edge of free land" it had maintained the democratic mobility and fluidity of American life; and second, there tended to grow up in frontier settlements a distinctively individualistic way of life which continually revitalized the democratic spirit in America. Though a view of the frontier resembling Turner's sometimes plays a role in the structure of more complex and serious Westerns, the central purport of the frontier in most Westerns has simply been its potential as a setting for exciting, epic conflicts. The Western formula tends to portray the frontier as "meeting point between civilization and savagery" because the clash of civilization ("law and order") with savagery, whether represented by Indians or lawless outlaws, generates dramatic excitement and striking antithesis without raising basic questions about American society or about life in general. In the Western formula savagery is implicitly understood to be on the way out. It made no difference whether the creator of the Western viewed savagery as a diabolical or criminal force (as in most of the dime novels) or as a meaningful way of life for which he felt a certain degree of elegaic nostalgia (an attitude in many Westerns from Cooper to the movies of John Ford), there was never a question that savagery might prevail, just as in the detective story there is never really a doubt that the criminal will ultimately be caught. While one might seriously seek to espouse certain "natural" values and to reject those of society (e.g. as in Thoreau's *Walden* or the poetry of Whitman) and while an American character in a novel by Henry James might be deeply torn between the European and American ways of life, the Western hero never has to make a basic choice like this, for, insofar as he is a hero it must be in relation to the victory of civilization over savagery, even if this victory, as it often does, puts him out of a job. Edwin Fussell suggests that in the first half of the nineteenth century,

the frontier retained enough of an air of mystery that it could represent a fundamental confrontation between human history and the possibility of a society transcending it. However, Fussell believes that as actual settlement progressed, the frontier lost its power as a fundamental moral antithesis to society. By 1850, according to Fussell, the frontier had ceased to be a major theme for the greatest American writers. Fussell's discussion supplements Henry Nash Smith's definition of the mythical West as the potential locus of a new and more natural human society. Like Fussell, Smith defines the early American conception of the frontier as a serious antithesis to existing society. However, Smith believes that the romanticization of nature implicit in this conception of the frontier could never support a serious literature. Thus, after Cooper, the Western story declined to a point where "devoid alike of ethical and social meaning, [it] could develop in no direction save that of a straining and exaggeration of its formulas."

Smith's treatment of the Western story is a bit harsh, ignoring as it does the rich flourishing of the Western in literature and on film in the twentieth century. However, Smith is essentially correct in pointing out that the Western formula has been an artistic device for resolving problems rather than confronting their irreconcilable ambiguities. Therefore the frontier setting and the role of the savage have invariably been defined in the formula as occasions for action rather than as the focus of the analysis. In other words, the Indian rarely stands for a possible alternative way of life which implies a serious criticism of American society. Instead he poses a problem for the hero. Leslie Fiedler points out how often the complex relationship between a young white boy and an Indian or Negro is the central theme of major American novels. In his recent study, *The Return of the Vanishing American,* Fiedler argues that the Indian way of life has become an important counter-cultural symbol for many young radicals. But the Indian never plays such a role in the formula Western, because he is always in the process of vanishing. In fact, the treatment of the Indian in the formula Western bears out Roy Harvey Pearce's analysis of the American idea of savagism. Pearce shows how the various seventeenth and eighteenth century views of the Indian with their complex dialectic between the Indian as devil and as noble savage quickly gave way in the nineteenth century to a definition of the Indian way of life as an inferior and earlier stage in the development of civilization. This redefinition of the Indian justified his assimilation or extermination and therefore served the need of nineteenth century American society for a philosophical rationale to justify its brutal elimination of the native Indian cultures. Even in Westerns quite sympathetic to the Indian, such as John Ford's version of Mari Sandoz' *Cheyenne Autumn,* the focus of the action usually shifts from the Indians themselves to the

5

291

dilemmas their situation poses for the white hero and heroine. In short, the Western formula seems to prescribe that the Indian be a part of the setting to a greater extent than he is ever a character in his own right. The reason for this is twofold: to give the Indian a more complex role would increase the moral ambiguity of the story and thereby blur the sharp dramatic conflicts; and second, if the Indian represented a significant way of life rather than a declining savagery, it would be far more difficult to resolve the story with a reaffirmation of the values of modern society.

Taken together, the work of Smith, Fussell, and Pearce suggest that   6 the Western formula emerged as American attitudes toward the frontier gradually underwent significant change around the middle of the nineteenth century. It was possible for Americans in the early nineteenth century to treat the frontier as a symbol of fundamental moral antitheses between man and nature, and, consequently, to use a frontier setting in fiction that engaged itself with a profound exploration of the nature and limitations of man and society. However, the redefinition of the frontier as a place where advancing civilization met a declining savagery changed the frontier setting into a locus of conflicts which were always qualified and contained by the knowledge that the advance of civilization would largely eliminate them. Or, to put it another way, the frontier setting now provided a fictional justification for enjoying violent conflicts and the expression of lawless force without feeling that they threatened the values or the fabric of society.

Thus, the social and historical aspects of setting are perhaps even   7 more important in defining the Western formula than geography. The Western story is set at a certain moment in the development of American civilization, namely at that point when savagery and lawlessness are in decline before the advancing wave of law and order, but are still strong enough to pose a local and momentarily significant challenge. In the actual history of the West, this moment was probably a relatively brief one in any particular area. In any case, the complex clashes of different interest groups over the use of Western resources and the pattern of settlement surely involved more people in a more fundamental way than the struggle with Indians or outlaws. Nonetheless, it is the latter which has become central to the Western formula. The relatively brief stage in the social evolution of the West when outlaws or Indians posed a threat to the community's stability has been erected into a timeless epic past in which heroic individual defenders of law and order without the vast social resources of police and courts stand poised against the threat of lawlessness or savagery. But it is also the nature of this epic moment that the larger forces of civilized society are just waiting in the wings for their cue. However threatening he may appear at the moment, the Indian is vanishing and the outlaw about to be superseded. It is because they too represent this epic moment that we are likely to think of such novels as Cooper's *Last of the Mohicans*, Bird's *Nick of the Woods*, or more recent historical novels like Walter Edmonds' *Drums Along the Mohawk* as Westerns, though they are not set in what we have come to know as the West.

Why then has this epic moment been primarily associated in fiction 8 with a particular West, that of the Great Plains and the mountains and deserts of the "Far West" and with a particular historical moment, that of the heyday of the open range cattle industry of the later nineteenth century? Westerns can be set at a later time—some of Zane Grey's stories take place in the twenties and some, like those of Gene Autry, Roy Rogers, or "Sky King" in the present—but even at those later dates the costumes and the way of life represented tend to be that of the later nineteenth century. Several factors probably contributed to this particular fixation of the epic moment. Included among these would be the ideological tendency of Americans to see the Far West as the last stronghold of certain traditional values, as well as the peculiar attractiveness of the cowboy hero. But more important than these factors, the Western requires a means of isolating and intensifying the drama of the frontier encounter between social order and lawlessness. For this purpose, the geographic setting of the Great Plains and adjacent areas has proved particularly appropriate, especially since the advent of film and television have placed a primary emphasis on visual articulation. Four characteristics of the Great Plains topography have been especially important: its openness, its aridity and general in-hospitality to human life, its great extremes of light and climate, and, paradoxically, its grandeur and beauty. These topographic features create an effective backdrop for the action of the Western because they exemplify in visual images the thematic conflict between civilization and savagery and its resolution. In particular, the Western has come to center about the image of the isolated town or ranch or fort surrounded by the vast open grandeur of prairie or desert and connected to the rest of the civilized world by a railroad, a stagecoach, or simply a trail. This tenuous link can still be broken by the forces of lawlessness, but never permanently. We can conceive it as a possibility that the town will be swept back into the desert—the rickety wooden buildings with their tottering false fronts help express the tenuousness of the town's posi-tion against the surrounding prairie—nonetheless we do not see the town solely as an isolated fort in hostile country—like an outpost of the French foreign legion in *Beau Geste*—but as the advance guard of an oncoming civilization. Moreover, while the prairie or desert may be inhospitable, it is not hostile. Its openness, freshness, and grandeur also play an important role in the Western. Thus, the open prairie around the town serves not only as a haven of lawlessness and savagery, but as a backdrop of epic magnitude and even, at times, as a source of regenerating power.

This characteristic setting reflects and helps dramatize the tripartite 9 division of characters that dominates the Western pattern of action. The townspeople hover defensively in their settlement, threatened by the outlaws or Indians who are associated with the inhospitable and uncontrollable elements of the surrounding landscape. The townspeople are static and largely incapable of movement beyond their little settlement. The outlaws or savages can move freely across the landscape. The hero, though a friend of the townspeople, has the lawless power of movement in that he, like the savages, is a horseman and possesses skills of wilderness existence. The moral character of the hero also appears symbolically in the Western setting. In its rocky aridity and climatic extremes the Great Plains landscape embodies the hostile savagery of Indians and outlaws, while its vast openness, its vistas of snow-covered peaks in the distance, and its great sunrises and sunsets (in the purple prose of Zane Grey, for example) suggest the epic courage and regenerative power of the hero. Thus, in every respect, Western topography helps dramatize more intensely the clash of characters and the thematic conflicts of the story. These dramatic resources of setting can of course be used more or less skillfully by the Western writer or film director, but even at their flattest they have a tendency to elevate rather commonplace plots into epic spectacles. When employed with conscious and skillfull intent, as in the Western films of John Ford, the lyrical and epic power of landscape can sometimes transcend even the inherent limitations of popular culture and raise escapist adventure to a level of high artistry.

The special qualities of the Western setting emerge still more 10 clearly from a comparison with the treatment of setting in the colonial adventure novels of English writers like H. Rider Haggard. Since it too involved adventures on the periphery of what its readers defined as civilization, the colonial adventure is the closest European analogue to the American Western. Like the Western setting, the tropical jungles of the colonial adventure have both hostile and attractive qualities. Haggard's African veldts, like the Western plains, contain savagery and raw nature which threaten the representatives of civilization. They are also full of exotic animals, beautiful natural spectacles, glamorous and mysterious cults, hidden treasures, and other exciting secrets. But, in contrast to the fresh and open grandeur of the Western landscape, these double qualities of the colonial jungle are superficially attractive, but essentially subversive and dangerous. They are associated not with a redeeming hero who saves civilization from the threat of lawlessness and savagery, but with temptations which undermine the hero's commitment to civilization. The Western landscape can become the setting for a regenerated social order once the threat of lawlessness has been overcome, but the colonial landscape remains alien. Its doubleness simply reflects the difference between the overt threat of savage hostility and the more insidious danger of the attractiveness of alien cults and exotic ways of life. Perhaps because it contains an unresolved antithesis between man and the jungle, the colonial adventure has inspired truly profound works of literature, as instanced by such examples as Joseph Conrad's "Heart of Darkness," while the Western formula has at best produced good novels like Wister's *The Virginian* or Clark's *The Ox-Bow Incident*.

The first major writer who brought together the tripartite division of 11 townsmen, savages, and intermediate hero with a vision of the landscape was James Fenimore Cooper, who thereby became the creator of the Western. Even though Cooper's novels are set in the eastern forests and many of his thematic emphases are quite different from the later Western, his landscapes show the same basic pattern. The new settlement *(The Pioneers)* or fort *(The Last of the Mohicans, The Pathfinder)* or "ranch" (Hutter's "castle" in *The Deerslayer*) is surrounded by miles of forested wilderness. It is clear, however, that civilization has irreversibly begun its advance. Like many later Western writers, Cooper liked frequently to call his reader's attention to the difference between the peaceful settlements of "today" and the dark mysterious forests of the earlier period of the story, thus insuring that the reader knew he was dealing with a stage of historical development which was definitely in the past. It is implicit in such a setting that the conflict between settlement and wilderness will soon be resolved. Cooper's wilderness also exemplifies the doubleness of the Western formula landscape. The forest is dark and frightening, but also the place where one gets the strongest feeling of the divine presence; it is the locus of the bloodthirsty and savage "Mingos" but also of the noble and heroic Delawares.

I have now discussed the effectiveness of the Western setting as 12 both background and source of dramatic conflicts and have indicated its potentiality both as a means of exploring certain historical themes and as a way of evoking a sense of epic grandeur. But we must not forget that one reason for the success of the Western as a popular form in the twentieth century has been its unique adaptability to film. Two major characteristics of the western setting turned out to have an enormous potential for cinematic expression: its great openness of space and its powerful visual contrasts.

The special openness of the topography of the Great Plains and 13 western desert has made it particularly expressive for the portrayal of movement. Against the background of this terrain, a skillful director can create infinite variations of space ranging from long panoramas to close-ups and he can clearly articulate movement across these various spaces. No matter how often one sees it, there is something inescapably effective about that scene, beloved of Western directors, in which a rider appears like an infinitely small dot at the far end of a great empty horizon and then rides toward us across the intervening space, just as there is a different thrill about the vision of a group of horses and men plunging pell-mell from the foreground into the empty distance. Nor is there anything which quite matches the feeling of suspense when the camera picks up a little group of wagons threading their way across the middle distance and then pans across the arid rocks and up the slopes of a canyon until it suddenly comes upon a group of Indians waiting in ambush. Moreover, the western landscape is uniquely adaptable to certain kinds of strong visual effects because of the sharp contrasts of light and shadow characteristic of an arid climate together with the topographical contrasts of plain and mountain, rocky outcrops and flat deserts, steep bare canyons and forested plateaus. The characteristic openness and aridity of the topography also makes the contrast between man and nature and between wilderness and society visually strong.

Perhaps no film exploits the visual resources of the western land- 14 scape more brilliantly than John Ford's 1939 *Stagecoach*. The film opens on a street in one of those western shantytowns characterized by rickety false fronts. By the rushing motion of horses and wagons along the street and by the long vista down the street and out into the desert we are immediately made aware of the surrounding wilderness and of the central theme of movement across it which will dominate the film. This opening introduction of the visual theme of fragile town contrasted with epic wilderness will be developed throughout the film in the contrast between the flimsy stagecoach and the magnificent landscape through which it moves. Similarly, the restless motion of the opening scene will be projected into the thrust of the stagecoach across the landscape. This opening is followed by several brief scenes leading up to the departure of the stagecoach. These scenes are cut at a rather breathless pace so that they do not slow down the sense of motion and flight generated by the opening. Visually, they dwell on two aspects of the town, its dark, narrow, and crowded interiors and its ramshackle sidewalks and storefronts, thus establishing in visual terms the restrictive and artificial character of town life. Then the stagecoach departs on its voyage and we are plunged into the vast openness and grandeur of the wilderness with the crowded wooden stagecoach serving as a visual reminder of the narrow town life it has left behind. Ford chose to shoot the major portion of the stagecoach's journey in Monument Valley, a brilliant choice because the visual characteristics of that topography perfectly embody the complex mixture of epic grandeur and savage hostility that the film requires. The valley itself is a large, flat desert between steep hills. Thrusting up out of the valley floor gigantic monoliths of bare rock dwarf the stagecoach as it winds across this vast panorama. This combination of large open desert broken by majestic upthrusts of rock and surrounded by threatening hills creates an enormously effective visual environment for the story, which centers around the way in which the artificial social roles and attitudes of the travellers break down under the impact of the wilderness. Those travellers who are able to transcend their former roles are regenerated by the experience: the drunken doctor delivers a baby, the meek salesman shows courage, the whore becomes the heroine of a romance, and the outlaw becomes a lover. By stunning photographic representation of the visual contrasts of desert, hills and moving stagecoach, Ford transforms the journey of the stagecoach into an epic voyage that transcends the film's rather limited romantic plot.

Costume—another feature of the Western setting—has also contrib- 15 uted greatly to the Western's success in film. Like topography, western costume gains effectiveness both from intrinsic interest and from the way writers and filmmakers have learned how to make it reflect character and theme. In simplest form, as in the B Westerns, costumes symbolized moral opposition. The good guy wears clean, well-pressed clothes and a white hat. The villain dresses sloppily in black. The importance of this convention, simple-minded as it was, became apparent when, to create a more sophisticated "adult" Western, directors frequently chose to dress their heroes in black. However, the tradition of western costume also contains more complex meanings. An important distinction marks off both hero and villain from the townspeople. The townspeople usually wear the ordinary street clothing associated with the later nineteenth century, suits for men and long dresses for women. On the whole this clothing is simple as compared to the more elaborate fashions of the period and this simplicity is one way of expressing the Westernness of the costume. However, in the midst of the desert, the townspeople's clothing has an air of non-utilitarian artificiality somewhat like the ubiquitous false fronts of the town itself. It is perhaps significant that even in Westerns purportedly set at a later date, the women tend to wear the full-length dresses of an earlier period.

The costumes associated with heroes and outlaws or savages are 16 more striking. Paradoxically, they are both more utilitarian and more artificial than those of the townspeople. The cowboy's boots, tight-fitting pants or chaps, his heavy shirt and bandanna, his gun, and finally his large ten-gallon hat all symbolize his adaptation to the wilderness. But utility is only one of the principles of the hero-outlaw's dress. The other is dandyism, that highly artificial love of elegance for its own sake. In the Western, dandyism sometimes takes the overt and obvious form of elaborate costumes laid over with fringes, tassels and scrollwork like a rococo drawing room. But it is more powerfully exemplified in the elegance of those beautifully tailored cowboy uniforms which John Wayne so magnificently fills out in the Westerns of John Ford and Howard Hawks.

The enormous attraction of this combination of naturalness and 17 artifice has played a significant role in both popular and avant-garde art since the middle of the nineteenth century. Baudelaire's fascination with the dandyism of the savage which he described as "the supreme incarnation of the idea of Beauty transported into the material world," is just one indication of the nineteenth century's fascination with the mixture of savagery and elegance which has been implicit in the costume of the Western hero from the beginning. Cooper's Leatherstocking even gained his name from his costume, suggesting the extent to which this particular kind of dress excited Cooper's imagination. Like later cowboys, Leatherstocking's costume combined nature and artifice. His dress was largely made of the skins of animals and it was particularly adapted to the needs of wilderness life. Yet at the same time it was subtly ornamented with buckskin fringes and porcupine quills "after the manner of the Indians." Still, it is important to note that Leatherstocking's costume is not that of the Indians, but rather a more utilitarian wilderness version of the settler's dress. Thus, costume exemplified the mediating role of the hero between civilization and savagery. Later the formula cowboy's costume developed along the same lines. In its basic outlines it resembled town dress more than that of the Indian, yet it was more functional for movement across the plains than that of the townspeople. At the same time, the cowboy dress had a dandyish splendor and elegance lacking in the drab fashions of the town and based on Indian or Mexican models. In later Westerns, the hero shared many of these qualities with the villain, just as Leatherstocking had a touch of the Indian, despite his repeated assurances that he was "a man without a cross," i.e. actual Indian kinship. But the hero's costume still differentiated him from the savage, whether Indian or outlaw, both by its basic resemblance to civilized dress and by its greater restraint and decorum. Thus costume, like setting, expressed the transcendent and intermediate quality of the hero. By lying between two ways of life, he transcended the restrictions and limitations of both. Or, to put it another way, the Western setting and costume embody the basic escapist principle of having your cake and eating it too. . . .

The Hero

The hero is a man with a horse and the horse is his direct tie to the 18 freedom of the wilderness, for it embodies his ability to move freely across it and to dominate and control its spirit. Through the intensity of his relationship to his horse, the cowboy excites that human fantasy of unity with natural creatures—the same fantasy seen in such figures as the centaurs of Greek mythology, in Siegfried's ability to understand the language of birds, and in a hero whose popularity was contemporaneous with the flourishing of the Western: Tarzan of the Apes.

The Western hero is also a man with a gun. The interaction of 19 American attitudes toward violence and the image of the Western hero as a gunfighter is so complex that it seems impossible to determine which causes the other. Critics of violence in the mass media believe that the heroic romanticized violence of the Western hero is a dangerous model for young people and stimulates them to imitation of the man with the gun. Defenders of the mass media argue that Westerns and other violent adventure dramas simply reflect the culture's fascination with guns. There have been many investigations of violence in the mass media and a large-scale government inquiry has recently been undertaken. Insofar as it seeks to determine the causal role of the Western hero in fostering violence among those who follow his adventures, this inquiry will probably be as inconclusive as the rest, for in my opinion both the tendency to admire gunfighter heroes and the actual social incidence of violence with guns are both symptoms of a more complex cultural force: the sense of decaying masculine potency which has long afflicted American culture. The American obsession with masculinity as often observed by Europeans and so evident in every aspect of our culture from serious artists like Ernest Hemingway to the immense range of gutsy men's magazines, *Playboy* images, and mass sports reflect a number of major social trends which undercut the sense of male security. Among the most important of these developments is the tendency of industrial work to depend increasingly on the superior potency of machines, the increasing importance of women in the industrial economy, the nationalizing trend of American life which has eroded local communities and the individual's sense of control over his life and finally, the decline of parental authority in the family which has undercut the basic source of masculine supremacy. Yet, at the same time, the American tradition has always emphasized individual masculine force; Americans love to think of themselves as pioneers, men who have conquered a continent and sired on it a new society. This radical discrepancy between the sense of eroding masculinity and the view of America as a great history of men against the wilderness has created the need for a means of symbolic expression of masculine potency in an unmistakable way. This means is the gun, particularly the six-gun.

Walter Prescott Webb suggests that the development of Colt's 20 revolver was the critical invention that made possible the American assault on the Great Plains. As Webb sees it, the Plains Indians with their horses and their extraordinary skill with the bow and arrow had a mobility and firepower unequalled until the adoption of the six-gun by the Texas Rangers. From that point on the Americans had a military advantage over the Plains Indians and the rapid development of the "Cattle Kingdom" followed. The historical and cultural significance of the gun as the means by which the cowboy drove out the Indian inhabitants of the plains and shaped a new culture happened to coincide with a long-standing tradition of heroism and masculine honor, that of the medieval knight, and its later offshoot, the code of the duel. For the westerner's six-gun and his way of using it in individual combat was the closest thing in the armory of modern violence to the knight's sword and the duellist's pistol. Thus in a period when violence in war was becoming increasingly anonymous and incomprehensible with massed attacks and artillery duels accounting for most of the casualties, the cowboy hero in his isolated combat with Indian or outlaw seemed to reaffirm the traditional image of masculine strength, honor, and moral violence. The cowboy hero with his six-gun standing between the uncontrolled violence of the savages and the evolving collective forces of the legal process played out in new terms the older image of chivalrous adventure. Not surprisingly an age which so enjoyed the historical romances of Sir Walter Scott would color the cowboy with tints freely borrowed from *Ivanhoe* and *Rob Roy*.

Many critics of the Western have commented upon the gun as a 21 phallic symbol, suggesting that the firing of the gun symbolizes the moment of ejaculation in a sexual act. Insofar as this is the case it bears out the emphasis on masculine potency already noted. However, this kind of phallic symbolism is an almost universal property of adventure heroes. The knight has his sword, the hard-boiled detective his automatic pistol, Buck Rogers his ray gun. The distinctive characteristic of the cowboy hero is not his possession of a symbolic weapon, but the way in which he uses it.

Where the knight encountered his adversary in bloody hand-to- 22 hand combat, the cowboy invariably meets his at a substantial distance and goes through the complex and rigid ritual of the "draw" before finally consummating the fatal deed. The most important implication of this killing procedure seems to be the qualities of reluctance, control, and elegance which it associates with the hero. Unlike the knight, the cowboy hero does not seek out combat for its own sake and he typically shows an aversion to the wanton shedding of blood. Killing is an act forced upon him and he carries it out with the precision and skill of a surgeon and the careful proportions of an artist. We might say that the six-gun is that weapon which enables the hero to show the largest measure of objectivity and detachment while yet engaging in individual combat. This controlled and aesthetic mode of killing is particularly important as the supreme mark of differentiation between the hero and the savage. The Indian or outlaw as savage delights in slaughter, entering into combat with a kind of manic glee to fulfill an uncontrolled lust for blood. The hero never engages in violence until the last moment and he never kills until the savage's gun has already cleared his holster. Suddenly it is there and the villain crumples.

This peculiar emphasis on the hero's skilled and detached killing 23 from a distance has been a part of the Western since its inception. One thinks, for example, of that climactic scene in *The Last of the Mohicans* where Leatherstocking picks the villainous Magua off the cliff top with a single shot from his unerring long rifle. The cowboy hero fights a little closer within the smaller range of the six-gun, but the same basic pattern of individual combat at a distance with the hero's last minute precision and control defeating the villain's undisciplined and savage aggression is the same. Careful staging of the final duel with all its elaborate protocol became a high point of the film Western, another example of an element of the literary Western which turned out to have even greater potential for the film.

The hero often fights with his fists, but he never kills in this kind of 24 direct hand-to-hand combat. Moreover, he rarely uses any weapon other than his fists, since knives and clubs suggest a more aggressive uncontrolled kind of violence which seems instinctively wrong for the character of the cowboy hero. Thus, the hero's special skill at gunfighting not only symbolizes his masculine potency, but indicates that his violence is disciplined and pure. Something like the old ideal of knightly purity and chastity survives in the cowboy hero's basic aversion to the grosser and dirtier forms of violence. In addition, the hero's reluctant but aesthetic approach to killing seems to reflect the ambiguity about violence which pervades modern society. Twentieth century America is perhaps the most ideologically pacifistic nation in history. Its political and social values are anti-militaristic, its legal ideals reject personal violence and it sees itself as a nation dedicated to world peace and domestic harmony through law and order. Yet this same nation supports one of the largest military establishments in history, its rate of violent crimes is enormously high, and it possesses the technological capacity to destroy the world. Perhaps one source of the cowboy hero's appeal is the way in which he resolves this ambiguity by giving a sense of moral significance and order to violence. His reluctance and detachment, the way in which he kills only when he forced to do so, the aesthetic order he imposes upon his acts of violence through the abstract ritual of the showdown, and finally, his mode of killing cleanly and purely at a distance through the magic of his six-gun cover the nakedness of violence and aggression beneath a skin of aesthetic grace and moral propriety.

Certain other characteristics are connected with the hero's role as 25 middleman between the pacifistic townspeople and the violent savages. There is his oft-noted laconic style, for example. Not all Western heroes are tight-lipped strong, silent types. Some, like Leatherstocking, are downright garrulous. But the laconic style is commonly associated with the Western hero, particularly in the twentieth century when movie stars like Gary Cooper, John Wayne, James Stewart, and Henry Fonda have vied for the prize as the Western hero who can say the fewest words with the least expression. Actually, tight lips are far more appropriate to the formula hero than the torrent of didacticism which flows from the lips of Natty Bumppo, and which most readers of Cooper resolutely ignore. Like his gun, language is a weapon the hero rarely uses, but when he does it is with precise and powerful effectiveness. In addition, the hero's reluctance with language reflects his social isolation and his reluctance to commit himself to the action which he knows will invariably lead to another violent confrontation.

Reluctance with words often matches the hero's reluctance toward 26 women. Cooper's Leatherstocking marked out one basic course that the Western hero would take with respect to the fair sex. The one girl Natty falls in love with, Mabel Dunham, in *The Pathfinder*, is too young and civilized to return his love and he gives her up to the younger, less wilderness-loving Jasper Western. On the other hand, the girl who falls in love with Natty, Judith Hutter in *The Deerslayer*, is too wild and too passionate to capture the affection of the chaste and pure Leatherstocking. This romantic situation reflects Natty's position as a man who mediates between civilization and wildness. Cooper found it increasingly difficult to resolve this antithesis and Natty remained caught in the middle between his beloved forest and the oncoming civilization which he had served. At other periods, writers have tried to make a romantic hero out of the cowboy, as in Wister's *The Virginian* and the many novels of Zane Grey. However, even when the hero does get the girl, the clash between the hero's adherence to the "code of the West" and the heroine's commitment to domesticity, social success, or other genteel values usually plays a role in the story. Heroes such as the Lone Ranger tend to avoid romance altogether. They are occasionally pursued by women, but generally manage to evade their clutches. . . .

Stephen Crane, "The Bride Comes to Yellow Sky"

I

The great Pullman was whirling onward with such dignity of motion 1
that a glance from the window seemed simply to prove that the plains
of Texas were pouring eastward. Vast flats of green grass, dull-hued
spaces of mesquite and cactus, little groups of frame houses, woods of
light and tender trees, all were sweeping into the east, sweeping over
the horizon, a precipice.

A newly married pair had boarded this coach at San Antonio. The 2
man's face was reddened from many days in the wind and sun, and a
direct result of his new black clothes was that his brick-colored hands
were constantly performing in a most conscious fashion. From time to
time he looked down respectfully at his attire. He sat with a hand on
each knee, like a man waiting in a barber's shop. The glances he
devoted to other passengers were furtive and shy.

The bride was not pretty, nor was she very young. She wore a dress 3
of blue cashmere, with small reservations of velvet here and there, and
with steel buttons abounding. She continually twisted her head to
regard her puff sleeves, very stiff, straight, and high. They embarrassed her. It was quite apparent that she had cooked, and that she
expected to cook, dutifully. The blushes caused by the careless scrutiny of some passengers as she had entered the car were strange to see
upon this plain, under-class countenance, which was drawn in placid,
almost emotionless lines.

They were evidently very happy. "Ever been in a parlor-car be- 4
fore?" he asked, smiling with delight.

"No," she answered; "I never was. It's fine, ain't it?" 5

"Great! And then after a while we'll go forward to the diner, and get 6
a big lay-out. Finest meal in the world. Charge a dollar."

"Oh, do they?" cried the bride. "Charge a dollar? Why, that's too 7
much—for us—ain't it, Jack?"

"Not this trip, anyhow," he answered bravely. "We're going to go 8
the whole thing."

Later he explained to her about the trains. "You see, it's a thousand 9
miles from one end of Texas to the other; and this train runs right
across it, and never stops but four times." He had the pride of an
owner. He pointed out to her the dazzling fittings of the coach; and in
truth her eyes opened wider as she contemplated the sea-green figured
velvet, the shining brass, silver, and glass, the wood that gleamed as
darkly brilliant as the surface of a pool of oil. At one end a bronze figure
sturdily held a support for a separated chamber, and at convenient
places on the ceiling were frescos in olive and silver.

To the minds of the pair, their surroundings reflected the glory of 10 their marriage that morning in San Antonio; this was the environment of their new estate; and the man's face in particular beamed with an elation that made him appear ridiculous to the negro porter. This individual at times surveyed them from afar with an amused and superior grin. On other occasions he bullied them with skill in ways that did not make it exactly plain to them that they were being bullied. He subtly used all the manners of the most unconquerable kind of snobbery. He oppressed them; but of this oppression they had small knowledge, and they speedily forgot that infrequently a number of travellers covered them with stares of derisive enjoyment. Historically there was supposed to be something infinitely humorous in their situation.

"We are due in Yellow Sky at 3:42," he said, looking tenderly into 11 her eyes.

"Oh, are we?" she said, as if she had not been aware of it. To evince 12 surprise at her husband's statement was part of her wifely amiability. She took from a pocket a little silver watch; and as she held it before her, and stared at it with a frown of attention, the new husband's face shone.

"I bought it in San Anton' from a friend of mine," he told her 13 gleefully.

"It's seventeen minutes past twelve," she said, looking up at him 14 with a kind of shy and clumsy coquetry. A passenger, noting this play, grew excessively sardonic, and winked at himself in one of the numerous mirrors.

At last they went to the dining-car. Two rows of negro waiters, in 15 glowing white suits, surveyed their entrance with the interest, and also the equanimity, of men who had been forewarned. The pair fell to the lot of a waiter who happened to feel pleasure in steering them through their meal. He viewed them with the manner of a fatherly pilot, his countenance radiant with benevolence. The patronage, entwined with the ordinary deference, was not plain to them. And yet, as they returned to their coach, they showed in their faces a sense of escape.

To the left, miles down a long purple slope, was a little ribbon of 16 mist where moved the keening Rio Grande. The train was approaching it at an angle, and the apex was Yellow Sky. Presently it was apparent that, as the distance from Yellow Sky grew shorter, the husband became commensurately restless. His brick-red hands were more insistent in their prominence. Occasionally he was even rather absent-minded and far-away when the bride leaned forward and addressed him.

As a matter of truth, Jack Potter was beginning to find the shadow of 17 a deed weigh upon him like a leaden slab. He, the town marshal of

Yellow Sky, a man known, liked, and feared in his corner, prominent person, had gone to San Antonio to meet a girl he believed he loved, and there, after the usual prayers, had actually induced her to marry him, without consulting Yellow Sky for any part of the transaction. He was now bringing his bride before an innocent and unsuspecting community.

Of course people in Yellow Sky married as it pleased them, in 18 accordance with a general custom; but such was Potter's thought of his duty to his friends, or of their idea of his duty, or of an unspoken form which does not control men in these matters, that he felt he was heinous. He had committed an extraordinary crime. Face to face with this girl in San Antonio, and spurred by his sharp impulse, he had gone headlong over all the social hedges. At San Antonio he was like a man hidden in the dark. A knife to sever any friendly duty, any form, was easy to his hand in that remote city. But the hour of Yellow Sky—the hour of daylight—was approaching.

He knew full well that his marriage was an important thing to his 19 town. It could only be exceeded by the burning of the new hotel. His friends could not forgive him. Frequently he had reflected on the advisability of telling them by telegraph, but a new cowardice had been upon him. He feared to do it. And now the train was hurrying him toward a scene of amazement, glee, and reproach. He glanced out of the window at the line of haze swinging slowly in toward the train.

Yellow Sky had a kind of brass band, which played painfully, to the 20 delight of the populace. He laughed without heart as he thought of it. If the citizens could dream of his prospective arrival with his bride, they would parade the band at the station and escort them, amid cheers and laughing congratulations, to his adobe home.

He resolved that he would use all the devices of speed and plains- 21 craft in making the journey from the station to his house. Once within that safe citadel, he could issue some sort of vocal bulletin, and then not go among the citizens until they had time to wear off a little of their enthusiasm.

The bride looked anxiously at him. "What's worrying you, Jack?" 22

He laughed again. "I'm not worrying, girl; I'm only thinking of 23 Yellow Sky."

She flushed in comprehension. 24

A sense of mutual guilt invaded their minds and developed a finer 25 tenderness. They looked at each other with eyes softly aglow. But Potter often laughed the same nervous laugh; the flush upon the bride's face seemed quite permanent.

The traitor to the feelings of Yellow Sky narrowly watched the 26 speeding landscape. "We're nearly there," he said.

Presently the porter came and announced the proximity of Potter's 27 home. He held a brush in his hand, and, with all his airy superiority gone, he brushed Potter's new clothes as the latter slowly turned this way and that way. Potter fumbled out a coin and gave it to the porter, as he had seen others do. It was a heavy and muscle-bound business, as that of a man shoeing his first horse.

The porter took their bag, and as the train began to slow they moved 28 forward to the hooded platform of the car. Presently the two engines and their long string of coaches rushed into the station of Yellow Sky.

"They have to take water here," said Potter, from a constricted 29 throat and in mournful cadence, as one announcing death. Before the train stopped his eye had swept the length of the platform, and he was glad and astonished to see there was none upon it but the station-agent, who, with a slightly hurried and anxious air, was walking toward the water-tanks. When the train had halted, the porter alighted first, and placed in position a little temporary step.

"Come on, girl," said Potter, hoarsely. As he helped her down they 30 each laughed on a false note. He took the bag from the negro, and bade his wife cling to his arm. As they slunk rapidly away, his hang-dog glance perceived that they were unloading the two trunks, and also that the station-agent, far ahead near the baggage-car, had turned and was running toward him, making gestures. He laughed, and groaned as he laughed, when he noted the first effect of his marital bliss upon Yellow Sky. He gripped his wife's arm firmly to his side, and they fled. Behind them the porter stood, chuckling fatuously.

II

The California express on the Southern Railway was due at Yellow 31 Sky in twenty-one minutes. There were six men at the bar of the Weary Gentleman saloon. One was a drummer who talked a great deal and rapidly; three were Texans who did not care to talk at that time; and two were Mexican sheepherders, who did not talk as a general practice in the Weary Gentleman saloon. The barkeeper's dog lay on the boardwalk that crossed in front of the door. His head was on his paws, and he glanced drowsily here and there with the constant vigilance of a dog that is kicked on occasion. Across the sandy street were some vivid green grass-plots, so wonderful in appearance, amid the sands that burned near them in a blazing sun, that they caused a doubt in the mind. They exactly resembled the grass mats used to represent lawns on the stage. At the cooler end of the railway station, a man without a coat sat in a tilted chair and smoked his pipe. The fresh-cut bank of the Rio Grande circled near the town, and there could be seen beyond it a great plum-colored plain of mesquite.

Save for the busy drummer and his companions in the saloon, 32 Yellow Sky was dozing. The newcomer leaned gracefully upon the bar, and recited many tales with the confidence of a bard who has come upon a new field.

"—and at the moment that the old man fell downstairs with the 33 bureau in his arms, the old woman was coming up with two scuttles of coal, and of course—"

The drummer's tale was interrupted by a young man who suddenly 34 appeared in the open door. He cried: "Scratchy Wilson's drunk, and has turned loose with both hands." The two Mexicans at once set down their glasses and faded out of the rear entrance of the saloon.

The drummer, innocent and jocular, answered: "All right, old man. 35 S'pose he has? Come in and have a drink, anyhow."

But the information had made such an obvious cleft in every skull in 36 the room that the drummer was obliged to see its importance. All had become instantly solemn. "Say," said he, mystified, "what is this?" His three companions made the introductory gesture of eloquent speech; but the young man at the door forestalled them.

"It means, my friend," he answered, as he came into the saloon, 37 "that for the next two hours this town won't be a health resort."

The barkeeper went to the door, and locked and barred it; reaching 38 out of the window, he pulled in heavy wooden shutters, and barred them. Immediately a solemn, chapel-like gloom was upon the place. The drummer was looking from one to another.

"But say," he cried, "what is this, anyhow? You don't mean there is 39 going to be a gunfight?"

"Don't know whether there'll be a fight or not," answered one man, 40 grimly; "but there'll be some shootin'—some good shootin'."

The young man who had warned them waved his hand. "Oh, there'll 41 be a fight fast enough, if anyone wants it. Anybody can get a fight out there in the street. There's a fight just waiting."

The drummer seemed to be swayed between the interest of a 42 foreigner and a perception of personal danger.

"What did you say his name was?" he asked. 43

"Scratchy Wilson," they answered in chorus. 44

"And will he kill anybody? What are you going to do? Does this 45 happen often? Does he rampage around like this once a week or so? Can he break in that door?"

"No; he can't break down that door," replied the barkeeper. "He's 46 tried it three times. But when he comes you'd better lay down on the floor, stranger. He's dead sure to shoot at it, and a bullet may come through."

Thereafter the drummer kept a strict eye upon the door. The time 47 had not yet been called for him to hug the floor, but, as a minor precaution, he sidled near to the wall. "Will he kill anybody?" he said again.

The men laughed low and scornfully at the question. 48

"He's out to shoot, and he's out for trouble. Don't see any good in 49 experimentin' with him."

"But what do you do in a case like this? What do you do?" 50

A man responded: "Why, he and Jack Potter—" 51

"But," in chorus the other men interrupted, "Jack Potter's in San 52 Anton'."

"Well, who is he? What's he got to do with it?" 53

"Oh, he's the town marshal. He goes out and fights Scratchy when 54 he gets on one of these tears."

"Wow!" said the drummer, mopping his brow. "Nice job he's got." 55

The voices had toned away to mere whisperings. The drummer 56 wished to ask further questions, which were born of an increasing anxiety and bewilderment; but when he attempted them, the men merely looked at him in irritation and motioned him to remain silent. A tense waiting hush was upon them. In the deep shadows of the room their eyes shone as they listened for sounds from the street. One man made three gestures at the barkeeper; and the latter, moving like a ghost, handed him a glass and a bottle. The man poured a full glass of whisky, and set down the bottle noiselessly. He gulped the whisky in a swallow, and turned again toward the door in immovable silence. The drummer saw that the barkeeper, without a sound, had taken a Winchester from beneath the bar. Later he saw this individual beckoning to him, so he tiptoed across the room.

"You better come with me back of the bar." 57

"No, thanks," said the drummer, perspiring; "I'd rather be where I 58 can make a break for the back door."

Whereupon the man of bottles made a kindly but peremptory 59 gesture. The drummer obeyed it, and, finding himself seated on a box with his head below the level of the bar, balm was laid upon his soul at sight of various zinc and copper fittings that bore a resemblance to armorplate. The barkeeper took a seat comfortably upon an adjacent box.

"You see," he whispered, "this here Scratchy Wilson is a wonder 60 with a gun—a perfect wonder; and when he goes on the war-trail, we hunt our holes—naturally. He's about the last one of the old gang that used to hang out along the river here. He's a terror when he's drunk. When he's sober he's all right—kind of simple—wouldn't hurt a fly— nicest fellow in town. But when he's drunk—whoo!"

There were periods of stillness. "I wish Jack Potter was back from 61

San Anton'," said the barkeeper. "He shot Wilson up once—in the leg—and he would sail in and pull out the kinks in this thing."

Presently they heard from a distance the sound of a shot, followed 62 by three wild yowls. It instantly removed a bond from the men in the darkened saloon. There was a shuffling of feet. They looked at each other. "Here he comes," they said.

III

A man in a maroon-colored flannel shirt, which had been purchased 63 for purposes of decoration, and made principally by some Jewish women on the East Side of New York, rounded a corner and walked into the middle of the main street of Yellow Sky. In either hand the man held a long, heavy, blue-black revolver. Often he yelled, and these cries rang through a semblance of a deserted village, shrilly flying over the roofs in a volume that seemed to have no relation to the ordinary vocal strength of a man. It was as if the surrounding stillness formed the arch of a tomb over him. These cries of ferocious challenge rang against walls of silence. And his boots had red tops with gilded imprints, of the kind beloved in winter by little sledding boys on the hillsides of New England.

The man's face flamed in a rage begot of whisky. His eyes, rolling, 64 and yet keen for ambush, hunted the still doorways and windows. He walked with the creeping movement of the midnight cat. As it occurred to him, he roared menacing information. The long revolvers in his hands were as easy as straws; they were moved with an electric swiftness. The little fingers of each hand played sometimes in a musician's way. Plain from the low collar of the shirt, the cords of his neck straightened and sank, straightened and sank, as passion moved him. The only sounds were his terrible invitations. The calm adobes preserved their demeanor at the passing of this small thing in the middle of the street.

There was no offer of fight—no offer of fight. The man called to the 65 sky. There were no attractions. He bellowed and fumed and swayed his revolvers here and everywhere.

The dog of the barkeeper of the Weary Gentleman saloon had not 66 appreciated the advance of events. He yet lay dozing in front of his master's door. At sight of the dog, the man paused and raised his revolver humorously. At sight of the man, the dog sprang up and walked diagonally away, with a sullen head, and growling. The man yelled, and the dog broke into a gallop. As it was about to enter an alley, there was a loud noise, a whistling, and something spat the ground directly before it. The dog screamed, and, wheeling in terror, galloped headlong in a new direction. Again there was a noise, a whistling, and sand was kicked viciously before it. Fear-stricken, the dog turned and flurried like an animal in a pen. The man stood laughing, his weapons at his hips.

Ultimately the man was attracted by the closed door of the Weary 67 Gentleman saloon. He went to it and, hammering with a revolver, demanded drink.

The door remaining imperturbable, he picked a bit of paper from 68 the walk, and nailed it to the framework with a knife. He then turned his back contemptuously upon this popular resort and, walking to the opposite side of the street and spinning there on his heel quickly and lithely, fired at the bit of paper. He missed it by a half-inch. He swore at himself, and went away. Later he comfortably fusilladed the windows of his most intimate friend. The man was playing with this town; it was a toy for him.

But still there was no offer of fight. The name of Jack Potter, his 69 ancient antagonist, entered his mind, and he concluded that it would be a glad thing if he should go to Potter's house, and by bombardment induce him to come out and fight. He moved in the direction of his desire, chanting Apache scalp-music.

When he arrived at it, Potter's house presented the same still front 70 as had the other adobes. Taking up a strategic position, the man howled a challenge. But this house regarded him as might a great stone god. It gave no sign. After a decent wait, the man howled further challenges, mingling with them wonderful epithets.

Presently there came the spectacle of a man churning himself into 71 deepest rage over the immobility of a house. He fumed at it as the winter wind attacks a prairie cabin in the North. To the distance there should have gone the sound of a tumult like the fighting of two hundred Mexicans. As necessity bade him, he paused for breath or to reload his revolvers.

IV

Potter and his bride walked sheepishly and with speed. Sometimes 72 they laughed together shamefacedly and low.

"Next corner, dear," he said finally.   73

They put forth the efforts of a pair walking bowed against a strong 74 wind. Potter was about to raise a finger to point the first appearance of the new home when, as they circled the corner, they came face to face with a man in a maroon-colored shirt, who was feverishly pushing cartridges into a large revolver. Upon the instant the man dropped his revolver to the ground and, like lightning, whipped another from its holster. The second weapon was aimed at the bridegroom's chest.

There was a silence. Potter's mouth seemed to be merely a grave for 75 his tongue. He exhibited an instinct to at once loosen his arm from the woman's grip, and he dropped the bag to the sand. As for the bride, her face had gone as yellow as old cloth. She was a slave to hideous rites, gazing at the apparitional snake.

The two men faced each other at a distance of three paces. He of the 76 revolver smiled with a new and quiet ferocity.

"Tried to sneak up on me," he said. "Tried to sneak up on me!" His 77 eyes grew more baleful. As Potter made a slight movement, the man thrust his revolver venomously forward "No; don't you do it, Jack Potter. Don't you move a finger toward a gun just yet. Don't you move an eyelash. The time has come for me to settle with you, and I'm goin' to do it my own way, and loaf along with no interferin'. So if you don't want a gun bent on you, just mind what I tell you."

Potter looked at his enemy. "I ain't got a gun on me Scratchy," he 78 said. "Honest, I ain't." He was stiffening and steadying, but yet some-where at the back of his mind a vision of the Pullman floated: the sea-green figured velvet, the shining brass, silver, and glass, the wood that gleamed as darkly brilliant as the surface of a pool of oil—all the glory of the marriage, the environment of the new estate. "You know I fight when it comes to fighting, Scratchy Wilson; but I ain't got a gun on me. You'll have to do all the shootin' yourself."

His enemy's face went livid. He stepped forward, and lashed his 79 weapon to and fro before Potter's chest. "Don't you tell me you ain't got no gun on you, you whelp. Don't tell me no lie like that. There ain't a man in Texas ever seen you without no gun. Don't take me for no kid." His eyes blazed with light, and his throat worked like a pump.

"I ain't takin' you for no kid," answered Potter. His heels had not 80 moved an inch backward. "I'm takin' you for a damn fool. I tell you I ain't got a gun, and I ain't. If you're goin' to shoot me up, you better begin now; you'll never get a chance like this again."

So much enforced reasoning had told on Wilson's rage; he was 81 calmer. "If you ain't got a gun, why ain't you got a gun?" he sneered. "Been to Sunday-school?"

"I ain't got a gun because I've just come from San Anton' with my 82 wife. I'm married," said Potter. "And if I'd thought there was going to be any galoots like you prowling around when I brought my wife home, I'd had a gun, and don't you forget it."

"Married!" said Scratchy, not at all comprehending.   83

"Yes, married. I'm married," said Potter, distinctly.   84

"Married?" said Scratchy. Seemingly for the first time, he saw the 85 drooping, drowning woman at the other man's side. "No!" he said. He was like a creature allowed a glimpse of another world. He moved a pace backward, and his arm, with the revolver, dropped to his side. "Is this the lady?" he asked.

"Yes; this is the lady," answered Potter.   86

There was another period of silence.   87

"Well," said Wilson at last, slowly, "I s'pose it's all off now."   88

"It's all off if you say so, Scratchy. You know I didn't make the   89
trouble." Potter lifted his valise.

"Well, I 'low it's off, Jack," said Wilson. He was looking at the   90
ground. "Married!" He was not a student of chivalry; it was merely that
in the presence of this foreign condition he was a simple child of the
earlier plains. He picked up his starboard revolver, and, placing both
weapons in their holsters, he went away. His feet made funnel-shaped
tracks in the heavy sand.

Stephen Crane, "The Blue Hotel"

I

The Palace Hotel at Fort Romper was painted a light blue, a shade   1
that is on the legs of a kind of heron, causing the bird to declare its
position against any background. The Palace Hotel, then, was always
screaming and howling in a way that made the dazzling winter
landscape of Nebraska seem only a grey swampish hush. It stood
alone on the prairie, and when the snow was falling the town two
hundred yards away was not visible. But when the traveller alighted
at the railway station he was obliged to pass the Palace Hotel before
he could come upon the company of low clapboard houses which
composed Fort Romper, and it was not to be thought that any
traveller could pass the Palace Hotel without looking at it. Pat Scully,
the proprietor, had proved himself a master of strategy when he
chose his paints. It is true that on clear days, when the great transcon-
tinental expresses, long lines of swaying Pullmans, swept through
Fort Romper, passengers were overcome at the sight, and the cult
that knows the brown reds and the subdivisions of the dark greens of
the East expressed shame, pity, horror, in a laugh. But to the citizens
of this prairie town and to the people who would naturally stop there,
Pat Scully had performed a feat. With this opulence and splendor,
these creeds, classes, egotisms, that streamed through Romper on
the rails day after day, they had no color in common.

As if the displayed delights of such a blue hotel were not suf-   2
ficiently enticing, it was Scully's habit to go every morning and
evening to meet the leisurely trains that stopped at Romper and work
his seductions upon any man that he might see wavering, gripsack in
hand.

One morning, when a snow-crusted engine dragged its long string   3 of freight cars and its one passenger coach to the station, Scully performed the marvel of catching three men. One was a shaky and quick-eyed Swede, with a great shining cheap valise; one was a tall bronzed cowboy, who was on his way to a ranch near the Dakota line; one was a little silent man from the East, who didn't look it, and didn't announce it. Scully practically made them prisoners. He was so nimble and merry and kindly that each probably felt it would be the height of brutality to try to escape. They trudged off over the creaking board sidewalks in the wake of the eager little Irishman. He wore a heavy fur cap squeezed tightly down on his head. It caused his two red ears to stick out stiffly, as if they were made of tin.

At last, Scully, elaborately, with boisterous hospitality, conducted 4
them through the portals of the blue hotel. The room which they entered was small. It seemed to be merely a proper temple for an enormous stove, which, in the center, was humming with godlike violence. At various points on its surface the iron had become luminous and glowed yellow from the heat. Beside the stove Scully's son Johnnie was playing High-Five with an old farmer who had whiskers both grey and sandy. They were quarrelling. Frequently the old farmer turned his face toward a box of sawdust—colored brown from tobacco juice—that was behind the stove, and spat with an air of great impatience and irritation. With a loud flourish of words Scully destroyed the game of cards, and bustled his son upstairs with part of the baggage of the new guests. He himself conducted them to three basins of the coldest water in the world. The cowboy and the Easterner burnished themselves fiery red with this water, until it seemed to be some kind of metal-polish. The Swede, however, merely dipped his fingers gingerly and with trepidation. It was notable that throughout this series of small ceremonies the three travellers were made to feel that Scully was very benevolent. He was conferring great favors upon them. He handed the towel from one to another with an air of philanthropic impulse.

Afterward they went to the first room, and, sitting about the stove, 5
listened to Scully's officious clamor at his daughters, who were preparing the midday meal. They reflected in the silence of experienced men who tread carefully amid new people. Nevertheless, the old farmer, stationary, invincible in his chair near the warmest part of the stove, turned his face from the sawdust-box frequently and addressed a glowing commonplace to the strangers. Usually he was answered in short but adequate sentences by either the cowboy or the Easterner. The Swede said nothing. He seemed to be occupied in making furtive estimates of each man in the room. One might have thought that he had the sense of silly suspicion which comes to guilt. He resembled a badly frightened man.

Later, at dinner, he spoke a little, addressing his conversation   6
entirely to Scully. He volunteered that he had come from New York,
where for ten years he had worked as a tailor. These facts seemed to
strike Scully as fascinating, and afterward he volunteered that he had
lived at Romper for fourteen years. The Swede asked about the crops
and the price of labor. He seemed barely to listen to Scully's extended replies. His eyes continued to rove from man to man.

Finally, with a laugh and a wink, he said that some of these   7
Western communities were very dangerous; and after his statement
he straightened his legs under the table, tilted his head, and laughed
again, loudly. It was plain that the demonstration had no meaning to
the others. They looked at him wondering and in silence.

II

As the men trooped heavily back into the front room, the two little   8
windows presented views of a turmoiling sea of snow. The huge arms
of the wind were making attempts—mighty, circular, futile—to
embrace the flakes as they sped. A gate-post like a still man with a
blanched face stood aghast amid this profligate fury. In a hearty voice
Scully announced the presence of a blizzard. The guests of the blue
hotel, lighting their pipes, assented with grunts of lazy masculine
contentment. No island of the sea could be exempt in the degree of
this little room with its humming stove. Johnnie, son of Scully, in a
tone which defined his opinion of his ability as a card-player, challenged the old farmer of both grey and sandy whiskers to a game
of High-Five. The farmer agreed with a contemptuous and bitter
scoff. They sat close to the stove, and squared their knees under
a wide board. The cowboy and the Easterner watched the game
with interest. The Swede remained near the window, aloof, but
with a countenance that showed signs of an inexplicable excitement.

The play of Johnnie and the grey-beard was suddenly ended by   9
another quarrel. The old man arose while casting a look of heated
scorn at his adversary. He slowly buttoned his coat, and then stalked
with fabulous dignity from the room. In the discreet silence of all the
other men the Swede laughed. His laughter rang somehow childish.
Men by this time had begun to look at him askance, as if they wished
to inquire what ailed him.

A new game was formed jocosely. The cowboy volunteered to   10
become the partner of Johnnie, and they all then turned to ask the
Swede to throw in his lot with the little Easterner. He asked some
questions about the game, and, learning that it wore many names,
and that he had played it when it was under an alias, he accepted the

invitation. He strode toward the men nervously, as if he expected to be assaulted. Finally, seated, he gazed from face to face and laughed shrilly. This laugh was so strange that the Easterner looked up quickly, the cowboy sat intent and with his mouth open, and Johnnie paused, holding the cards with still fingers.

Afterward there was a short silence. Then Johnnie said, "Well, 11 let's get at it. Come on now!" They pulled their chairs forward until their knees were punched under the board. They began to play, and their interest in the game caused the others to forget the manner of the Swede.

The cowboy was a board-whacker. Each time that he held superior 12 cards he whanged them, one by one, with exceeding force, down upon the improvised table, and took the tricks with a glowing air of prowess and pride that sent thrills of indignation into the hearts of his opponents. A game with a board-whacker in it is sure to become intense. The countenances of the Easterner and the Swede were miserable whenever the cowboy thundered down his aces and kings, while Johnnie, his eyes gleaming with joy, chuckled and chuckled.

Because of the absorbing play none considered the strange ways of 13 the Swede. They paid strict heed to the game. Finally, during a lull caused by a new deal, the Swede suddenly addressed Johnnie: "I suppose there have been a good many men killed in this room." The jaws of the others dropped and they looked at him.

"What in hell are you talking about?" said Johnnie. 14

The Swede laughed again his blatant laugh, full of a kind of false 15 courage and defiance. "Oh, you know what I mean all right," he answered.

"I'm a liar if I do!" Johnnie protested. The card was halted, and the 16 men stared at the Swede. Johnnie evidently felt that as the son of the proprietor he should make a direct inquiry. "Now, what might you be drivin' at, mister?" he asked. The Swede winked at him. It was a wink full of cunning. His fingers shook on the edge of the board. "Oh, maybe you think I have been to nowheres. Maybe you think I'm a tenderfoot?"

"I don't know nothing' about you," answered Johnnie, "and I don't 17 give a damn where you've been. All I got to say is that I don't know what you're driving at. There hain't never been nobody killed in this room."

The cowboy, who had been steadily gazing at the Swede, then 18 spoke: "What's wrong with you, mister?"

Apparently it seemed to the Swede that he was formidably 19 menaced. He shivered and turned white near the corners of his mouth. He sent an appealing glance in the direction of the little Easterner. During these moments he did not forget to wear his air of advanced pot-valor. "They say they don't know what I mean," he remarked mockingly to the Easterner.

The latter answered after prolonged and cautious reflection. "I 20 don't understand you," he said, impassively.

The Swede made a movement then which announced that he 21 thought he had encountered treachery from the only quarter where he had expected sympathy, if not help. "Oh, I see you are all against me. I see—"

The cowboy was in a state of deep stupefaction. "Say," he cried, as 22 he tumbled the deck violently down upon the board, "say, what are you gittin' at, hey?"

The Swede sprang up with the celerity of a man escaping from a 23 snake on the floor. "I don't want to fight!" he shouted, "I don't want to fight!"

The cowboy stretched his long legs indolently and deliberately. 24 His hands were in his pockets. He spat into the sawdust-box. "Well, who the hell thought you did?" he inquired.

The Swede backed rapidly toward a corner of the room. His hands 25 were out protectingly in front of his chest, but he was making an obvious struggle to control his fright. "Gentlemen," he quavered, "I suppose I am going to be killed before I can leave this house! I suppose I am going to be killed before I can leave this house!" In his eyes was the dying-swan look. Through the windows could be seen the snow turning blue in the shadow of dusk. The wind tore at the house, and some loose thing beat regularly against the clapboards like a spirit tapping.

A door opened, and Scully himself entered. He paused in surprise 26 as he noted the tragic attitude of the Swede. Then he said, "What's the matter here?"

The Swede answered him swiftly and eagerly: "These men are 27 going to kill me."

"Kill you!" ejaculated Scully. "Kill you! What are you talkin'?" 28

The Swede made the gesture of a martyr. 29

Scully wheeled sternly upon his son. "What is this, Johnnie?" 30

The lad had grown sullen. "Damned if I know," he answered. "I 31 can't make no sense to it." He began to shuffle the cards, fluttering them together with an angry snap. "He says a good many men have been killed in this room, or something like that. And he says he's goin' to be killed here too. I don't know what ails him. He's crazy, I shouldn't wonder."

Scully then looked for explanation to the cowboy, but the cowboy 32 simply shrugged his shoulders.

"Kill you?" said Scully again to the Swede. "Kill you? Man, you're 33 off your nut."

"Oh, I know," burst out the Swede. "I know what will happen.   34
Yes, I'm crazy—yes. Yes, of course, I'm crazy—yes. But I know one
thing—" There was a sort of sweat of misery and terror upon his face.
"I know I won't get out of here alive."

The cowboy drew a deep breath, as if his mind was passing into the   35
last stages of dissolution. "Well, I'm doggoned," he whispered to
himself.

Scully wheeled suddenly and faced his son. "You've been troublin'   36
this man!"

Johnnie's voice was loud with its burden of grievance. "Why, good   37
Gawd, I ain't done nothin' to 'im."

The Swede broke in. "Gentlemen, do not disturb yourselves. I will   38
leave this house. I will go away, because"—he accused them dramatically with his glance— "because I do not want to be killed."

Scully was furious with his son. "Will you tell me what is the   39
matter, you young divil? What's the matter, anyhow? Speak out!"

"Blame it!" cried Johnnie in despair, "don't I tell you I don't know?   40
He—he says we want to kill him, and that's all I know. I can't tell
what ails him."

The Swede continued to repeat: "Never mind, Mr. Scully; never   41
mind. I will leave this house. I will go away, because I do not wish to
be killed. Yes, of course, I am crazy—yes. But I know one thing! I
will go away. I will leave this house. Never mind, Mr. Scully; never
mind. I will go away."

"You will not go 'way," said Scully. "You will not go 'way until I   42
hear the reason of this business. If anybody has troubled you I will
take care of him. This is my house. You are under my roof, and I will
not allow any peaceable man to be troubled here." He cast a terrible
eye on Johnnie, the cowboy, and the Easterner.

"Never mind, Mr. Scully; never mind. I will go away. I do not   43
wish to be killed." The Swede moved toward the door which opened
upon the stairs. It was evidently his intention to go at once for his
baggage.

"No, no," shouted Scully peremptorily; but the white-faced man   44
slid by him and disappeared. "Now," said Scully severely, "what does
this mane?"

Johnnie and the cowboy cried together: "Why, we didn't do   45
nothin' to 'im!"

Scully's eyes were cold. "No," he said, "you didn't?"   46

Johnnie swore a deep oath. "Why, this is the wildest loon I ever   47
see. We didn't do nothin' at all. We were jest sittin' here playin'
cards, and he—"

The father suddenly spoke to the Easterner. "Mr. Blanc," he   48
asked, "what has these boys been doin'?"

The Easterner reflected again. "I didn't see anything wrong at all," 49
he said at last, slowly.

Scully began to howl. "But what does it mane?" He stared fero- 50
ciously at his son. "I have a mind to lather you for this, me boy."

Johnnie was frantic. "Well, what have I done?" he bawled at his 51
father.

III

"I think you are tongue-tied," said Scully finally to his son, the 52
cowboy, and the Easterner; and at the end of this scornful sentence
he left the room.

Upstairs the Swede was swiftly fastening the straps of his great 53
valise. Once his back happened to be half turned toward the door,
and, hearing a noise there, he wheeled and sprang up, uttering a loud
cry. Scully's wrinkled visage showed grimly in the light of the small
lamp he carried. This yellow effulgence, streaming upward, colored
only his prominent features, and left his eyes, for instance, in
mysterious shadow. He resembled a murderer.

"Man! man!" he exclaimed, "have you gone daffy?" 54

"Oh, no! Oh, no!" rejoined the other. "There are people in this 55
world who know pretty nearly as much as you do—understand?"

For a moment they stood gazing at each other. Upon the Swede's 56
deathly pale cheeks were two spots brightly crimson and sharply
edged, as if they had been carefully painted. Scully placed the light
on the table and sat himself on the edge of the bed. He spoke
ruminatively. "By cracky, I never heard of such a thing in all my life.
It's a complete muddle. I can't, for the soul of me, think how you ever
got this idea into your head." Presently he lifted his eyes and asked:
"And did you sure think they were going to kill you?"

The Swede scanned the old man as if he wished to see into his 57
mind. "I did," he said at last. He obviously suspected that this answer
might precipitate an outbreak. As he pulled on a strap his whole arm
shook, the elbow wavering like a bit of paper.

Scully banged his hand impressively on the footboard of the bed. 58
"Why, man, we're goin' to have a line of ilictric streetcars in this town
next spring."

"'A line of electric streetcars,'" repeated the Swede, stupidly. 59

"And," said Scully, "there's a new railroad goin' to be built down 60
from Broken Arm to here. Not to mintion the four churches and the
smashin' big brick schoolhouse. Then there's the big factory, too.
Why, in two years Romper'll be a met-tro-*pol*-is."

Having finished the preparation of his baggage, the Swede 61
straightened himself. "Mr. Scully," he said, with sudden hardihood,
"how much do I owe you?"

"You don't owe me anythin'," said the old man, angrily. 62

"Yes, I do," retorted the Swede. He took seventy-five cents from 63
his pocket and tendered it to Scully; but the latter snapped his fingers
in disdainful refusal. However, it happened that they both stood
gazing in a strange fashion at three silver pieces on the Swede's open
palm.

"I'll not take your money," said Scully at last. "Not after what's 64
been goin' on here." Then a plan seemed to strike him. "Here," he
cried, picking up his lamp and moving toward the door. "Here! Come
with me a minute."

"No," said the Swede, in overwhelming alarm. 65

"Yes," urged the old man. "Come on! I want you to come and see a 66
picter—just across the hall—in my room."

The Swede must have concluded that his hour was come. His jaw 67
dropped and his teeth showed like a dead man's. He ultimately
followed Scully across the corridor, but he had the step of one hung in
chains.

Scully flashed the light high on the wall of his own chamber. There 68
was revealed a ridiculous photograph of a little girl. She was leaning
against a balustrade of gorgeous decoration, and the formidable bang
to her hair was prominent. The figure was as graceful as an upright
sled-stake, and, withal, it was of the hue of lead. "There," said Scully,
tenderly, "that's the picter of my little girl that died. Her name was
Carrie. She had the purtiest hair you ever saw! I was that fond of her,
she—"

Turning then, he saw that the Swede was not contemplating the 69
picture at all, but, instead, was keeping keen watch on the gloom in
the rear.

"Look, man!" cried Scully, heartily. "That's the picter of my little 70
gal that died. Her name was Carrie. And then here's the picter of my
oldest boy, Michael. He's a lawyer in Lincoln, an' doin' well. I gave
that boy a grand eddication, and I'm glad for it now. He's a fine boy.
Look at 'im now. Ain't he bold as blazes, him there in Lincoln, an
honored an'respicted gintleman! An honored and respicted gintleman," concluded Scully with a flourish. And, so saying, he smote the
Swede jovially on the back.

The Swede faintly smiled. 71

"Now," said the old man, "there's only one more thing." He 72
dropped suddenly to the floor and thrust his head beneath the bed.
The Swede could hear his muffled voice. "I'd keep it under me piller
if it wasn't for that boy Johnnie. Then there's the old woman—Where
is it now? I never put it twice in the same place. Ah, now come out
with you!"

Presently he backed clumsily from under the bed, dragging with 73

319

him an old coat rolled into a bundle. "I've fetched him," he muttered. Kneeling on the floor, he unrolled the coat and extracted from its heart a large yellow-brown whisky bottle.

His first maneuver was to hold the bottle up to the light. Reas- 74
sured, apparently, that nobody had been tampering with it, he thrust it with a generous movement toward the Swede.

The weak-kneed Swede was about to eagerly clutch this element of 75
strength, but he suddenly jerked his hand away and cast a look of horror upon Scully.

"Drink," said the old man affectionately. He had risen to his feet, 76
and now stood facing the Swede.

There was a silence. Then again Scully said: "Drink!" 77

The Swede laughed wildly. He grabbed the bottle, put it to his 78
mouth; and as his lips curled absurdly around the opening and his throat worked, he kept his glance, burning with hatred, upon the old man's face.

IV

After the departure of Scully the three men, with the card-board 79
still upon their knees, preserved for a long time an astounded silence. Then Johnnie said: "That's the doddangedest Swede I ever see."

"He ain't no Swede," said the cowboy, scornfully. 80

"Well, what is he then?" cried Johnnie. "What is he then?" 81

"It's my opinion," replied the cowboy deliberately, "he's some 82
kind of a Dutchman." It was a venerable custom of the country to entitle as Swedes all light-haired men who spoke with a heavy tongue. In consequence the idea of the cowboy was not without its daring. "Yes, sir," he repeated. "It's my opinion this feller is some kind of a Dutchman."

"Well, he says he's a Swede, anyhow," muttered Johnnie, sulkily. 83
He turned to the Easterner: "What do you think, Mr. Blanc?"

"Oh, I don't know," replied the Easterner. 84

"Well, what do you think makes him act that way?" asked the 85
cowboy.

"Why, he's frightened." The Easterner knocked his pipe against a 86
rim of the stove. "He's clear frightened out of his boots."

"What at?" cried Johnnie and the cowboy together. 87

The Easterner reflected over his answer. 88

"What at?" cried the others again. 89

"Oh, I don't know, but it seems to me this man has been reading 90
dime novels, and he thinks he's right out in the middle of it—the shootin' and stabbin' and all."

"But," said the cowboy, deeply scandalized, "this ain't Wyoming, 91
ner none of them places. This is Nebrasker."

"Yes," added Johnnie, "an' why don't he wait till he gits *out West?*" 92

The travelled Easterner laughed. "It isn't different there even— 93
not in these days. But he thinks he's right in the middle of hell."

Johnnie and the cowboy mused long. 94

"It's awful funny," remarked Johnnie at last. 95

"Yes," said the cowboy. "This is a queer game. I hope we don't git 96
snowed in, because then we'd have to stand this here man bein'
around with us all the time. That wouldn't be no good."

"I wish pop would throw him out," said Johnnie. 97

Presently they heard a loud stamping on the stairs, accompanied 98
by ringing jokes in the voice of old Scully, and laughter, evidently
from the Swede. The men around the stove stared vacantly at each
other. "Gosh!" said the cowboy. The door flew open, and old Scully,
flushed and anecdotal, came into the room. He was jabbering at the
Swede, who followed him, laughing bravely. It was the entry of two
roisterers from a banquet hall.

"Come now," said Scully sharply to the three seated men, "move 99
up and give us a chance at the stove." The cowboy and the Easterner
obediently sidled their chairs to make room for the newcomers.
Johnnie, however, simply arranged himself in a more indolent attitude, and then remained motionless.

"Come! Git over there," said Scully. 100

"Plenty of room on the other side of the stove," said Johnnie. 101

"Do you think we want to sit in the draft?" roared the father. 102

But the Swede here interposed with a grandeur of confidence. 103
"No, no. Let the boy sit where he likes," he cried in a bullying voice
to the father.

"All right! All right!" said Scully, deferentially. The cowboy and 104
the Easterner exchanged glances of wonder.

The five chairs were formed in a crescent about one side of the 105
stove. The Swede began to talk; he talked arrogantly, profanely,
angrily. Johnnie, the cowboy, and the Easterner maintained a morose
silence, while old Scully appeared to be receptive and eager, breaking in constantly with sympathetic ejaculations.

Finally the Swede announced that he was thirsty. He moved in his 106
chair, and said that he would go for a drink of water.

"I'll git it for you," cried Scully at once. 107

"No," said the Swede, contemptuously. "I'll get it for myself." He 108
arose and stalked with the air of an owner off into the executive parts
of the hotel.

As soon as the Swede was out of hearing Scully sprang to his feet 109 and whispered intensely to the others: "Upstairs he thought I was tryin' to poison 'im."

"Say," said Johnnie, "this makes me sick. Why don't you throw 'im out in the snow?" 110

"Why, he's all right now," declared Scully. "It was only that he was from the East, and he thought this was a tough place. That's all. He's all right now." 111

The cowboy looked with admiration upon the Easterner. "You were straight," he said. "You were on to that there Dutchman." 112

"Well," said Johnnie to his father, "he may be all right now, but I don't see it. Other time he was scared, but now he's too fresh." 113

Scully's speech was always a combination of Irish brogue and idiom, Western twang and idiom, and scraps of curiously formal diction taken from the storybooks and newspapers. He now hurled a strange mass of language at the head of his son. "What do I keep? What do I keep? What do I keep?" he demanded, in a voice of thunder. He slapped his knee impressively, to indicate that he himself was going to make reply, and that all should heed. "I keep a hotel," he shouted. "A hotel, do you mind? A guest under my roof has sacred privileges. He is to be intimidated by none. Not one word shall he hear that would prijudice him in favor of goin' away. I'll not have it. There's no place in this here town where they can say they iver took in a guest of mine because he was afraid to stay here." He wheeled suddenly upon the cowboy and the Easterner. "Am I right?" 114

"Yes, Mr. Scully," said the cowboy, "I think you're right." 115

"Yes, Mr. Scully," said the Easterner, "I think you're right." 116

V

At six-o'clock supper, the Swede fizzed like a fire-wheel. He sometimes seemed on the point of bursting into riotous song, and in all his madness he was encouraged by old Scully. The Easterner was encased in reserve; the cowboy sat in wide-mouthed amazement, forgetting to eat, while Johnnie wrathily demolished great plates of food. The daughters of the house, when they were obliged to replenish the biscuits, approached as warily as Indians, and, having succeeded in their purpose, fled with ill-concealed trepidation. The Swede domineered the whole feast, and he gave it the appearance of a cruel bacchanal. He seemed to have grown suddenly taller; he gazed, brutally disdainful, into every face. His voice rang through the room. Once when he jabbed out harpoon-fashion with his fork to pinion a biscuit, the weapon nearly impaled the hand of the Easterner, which had been stretched quietly out for the same biscuit. 117

After supper, as the men filed toward the other room, the Swede 118

322

smote Scully ruthlessly on the shoulder. "Well, old boy, that was a good, square meal." Johnnie looked hopefully at his father; he knew that shoulder was tender from an old fall; and, indeed, it appeared for a moment as if Scully was going to flame out over the matter, but in the end he smiled a sickly smile and remained silent. The others understood from his manner that he was admitting his responsibility for the Swede's new viewpoint.

Johnnie, however, addressed his parent in an aside. "Why don't 119 you license somebody to kick you downstairs?" Scully scowled darkly by way of reply.

When they were gathered about the stove, the Swede insisted on 120 another game of High-Five. Scully gently deprecated the plan at first, but the Swede turned a wolfish glare upon him. The old man subsided, and the Swede canvassed the others. In his tone there was always a great threat. The cowboy and the Easterner both remarked indifferently that they would play. Scully said that he would presently have to go to meet the 6:58 train, and so the Swede turned menacingly upon Johnnie. For a moment their glances crossed like blades, and then Johnnie smiled and said, "Yes, I'll play."

They formed a square, with the little board on their knees. The 121 Easterner and the Swede were again partners. As the play went on, it was noticeable that the cowboy was not board-whacking as usual. Meanwhile, Scully, near the lamp, had put on his spectacles and, with an appearance curiously like an old priest, was reading a newspaper. In time he went out to meet the 6:58 train, and, despite his precautions, a gust of polar wind whirled into the room as he opened the door. Besides scattering the cards, it chilled the players to the marrow. The Swede cursed frightfully. When Scully returned, his entrance disturbed a cosy and friendly scene. The Swede again cursed. But presently they were once more intent, their heads bent forward and their hands moving swiftly. The Swede had adopted the fashion of board-whacking.

Scully took up his paper and for a long time remained immersed in 122 matters which were extraordinarily remote from him. The lamp burned badly, and once he stopped to adjust the wick. The newspaper, as he turned from page to page, rustled with a slow and comfortable sound. Then suddenly he heard three terrible words: "You are cheatin'!"

Such scenes often prove that there can be little of dramatic import 123 in environment. Any room can present a tragic front; any room can be comic. This little den was now hideous as a torture-chamber. The new faces of the men themselves had changed it upon the instant. The Swede held a huge fist in front of Johnnie's face, while the latter looked steadily over it into the blazing orbs of his accuser. The

Easterner had grown pallid; the cowboy's jaw had dropped in that expression of bovine amazement which was one of his important mannerisms. After the three words, the first sound in the room was made by Scully's paper as it floated forgotten to his feet. His spectacles had also fallen from his nose, but by a clutch he had saved them in air. His hand, grasping the spectacles, now remained poised awkwardly and near his shoulder. He stared at the card-players.

Probably the silence was while a second elapsed. Then, if the floor 124 had been suddenly twitched out from under the men they could not have moved quicker. The five had projected themselves headlong toward a common point. It happened that Johnnie, in rising to hurl himself upon the Swede, had stumbled slightly because of his curiously instinctive care for the cards and the board. The loss of the moment allowed time for the arrival of Scully, and also allowed the cowboy time to give the Swede a great push which sent him staggering back. The men found tongue together, and hoarse shouts of rage, appeal, or fear burst from every throat. The cowboy pushed and jostled feverishly at the Swede, and the Easterner and Scully clung wildly to Johnnie; but through the smoky air, above the swaying bodies of the peace-compellers, the eyes of the two warriors ever sought each other in glances of challenge that were at once hot and steely.

Of course the board had been overturned, and now the whole 125 company of cards was scattered over the floor, where the boots of the men trampled the fat and painted kings and queens as they gazed with their silly eyes at the war that was waging above them.

Scully's voice was dominating the yells. "Stop now! Stop, I say! 126 Stop, now—"

Johnnie, as he struggled to burst through the rank formed by 127 Scully and the Easterner, was crying, "Well, he says I cheated! He says I cheated! I won't allow no man to say I cheated! If he says I cheated he's a — —!"

The cowboy was telling the Swede, "Quit, now! Quit, d'ye hear—" 128

The screams of the Swede never ceased: "He did cheat! I saw him! 129 I saw him—"

As for the Easterner, he was importuning in a voice that was not 130 heeded: "Wait a moment, can't you? Oh, wait a moment. What's the good of a fight over a game of cards? Wait a moment—"

In this tumult no complete sentences were clear. "Cheat"— 131 "Quit"—"He says"—these fragments pierced the uproar and rang out sharply. It was remarkable that, whereas Scully undoubtedly made the most noise, he was the least heard of any of the riotous band.

Then suddenly there was a great cessation. It was as if each man 132 had paused for breath; and although the room was still lighted with the anger of men, it could be seen that there was no danger of immediate conflict, and at once Johnnie, shouldering his way forward, almost succeeded in confronting the Swede. "What did you say I cheated for? What did you say I cheated for? I don't cheat, and I won't let no man say I do!"

The Swede said, "I saw you! I saw you!" 133

"Well," cried Johnnie, "I'll fight any man what says I cheat!" 134

"No, you won't," said the cowboy. "Not here." 135

"Ah, be still, can't you?" said Scully, coming between them. 136

The quiet was sufficient to allow the Easterner's voice to be heard. 137 He was repeating, "Oh, wait a moment, can't you? What's the good of a fight over a game of cards? Wait a moment!"

Johnnie, his red face appearing above his father's shoulder, hailed 138 the Swede again. "Did you say I cheated?"

The Swede showed his teeth. "Yes." 139

"Then," said Johnnie, "we must fight." 140

"Yes, fight," roared the Swede. He was like a demoniac. "Yes, 141 fight! I'll show you what kind of man I am! I'll show you who you want to fight! Maybe you think I can't fight! Maybe you think I can't! I'll show you, you skin, you card-sharp! Yes, you cheated! You cheated! You cheated!"

"Well, let's go at it, then, mister," said Johnnie, coolly. 142

The cowboy's brow was beaded with sweat from his efforts in 143 intercepting all sorts of raids. He turned in despair to Scully. "What are you goin' to do now?"

A change had come over the Celtic visage of the old man. He now 144 seemed all eagerness; his eyes glowed.

"We'll let them fight," he answered, stalwartly. "I can't put up 145 with it any longer. I've stood this damned Swede till I'm sick. We'll let them fight.

VI

The men prepared to go out of doors. The Easterner was so 146 nervous that he had great difficulty in getting his arms into the sleeves of his new leather coat. As the cowboy drew his fur cap down over his ears his hands trembled. In fact, Johnnie and old Scully were the only ones who displayed no agitation. These preliminaries were conducted without words.

Scully threw open the door. "Well, come on," he said. Instantly a 147 terrific wind caused the flame of the lamp to struggle at its wick, while a puff of black smoke sprang from the chimney-top. The stove was in mid-current of the blast, and its voice swelled to equal the roar of the storm. Some of the scarred and bedabbled cards were caught up from the floor and dashed helplessly against the farther wall. The men lowered their hands and plunged into the tempest as into a sea.

No snow was falling, but great whirls and clouds of flakes, swept 148 up from the ground by the frantic winds, were streaming southward with the speed of bullets. The covered land was blue with the sheen of an unearthly satin, and there was no other hue save where, at the low, black railway station—which seemed incredibly distant—one light gleamed like a tiny jewel. As the men floundered into a thigh-deep drift, it was known that the Swede was bawling out something. Scully went to him, put a hand on his shoulder, and projected an ear. "What's that you say?" he shouted.

"I say," bawled the Swede again, "I won't stand much show against 149 this gang. I know you'll all pitch on me."

Scully smote him reproachfully on the arm. "Tut, man!" he yelled. 150 The wind tore the words from Scully's lips and scattered them far alee.

"You are all a gang of—" boomed the Swede, but the storm also 151 seized the remainder of this sentence.

Immediately turning their backs upon the wind, the men had 152 swung around a corner to the sheltered side of the hotel. It was the function of the little house to preserve here, amid this great devastation of snow, an irregular V-shape of heavily encrusted grass, which crackled beneath the feet. One could imagine the great drifts piled against the windward side. When the party reached the comparative peace of this spot it was found that the Swede was still bellowing.

"Oh, I know what kind of a thing this is! I know you'll all pitch on 153 me. I can't lick you all!"

Scully turned upon him panther-fashion. "You'll not have to whip 154 all of us. You'll have to whip my son Johnnie. An' the man what troubles you durin' that time will have me to dale with."

The arrangements were swiftly made. The two men faced each 155 other, obedient to the harsh commands of Scully, whose face, in the subtly luminous gloom, could be seen set in the austere impersonal lines that are pictured on the countenances of the Roman veterans. The Easterner's teeth were chattering, and he was hopping up and down like a mechanical toy. The cowboy stood rock-like.

The contestants had not stripped off any clothing. Each was in his 156 ordinary attire. Their fists were up, and they eyed each other in a calm that had the elements of leonine cruelty in it.

During this pause, the Easterner's mind, like a film, took lasting 157 impressions of three men—the iron-nerved master of the ceremony; the Swede, pale, motionless, terrible; and Johnnie, serene yet ferocious, brutish yet heroic. The entire prelude had in it a tragedy greater than the tragedy of action, and this aspect was accentuated by the long, mellow cry of the blizzard, as it sped the tumbling and wailing flakes into the black abyss of the south.

"Now!" said Scully.   158

The two combatants leaped forward and crashed together like 159 bullocks. There was heard the cushioned sound of blows, and of a curse squeezing out from between the tight teeth of one.

As for the spectators, the Easterner's pent-up breath exploded 160 from him with a pop of relief, absolute relief from the tension of the preliminaries. The cowboy bounded into the air with a yowl. Scully was immovable as from supreme amazement and fear at the fury of the fight which he himself had permitted and arranged.

For a time the encounter in the darkness was such a perplexity of 161 flying arms that it presented no more detail than would a swiftly revolving wheel. Occasionally a face, as if illumined by a flash of light, would shine out, ghastly and marked with pink spots. A moment later, the men might have been known as shadows, if it were not for the involuntary utterance of oaths that came from them in whispers.

Suddenly a holocaust of warlike desire caught the cowboy, and he 162 bolted forward with the speed of a bronco. "Go it, Johnnie! Go it! Kill him! Kill him!"

Scully confronted him. "Kape back," he said; and by his glance the 163 cowboy could tell that this man was Johnnie's father.

To the Easterner there was a monotony of unchangeable fighting 164 that was an abomination. This confused mingling was eternal to his sense, which was concentrated in a longing for the end, the priceless end. Once the fighters lurched near him, and as he scrambled hastily backward he heard them breathe like men on the rack.

"Kill him, Johnnie! Kill him! Kill him! Kill him!" The cowboy's face 165 was contorted like one of those agony masks in museums.

"Keep still," said Scully, icily.   166

Then there was a sudden loud grunt, incomplete, cut short, and 167 Johnnie's body swung away from the Swede and fell with sickening heaviness to the grass. The cowboy was barely in time to prevent the mad Swede from flinging himself upon his prone adversary. "No, you don't," said the cowboy, interposing an arm. "Wait a second."

Scully was at his son's side. "Johnnie! Johnnie, me boy!" His voice 168 had a quality of melancholy tenderness. "Johnnie! Can you go on with it?" He looked anxiously down into the bloody, pulpy face of his son.

There was a moment of silence, and then Johnnie answered in his 169 ordinary voice, "Yes, I—it—yes."

Assisted by his father he struggled to his feet. "Wait a bit now till 170 you git your wind," said the old man.

A few paces away the cowboy was lecturing the Swede. "No, you 171 don't! Wait a second!"

The Easterner was plucking at Scully's sleeve. "Oh, this is 172 enough," he pleaded. "This is enough! Let it go as it stands. This is enough!"

"Bill," said Scully, "git out of the road." The cowboy stepped aside. 173 "Now." The combatants were actuated by a new caution as they advanced toward collision. They glared at each other, and then the Swede aimed a lightning blow that carried with it his entire weight. Johnnie was evidently half stupid from weakness, but he miraculously dodged, and his fist sent the overbalanced Swede sprawling.

The cowboy, Scully, and the Easterner burst into a cheer that was 174 like a chorus of trimphant soldiery, but before its conclusion the Swede had scuffled agilely to his feet and come in berserk abandon at his foe. There was another perplexity of flying arms, and Johnnie's body again swung away and fell, even as a bundle might fall from a roof. The Swede instantly staggered to a little wind-waved tree and leaned upon it, breathing like an engine, while his savage and flame-lit eyes roamed from face to face as the men bent over Johnnie. There was a splendor of isolation in his situation at this time which the Easterner felt once when, lifting his eyes from the man on the ground, he beheld that mysterious and lonely figure, waiting.

"Are you any good yet, Johnnie?" asked Scully in a broken voice. 175

The son gasped and opened his eyes languidly. After a moment 176 he answered, "No—I ain't—any good—any—more." Then, from shame and bodily ill, he began to weep, the tears furrowing down through the blood stains on his face. "He was too—too—too heavy for me."

Scully straightened and addressed the waiting figure. "Stranger," 177 he said, evenly, "it's all up with our side." Then his voice changed into that vibrant huskiness which is commonly the tone of the most simple and deadly announcements. "Johnnie is whipped."

Without replying, the victor moved off on the route to the front 178 door of the hotel.

The cowboy was formulating new and unspellable blasphemies. 179 The Easterner was startled to find that they were out in a wind that seemed to come direct from the shadowed arctic floes. He heard again the wail of the snow as it was flung to its grave in the south. He knew now that all this time the cold had been sinking into him deeper and deeper, and he wondered that he had not perished. He felt indifferent to the condition of the vanquished man.

"Johnnie, can you walk?" asked Scully. 180

"Did I hurt—hurt him any?" asked the son. 181

"Can you walk, boy? Can you walk?" 182

Johnnie's voice was suddenly strong. There was a robust impa- 183 tience in it. "I asked you whether I hurt him any!"

"Yes, yes, Johnnie," answered the cowboy, consolingly; "he's hurt 184 a good deal."

They raised him from the ground, and as soon as he was on his feet 185 he went tottering off, rebuffing all attempts at assistance. When the party rounded the corner they were fairly blinded by the pelting of the snow. It burned their faces like fire. The cowboy carried Johnnie through the drift to the door. As they entered, some cards again rose from the floor and beat against the wall.

The Easterner rushed to the stove. He was so profoundly chilled 186 that he almost dared to embrace the glowing iron. The Swede was not in the room. Johnnie sank into a chair and, folding his arms on his knees, buried his face in them. Scully, warming one foot and then the other at a rim of the stove, muttered to himself with Celtic mournfulness. The cowboy had removed his fur cap, and with a dazed and rueful air he was running one hand through his tousled locks. From overhead they could hear the creaking of boards, as the Swede tramped here and there in his room.

The sad quiet was broken by the sudden flinging open of a door 187 that led toward the kitchen. It was instantly followed by an inrush of women. They precipitated themselves upon Johnnie amid a chorus of lamentation. Before they carried their prey off to the kitchen, there to be bathed and harangued with that mixture of sympathy and abuse which is a feat of their sex, the mother straightened herself and fixed old Scully with an eye of stern reproach. "Shame be upon you, Patrick Scully!" she cried. "Your own son, too. Shame be upon you!"

"There, now! Be quiet now!" said the old man, weakly. 188

"Shame be upon you, Patrick Scully!" The girls, rallying to this 189 slogan, sniffled disdainfully in the direction of those trembling accomplices, the cowboy and the Easterner. Presently they bore Johnnie away, and left the three men to dismal reflection.

VII

"I'd like to fight this here Dutchman myself," said the cowboy, 190 breaking a long silence.

Scully wagged his head sadly. "No, that wouldn't do. It wouldn't 191 be right. It wouldn't be right."

"Well, why wouldn't it?" argued the cowboy. "I don't see no harm 192 in it."

"No," answered Scully, with mournful heroism. "It wouldn't be 193 right. It was Johnnie's fight, and now we mustn't whip the man just because he whipped Johnnie."

"Yes, that's true enough," said the cowboy; "but—he better not get 194 fresh with me, because I couldn't stand no more of it."

"You'll not say a word to him," commanded Scully, and even then 195
they heard the tread of the Swede on the stairs. His entrance was
made theatric. He swept the door back with a bang and swaggered to
the middle of the room. No one looked at him. "Well," he cried,
insolently, at Scully, "I s'pose you'll tell me now how much I owe
you?"

The old man remained stolid. "You don't owe me nothin'." 196

"Huh!" said the Swede, "huh! Don't owe 'im nothin'." 197

The cowboy addressed the Swede. "Stranger, I don't see how you 198
come to be so gay around here."

Old Scully was instantly alert. "Stop!" he shouted, holding his 199
hand forth, fingers upward. "Bill, you shut up!"

The cowboy spat carelessly into the sawdust-box. "I didn't say a 200
word, did I?" he asked.

"Mr. Scully," called the Swede, "how much do I owe you?" It was 201
seen that he was attired for departure, and that he had his valise in his
hand.

"You don't owe me nothin'," repeated Scully in the same im- 202
perturbable way.

"Huh!" said the Swede. "I guess you're right. I guess if it was any 203
way at all, you'd owe me somethin'. That's what I guess." He turned
to the cowboy. " 'Kill him! Kill him! Kill him!' " he mimicked, and
then guffawed victoriously. " 'Kill him!' " He was convulsed with
ironical humor.

But he might have been jeering the dead. The three men were 204
immovable and silent, staring with glassy eyes at the stove.

The Swede opened the door and passed into the storm, giving one 205
derisive glance backward at the still group.

As soon as the door was closed, Scully and the cowboy leaped to 206
their feet and began to curse. They trampled to and fro, waving their
arms and smashing into the air with their fists. "Oh, but that was a
hard minute!" wailed Scully. "That was a hard minute! Him there
leerin' and coofffin'! One bang at his nose was worth forty dollars to me
that minute! How did you stand it, Bill?"

"How did I stand it?" cried the cowboy in a quivering voice. "How 207
did I stand it? Oh!"

The old man burst into sudden brogue. "I'd loike to take that 208
Swade," he wailed, "and hold 'im down on a shtone floor and bate 'im
to a jelly wid a shtick!"

The cowboy groaned in sympathy. "I'd like to git him by the neck 209
and ha-ammer him"—he brought his hand down on a chair with a
noise like a pistol-shot—"hammer that there Dutchman until he
couldn't tell himself from a dead coyote!"

"I'd bate 'im until he—" 210

"I'd show *him* some things—"   211
And then together they raised a yearning, fanatic cry— "Oh-o-oh! 212
if we only could—"
  "Yes!   213
  "Yes!"   214
  "And then I'd—"   215
  "O-o-oh!"   216

VIII

The Swede, tightly gripping his valise, tacked across the face of the 217
storm as if he carried sails. He was following a line of little naked,
grasping trees which, he knew, must mark the way of the road. His
face, fresh from the pounding of Johnnie's fists, felt more pleasure
than pain in the wind and the driving snow. A number of square
shapes loomed upon him finally, and he knew them as the houses of
the main body of the town. He found a street and made travel along
it, leaning heavily upon the wind whenever, at a corner, a terrific
blast caught him.

He might have been in a deserted village. We picture the world as 218
thick with conquering and elate humanity, but here, with the bugles
of the tempest pealing, it was hard to imagine a peopled earth. One
viewed the existence of man then as a marvel, and conceded a glamor
of wonder to these lice which were caused to cling to a whirling,
fire-smitten, ice-locked, disease-stricken, space-lost bulb. The con-
ceit of man was explained by this storm to be the very engine of life.
One was a coxcomb not to die in it. However, the Swede found a
saloon.

In front of it an indomitable red light was burning, and the 219
snowflakes were made blood-color as they flew through the circums-
cribed territory of the lamp's shining. The Swede pushed open the
door of the saloon and entered. A sanded expanse was before him,
and at the end of it four men sat about a table drinking. Down one
side of the room extended a radiant bar, and its guardian was leaning
upon his elbows listening to the talk of the men at the table. The
Swede dropped his valise upon the floor and, smiling fraternally upon
the barkeeper, said, "Gimme some whisky, will you?" The man
placed a bottle, a whisky-glass, and a glass of ice-thick water upon the
bar. The Swede poured himself an abnormal portion of whisky and
drank it in three gulps. "Pretty bad night," remarked the bartender,
indifferently. He was making the pretension of blindness which is
usually a distinction of his class; but it could have been seen that he
was furtively studying the half-erased blood stains on the face of the
Swede. "Bad night," he said again.

"Oh, it's good enough for me," replied the Swede, hardily, as he 220 poured himself some more whisky. The bartender took his coin and maneuvered it through its reception by the highly nickelled cash-machine. A bell rang; a card labelled "20 cts." had appeared.

"No," continued the Swede, "this isn't too bad weather. It's good 221 enough for me."

"So?" murmured the barkeeper, languidly. 222

The copious drams made the Swede's eyes swim, and he breathed 223 a trifle heavier. "Yes, I like this weather. I like it. It suits me." It was apparently his design to impart a deep significance to these words.

"So?" murmured the bartender again. He turned his gaze dreamily 224 at the scroll-like birds and bird-like scrolls which had been drawn with soap upon the mirrors in back of the bar.

"Well, I guess I'll take another drink," said the Swede, presently. 225 "Have something?"

"No, thanks; I'm not drinkin'," answered the bartender. Afterward 226 he asked, "How did you hurt your face?"

The Swede immediately began to boast loudly. "Why, in a fight. I 227 thumped the soul out of a man down here at Scully's hotel."

The interest of the four men at the table was at last aroused. 228

"Who was it?" said one. 229

"Johnnie Scully," blustered the Swede. "Son of the man what runs 230 it. He will be pretty near dead for some weeks, I can tell you. I made a nice thing of him, I did. He couldn't get up. They carried him in the house. Have a drink?"

Instantly the men in some subtle way encased themselves in 231 reserve. "No, thanks," said one. The group was of curious formation. Two were prominent local businessmen; one was the district attorney; and one was a professional gambler of the kind known as "square." But a scrutiny of the group would not have enabled an observer to pick the gambler from the men of more reputable pursuits. He was, in fact, a man so delicate in manner, when among people of fair class, and so judicious in his choice of victims, that in the strictly masculine part of the town's life he had come to be explicitly trusted and admired. People called him a thoroughbred. The fear and contempt with which his craft was regarded were undoubtedly the reason why his quiet dignity shone conspicuous above the quiet dignity of men who might be merely hatters, billiard-markers, or grocery clerks. Beyond an occasional unwary traveller who came by rail, this gambler was supposed to prey solely upon reckless and senile farmers, who, when flush with good crops, drove into town in all the pride and confidence of an absolutely invulnerable stupidity. Hearing at times in circuitous fashion of the despoilment of such a farmer, the important men of Romper invariably laughed in contempt of the victim, and if they thought of the wolf at all, it was with a kind of pride at the knowledge that he would never dare think of attacking their wisdom and courage. Besides, it was popular that this gambler had a real wife and two real children in a neat cottage in a suburb, where he led an exemplary home life; and when anyone even suggested a discrepancy in his character, the crowd immediately vociferated descriptions of this virtuous family circle. Then men who led exemplary home lives, and men who did not lead exemplary home lives, all subsided in a bunch, remarking that there was nothing more to be said.

However, when a restriction was placed upon him—as, for instance, when a strong clique of members of the new Pollywog Club refused to permit him, even as a spectator, to appear in the rooms of the organization—the candor and gentleness with which he accepted the judgment disarmed many of his foes and made his friends more desperately partisan. He invariably distinguished between himself and a respectable Romper man so quickly and frankly that his manner actually appeared to be a continual broadcast compliment. 232

And one must not forget to declare the fundamental fact of his entire position in Romper. It is irrefutable that in all affairs outside his business, in all matters that occur eternally and commonly between man and man, this thieving card-player was so generous, so just, so moral, that, in a contest, he could have put to flight the consciences of nine tenths of the citizens of Romper. 233

And so it happened that he was seated in this saloon with the two prominent local merchants and the district attorney. 234

The Swede continued to drink raw whisky, meanwhile babbling at the barkeeper and trying to induce him to indulge in potations. "Come on. Have a drink. Come on. What—no? Well, have a little one, then. By gawd, I've whipped a man tonight, and I want to celebrate. I whipped him good, too. Gentlemen," the Swede cried to the men at the table, "have a drink?" 235

"Ssh!" said the barkeeper. 236

The group at the table, although furtively attentive, had been pretending to be deep in talk, but now a man lifted his eyes toward the Swede and said, shortly, "Thanks. We don't want any more." 237

At this reply the Swede ruffled out his chest like a rooster. "Well," he exploded, "it seems I can't get anybody to drink with me in this town. Seems so, don't it? Well!" 238

"Ssh!" said the barkeeper. 239

"Say," snarled the Swede, "don't you try to shut me up. I won't have it. I'm a gentleman, and I want people to drink with me. And I want 'em to drink with me now. *Now*—do you understand?" He rapped the bar with his knuckles. 240

Years of experience had calloused the bartender. He merely grew 241
sulky. "I hear you," he answered.

"Well," cried the Swede, "listen hard then. See those men over 242
there? Well, they're going to drink with me, and don't you forget it.
Now you watch."

"Hi!" yelled the barkeeper, "this won't do!" 243

"Why won't it?" demanded the Swede. He stalked over to the 244
table, and by chance laid his hand upon the shoulder of the gambler.
"How about this?" he asked wrathfully. "I asked you to drink with
me."

The gambler simply twisted his head and spoke over his shoulder. 245
"My friend, I don't know you."

"Oh, hell!" answered the Swede, "come and have a drink." 246

"Now, my boy," advised the gambler, kindly, "take your hand off 247
my shoulder and go 'way and mind your own business." He was a
little, slim man, and it seemed strange to hear him use this tone of
heroic patronage to the burly Swede. The other men at the table said
nothing.

"What! You won't drink with me, you little dude? I'll make you, 248
then! I'll make you!" The Swede had grasped the gambler frenziedly
at the throat, and was dragging him from his chair. The other men
sprang up. The barkeeper dashed around the corner of his bar. There
was a great tumult, and then was seen a long blade in the hand of the
gambler. It shot forward, and a human body, this citadel of virtue, wisdom, power, was pierced as easily as if it had been a melon.
The Swede fell with a cry of supreme astonishment.

The prominent merchants and the district attorney must have at 249
once tumbled out of the place backward. The bartender found himself hanging limply to the arm of a chair and gazing into the eyes of a
murderer.

"Henry," said the latter, as he wiped his knife on one of the towels 250
that hung beneath the bar rail, "you tell 'em where to find me. I'll be
home, waiting for 'em." Then he vanished. A moment afterward the
barkeeper was in the street dinning through the storm for help and,
moreover, companionship.

The corpse of the Swede, alone in the saloon, had its eyes fixed 251
upon a dreadful legend that dwelt atop of the cash-machine: "This
registers the amount of your purchase."

IX

Months later, the cowboy was frying pork over the stove of a little 252
ranch near the Dakota line, when there was a quick thud of hoofs

outside, and presently the Easterner entered with the letters and the papers.

"Well," said the Easterner at once, "the chap that killed the Swede 253 has got three years. Wasn't much was it?"

"He has? Three years?" The cowboy poised his pan of pork, while 254 he ruminated upon the news. "Three years. That ain't much."

"No. It was a light sentence," replied Easterner as he unbuckled 255 his spurs. "Seems there was a good deal of sympathy for him in Romper."

"If the bartender had been any good," observed the cowboy, 256 thoughtfully, "he would have gone in and cracked that there Dutchman on the head with a bottle in the beginnin' of it and stopped all this here murderin'."

"Yes, a thousand things might have happended," said the Eastern- 257 er, tartly.

The cowboy returned his pan of pork to the fire, but his philosophy 258 continued. "It's funny, ain't it? If he hadn't said Johnnie was cheatin' he'd be alive this minute. He was an awful fool. Game played for fun, too. Not for money. I believe he was crazy."

"I feel sorry for the gambler," said the Easterner. 259

"Oh, so do I," said the cowboy. "He don't deserve none of it for 260 killin' who he did."

"The Swede might not have been killed if everything had been 261 square."

"Might not have been killed?" exclaimed the cowboy. "Everythin' 262 square? Why, when he said that Johnnie was cheatin' and acted like such a jackass? And then in the saloon he fairly walked up to git hurt?" With these arguments the cowboy browbeat the Easterner and reduced him to a rage.

"You're a fool!" cried the Easterner, viciously. "You're a bigger 263 jackass than the Swede by a million majority. Now let me tell you one thing. Let me tell you something. Listen! Johnnie *was* cheating!"

" 'Johnnie,' " said the cowboy, blankly. There was a minute of 264 silence, and then he said, robustly, "Why, no. The game was only for fun."

"Fun or not," said the Easterner, "Johnnie was cheating. I saw 265 him. I know it. I saw him. And I refused to stand up and be a man. I let the Swede fight it out alone. And you—you were simply puffing around the place and wanting to fight. And then old Scully himself! We are all in it! This poor gambler isn't even a noun. He is kind of an adverb. Every sin is the result of a collaboration. We, five of us, have collaborated in the murder of this Swede. Usually there are from a dozen to forty women really involved in every murder, but in this case it seems to be only five men—you, I, Johnnie, old Scully; and that fool of an unfortunate gambler came merely as a culmination, the apex of a human movement, and gets all the punishment."

The cowboy, injured and rebellious, cried out blindly into this fog 266 of mysterious theory: "Well, I didn't do anythin', did I?"

PRACTICE

Stephen Crane and the Western Formula

Your assignment here is to use the Western formula discussed in John Cawelti's essay to analyze the two stories by Stephen Crane, and to arrive at a thesis for your essay.

First, you should read through the material carefully, and you should make notes of what you consider to be Cawelti's main points about setting and heroes in the Western. In reading Crane's stories, you should also make notes of your responses to the stories, of passages you consider important, and of connections or contrasts you find between the stories and Cawelti's essay.

A general approach to the Crane stories might consider one of the following:

1. In what ways do Crane's stories exemplify Cawelti's formula?
2. In what ways do these stories deviate from the formula of the tradition-al Western?
3. In what ways do the stories comment on the traditional Western code?

From such general considerations you can narrow your approach to an analysis of setting or of heroes (or the lack of them) in the stories. You might compare and contrast aspects of setting or of characters in the stories to illustrate a thesis about the traditional or nontraditional treatment of char-acter or setting. You might want to investigate the clash of civilization and wilderness, or consider the stories as commentaries on masculine rituals or mythic ideas about the West.

But remember: while Calwelti's essay will provide a frame through which to read the stories as well as a number of possible theses to investigate, your choice of a thesis and your effective development of it will depend on your own careful reading and gathering of evidence from the stories.

PRACTICE

Crane: The Man and the Stories

What relation has Stephen Crane's life to the fiction he wrote? To in-vestigate this question, you should look at the biographical material on

Crane in Chapter 6, pp. 102–109.[1] Consider what sort of man Crane was, and why the American West would have interested him as a topic for his fiction. In reading the two stories reprinted in this chapter, consider what attitude toward the West is expressed. Given what you know of Crane's life, is it possible to say that any of the characters in the stories reflect his point of view?

Your instructor can decide whether further research into Crane's trip to the West in 1895 is necessary, or whether you might read Crane's Western nonfiction to see whether any of his own experiences were transformed into such fiction as "The Bride Comes to Yellow Sky" or "The Blue Hotel."

READING AND PRACTICE

Men and Women on Love: A Collection of Poems

The material for this synthesis project consists of twelve poems about love. To discover an hypothesis for a synthesis paper, consider your responses to these poems as well as the features that make these poems similar to or different from one another in both form and content.

A good way to begin this project is to make sense of each poem. After reading a poem, consider the following questions: Who is speaking? to whom? when? where? about what? how? why? to what effect? In analyzing the "how" of each poem, you might find that some of the terms we've used in this book are helpful.

To generate an hypothesis about these love poems, you will need to consider similar features of form, point, and purpose as well as what differentiates one or more poems from the others. You may also want to speculate about the reasons for the similarities and differences that you find most significant. Here are some additional questions that may help you to generate an hypothesis:

1. Is one of these poems more intriguing or effective than the others? If so, what makes it more intriguing or effective?
2. What aspects of love do these poems tend to emphasize? What aspects of love do they tend to marginalize or ignore?
3. Have poetic ways of figuring (out) love changed over time? If so, how so? If not, in what ways have they remained the same?
4. Does a poet's gender affect the way the experience of love is represented? If so, how so? If not, how not?

---

[1]Also relevant is Crane's "The Last of the Mohicans," pp. 154–156.

---

5. As you see it, what is the major problem poets confront when writing about love? How do they deal with this problem? Are some ways of dealing better than others?

As you work through these questions—and any others you have thought of—remember that your task is to come up with an hypothesis that is relevant to these poems and that can therefore be explored, explained, and supported by reference to specific poems. In the end, love may be impossible to explain or understand. But love poetry is something else. Or is it? What do you think?

Sonnet 138

When my love swears that she is made of truth,
I do believe her, though I know she lies,
That she might think me some untutored youth,
Unlearned in the world's false subtleties.
Thus vainly thinking that she thinks me young,   5
Although she knows my days are past the best,
Simply I credit her false-speaking tongue:
On both sides thus is simple truth suppressed.
But wherefore says she not she is unjust?
And wherefore say not I that I am old?   10
Oh, love's best habit is in seeming trust,
And age in love loves not to have years told.
Therefore I lie with her and she with me,
And in our faults by lies we flattered be.

      —WILLIAM SHAKESPEARE, 1609

To My Dear and Loving Husband

If ever two were one, then surely we.
If ever man were loved by wife, then thee;
If ever wife was happy in a man,
Compare with me, ye women, if you can.
I prize thy love more than whole mines of gold   5
Or all the riches that the East doth hold.
My love is such that rivers cannot quench,
Nor ought but love from thee, give recompense.
Thy love is such I can no way repay,
The heavens reward thee manifold, I pray.   10
Then while we live, in love let's so persevere
That when we live no more, we may live ever.

      —ANNE BRADSTREET, 1671

To His Coy Mistress

    Had we but world enough, and time,
This coyness, lady, were no crime.
We would sit down, and think which way
To walk, and pass our long love's day.
Thou by the Indian Ganges' side   5
Shouldst rubies find; I by the tide
Of Humber would complain.[1] I would
Love you ten years before the flood,
And you should, if you please, refuse
Till the conversion of the Jews.[2]   10
My vegetable love should grow
Vaster than empires and more slow;
An hundred years should go to praise
Thine eyes, and on thy forehead gaze;
Two hundred to adore each breast,   15
But thirty thousand to the rest;
An age at least to every part,
And the last age should show your heart.
For, lady, you deserve this state,
Nor would I love at lower rate.   20
    But at my back I always hear
Time's wingéd chariot hurrying near;
And yonder all before us lie
Deserts of vast eternity.
Thy beauty shall no more be found.   25
Nor, in thy marble vault, shall sound
My echoing song; then worms shall try
That long-preserved virginity,
And your quaint honor turn to dust,
And into ashes all my lust: 30
The grave's a fine and private place,
But none, I think, do there embrace.
    Now therefore, while the youthful hue
Sits on thy skin like morning dew,
And while thy willing soul transpires[3]   35
At every pore with instant fires,
Now let us sport us while we may,

---

[1]*Humber:* a stream flowing through Hull, Marvell's home town. *complain:* to sing plaintively.
[2]The Jews were to be converted just before the Last Judgment.
[3]*transpires:* breathes out.

And now, like amorous birds of prey,
Rather at once our time devour
Than languish in his slow-chapped[4] power.   40
Let us roll all our strength and all
Our sweetness up into one ball,
And tear our pleasures with rough strife
Thorough the iron gates of life:
Thus, though we cannot make our sun   45
Stand still, yet we will make him run.

—ANDREW MARVELL, 1681

A Song

What torments must the virgin prove
That feels the pangs of hopeless love.
What endless cares must rack the breast
That is by sure despair possessed.

When love in tender bosoms reigns,   5
With all its soft, its pleasing pains,
Why should it be a crime to own
The fatal flame we cannot shun?

The soul by nature formed sincere
A slavish forced disguise must wear,   10
Lest the unthinking world reprove
The heart that glows with generous love.

But oh! in vain the sigh's repressed,
That gently heaves the pensive breast,
The glowing blush, the falling tear,   15
The conscious wish, and silent fear.

Ye soft betrayers, aid my flame,
And give my new desires a name;
Some power my gentle griefs redress,
Reveal, or make my passion less.   20

—CHARLOTTE LENNOX, 1747

---

[4]*slow-chapped:* slow-jawed; to chew slowly.

Love's Philosophy

The fountains mingle with the river
    And the rivers with the Ocean,
The winds of Heaven mix for ever
    With a sweet emotion;
Nothing in the world is single;   5
    All things by a law divine
In one spirit meet and mingle.
    Why not I with thine?—

See the mountains kiss high Heaven
    And the waves clasp one another;   10
No sister-flower would be forgiven
    If it disdained its brother;
And the sunlight clasps the earth
    And the moonbeams kiss the sea:
What is all this sweet work worth   15
    If thou kiss not me?

        —PERCY BYSSHE SHELLEY, 1819

Sonnet 43, from *Sonnets from the Portuguese*

How do I love thee? Let me count the ways.
I love thee to the depth and breadth and height
My soul can reach, when feeling out of sight
For the ends of Being and ideal Grace.
I love thee to the level of everyday's   5
Most quiet need, by sun and candlelight.
I love thee freely, as men strive for Right;
I love thee purely, as they turn from Praise.
I love thee with the passion put to use
In my old griefs, and with my childhood's faith.   10
I love thee with a love I seemed to lose
With my lost saints—I love thee with the breath,
Smiles, tears, of all my life!—and, if God choose,
I shall but love thee better after death.

        —ELIZABETH BARRETT BROWNING, 1850

When You Have Forgotten Sunday: The Love Story

——And when you have forgotten the bright bedclothes on a
  Wednesday and a Saturday,
And most especially when you have forgotten Sunday—
When you have forgotten Sunday halves in bed,
Or me sitting on the front-room radiator in the limping afternoon
Looking off down the long street   5
To nowhere,
Hugged by my plain old wrapper of no-expectation
And nothing-I-have-to-do and I'm-happy-why?
And if-Monday-never-had-to-come—
When you have forgotten that, I say,   10
And how you swore, if somebody beeped the bell,
And how my heart played hopscotch if the telephone rang;
And how we finally went in to Sunday dinner,
That is to say, went across the front room floor to the ink-spotted table
  in the southwest corner
To Sunday dinner, which was always chicken and noodles   15
Or chicken and rice
And salad and rye bread and tea
And chocolate chip cookies—
I say, when you have forgotten that,
When you have forgotten my little presentiment   20
That the war would be over before they got to you;
And how we finally undressed and whipped out the light and flowed
  into bed,
And lay loose-limbed for a moment in the week-end
Bright bedclothes,
Then gently folded into each other—   25
When you have, I say, forgotten all that,
Then you may tell,
Then I may believe
You have forgotten me well.

                —GWENDOLYN BROOKS, 1945

Love Poem

My clumsiest dear, whose hands shipwreck vases,
At whose quick touch all glasses chip and ring,
Whose palms are bulls in china, burs in linen,
And have no cunning with any soft thing

Except all ill-at-ease fidgeting people: 5
The refugee uncertain at the door
You make at home; deftly you steady
The drunk clambering on his undulant floor.

Unpredictable dear, the taxi drivers' terror,
Shrinking from far headlights pale as a dime   10
Yet leaping before red apoplectic streetcars—
Misfit in any space. And never on time.

A wrench in clocks and the solar system. Only
With words and people and love you move at ease.
In traffic of wit expertly manoeuvre   15
And keep us, all devotion, at your knees.

Forgetting your coffee spreading on our flannel,
Your lipstick grinning on our coat,
So gayly in love's unbreakable heaven
Our souls on glory of spilt bourbon float.   20

Be with me, darling, early and late. Smash glasses—
I will study wry music for your sake.
For should your hands drop white and empty
All the toys of the world would break.

                    —JOHN FREDERICK NIMS, 1947

Living in Sin

She had thought the studio would keep itself;
no dust upon the furniture of love.
Half heresy, to wish the taps less vocal,
the panes relieved of grime. A plate of pears,
a piano with a Persian shawl, a cat   5
stalking the picturesque amusing mouse
had risen at his urging.
Not that at five each separate stair would writhe
under the milkman's tramp; that morning light
so coldly would delineate the scraps   10
of last night's cheese and three sepulchral bottles;
that on the kitchen shelf among the saucers
a pair of beetle-eyes would fix her own—
Envoy from some village in the moldings . . .
Meanwhile, he, with a yawn,   15
sounded a dozen notes upon the keyboard,
declared it out of tune, shrugged at the mirror,
rubbed at his beard, went out for cigarettes;
while she, jeered by the minor demons,

pulled back the sheets and made the bed and found 20
a towel to dust the table-top,
and let the coffee-pot boil over on the stove.
By evening she was back in love again,
though not so wholly but throughout the night
she woke sometimes to feel the daylight coming 25
like a relentless milkman up the stairs.

—ADRIENNE RICH, 1955

Love Song: I and Thou

Nothing is plumb, level or square:
    the studs are bowed, the joists
are shaky by nature, no piece fits
    any other piece without a gap
or pinch, and bent nails 5
    dance all over the surfacing
like maggots. By Christ
    I am no carpenter, I built
the roof for myself, the walls
    for myself, the floors 10
for myself, and got
    hung up in it myself. I
danced with a purple thumb
    at this house-warming, drunk
with my prime whiskey: rage. 15
    Oh I spat rage's nails
into the frame-up of my work:
    it held. It settled plumb,
level, solid, square and true
    for that great moment. Then 20
it screamed and went on through
    skewing as wrong the other way.
God damned it. This is hell,
    but I planned it, I sawed it,
I nailed it, and I 25
    will live in it until it kills me.
I can nail my left palm
    to the left-hand cross-piece but
I can't do everything myself.
    I need a hand to nail the right, 30
a help, a love, a you, a wife.

—ALAN DUGAN, 1961

Now Ain't That Love?

who would
who could
understand that
when i'm near him
i am a skinny, dumb, knock-kneed   5
lackey, drooling on the words of
my maharajah (or what/ever they call them
      in those jive textbooks)

me. i am a bitch. hot.
panting for a pat from his hand   10
so i can wag my
love in front of his
    face. a princess, black.
dopey with lust, waiting
for the kiss of action from my   15
   prince. now i know that this
whole scene is not
   cool, but it's real!
so a-live—dig it! sometimes we be so close
   i can cop his pulse   20
and think it's my heart that i
   hear
in my ears. uh. now ain't that love?

          —CAROLYN M. RODGERS, 1968

Unabashed

Unabashed
as some landscapes are
(a lakeshape, say,
lying and lifting
under a cupping sky)   5
   so angels are,
entire with each other,
their wonderful bodies
obedient, their strengths
interchanging—
or so   10
   we imagine them
   hoping
by saying these things of them
to invent human love.   15

      —MARIE PONSOT, 1981

Acknowledgments

Arnold, Eve. Excerpts from *The Unretouched Woman* by Eve Arnold (1976). Reprinted by permission of Eve Arnold/Magnum Photos.

Auden, W. H. "Musée des Beaux Arts," copyright 1940 and renewed 1968 by W. H. Auden. Reprinted from *W. H. Auden: Collected Poems*. Edited by Edward Mendelson, by permission of Random House, Inc. and Faber and Faber Ltd.

Baker, Russell. Reprinted from *Growing Up* by Russell Baker, © 1982. Used with permission of Congdon & Weed, Inc., Chicago.

Baldridge, Letitia. Excerpt from Letitia Baldridge, *Amy Vanderbilt's Everyday Etiquette* (1978), Bantam edition (1981). Reprinted by permission of Doubleday, a division of Bantam, Doubleday, Dell Publishing Group, Inc.

Barthes, Roland. Excerpt form *A Lover's Discourse* by Roland Barthes, translated by Richard Howard. Translation copyright © 1979 by Farrar, Straus & Giroux, Inc. Reprinted by permission of Hill & Wang, a division of Farrar, Straus & Giroux. Excerpt from chapter 28 from *Camera Lucida* by Roland Barthes, translated by Richard Howard. Translation copyright © 1981 by Farrar, Straus & Giroux, Inc. Reprinted by permission of Hill & Wang, a division of Farrar, Straus & Giroux.

Berger, John. "On the Use of Photography" from *About Looking* by John Berger. Copyright © 1980 by John Berger. Reprinted by permission of Pantheon Books, a division of Random House, Inc. "A Photo and Some Reactions" and "John Berger Reads a Photograph" from *Another Way of Telling* by John Berger and Jean Mohr. Copyright © 1982 by John Berger and Jean Mohr. Reprinted by permission of Pantheon Books, a division of Random House, Inc.; excerpt from *Ways of Seeing* by John Berger. Copyright © 1972 by Penguin Books Ltd. Used by permission of Viking Penguin, a division of Penguin Books USA Inc.

Blake, William. "The Clod & The Pebble." Reprinted from *The Poetry and Prose of William Blake*, ed. David Erdman, published by Bantam Doubleday Dell.

Booth, Pat. Excerpt from an interview with Eve Arnold. From *Master Photographers* by Pat Booth. Copyright © 1983 by Pat Booth. Reprinted by permission of Crown Publishers, Inc. and Macmillan London.

Bradstreet, Anne. "To My Dear and Loving Husband." Reprinted by permission of the publishers from *The Works of Anne Bradstreet*, edited by Jeannine Hensley, Cambridge, Mass.: The Belknap Press of Harvard University Press, Copyright © 1967 by the President and Fellows of Harvard College.

Brooks, Gwendolyn. "When You Have Forgotten Sunday: The Love Story," from *Blacks*, 1991, Third World Press, Chicago. Copyright © 1991 by Gwendolyn Brooks. Reprinted by permission of the author.

Browning, Elizabeth Barrett. "Sonnet XLIII." Reprinted from *Sonnets from the Portuguese*, published by Bantam Doubleday Dell.

Bush, Martin. Excerpts from an interview with Gordon Parks in *The Photographs of Gordon Parks* by Martin Bush. Copyright © 1983 by Wichita State University. Reprinted by permission of The Edwin A. Ulrich Museum of Art, Wichita State University, Wichita, Kansas.

Capellanus, Andreas. Excerpt from *The Art of Courtly Love*, trans. by John Jay Parry. © 1990 by Columbia University Press, New York. Reprinted with permission of the publisher.

Cawelti, John. From *The Six-Gun Mystique*. Copyright 1970 by The Popular Press. Reprinted by permission of the publisher.

Claiborne, Craig. "Basic Pie Pastry" from *The New York Times Cookbook* by Craig Claiborne. Copyright © 1961 by Craig Claiborne. Reprinted by permission of HarperCollins Publishers, Inc.

de Pizan, Christine. Excerpt from *A Medieval Woman's Mirror of Honor: The Treasury Of The City of Ladies* by Christine de Pizan, translated by Charity Cannon Willard. Copyright © 1989 by Bard Hall Press and Persea Books, Inc. Reprinted by permission of Persea Books, Inc.

DeSalvo, Louise A. Excerpt from "A Portrait of the Puttana as a Middle-Aged World Scholar," in *Between Women*, eds. Carol Ascher, Louise DeSalvo, and Sara Rudnick. Copyright © 1983 Louise A. DeSalvo. Reprinted by permission of the author.

Dinesen, Isak. "Iguana," from *Out of Africa* by Isak Dinesen. Copyright © 1937 by Random House, Inc. and renewed 1965 by Rungstedlundfonden. Reprinted by permission of Random House, Inc. and the Rungstedlund Foundation.

Doisneau, Robert. Excerpt from "Robert Doisneau" from *Dialogue with Photography* by Paul Hill and Thomas Cooper. Copyright © 1979 by Paul Hill and Thomas Cooper. Reprinted by permission of Farrar, Straus & Giroux, Inc.

Dugan, Alan. "Love Song: I and Thou." Copyright © 1961, 1962, 1968, 1972, 1973, 1974, 1983, by Alan Dugan. From *New and Collected Poems 1961–1983* by Alan Dugan, published by The Ecco Press. Reprinted by permission.

Ehrenreich, Barbara. From "Is Success Dangerous to Your Health?" *Ms.* Magazine, May 1979. Reprinted by permission of the author.

Elbow, Peter. Excerpt from *Writing with Power: Techniques for Mastering the Writing Process* by Peter Elbow. Copyright © 1981 by Oxford University Press, Inc. Reprinted by permission.

Erdrich, Louise. From *The Beet Queen* by Louise Erdrich. Copyright © 1986 by Louise Erdrich. Reprinted by permission of Henry Holt and Company, Inc.

Freund, Gisele. "On Doisneau's Photograh" by Gisele Freund. From *Photography and Society* by Gisele Freund. Reprinted by permission of Joan Daves Agency.

Gass, William. From *On Being Blue* by William Gass. Copyright © 1976 by William Gass. Reprinted by permission of David R. Godine, Publisher.

Giovanni, Nikki. Reprinted with the permission of Macmillan Publishing Company from *Gemini* by Nikki Giovanni. Originally published by The Bobbs-Merrill Company, Inc. Copyright © 1971 by Nikki Giovanni.

Gonzalez, Angelo. "Bilingualism Pro: The Key to Basic Skills," by Angelo Gonzalez. Copyright © 1985 by The New York Times Company. Reprinted by permission.

Goodman, Ellen. From "Phone Calls Are for Talk, Talk, Talk—But Not for Remembering." Copyright © 1987, The Boston Globe Newspaper Company. Reprinted with permission.

Gould, Stephen J. "Integrity and Mr. Rifkin" is reprinted from *An Urchin in the Storm, Essays about Books and Ideas* by Stephen Jay Gould, by permission of W. W. Norton & Company, Inc. Copyright © 1987 by Stephen Jay Gould.

Gullason, Thomas A. "Stephen Crane—A Chronology," from *Stephen Crane's Career: Perspectives and Evaluations*, edited with Introduction and Notes, by Thomas A. Gullason (New York: New York University Press, 1972). Reprinted by permission of the author.

Joyce, James. "The End of Molly's Soliloquy" and "A Restaurant," from *Ulysses* by James Joyce, published by Random House and The Bodley Head. Copyright © 1934 and renewed 1962 by Lucia & George Joyce. Reprinted by permission of Random House, Inc.

Kincaid, Jamaica. Excerpt retitled as "A Tourist's Arrival" from *Annie John* by Jamaica Kincaid. Copyright © 1985 by Jamaica Kincaid. Reprinted by permission of Farrar, Straus & Giroux, Inc.

Lebowitz, Fran. "How to be a Directory Assistance Operator: A Manual," from

Back Country. Copyright © 1968 by Gary Snyder. Reprinted by permission of New Directions Publishing Corporation.

Spender, Dale. Excerpt from *Man Made Language* by Dale Spender. Reprinted by permission of Routledge & Kegan Paul.

Staples, Brent. "Just Walk on By: A Black Man Ponders His Power to Alter Public Space," as appeared in *Ms.* Magazine, September 1986. Reprinted by permission of the author.

Terkel, Studs. From *Working: People Talk about What They Do All Day and How They Feel about What They Do*. Copyright © 1972, 1974 by Studs Terkel. Reprinted by permission of Pantheon Books, a division of Random House, Inc.

Tompkins, Jane. "Fishing Words: Unlearning to Write the Critical Essay." Appeared in *The Georgia Review*, 1988. Copyright © 1988 Jane Tompkins. Reprinted by permission of the author.

Williams, William Carlos. "Landscape with the Fall of Icarus." From William Carlos Williams, *The Collected Poems of William Carlos Williams, 1939–1962, vol. II*. Copyright © 1958 by William Carlos Williams. Reprinted by permission of New Directions Publishing Corporation.

Wright, James. "Lying in a Hammock at William Duffy's Farm in Pine Island, Minnesota." Reprinted from *The Branch Will Not Break* © 1963 by James Wright, Wesleyan University Press. By permission of University Press of New England.

Wright, John W. "T.V. Commercials That Move the Merchandise," excerpted from *The Commercial Connection: Advertising and the Mass Media*, edited by John W. Wright. Copyright © 1979 by John W. Wright and reprinted by permission of the editor.

Wright, Richard. Excerpt from Richard Wright, "The Man Who Lived Underground." From the book *Eight Men* by Richard Wright. Copyright © 1987 by the Estate of Richard Wright. Used by permission of the publisher, Thunder's Mouth Press.

Photographs and Art

Arnold, Eve. Photos of "Marlene Dietrich" and "Teacher in a literary class in Abu Dhabi." Courtesy of Eve Arnold/Magnum Photos.

Barris, George. Photo of "Marilyn Monroe." World copyright by: George Barris. Courtesy of the photographer.

"Bisou Bisou" advertisement, 1993. Mark Hanaeur. © Bisou Bisou/No Comment! Reproduced with permission.

Bruegel, Pieter, *The Fall of Icarus*, Coll. Van Bueren. Scala/Art Resource, N.Y.

Cartier-Bresson, Henri. *Athens*. Reprinted by permission of Henri Cartier-Bresson/Magnum Photos.

"Charlie" advertisement. © 1987 Revlon, Inc. Courtesy of Revlon, Inc.

Cosmopolitan **advertisement,** 1966. Reprinted with permission of *Cosmopolitan* magazine.

Da Vinci, Leonardo. *Mona Lisa*, Louvre, Paris. Alinari/Art Resource, N.Y.

Doisneau, Robert. "A Parisian Cafe" and "Sidelong Glance" photographs. Courtesy of Robert Doisneau/Black Star/Rapho.

Filo, John Paul. "Kent State—Girl Screaming Over Dead Body, May 4, 1970." © 1970 John Paul Filo. Courtesy of the photographer.

Fly-tox advertisement. From *Ladies Home Journal*, June 1926. General Research Division, The New York Public Library. Astor, Lenox, and Tilden Foundations.

Groening, Matt. "The Simpsons—Bart Simpson character." The Simpsons © & ™ Twentieth Century Fox Film Corporation. Used by permission.

Heckel, Eric. *Head of a Girl*, 1912. Pencil on paper: 17 ⅝ × 13 ¼ in. Sheldon Memorial Art Gallery, University of Nebraska–Lincoln, F. M. Hall Collection.

Hogarth. *Noon* and *London*. Courtesy of The Granger Collection, New York.

John Goodman as Dan Conner (from *Roseanne*). Courtesy: Cadette/Viacom.

Kertész, André. "Elizabeth & I, Paris, 1931" and "Red Hussard Leaving, June 1919, Budapest." © Ministère de la Culture – France. Courtesy of Mission du Patrimoine Photographique, Paris.

Lange, Dorothea. *Drought Refugees Hoping for Cotton Work*, Library of Congress.

MacNelly, Jeff. "Shoe." Reprinted by permission of Jefferson Communications, Inc., Reston, VA.

"Marlboro Man" advertisement. Reprinted by permission of Philip Morris Incorporated.

Martin, Charles. "Window Dressing" (1989). © Charles Martin. Reproduced with permission of Charles Martin.

Mestach, Jean Willy. Figure from Songye Zaire. Collection J. W. Mestach, Brussels. Reproduced with the permission of the artist.

"Mirage Jet," July 14, 1967. Anonymous. Courtesy of Time Inc. Picture Collection.

Mohr, Jean. Photograph from *Another Way of Telling* by John Berger and Jean Mohr. Copyright © 1982 by John Berger and Jean Mohr. Reprinted by permission of Pantheon Books, a division of Random House, Inc.

Munch, Edvard. Norwegian, 1863–1944. *The Cry*. Lithograph on pink paper: 14 ½ × 9 ⅞ in. Courtesy of the Museum of Fine Arts, Boston. William Francis Warden Fund.

Parks, Gordon. "American Gothic," Washington, D.C. 1942 and "Muslim School Children," 1963. Photographs courtesy of the Edwin A. Ulrich Museum of Art, The Wichita State University, Kansas. Reprinted by permission of Gordon Parks.

Redbook **advertisement,** 1977. Reprinted by permission of *Redbook* Magazine. Copyright © 1993 by The Hearst Corporation. All rights reserved.

Russia at War, 1941–1945. © 1987 The Vendome Press.

Smith, Eugene W. *Tomoko in the Bath*. Courtesy of Black Star.

"South Vietnam/U.S. Wounded." Courtesy of AP/Wide World Photos.

Ut, Huynh Cong (Nick). "Children Fleeing a Napalm Strike," June 8, 1972. Courtesy of AP/Wide World Photos.

INDEX

About Looking (Berger), 249
Advertising
  analysis of, 161–75
  argumentation and, 176, 177
  classification and, 144–49
  persuasion in, 70, 71–77, 176
  women in, 165–75
American Gothic (Parks), 256
Amy Vanderbilt's Everyday Etiquette
    (Baldridge), 64–65
Analysis, 10, 153–75
  of advertising, 161–75
  comparison and contrast and, 153–
    61
  defined, 153
  dialectical, 153–54, 161–75
  of painting, 157–61
  practice in writing of, 156–61, 163,
    165–75
  synthesis and, 243
Another Way of Telling, 244–46,
    247–49
Anxiety, and writing, 13, 21
"Arbor, An" (Momaday), 120–21
Argumentation, 10–11, 176–241
  advertising and, 176, 177
  on bilingual education, 210–19
  complexity of, 178
  on criminal justice, 219–34
  diagram or outline of, 187
  experimenting and, 15, 240–41
  features of, 178

feminist, 188–93, 199–209
persuasion vs., 10, 70, 176
philosophical, 176–78
political, 176
practice in writing of, 187–88, 193,
    199–209, 218–19, 233–34, 240–
    41
reflection vs., 177
scientific, 178–88
on socioeconomic class, 193–99
statistics and, 193–209
synthesis vs., 242
on violence, 234–41
Arnold, Eve, 259–63, 267
Art
  analysis of, 157–61
  description of, 127–30
  self-expression through, 25–28
Art of Courtly Love, The (Capella-
    nus), 61–62
Association, expression through, 23–
    24
Athens (Cartier-Bresson), 274
Auden, W. H., 160
*Automatic Reconnaissance Camera,
    Mirage Jet*, 275

Baker, Russell, 37, 40–42, 60
Baldridge, Letitia, 64–65
Barthes, Roland, 33, 44–46, 162
Beet Queen, The (Erdrich), 99–100
Bell Jar, The (Plath), 29–30

Berger, John, 137, 163–65, 247–50
Bilingual education, argumentation
    on, 210–19
"Bilingualism Pro: The Key to Basic
    Skills" (Gonzalez), 216–18
Biography
    narration in, 102–9
    synthesis and, 336–37
Biological classification, 137–38
Bisou Bisou advertisement. 175
"Blue Hotel, The" (Crane), 312–36
Bradstreet, Anne, 338
"Bride Comes to Yellow Sky, The"
    (Crane), 303–12
Bronx Primitive (Simon), 120
Brooks, Gwendolyn, 342
Browning, Elizabeth Barrett, 341
Brueghel, Pieter, 157–61
Bush, Martin, 254–58

Capellanus, Andreas, 61–62
Carter, Joan, 285–86
Cartier-Bresson, Henri, 274
Cather, Willa, 94–95
Cawelti, John, 288–302, 336
Children Fleeing a Napalm Strike,
    June 8, 1972 (Huynh Cong
    Ut), 270
Classification, 10, 136–52
    advertising and, 144–49
    biological, 137–38
    comparing and contrasting and,
        136
    defined, 136
    experimenting and, 15
    of forms of power, 149–52
    practice in writing of, 139–40, 143–
        44, 148–49, 151–52
    purpose of, 136
    in social sciences, 136–37, 138–44
    of student body, 140–44
    synthesis and, 243
"Class in America: Myths and Reali-
    ties" (Mantsios), 194–99
Clinton, Bill, 77–81
Commercials, classification of, 144–
    49. See also Advertising

Communication, 3–5. See also Writ-
    ing
Comparison and contrast
    analysis and, 153–61
    classification and, 136
    poetry and, 157–61
    in writing about visual images, 264
Concept of Mind, The (Ryle), 178
Conduct, directions on, 60–66
Confidence, and writing, 12–13, 17–
    18
Contrast. See Comparison and con-
    trast
Cookbooks, directions in, 57–58
Cosmopolitan (magazine), 166, 172
"Cousin Mary" (Erdrich), 99–100
Crane, Stephen, 102–9, 154–56, 303–
    37
"Crime of Punishment, The"
    (Menninger), 220–26
Criminal justice, argumentation on,
    219–34
Cry, The (Munch), 26

Data
    organizing (See Classification)
    playing with, 137
    synthesis and, 243
De Salvo, Louise, 37–40
Description, 10, 117–35
    of faces, 131–35
    narration vs., 93, 117
    order in, 117
    organization of space in, 117–18,
        121
    of pictures, 127–35
    of place with history, 121–27
    point of view in, 117–21
    practice in writing of, 121, 126–27,
        129, 132–33, 134–35
    problems with writing of, 117
    purpose and, 118
Diagramming arguments, 187
Dialectical analysis, 153–54, 161–75
Dialogue with Photography, 251–54
Dietrich, Marlene, 261
Dinesen, Isak, 47–48, 49

Directions, 9, 57–69
  through the ages, 60–66
  on conduct, 60–66
  in cookbooks, 57–58
  indirection and, 66–69
  to make or do something, 59–60
  persuasion vs., 57
  revising, 60
  rules for, 58–59
Division Street: America (Terkel), 278
Doisneau, Robert, 250–54, 265
Drafting, in act of writing, 15–16
Drought Refugees Hoping for Cotton Work (Lange), 272
Dugan, Alan, 344

Education, bilingual, 210–19
Ehrenreich, Barbara, 284
Elbow, Peter, 22–23, 36
Elizabeth and I (Kertész), 271
Emotion, and narration, 93–94, 96
"End of Molly's Soliloquy, The" (Joyce), 100–102
Erdrich, Louise, 99–100
Events, narration of, 110–16
Experience
  fiction vs., 156–57
  reflection on, 47–52
Experimenting
  argumentation and, 15, 240–41
  classification and, 15
  narration and, 14–15
"Experts in a Free Society" (Feyerabend), 177
Expression, 8, 21–34
  through art, 25–28
  through association, 23–24
  freedom of, 21–22
  of ideas, 31–34
  of mood, 29–31
  open-ended writing process and, 22–23
  reflection vs., 35

Faces, description of, 131–35
Fall of Icarus, The (Brueghel), 157–61

Father's Legacy to His Daughters, A (Gregory), 63
Fellini, Federico, 32–33
Fellini on Fellini (Fellini), 32–33
Feminist argumentation, 188–93, 199–209
Feyerabend, Paul, 177
Fiction, vs. experience, 156–57
"Fighting Words: Unlearning to Write the Critical Essay" (Tompkins), 235–40
Filo, John Paul, 269
Fly-Tox advertisement, 71–73
Follis, Ann, 284
Forms of writing, 6–13
  reader-oriented, 9, 55–89
  reading and practice, 11–12
  topic-oriented, 9–11 (*See also* Topic–oriented forms)
  writer-oriented, 8, 19–53
"400 Mulvaney Street" (Giovanni), 121–26
Freedom of expression, 21–22
Freud, Sigmund, 4
Freund, Gisèle, 250–51

Gass, W. H., 23–24
General Electric advertisement, 170
Giovanni, Nikki, 121–26, 127
Gonzalez, Angelo, 216–18
Good Housekeeping (magazine), 166
Goodman, Ellen, 31–32
Goodman, John, 134, 135
Gould, Stephen Jay, 136–37, 179–88
Gregory, John, 63
Growing Up (Baker), 40–42
Guess jeans advertising, 161–63

Hamlet (Shakespeare), 66
Hard Times (Terkel), 278
Harrison, Constance Cary, 63–64
Head of Girl (Heckel), 27
Heckel, Erich, 27
Hemingway, Ernest, 162
Henfrey, Colin, 283–84
Herrick, Barbara, 281–82
Hogarth, William, 127–30
Housekeeping (Robinson), 119

Howell, Richard, 286
"How to Be a Directory Assistance
    Operator: A Manual" (Lebo-
    witz), 66–69
"Humanitarian Theory of Punish-
    ment, The" (Lewis), 226–33
Hundley, Dave, 286
Huynh Cong (Nick) Ut, 270
Hypothesis, 242, 243, 337–38

Ibsen, Henrik, 77
Icarus, 157–61
Ideas, expression of, 31–34
"I Go Back to May 1937" (Olds), 44
"Iguana, The" (Dinesen), 47–48
"Inaugural Address" (Clinton), 77–81
Indirection, 66–69
"Integrity and Mr. Rifkin" (Gould),
    179–88
Interviews, 278–88
"Is Success Dangerous to Your
    Health?" (Ehrenreich), 284

Job letter, writing of, 83, 85–89
Johnson, Susan, 284
Joyce, James, 100–102, 119–20
"Just Walk on By: A Black Man
    Ponders His Power to Alter
    Public Space" (Staples), 49–53

Kertész, André, 247–49, 271
Kincaid, Jamaica, 97–99
"Kitchen, A" (Robinson), 119
Klein, Robert, 285–86

Ladies' Home Journal (magazine), 166
"La Gioconda," 133–34
"Landscape with the Fall of Icarus"
    (Williams), 160–161
Lange, Dorothea, 272
Language, 3–4
"Last of the Mohicans, The" (Crane),
    154–56
Lebowitz, Fran, 66–69
Lefevre, Mike, 279–81
Lennox, Charlotte, 340
Letters, job, 83, 85–89
Lewis, C. S., 226–33

Listerine advertisement, 171
Literacy Teacher in Abu Dhabi, A
    (Arnold), 267
"Living in Sin" (Rich), 343–44
Logic, organizing by. See Classifica-
    tion
"Looking at Pictures to Be Put
    Away" (Snyder), 43
"Looking for My Mother" (Barthes),
    44–46
Love poem(s), 337–45
"Love Poem" (Nims), 342–43
Lover's Discourse, A (Barthes), 33
"Love Song: I and Thou" (Dugan),
    344
"Love's Philosophy" (Shelley), 341
Lux Soap advertisement, 169
"Lying in a Hammock at William
    Duffy's Farm in Pine Island,
    Minnesota" (Wright), 29
Lynd, Helen, 141–43
Lynd, Robert, 141–43

MacNelly, Jeff, 158
Maggie: A Girl of the Streets
    (Crane), 104, 106–7
Man Made Language (Spender), 188–
    93
Manscapes (Henfrey), 283–84
Mantsios, Gregory, 137, 194–99
"Man Who Lived Underground, The"
    (Wright), 96–97
Marciano, Georges, 161, 162
Marilyn Monroe (McCann), 131–32
Marlboro Man advertisement, 75, 76
Marlene Dietrich (Arnold), 261
Márquez, Gabriel García, 110–16
Martin, Charles, 277
Martineau, Pierre, 75
Marvell, Andrew, 339–40
Master Photographers, 260–63
McCann, Graham, 131–32
Menninger, Karl, 220–26
Middletown (Lynd and Lynd), 141–43
Minimata (Smith), 276
Mirror of Honor, The (Pizan), 62–63
Mohr, Jean, 244–46
Momaday, Scott, 120–21

Mona Lisa (Da Vinci), 133–34
Monroe, Marilyn, 131–32
Mood, expression of, 29–31
Motivation in Advertising (Martineau), 75
Munch, Edvard, 26
"Musée des Beaux Arts" (Auden), 159
Muslim School Children (Parks), 266
My Philosophical Development (Russell), 176

Narration, 10, 93–116
  in biography, 102–9
  defined, 93
  description vs., 93, 117
  emotional effect of, 93–94, 96
  of events, 110–16
  experimenting and, 14–15
  level of detail in, 93, 94
  point of view in, 94, 97
  practice in writing of, 109–10, 116
  stream-of-consciousness, 100–101
Nation of Strangers, A (Packard), 138–39
Nelson, Ruth, 283
New York Times Cook Book, 57–58
Nims, John Frederick, 342–43
"Noon" (Hogarth), 127–29
"Now Ain't That Love?" (Rodgers), 345

Olds, Sharon, 44
On Being Blue (Gass), 23–24
"On the Invention of Photographic Meaning" (Sekula), 246–47
Open-ended writing, 22–23
O Pioneers (Cather), 94–95
Oral text, vs. written text, 5
Organization
  by data, 136–52
  spatial, 117–35
  temporal, 93–116
Outlines
  of argument, 187
  drafting and, 15, 16

Packard, Vance, 138–39
Paintings. *See* Art

Paratrooper Works to Save the Life of a Buddy, A, 268
Parisian Café, A (Doisneau), 252
Parks, Gordon, 254–58, 266
Pater, Walter, 133–34
Peaslee, Clarence Loomis, 105–6
Persuasion, 9, 70–89
  in advertising, 70, 71–77, 176
  argumentation vs., 10, 70, 176
  direction vs., 57
  in job letter and résumé, 83–89
  political, 70, 77–83
  synthesis vs., 242
Philosophical argument, 176–78
"Photo and Some Reactions, A" (Mohr), 244–46
Photographs
  description of, 131–32
  reflection on, 43–47
  synthesis and, 243–77
Photographs of Gordon Parks, The, 254–58
Photography & Society (Freund), 250–51
Pizan, Christine de, 62–63
Place
  description of, 121–27
  mood in, 30–31
Plath, Sylvia, 29–30
Poetry
  comparing and contrasting, 157–61
  of love, 337–45
  reflection and, 43–44
  synthesis and, 337–45
Point of view
  in description, 117–21
  in narration, 94, 97
Political argumentation, 176
Political persuasion, 70, 77–83
"Politicization of the Schools: The Case of Bilingual Education" (Ravitch), 210–16
Ponsot, Marie, 345
"Portrait of the *Puttana* as a Middle-Aged Woolf Scholar, A" (De Salvo), 37–40
Potter, Jane, 286–87
Potter, Linda, 286–87

Power (Russell), 149–51
Power, classification of forms of, 149–
52
Proofreading, 17
Punishment, of criminals, 219–34

Ravitch, Diane, 210–16
Reader-oriented forms, 9, 55–89
    direction, 9, 57–69
    persuasion, 9, 57, 70–89, 176, 242
    practice in writing of, 59–60, 66,
        69, 74–77, 81–83, 87–89
Reading, and forms of writing, 11–12
Red Badge of Courage, The (Crane),
    102, 104, 106
Redbook (magazine), 166, 173
*Red Hussar leaving, June 1919,
    Budapest* (Kertész), 247–49
Reflection, 8, 35–53
    argumentation vs., 177
    on experience, 47–52
    expression vs., 35
    on photographs, 43–47
    poetry and, 43–44
    as revision, 36–43
    role of, 35–36
    on school days, 37–43
    synthesis vs., 242
    time and, 35, 46, 47
Renaissance, The (Pater), 134
Resinol Soap advertisement, 168
"Restaurant, A" (Joyce), 119–20
Résumé writing, 83, 84
Revising
    in act of writing, 16–17
    reflection as, 36–47
    in writing directions, 60
Revlon advertisement, 173
Rich, Adrienne, 343–44
Rifkin, Jeremy, 179–87
Robinson, Marilynne, 119
Rodgers, Carolyn M., 345
Rogers, Marc, 287–88
Role-player, writer as, 17–18
Roman, Fred, 282–83
Russell, Bertrand, 149–51, 176–77

*Russian and American troops meet at
    Torgau on the Elbe, April 27,
    1945,* 273
Ryle, Gilbert, 178

Sartre, Jean-Paul, 17–18
Saturday's Child (Seed), 283
School days, reflection on, 37–43
Schoolgirl (Mohr), 244, 245
Science, and argumentation, 178–88
Seed, Suzanne, 283
Sekula, Allan, 246–47
Shakespeare, William, 66, 338
Shaw, Donna, 287–88
Shelley, Percy Bysshe, 341
"Shooting, A" (Cather), 95
Shredded Wheat advertisement, 167
Sidelong Glance (Doisneau), 265
Simon, Kate, 120
Simpson, Bart, 134, 135
Six-Gun Mystique, The (Cawelti),
    288–302
Slotnik, Jacob, 283–84
Small Place, A (Kincaid), 97–99
Smith, Langdon, 108
Smith, W. Eugene, 276
Snyder, Gary, 43
Social sciences, classification in, 136–
    37, 138–44
Socioeconomic class, argumentation
    on, 193–99
"Song, A" (Lennox), 340
"Sonnet 43" (Browning), 341
"Sonnet 138" (Shakespeare), 338
Sonnets from the Portuguese (Brown-
    ing), 341
Space, organizing. *See* Description
Speech
    political, 77–83
    thought vs., 3
    writing vs., 4–5
Spender, Dale, 188–93
Staples, Brent, 49–53
Statistics, and argumentation, 193–
    209
Stream-of-consciousness narration,
    100–101

"Street, A" (Simon), 120
Street Scene (Hogarth), 129, 130
Student body, classification of, 140–44
Student Killed by National Guardsmen, Kent State University (Filo), 269
Subject. *See* Topic
Synthesis, 11, 242–345
  analysis and, 243
  argument vs., 242
  biography and, 336–37
  classification and, 243
  interviews and, 278–88
  love poems and, 337–45
  persuasion vs., 242
  practice in writing of, 243–345
  "reading" photographs and, 243–77
  reflection vs., 242
  requirements of, 242–43
  westerns and, 288–337

Terkel, Studs, 278, 279–83
Thesis, of synthetic essay, 242–43. *See also* Argumentation
Thought, vs. speech, 3
Time
  organizing (*See* Narration)
  reflection and, 35, 46, 47
"To His Coy Mistress" (Marvell), 339–40
Tomoko in the Bath (Smith), 276
Tompkins, Jane, 234–40
"To My Dear and Loving Husband" (Bradstreet), 338
Topic, 6
  experimenting and, 14–15
  testing, 15
Topic-oriented forms, 9–11, 91–345
  analysis, 10, 153–75, 243
  argumentation, 10–11, 15, 70, 176–241
  classification, 10, 15, 136–52, 243
  description, 10, 93, 117–35
  narration, 10, 14–15, 93–116, 117
  synthesis, 11, 242–345

"Tourist's Arrival, The" (Kincaid), 98–99
"TV Commercials That Move the Merchandise" (Wright), 144–48

Ulysses (Joyce), 100–102, 119–20
"Unabashed" (Ponsot), 345
Universals, 4
Unretouched Woman, The (Arnold), 259–60
Ut, Huynh Cong (Nick), 270

Vanity Fair (magazine), 161–63
"Very Old Man with Enormous Wings, A" (Márquez), 110–16
Vietnam War photographs, 268–70
Vinci, Leonardo Da, 133–34
Violence, argumentation on, 234–41

War photographs, 268–70
Ways of Seeing (Berger), 163–65
Way to Rainy Mountain, The (Momaday), 120–21
Weatherby, W. J., 132
Well-Bred Girl in Society, The (Harrison), 63–64
Westerns, and synthesis, 288–337
"When You Have Forgotten Sunday: The Love Story" (Brooks), 342
Williams, William Carlos, 159, 161
Window Dressing (Martin), 277
Women
  in advertising, 165–75
  feminist argumentation and, 188–93, 199–209
  statistics on education, employment, and income of, 199–209
Words, 3–4
Working (Terkel), 278, 279–83
Wright, James, 29
Wright, John W., 144–48
Wright, Richard, 96–97
Writer-oriented forms, 8, 19–53
  expression, 8, 21–34
  practice in writing of, 23, 24–25, 30–31, 34, 36–37, 43, 46–47, 48–49, 53

Index

Writer-oriented forms (*continued*)
  reflection, 8, 35–53, 177, 242
Writing, 13–17
  anxiety and, 13, 21
  drafting in, 15–16
  experimenting in, 14–15, 240–41
  forms of (*See* Forms of writing)

  revising in, 16–17
  role-playing and, 17–18
  speaking vs., 4–5
Writing situation, 6–7
Writing with Power (Elbow), 22–23

Zaire wood figure, 28

Instructor's Manual to Accompany

THE PRACTICE OF WRITING

FOURTH EDITION

Robert Scholes • Nancy R. Comley • Janice Peritz

Manufactured in the United States of America.

8 7 6 5 4
f e d c b a

For information, write:
St. Martin's Press, Inc.
175 Fifth Avenue
New York, NY 10010

ISBN: 0-312-10313-1

CONTENTS

A Few Words about *The Practice of Writing* ii

Preparing Yourself to Teach Writing iii

Suggested Syllabi iv

A 15-Week Syllabus Using an Issue plus Modified Portfolio Approach v

A 12-Week Syllabus viii

PART ONE: WRITING AS A HUMAN ACT 1

Chapter 1   Practicing Writing: Situation, Form, Process 1

PART TWO: WRITER-ORIENTED FORMS: DISCOURSE AND THE SELF 3

Chapter 2   Expression: Your Self as Subject 3

Chapter 3   Reflection: Your Self as Object 8

PART THREE: READER-ORIENTED FORMS: DISCOURSE AND POWER 15

Chapter 4   Direction: Guiding Your Reader 15

Chapter 5   Persuasion: Moving Your Reader 19

PART FOUR: TOPIC-ORIENTED FORMS: DISCOURSE AND KNOWLEDGE 24

Chapter 6   Narration: Organizing Time 24

Chapter 7   Description: Organizing Space 30

Chapter 8   Classification: Organizing Data 34

Chapter 9   Analysis: Taking Things Apart 40

Chapter 10   Argumentation: Presenting a Thesis 47

Chapter 11   Synthesis: Putting Things Together 57

A Few Words about THE PRACTICE OF WRITING

This manual is addressed primarily to the person who needs it most, the instructor with relatively little experience in the composition classroom. We hope that some of the material here will be of use as well to the battle-scarred veteran of a thousand classes, but we must cheerfully run the risk of boring the experienced teacher in order to give the newcomer the sort of assistance that he or she will need in teaching writing.

It is a truism of marine architecture that no boat can be built for comfort and speed. It is similar with composition texts and, indeed, with composition courses. No teacher can teach everything about writing in one quarter or one semester, and no textbook can cover every aspect of writing successfully. It is with books as it is with boats: much better for all concerned if the makers are honest about what their creation is intended to accomplish.

The Practice of Writing undertakes to solve one major problem that besets all writing classrooms--the morale problem. All language teaching includes some degree of repetition. To this, writing adds an element of psychological stress for the student and the burden of reading and responding for the teacher. And yet, the creation of written works, like all constructive processes, has a dimension of pleasure and satisfaction that is the true reward for the effort required. As we saw it, our task was to find a way of locating and using the compositional joy that is locked into every well-made piece of writing.

By emphasizing the pleasure of composition we do not mean to slight the results that a writing course should achieve. Rather, we wish to assert that promoting a healthy and appreciative *attitude* toward writing is a major goal of teaching English. The student's growth as a writer does not end with the completion of a course. We hope that students--ours and yours--will show visible improvement after working with us, and that they will want to become better writers still. Above all, we hope that they can see how their own practice is the key to improvement.

In composing this fourth edition of our text we have continued to emphasize visual material because we think the ability to read visual texts critically is crucially important. The visual texts and the other readings are the points of departure for practice in writing. We have included a number of texts from the fields of advertising, art, literature, and photography, as well as the more expository and argumentative kinds of writing. The readings are designed both to provide interesting texts for class discussion and to function as bases for written assignments. There is enough reading here so that no "reader" is needed to accompany this text, and we usually provide questions to help you get class discussion going. The questions aim to treat the readings as a writing instructor must--that is, to emphasize *how* the text can be used by a writer rather than *what* it means to a literary critic.

The Practice of Writing is not a handbook of grammar, and you may well wish to order one for that aspect of your composition course. This is also not a text that concentrates on a single form of discourse or seeks to develop the student's skill at a single method of composition. We have emphasized range and variety. We have sacrificed tidiness of focus. But we have tried to arrange things so as to lead up to and emphasize the kind of argumentative and synthetic writing most required of the college student, while providing variety and even amusement along the way.

The authors are deeply indebted to Lori Lefkovitz, whose journal of her first semester of teaching as a graduate assistant at Brown University provided us with good suggestions for improving *The Practice of Writing* and for using the text effectively in the classroom. You will find L. L.'s experiences interspersed with our own throughout this manual.

Preparing Yourself to Teach Writing

It would be unthinkable for a teacher to enter a literature class without some training in the history and theory of the subject. Yet teachers enter composition classes every year with nothing but their native wit and their own history as writers to guide them. The occasional genius aside--this is not enough. To manage a writing classroom with the confidence that brings ease and allows the students to relax and grow, some preparation is needed. Formal course work in language and discourse is the ideal solution, but the ideal is not always attainable. Therefore we list a few texts here that we recommend most strongly to every writing teacher. These are works that even seasoned veterans will wish to dip into on occasion for inspiration and encouragement.

1. William F. Irmscher, Teaching Expository Writing (New York: Holt, Rinehart and Winston, 1979). Especially useful for the new teacher because of its good advice on practical matters.
2. James Moffett, *Teaching the Universe of Discourse* (Boston: Houghton Mifflin, 1968). This text is very helpful for giving a strong sense of the classroom and the ways that human interaction can be related to composition. The sections on dramatic aspects of writing are excellent. Those on narration are less helpful.
3. Theresa Enos, ed., *A Sourcebook for Basic Writing Teachers* (New York: Random House, 1987).
4. For further reading in theory and practice, these two collections are useful: Richard Graves, ed., *Rhetoric and Composition: A Sourcebook for Teachers and Writers* (Upper Montclair, N. J.: Boynton/Cook, 1984); and Gary Tate and Edward P. J. Corbett, eds., *The Writing Teacher's Sourcebook* (New York: Oxford University Press, 1988).
5. *Focus on Collaborative Learning*. (Urbana, Ill.: NCTE, 1988).
6. Chris Anson, ed., *Writing and Response: Theory, Practice, and Research*. (Urbana, Ill.: NCTE, 1988).

7. Gary Tate, ed., *Teaching Composition: Twelve Bibliographic Essays* (Fort Worth: Texas Christian University Press, 1987). See also Patricia Bizzell and Bruce Herzberg, *The Bedford Bibliography for Teachers of Writing* (Boston: Bedford/St. Martin's, 1987).
8. On composing, see Patricia Bizzell, "Composing Processes: An Overview," in Bizzell's *Academic Discourse and Critical Consciousness* (Pittsburgh: University of Pittsburgh Press, 1992).
9. Amy Tucker, *Decoding ESL* (New York: McGraw-Hill, 1991). Well-researched critical discussion of teaching writing to students of diverse linguistic backgrounds. Especially helpful for understanding how cultural difference manifests itself rhetorically.

10. Lester Faigley, *Fragments of Rationality: Postmodernity and the Subject of Composition* (Pittsburgh: University of Pittsburgh Press, 1992). A survey of contemporary theories and their pedagogical implications. Stimulating discussions of the student's writing "self," computer networking, teacher authority.

11. *Journals*. Writing teachers should see regularly two journals available to members of the National Council of Teachers of English: *College English*, which frequently publishes important essays on writing, and *College Composition and Communication*, which is devoted primarily to this field. *The Journal of Advanced Composition* is also highly recommended.

Suggested Syllabi

We present here a syllabus for a 15-week course and one for a 12-week course. You will want to develop your own syllabus according to the needs of your students. In planning your syllabus for a semester's work, start with a general outline of what you want to cover. After you are better acquainted with your students' writing abilities, you will be able to refine the syllabus. During the first few weeks of the course, have your students writing frequently, both in class and out so that you can make an early assessment. If your students work easily with writer-oriented forms, you may wish to spend more time with reader- and topic-oriented writing. On the other hand, if your students come to you after having been drilled in what might be called teacher-oriented writing ("never use I or you"; passive constructions; more generalities than specifics), they will benefit from the time spent on writer- and reader-oriented writing. Such writing will help them develop more confidence in their own voices and ideas.

In each syllabus, we have tried to leave adequate time for discussion of the readings and of strategies for approaching the writing assignments, and for discussion of student papers. We have also included suggestions for writing practice in the classroom. Students need experience in writing under time limitations (especially for essay exams in other courses), and shorter practices can usefully provide this experience. Starting a writing practice in class is also valuable. The instructor is available for help during the composing process, and thus serves a more creative and helpful role than when he or she functions simply as judge of final products.

Remember that you can't accomplish everything you wish to in one semester. In writing up these suggested syllabi, we are fully aware of our own practice of adjusting a syllabus during the semester as we discover more about our students' strengths and weaknesses--and interests. Also, there will be days when you will find it necessary to deviate from your syllabus to attack an epidemic of sentence fragments, or discuss the whys and wherefores of the semicolon; and days when your students get so involved in a discussion of some issue that you will let them go on because you see them teaching each other what argumentation is all about. Such days are not wasted, so allow for them when designing your own syllabus.

A 15-Week Syllabus Using an Issue plus Modified Portfolio Approach

I. **Discourse and the Self: Expression and Reflection (Weeks 1-4)**

WEEK 1
First day writing sample: "An Experience in Your Life" (that angered, frightened, or confused you). Read Part One, "Writing as a Human Act" and chapter introductions to Expression and Reflection.

Introduce freewriting and writing portfolio. Do "The Open-ended Writing Process" (reading and practice). Small-group work on "Experience in Your Life," Part B. Assign "Reflection as Revision" practice.

WEEK 2
Begin class with a five-minute freewrite in portfolio (standard procedure from now on). Do "Self-Expression through Art" and "Looking at Pictures." Assign "Reflecting on a Photograph" practice for homework.

Peer Response Groups: on "Reflecting on a Photograph" practice.

WEEK 3
Discuss "Ideas about the Telephone" and "From Thing to Thought." Assign "Ideas about a Common Object" practice.

Peer Response Groups: on "Common Object" practice. Begin working with the first Reading and Practice in the Narration chapter.

WEEK 4

Discuss reading in "From Experience to Thought" and assign practice as a revision of the "Experience in Your Life" assignment.

Peer Review for revising and editing draft of paper 1: a reflective essay on an experience in your life.

II. **Discourse and Power: Direction and Persuasion (Weeks 5-7)**

WEEK 5

Paper 1 plus portfolio due. Introduce Direction and do "How to Make or Do Something" as an in-class practice. Discuss "Direction through the Ages" and "How to Be a Directory Assistance Operator." For homework, students choose either the "How to Conduct Yourself" or the "How to Be a _____" practice.

WEEK 6

Peer Response Groups: on "How to Conduct/Be" practices. Discuss chapter introduction to Persuasion, the Fly-Tox Advertisement, and Clinton's inaugural speech.

For homework, students choose one of the following practices: the "Ghastly Resort Hotel," "Changing the Persuasive Pattern," or "The Difficult Campaign Speech."

WEEK 7

Peer review for revising and editing paper 2: either a directive or a persuasive paper.

Discuss chapter introduction to Description and examples of Point of View in Description.

III. **Discourse and Knowledge (Weeks 8-15)**

WEEK 8

Paper 2 plus portfolio due. Discuss "A Critic Describes a Face" and "La Gioconda." For homework, students choose either "Describing a Famous Face" or "Il Giocondo."

Discuss chapter introduction to Analysis and "Analyzing an Advertisement." As a class, analyze an advertisement.

WEEK 9

Discuss Crane's "The Last of the Mohicans" by doing the "Analysis of a Comparative Analysis" practice.

Discuss "A Critic Theorizes about Advertising." For homework, students choose either "Two Poets and a Painting" or "Analyzing Images of Women in Advertising."

WEEK 10
Discuss introduction to Classification and "Social Groups in a Town." In class, small group work on "Social Categories in an Institution." For homework, assign reading and practice on "The Student Body."
Peer review for revising and editing paper 3: an analysis or classification paper.

WEEK 11
Paper 3 plus portfolio due. Library orientation and exercise. For homework, choose one of the projects in the Synthesis chapter and begin working on it.
Introduce Argumentation and discuss Gould's "Integrity and Mr. Rifkin" by working on "Reconstructing, Summarizing, and Evaluating Gould's Argument." Finish this practice at home.

WEEK 12
Discuss "An Educator Considers Class Myths and Realities." In small groups, generate theses based on "Arguing about Statistics" material.
Small group discussion of synthesis projects. Class discussion of "A Feminist Discusses Women and Names." Assign "Arguing about Men and Women" practice.

WEEK 13
Class discussion about making informed, reasonable arguments and about the importance of primary and secondary research. Peer Response Groups: on "Arguing about Men and Women" practice. Assign research exercise: bibliography of ten sources that might be worth consulting to make your argument about men and women more informed and reasonable.
Small group work on planning and drafting synthesis papers. For homework: draft a synthesis paper.

WEEK 14
Peer review of paper 4: Synthesis. Discuss "A Critic Reflects on the Violence of Western Reason" and in class, do a dialogue for "Is There a Better Way?"

WEEK 15
Paper 4 and portfolio due.

A 12-Week Syllabus

WEEK 1
For a writing sample, use "An Experience in Your Life." Read and discuss some of
these. Read and discuss "Writing as a Human Act," and the introduction to
Expression. (This syllabus assumes the reading and discussion of each chapter
introduction.)

WEEK 2
Expression (Chapter 2). "The Open-ended Writing Process." The freewriting may
be focused on areas of the "Experience" papers that need further development, or
"Expression through Association" or "Self-Expression through Art" may be done in
class.

WEEK 3
Revised "Experience" papers due.
    Reflection (Chapter 3). "Reflection as Revision." Freewriting on Gass or art
responses can be revised. Discussion of poems and strategies for "Reflecting on a
Photograph."

WEEK 4
"Photograph" papers due. Read and discuss in class.
    Direction (Chapter 4). "Direction through the Ages." Discussion of
examples and approaches to "How to Conduct Yourself."

WEEK 5
"How to" papers due. Read and discuss in class.
    Persuasion (Chapter 5). "Persuasion in Advertising." Discuss Fly-Tox ad
and approaches to "The Ghastly Resort Hotel."

WEEK 6
"Ghastly" papers due. Read and discuss in class, or have students assume the role
of the copywriter's boss and write critiques of one another's papers. Discuss "The
Job Letter and Résumé."

WEEK 7
Job letters due. Read and discuss in class.
    Narration (Chapter 6). Discuss opening short selections before moving on to
the García-Márquez story and "Narrating an Event."

WEEK 8
Narratives due. Read and discuss in class.
    Classification (Chapter 8). "Social Groups in a Town." "Social Types in a
Particular Place" started in class.

WEEK 9
"Social Types" paper due. Read and discuss in class.
    Argumentation (Chapter 10). "A Scientist Argues about Means and Ends" and "Reconstructing . . . Gould's Argument." This practice can be started in class and completed as homework.

WEEK 10
"A Feminist Discusses Women and Names" and "Arguing about Men and Women." Discussion of Spender and approaches to writing practice due Week 11.

WEEKS 11 and 12
Analysis and Synthesis (Chapters 9 and 11). "Two Poets Look at a Painting" and "Men and Women on Love"; or "Analyzing an Advertisement" and "Images of Women in Advertising"; or "How Should Photographs Be Read?"

PART ONE
WRITING AS A HUMAN ACT

Chapter 1
Practicing Writing: Situation, Form, Process

We do not believe that reading about writing does much to help students to become better writers. That is why this book emphasizes practice. In this first chapter, then, we are not telling students how to write but explaining--very briefly--how writing works and why this book has the shape it has. Above all, this chapter is designed to help the student understand *why* certain kinds of assignments will be made later on, and how the forms of writing and the process of writing are related. Our experience in the classroom has shown that students work much better when they understand fully the purpose of the work they are doing. In a writing course, the student's *effort* to improve is the crucial ingredient. Without that, everything else will fail. It is important for *you* to understand this chapter as well. Knowing what is here, you can decide what to emphasize for your students. In our opinion, the material about the forms of writing should probably *not* be stressed at the beginning of the semester. On the other hand, the material on the writing process, beginning with "Reading and Practice' and continuing to the end of the chapter, is likely to be very useful to your students, especially the three stages of writing that are discussed in "The Act of Writing." We have provided a Practice very early in this chapter, so that you can get your students engaged in the writing process as soon as possible. Following are some thoughts about the Practice in Chapter 1.

PRACTICE: An Experience in Your Life (p. 5)

This assignment serves to emphasize the difference between ordinary speech and the formality of written English. Students may ask if they really are free to use the language they'd use with a group of friends. They should be encouraged to do so for part A, for the resulting narrative is much livelier if they feel unrestrained. Students who have access to tape recorders may enjoy transcribing their own speech patterns, and for those who don't have tape recorders, suggest that they really listen to other people's speech patterns. Remind them that even *you* don't always speak in beautifully formed sentences. You might also suggest that they look at the interviews in the "Working People" assignment in Chapter 11 to get an idea of how speech is transcribed.

    In response to part A, most students produce interesting and lively narratives. But students who are unsure of themselves as writers tend to think that their experiences are not valuable and produce very short narratives.

Part B. Early in the semester, students are shy about commenting on one another's writing. You can help the revision process of part B along by reading a good part-A sample to the class and asking them what's good about the narrative, and what areas need clarification. If your students remain silent, ask your own questions of the narrative to give them an idea of how to respond to one another.

In your own written response to part B, we suggest you point your comments toward further revision. You may want to assign another revision later in the semester, possibly after discussing narrative strategies (Chapter 6). Our experience has shown that students prefer--and in fact, enjoy--revising personal narratives. Perhaps it's because they keep learning more about themselves as they do so. The trick in teaching revision is to get them to realize that revision involves further discoveries with respect to any topic. (Make sure that students present all versions of their narratives with each revision, so that you can see whether they've really revised and not simply edited.)

PART TWO
WRITER-ORIENTED FORMS: DISCOURSE AND THE SELF

Chapter 2
Expression: Your Self as Subject

The materials in this chapter are designed to emphasize two aspect of writing: the satisfactions of self-expression and the ways that writers begin to write. There is a mechanical dimension to self-expression as well as a playful dimension. Writing in the expressive mode helps students learn how to get their minds in gear. Once they learn how to *begin*, they will experience the satisfaction of discovering that they have something to say that expresses their own thoughts and feelings.

READING: The Open-ended Writing Process (p. 22)
           Peter Elbow, from *Writing with Power* (p. 22)
PRACTICE: Open-ended Writing (p. 23)

If your students have had no experience with freewriting (unfocused writing) or open-ended writing, you might consider incorporating this kind of practice into a number of your class sessions. Students should know how to use such focused and unfocused writing as a part of their composing process, to help them start on a topic, develop it, or unblock themselves at difficult points.

        The purpose of this Practice is to introduce open-ended writing as a means of expression. In writing about "anything at all," many students will be surprised at what they discover. If your students will be using this writing for further development in Chapter 3 ("Reflection"), you might ask them to do more open-ended writing as homework. This will give them more than one choice of focus or allow them to develop their original focus a bit more.

READING: Expression through Association (p. 23)
          W. H. Gass, from *On Being Blue* (p. 23)

Play with this text in class, seeing if, collectively, the group can "get" every item listed--that is, understand its reference, explaining what blue laws and blue movies, etc., are. You need not know all the answers yourself. This is your chance to admit that you don't know everything and for class members to show that they know something. (The German phrase is puzzling: literally, "in the blue into," it means something like "at random.") In playing with these blue terms, try to bring out the different levels of blueness, literal and figurative, that they incorporate. (This will be a good place to discuss those basic rhetorical terms themselves.) This whole exercise is a game designed to heighten the student's awareness of language.

PRACTICE: On Being _____ (p. 24)

This is probably better done at home, individually, than in a group. The student may wish to look at a dictionary for inspiration and should feel free to ask other people to help with free association of things in the chosen color. Remind your students that they are not being asked to simply call things a certain color but to find things that are already so called in language (red-eye, yellowbelly, blackfeet). The idea is to take some time listing, exploring, and thinking.

READING AND PRACTICE: Self-Expression through Art (p. 25)
Edvard Munch, "The Cry" (p. 26)
Erich Heckel, "Head of Girl" (p. 27)
Wood figure, Zaire (p. 28)

As this assignment has three parts, one for each picture, you may well wish to use the first one in class as a group exercise to illustrate various ways of using each picture as a vehicle for self-expression. You could, for instance, divide into four groups and ask each group to produce a collective reading of the first picture--one group using the pronoun *I*, another using *you*, another *he*, and the last *she*. If you have more groups, you can use alternatives to the present tense as well. Four pronouns and two tenses will give you eight combinations, if you need them.

A major point to emphasize is that the picture should not be the limit or boundary of what is said; it is just the point of departure, a way of establishing a mood that can be expanded out of the writer's own repertory of thoughts and feelings. For example, with respect to the first picture--by Edvard Munch (pronounced Moonk)--the writer need not try to capture what the artist's subject is actually experiencing, but only what the person *might* be experiencing that could account for such an expression. Even better, what does the picture lead students to think and feel themselves?

In the second picture, the girl is obviously thinking about *something*, but the writer is not supposed to guess what. The writer's job is to produce a coherent stream of reflection that *might* be attributed to such a girl. Remind students that the main constraint on them is that they should try to maintain a consistent mood, not that they should stick to a single image or--above all--that they should attempt to tell a story. The writing goal is to present thoughts and feelings, not to recount events. Explain that there is no question of getting the "right" thoughts and feelings. The idea is to produce the richest, most coherent stream of thoughts and feelings that one can.

The third figure, made of wood, metal, and feathers, comes from Zaire and is probably a fertility figure. Note the distended abdomen and the presence of male and female sexual characteristics. We found this figure in William Rubin's *"Primitivism" in 20th-Century Art* (1984), a catalogue of a show at the Museum of Modern Art in New York that considered the effects of non-Western art on Western artists such as Picasso, Gauguin, and Klee. Some students may respond (as modernist artists did) to the "otherness" of this figure; some may meditate on its smile.

You may wish to let students choose to write about whichever picture stimulates them most--in which case you may prefer *not* to discuss the first one in a way that makes it unsuitable for a writing assignment. If all students want to write about the first or second picture, then use the third for practice in class. We suggest reminding students before they write to check the directions in paragraph 3 again, or you may want to discuss the directions in class. With an assignment like this, we teachers need to curb our tendency to suggest that there is a right answer. The point of the exercise is to get students' creative juices flowing.

READING: TWO EXPRESSIONS OF MOOD (p. 29)
James Wright, "Lying in a Hammock at William Duffy's
Farm in Pine Island, Minnesota" (p. 29)

1.   The movement of the speaker's eyes takes in his world: the butterfly, the framed field, the horse droppings, the chicken hawk: all images of nature. Sight predominates, and distant cowbells are the only sound.

2.   The interest and subtlety of the poem lies in *how* these objects are seen and heard: if the butterfly is given a "weighty" color (bronze), it has through comparison with a leaf retained its own lightness, a weightlessness echoed in the floating chicken hawk. Perhaps the most remarkable transformation is that of old horse droppings into "golden stones." The imagery is bucolic, pleasant, serene but for the "blazing up" of those horse droppings--an arresting and unusual image of something usually considered worthless, dull, and foul becoming valuable, bright, and beautiful.

3.   We might ask whether one who experiences the natural world as the speaker does can be considered to have "wasted" his life. "Lying in a hammock" bears connotations of leisure, comfort, laziness. The speaker might be said to be doing nothing, but is this a waste of time? Similarly, we might ask whether that "empty house" signifies loneliness, or whether the speaker (and perhaps others) have simply left it, preferring to spend the day outside, in the natural world.

READING: Sylvia Plath, from *The Bell Jar* (p. 29)

1.   Her dominant mood is one of strangeness or alienation. She sees no place for herself in the world of mothers and babies.
2.   She is nervous, clever, frightened, sensitive. Her view of the world in the last sentence of paragraph 1 is a good place to start. The changes of attitude from sentence to sentence in paragraph 2 are also important.
3.   Consider the last sentence in paragraph 2. Notice how the adjectives (*fat puling*) qualify Dodo Conway's attitude. An attitude toward *Baby Talk* is also established by descriptive details and adjectives.
4.   The main idea here is the one stated in paragraph 3, where the question is raised as to whether Esther or those who "wait on" babies are the maddest.
5.   Her moods certainly fluctuate, even from paragraph 3 to paragraph 4, but they fluctuate in a coherent and convincing way. She does and does not wish she was like the others.
6.   The descriptive sentence in paragraph 1 is the longest; the personal statement in paragraph 3 is the shortest.

PRACTICE: Mood in a Place (p. 30)

There are two ways to go wrong in this Practice. One is to simply state the mood as a fact: "I felt sad." The other is to simply list or describe the details that can be recorded in the chosen place. Remind your students to select details that *express* the mood they want to convey.

READING: Ideas about the Telephone (p. 31)
Ellen Goodman, from a newspaper column (p. 31)
Federico Fellini, from *Fellini on Fellini* (p. 32)
Roland Barthes, from *A Lover's Discourse* (p. 33)

This is a more complex and challenging exercise than the first two. You may wish to skip it, but if your students found the other exercises obvious, they may be stimulated by this one.
1.   Goodman is thoughtful, emotional, argumentative. In her use of *we*, she assumes the confidence of her reader. Note also her use of parallel structure in paragraphs 5 and 8 as a means of emphasizing her points. Fellini is self-justifying, lively, emotional; words like *joy, terror, charm, dullest, silliest* are crucial to him. Barthes is both emotional *and* intellectual, feeling and analyzing at the same time. Subtlety is both his method and his problem--see his words on what he lacks: spontaneity.

As to which text is most revealing--let that question provoke discussion. It cannot be settled.

2. Goodman is probably a businesslike caller; Fellini is a person likely to be called; and Barthes a potential caller afraid to call.

3. Goodman is comparing and contrasting the telephone's immediate demand for talk with the letter's leisurely time for telling. She accepts the phone as "the tool of these times," but she emphasizes the ephemerality of talk. Fellini says that telephone communication is superior to direct encounters; Barthes says that anxieties about communicative behavior are endless and paralyzing. We don't agree with any of them, though one of us sympathizes with Barthes. And you?

4. These are not analytic questions but matters of opinion. We find Barthes most difficult and most thoughtful.

5. They are about communication: its ways, its joys, its terrors. The telephone serves to concentrate and make concrete the larger issues.

PRACTICE: Ideas about a Common Object (p. 34)

Ideas are a lot less common than objects. In assigning this exercise, you will want to talk about how ideas are generated. Encourage your students to think about the approaches of Goodman, Fellini, and Barthes. One can consider the history of an object, its use, and what it allows, promises, and threatens. Above all, your students should concentrate on what the object means to *them*: how it affects their lives, what they think about it. The best papers will use the writer's own experience as the basis for more general ideas about the meaning and use of the object.

Chapter 3
Reflection: Your Self as Object

Teaching reflective writing has two main functions. At the level of thought, it helps students learn how to objectivize, and at the level of composition, it puts a special emphasis on revision. Looking in a mirror each of us sees our own self as an object, out there, reflected. In writing, this objectivization is not done in space but in time. We reflect by looking back at an earlier self.

Some discussion of reflection as a process will help your students understand why they are being asked to write in this mode. The first Practice should help them to see what reflection has to do with revising their own writing.

READING: Your Own Expressive Writing (p. 36)
PRACTICE: Reflection as Revision (p. 36)

This is an assignment that can make a great difference in a student's sense of the purposes and possibilities of writing. It can be begun in class and finished at home. You may wish to ask students to keep all their rough drafts and false starts. The idea is to get them to feel how writing and revising are integrated in developing ideas.

Your students may not yet have a grasp of the developmental structure of argument, but this is not the place to emphasize that. Look for and encourage signs of refinement of thought or feeling by the refinement of word selection and sentence structure from one draft to the next. This is a time to be rewarding progress, not penalizing errors.

READING: School Days Revisited (p. 37)
           Louise De Salvo, from "A Portrait of the *Puttana* as a
              Middle-Aged Woolf Scholar" (p. 37)

1.   The writer gives a specific time in the past (Autumn, 1963), but writes in the present tense: "I am a senior." She switches to the present perfect--"I have studied"--to include time previous. Again, in the second paragraph, she contrasts the present of that time--"She is talking"--with time gone before: "I have never . . . ". Both shifts emphasize the importance of her experience. In the third paragraph, she switches to the simple present, indicative mood ("I learn," "I observe") to summarize the effects of her experience.
2.   By using the present in the past, she gives a sense of immediacy to her 1963 experiences, as if she wants the reader to experience them with her. Her textual breaks between paragraphs 3 and 4, 5 and 6, 7 and 8, 11 and

12, and 13 and 14 indicate larger shifts in time, setting out particular moments from the past.

Russell Baker, from *Growing Up* (p. 40)

1. In paragraph 1, Baker reflects on the period of time he had been interested in being a writer--a period during which he had "been bored with everything associated with English courses." In paragraph 2, he reflects on the very beginning of his third-year English class, and his anticipation at that time for "another grim year," given Mr. Fleagle's reputation.

2. Baker shows us what he was like at age 16, keeping the reader over his shoulder as he narrates chronologically. By allowing the reader to experience his views and his surprise as he did, the reader participates in Baker's education, in his growing up.

3. The process of memory--the first step in reflective writing--is presented in paragraphs 7 and 8. The rewards of such writing appear in paragraph 8: "It was a moment I wanted to recapture and hold for myself. I wanted to relive the pleasure of an evening at New Street." The result of his writing--the effect of his words on others--is presented in paragraph 11, where he finds himself successful in making others see that moment in the past as he did.

PRACTICE: Reflection on Your School Days (p. 43)

Students usually have no difficulty recalling past events of their school days, so the first draft, expressing their thoughts about the event and the particulars of the experience, should pose few problems. Reflecting on the events may be more difficult, especially for the writer for whom the event is still charged with emotion (e.g., the paper on receiving a poor grade, with the reflection amounting to, "Teachers should not be unfair graders"). Here, the instructor should help with comments and questions that will help the student objectify the experience.

Because these papers are usually so interesting, you should plan to have students read them in class. And because of the students' interest in the topic, such papers are prime candidates for revision (if that proves to be necessary). Furthermore, you can count on a lively discussion of pedagogical practices and philosophies of education arising from the students' reactions to one another's experiences.

READING: Looking at Pictures (p. 43)
Gary Snyder, "Looking at Pictures to Be Put Away"
(p. 43)
Sharon Olds, "I Go Back to May 1937" (p. 44)
Roland Barthes, "Looking for My Mother" (p. 44)

These short readings should be gone over carefully in class. The Snyder poem is easy to understand but tricky to interpret. It can be read in different ways, depending on who you think says *we* in line 5, where and when you think it is said, and to whom it is said. The Barthes piece is more complex on the surface but the direction of the thought is straightforward.

1.   *Who* looks to the past, implying "I have forgotten." *What* looks to the future, implying "we will forget." Both have to do with the frailty of memory.

2.   She *looks* (in the present tense) because the picture has frozen her in its eternal present. *Who was* (in the past) asks about the real girl behind the photographic image. The picture captures part of a forgotten story. It makes the poet wonder about the future: *What will . . . ."*

3.   Eating *can* make us fat, heavy, thick, but loving can't. The physical thickness becomes a metaphor for the way that repetition dulls our feelings and thoughts, making us insensitive, thick.

4.   *We* could be the poet and the girl, but your editors don't think so. They think that *we* refers to the poet in his own present tense and someone close to him who is looking at the pictures with him. He asks, either out loud or to himself, whether another picture, taken now, at the moment of looking at the first picture, could be looked at twenty years later without the same question--who were those people? being asked. The last three lines are the reflection stimulated by the photograph.

5.   Most obviously, there are two kinds of innocence: the innocence of youth untouched sexually and by worldly experience; and the innocence that contrasts with guilt: in this case, their intent not to "hurt anybody." The writer, of course, suggests that these innocent "kids" will go on to hurt their own, as well as themselves.

6.   There's some violent imagery here: "the/red tiles glinting like bent/plates of blood"; the gate, "its/sword-tips black," in contrast with the softness of "May air" and "May sunlight." The banging together of these paper doll images "at the hips like chips of flint" is a perversion of childhood play and suggests the violence of the parents' eventual sexual congress--and certainly of the speaker's assessment of it.

7. The injection of the child-grown-up into the poem, especially in lines 13ff., with their litany of the unpleasantness that is to come (that has, in fact taken place) makes this a painful reflection, especially with its contrast of the last moment of her parents' innocence and her assessment of what happened afterwards, all of which she must accept as the price paid for her coming into being.

8. It is a paradox because assertiveness and gentleness are usually considered opposed qualities. But she was persistent in her gentleness, strongly gentle.

9. He means something like a critical remark about another person, an aggressive comment such as fathers are fond of making.

10. A *just* image goes beyond the things represented to reveal the truth behind them: accuracy plus justice. Barthes is playing on the realistic novelist's search for the *mot juste*, the accurate word (Flaubert).. He wants more than accuracy, he wants justice in his *justesse*. And he finds it in this one picture.

PRACTICE: Reflecting on a Photograph (p. 46)

In this Practice, students are asked to write for a reader who will *not* have the photograph they are writing about. This is not an exercise in description. The photograph is meant to be a stimulus to reflection rather than an object to be described. Still, the students' reflections will be more productive if they have some idea how to "read" a picture, as indicated in the following reflective report by N. R. C. on her teaching of this Practice:

> Students are curious about photos used by others. My students read their essays to the class and then showed the photograph to others. This was a much-enjoyed assignment. The problem for my basic writers (adults) was organizing their essays. Some started with a reading of the picture (what was there for them) and continued with a reflection on the people in the picture and/or the situation surrounding the taking of the picture. The least successful papers (and there weren't many) came from those who had difficulty reading the photo; they overlooked such things as the stance of the subject, or the closeness or distance of one or more subjects from one another. In conferences on revision, I helped students with such reading, and though their revisions were successful in the sense of organization and expansion of description and reflection, I regretted having to manipulate, or influence, what they might see themselves. What I should have done in class was go over a photograph with them. They hadn't had enough experience in reading visual texts.

READING: From Thing to Thought (p. 47)
Isak Dinesen, "The Iguana" (p. 47)

The questions for this Reading direct the student to its organization, especially to its movement from description through reflection to advice. You may wish to supplement them with questions of your own that point to Dinesen's descriptive and expressive power. This is a strong bit of writing.

1. Paragraph 1:   description of Iguana
    Paragraph 2:   narration of shooting
    Paragraph 3:   narration of bracelet incident (but notice first sentence raising Iguana to the level of a symbol ("in some sort")
    Paragraph 4:   reflection on bracelet
    Paragraph 5:   advice about dealing with "foreign" things
2. Note and discuss expressions like *sometimes* (paragraph 1), *Once* (paragraph 2), and *Often since* (paragraph 3) as markers of time, and the complexities of paragraph 3--"had it come . . . now . . . had been." The last paragraph is in the present and gives advice about the future: "shoot not."
3. The last question should help students see how dependent the advice is upon the illustrations that precede it. The change from life to death must be brought home to us vividly for the advice to take effect when it is offered.

PRACTICE: Reflecting on Experience (p. 48)

The experimenting part of this assignment is crucial. Encourage students to take some time making their lists. It might be a good idea to begin by separating into small groups in which all members can talk about some occasion when they did something that led to their learning from a mistake or from careless or thoughtless behavior. The idea is to make the notion of this kind of learning by trial and error clear enough to stimulate each student's memory. One way to get the memory working is to search by categories: events in sports, events in school, events with parents, events with friends, events with strangers. Another good way to search is by years or by school grades. The best papers are likely to come from students whose lists provide enough material that they can select specific events which will make a coherent essay.

In the actual writing, the hard part will be to move beyond merely telling what happened in order to describe the events as typical of a pattern of behavior-- of something that happened more than once, in different circumstances. This will depend on the writer's discovery of the patterns, which may happen during the making of the list, or it may happen only during the actual writing. Sometimes the writing will stimulate recollection of related events that can be added to the list.

Reflection is this whole process of remembering, evaluating, relating, describing, and drawing conclusions. The process itself should be discussed with the whole group. You might ask the class to imagine how Dinesen came to write what she wrote. Ask them to think of her as having certain experiences that gave her an idea for a reflective essay. They should try to see her becoming able to write the essay as she came to understand the pattern that made each of her experiences one version of a single kind of experience. Ideally, your students should see that such writing is not random but is actually a highly structured process that is driven by what we are calling reflection: thinking over certain experiences until the way they fit together emerges from our reflection. The conclusion to Dinesen's essay could be written only after she understood the meaning of her experiences. A writer may begin writing with such a conclusion already in mind--or may find it only after beginning to write, in which case it must have been lurking in the unconscious mind before it was discovered. Reflection means, among other things, finding what one really thinks about things by getting beneath the superficial level and seeing the patterns that make up one's character and the characters of others. Reflection also means trying to judge or evaluate the patterns discovered. Ask your students whether they keep making the same mistakes or have the same kind of learning experiences over and over. If they do, ask them to reflect on why the pattern recurs in the way that it does.

READING: **From Experience to Thought (p. 49)**
Brent Staples, "Just Walk on By: A Black Man Ponders
His Power to Alter Public Space (p. 49)

1.   Here are the various shifts in time, paragraph by paragraph:
      1:   what happened more than a decade ago
      2:   shift to reflection on that event
      3:   shift to past events
      4:   shift to present situation
      5:   shift to reflection
      6:   to reflection on present
      7:   shift to past events (boyhood)
      8:   to reflection on events
      9:   to past events and their effect
    10:   shift to recent past events as reporter
    11:   shift to recent past events as reporter continued
    12:   shift to reflection
    13:   shift to present events
    14:   shift to present events

2. Podhoretz's terror and nervousness re blacks in his 1963 essay on black men's "firm place in New York mugging literature" and on black men's "paranoid touchiness" provides a point of view for Staples to work with (and in fact against). Staples shows in his essay that such "touchiness" does not result from paranoia, but is induced by society's perception of black men, a position amply demonstrated by Podhoretz. Perhaps it is he who may be considered paranoid.

3. Staples's reflection on a black man's "power to alter public space," gets to the heart of racism and white fear of the big black man. Staples shows how one kind of paranoia can breed another. Though Staples's rage may be under control, it manifests itself in the form of irony, as in the opening of the essay: "My first victim was a woman." He himself has become victimized.

PART THREE
<u>READER-ORIENTED FORMS: DISCOURSE AND POWER</u>

Chapter 4
<u>Direction: Guiding Your Reader</u>

The main thing that must be emphasized in this section is the need for the writer to *imagine the reader*. You will want to repeat this emphasis with every assignment. Directive discourse depends on the writer seeing things from the reader's point of view. Discussion of the pie/pastry recipe will make it clear to those who bake how inadequate the directions are for those who have never baked.

PRACTICE: How to Make or Do Something (p. 59)

Students generally have few problems coming up with a topic. Even those who feel they don't know how to do anything "special" can produce successful papers on "How to Parallel-Park a Car" or "How to Catch a Ball."

In testing one another's directions, students should look for undefined terminology and proper sequence. Directive writing tests syntactical skills, and unclear or confusing sentences should be pointed out. Certain types of directions can be tested in class as well, with one student trying to follow another's directions.

READING: The Art of Eating Spaghetti (p. 60)
PRACTICE: The Art of Eating _____ (p. 60)

Baker does not describe his essay, but reflects on the people and the events that the topic brought to mind. He does provide some cues for thinking about the assignment and its audience. You might encourage students to recall the first time they encountered a "difficult" or exotic food, and to transfer their memories of embarrassment or disaster to the topic. As in the previous assignment, it is crucial to keep an inexperienced audience in mind while writing.

READING: Direction through the Ages: How to Conduct Yourself
(p. 60)
from *The Art of Courtly Love* (p. 61)
from *The Mirror of Honor* (p. 62)
from *A Father's Legacy to His Daughters* (p. 63)
from *The Well-Bred Girl in Society* (p. 63)
from *Amy Vanderbilt's Everyday Etiquette* (p. 64)

Most students will find these excerpts accessible, although some may have trouble with Gregory's diction and Harrison's complicated syntax. In the former instance, you should be prepared to gloss and exemplify such terms as "double *entendre*" and "dissoluteness." However, we suggest that you let the excerpt define its key terms such as "virgin purity" and "delicacy." In the latter instance, an oral reading in *propria persona* can be helpful--and amusing. To get discussion going, any one of the first three questions will do. The fourth question is worth considering but we do not recommend that you use it to begin discussion.

1. To come up with subtitles, students have to posit some kind of topical unity or coherent purpose for each excerpt. They are likely to have problems relating each excerpt's specifics to some more general issue or abstract idea. Word choice also poses problems since students not only have to negotiate the gap between their terms and those of the writer but also have to decide which terms in the excerpt are key. You can address these problems--and get discussion going--by putting suggested subtitles on the board and evaluating their appropriateness. Here is one possible set of subtitles for the excerpts: The Art of Retaining Love, The Honorable Art of Caring for Your Lord, The Art of Delicate Conversation, The Art of Visible Innocence, and How to Be a Well-Mannered Date.

2. We think that excerpt five is most like our description of basic directive writing; that the purpose of excerpt three and the style of excerpt four make them least like basic directive writing; and that excerpt three's emphasis on abstract ideals makes it verge on being nondirective.

3. This question should provoke debate on what it means to "attend" to the reader. Although each writer attends to the reader, they do so in different ways. Capellanus, Pizan, and Harrison clearly imagine their readers as actual performers or actors. Not so Gregory, who seems more concerned with his daughters' morale. Baldridge certainly informs her readers, but her step-by-step approach suggests a rather mechanical image of their possibilities.

4. This question invites students to consider these excerpts as sociocultural documents which can tell us something about the history and structure of relations between the sexes, of class positions, and of producing a self.

PRACTICE: How to Conduct Yourself (p. 66)

Although students often give each other advice in private, they may be uncomfortable about going public with what they know. You can ease their way into this assignment by asking them to help you imagine--and understand--what it's like to be a new student on campus. As the class constructs a general image of the newcomer, you'll want to encourage them to imagine specific situations that are likely to pose problems for that newcomer and to think about what the newcomer needs in order to deal with those situations. Would insider information help? What about a set of rules to follow? Is morale boosting important; if so, is sympathy likely to be more or less encouraging than humor or irony? Imagining a reader different from one's self or the teacher is crucial to the success of this assignment.

READING: Indirection (p. 66)
                Fran Lebowitz, "How to Be a Directory Assistance
                    Operator: A Manual" (p. 66)

This reading is meant to be a model for the accompanying practice. However, its witty take on directive writing is well worth considering, even if you don't plan to assign the accompanying practice.

1.   We think that Lebowitz follows all the rules except for the "--and no more" caveat in rule number 2. For example, the Russian Tea Room example is not only unnecessary but also excessive--and therefore humorous.

2.   This question is designed to get students to look more carefully at how Lebowitz works. So, there are not right answers, just occasions for talking about how specific words, lines, and passages function. For us, the word "grave" in the second sentence is the first tip-off; it's just too excessive and clichéd to be taken seriously.

3.   Explicitly, Lebowitz says directory assistance operators should "give them the number" (paragraph 1). If students say something similar in answer to this question, you can point out that this direction is explicitly rather than implicitly articulated and that it covers up a number of problems, including a certain mechanical notion of service that dehumanizes social interactions. Implicitly, Lebowitz suggests a number of ways--including humor--that communication can be made more human.

4.   This question is another way to get at some of the issues question 3 raises-- including the rise of a "service" economy, the dehumanization of communicative interactions, and the subtle yet very real power struggles involved in giving and following directions.

PRACTICE: How to Be a _____ : A Manual (p. 69)

Topic and format are unlikely to be problems for students working through this practice. But there are bound to be lots of problems with the art and aim of indirection unless ample class time is devoted to working through question 2 and either question 3 or question 4 above. Once students see that Lebowitz uses specific techniques to make her point indirectly, they can try some of the same techniques themselves. And if they understand that her aim cannot be reduced to a simple message (i.e. to "give them the number"), then they may be more inclined to write with good humor rather than with petty sarcasm. Sarcasm is not out of play; but students should be encouraged to make it human rather than hurtful. And that means imagining that those who have served us ill are also persons.

Chapter 5
Persuasion: Moving Your Reader

First of all, we certainly do not wish to advocate lying, misrepresenting, deceiving, or any other form of unethical behavior. But no citizen can afford to be unaware of the workings of persuasion. This sort of discourse *must* be studied, and there is no way to understand it fully without using it in the gamelike situations we have devised here. Good causes need persuasive presentation. Our legal system is based on an adversary structure, wherein different persuasive discourses contend for the opinions of judges and juries. We even persuade ourselves frequently against our better judgment. To hide from persuasion is to become the victim of it. By all means, make your ethical position clear to your students, and choose the assignments here that you find most congenial. But do not pass over this without giving the techniques of persuasion some attention.

Since the days of Socrates and the Sophists, the moral issues involved in persuasive discourse have been argued. Certainly, today many teachers will have some questions about the ethical propriety of teaching persuasive discourse. This being the case, we wanted to make our own position on these issues clear.

READING: Persuasion in Advertising (p. 71)
Fly-Tox Advertisement, 1926 (p. 71)

1.   The picture of the living room and the text suggest an audience of middle-to-upper-class families who live in (or desire to live in) "finely appointed homes." The reference to the Mellon Institute suggests that such an audience is educated enough to believe in progress through science. And certainly, this is an audience who wants the best for their children.

2.   The ad works on the anxieties of both the housewife and the parent. The standards are "good housekeeping" on the one hand and the prevention of suffering in little children on the other. The reader is encouraged to feel revulsion and hatred for insects and pride in a well-kept, "finely appointed" home.

3.   The passages descriptive of the fly and the mosquito are the most useful here. The "assassin" insect is contrasted with the "devoted" parent who proves devotion by paying for Fly-Tox. We learn nothing about the composition of the product. Can it really be so deadly and be as "harmless to humans" as it claims? Sizes and prices are the most accurately given information.

4.   The main image shows a delicate child about to eat a fly-infected sandwich. The love of children and desire to protect them is the basis for this image. Another shows a well-appointed home, appealing to pride and/or envy. The

determined woman is meant as a model for others. The product is shown so it may be recognized.

PRACTICE: The Ghastly Resort Hotel (p. 74)

The game here is to remain faithful to the denotative level while producing copy that connotes pleasure to the reader. Students really enjoy this assignment, even though they find the transformation of the twelve ghastly features very challenging. Working out the possibilities for one of the ghastly features in class is a good idea. For example, what about those barracudas? One student's solution was this: "You'll be astounded when you find yourself swimming amongst our beautiful and world-famous sea life! Some people have even gone out and fed these magnificent fish!"

You should also stress the organization of the twelve features. For example, one paragraph might be devoted to the features of the hotel; a second paragraph might decide waterfront activities; a third, nightlife; and so on. To aid in this organization, you should suggest that students have a specific audience in mind, such as honeymooners, adventure lovers, those who enjoy the unexpected, those who appreciate unspoiled primitive cultures.

Alternative approach: If you have used this assignment before and are tired of reading about this hotel, have your students make up alternative ghastly places. They can work in groups devising lists of unattractive features for restaurants, summer camps, colleges, and so on. The groups can then swap these lists, and write up attractive copy. Each originating group can critique the papers of the group they've swapped with.

READING: Reaching a Different Audience (p. 75)
The Marlboro Man, 1954 (p. 76)

Though the intended appeal of this advertisement is pretty obvious, you should spend some time discussing it in class to make sure students see all of its "virile" qualities. Besides the anchor tattoo (military), note the butch haircut, cigarette at side of mouth, tank-top undershirt revealing muscles and hairy chest, the whistle (authority), the square jaw (tough), the slightly furrowed brow (serious), the squinting-eyed (penetrating, perhaps threatening?) gaze.

PRACTICE: Changing the Persuasive Pattern (p. 75)

Encourage students to name some current products undergoing a "gender" change, such as male underwear (briefs and tank tops) transformed by Calvin Klein for trendy young women; or cosmetics for men; and whiskey being promoted in ads featuring women. Students may also recall the "urban cowboy" craze and the selling of boots and Stetsons to an urban audience. To get them started, ask your students how they might sell chewing tobacco to a New York stockbroker of either sex.

Students usually have no difficulty creating ads, but this assignment requires a special leap of imagination. If your students seem bereft of ideas, have them work in groups to come up with a product, an audience, and possible campaign strategies (this is how it's done on Madison Avenue). Each member of a group can submit an ad, and these can be exchanged and critiqued within each group.

READING: Political Persuasion (p. 77)
Bill Clinton, "Inaugural Address, 1993" (p. 77)

This is not an imposingly powerful piece of political persuasion, perhaps because it is less partisan than other kinds of political discourse like campaign speeches. Yet that is one of the reasons why we chose it for analysis; we wanted to decrease the chance that this reading would be used as an occasion to parade party loyalties. While it is true that Clinton received only 43 percent of the popular vote, he is addressing the nation as a whole in this speech. Does America have a consensual mode of political discourse? This is one question you might raise with your students.

Two other considerations prompted us to choose this piece: Students probably know something about the state of the nation at the time of Clinton's address, and they may well have seen the speech broadcast on television. Before taking up the questions below, the class should list significant events and conditions of 1992 (i.e., the aftermath of the Persian Gulf War, the L. A. riots, economic recession, dismemberment of the Soviet and the communist bloc, ethnic violence in the former Yugoslavia.

1. Clinton is trying to persuade his audience to believe in the idea that by working together and embracing change, Americans can and will revitalize their country, if not the world.

2. *We/us* are by far the most dominant pronouns--as you would expect them to be in a speech addressed to the nation and intent on producing consensus. Hence, you might want to look more closely at those instances when *we/us* is not used. Or draw the students' attention to paragraphs 21 and 22 and discuss how and why Clinton moves from *you* to *I* to *we*.

3. Both use a "this *but* that" structure which might be called contrastive, antithetical, or balanced; we like to call it the "but" pattern so that by way of a but/butt pun, we can suggest how closely it is related to the point--or butt--of each paragraph: that these are contradictory times (cf. "the best of times/worst of times" formula that opens Dickens' *A Tale of Two Cities*).

This "but" structure informs the whole speech, appearing at the sentence level (i.e., the opening line of paragraph 17); at the paragraph level (often explicitly but sometimes implicitly as in paragraphs 4 and 11); and at the section level (i.e., the "Assuming the Mantle" section begins in "triumph" and after a number of ups and downs, ends with both a threatening earthquake image and the word "enemy"). Yet Clinton varies the effect of the pattern, sometimes using it to go from negative to positive (i.e., paragraph 1) and at other times turning it the other way--from positive to negative (i.e., paragraph 5). We think he began with paragraph 1 rather than 5 for the following reasons. Although "The economy, stupid" (paragraph 5) suited well the partisan purposes of the campaign, the purpose of this speech is political consensus rather than victory at the polls. This purpose also accounts for the stylistic difference between the two paragraphs. Paragraph 1 is much more explicitly metaphorical than paragraph 5 not only because Clinton wants to effect a change from negative to positive that, materially speaking, has not yet occurred, but also because metaphor emphasizes resemblance over difference--an emphasis that makes it quite useful to those interested in promoting consensus or mediating contradictions.

4. He appeals to (the laws of) Nature; the founding fathers (specifically, Washington and Jefferson); to Scripture and the "Almighty"; to the American spirit of adventure (see his repeated use of the word "bold" and terms associated with it); to the tradition of progress; to the "work ethic" and to a social service ideal. In our opinion, no one of these appeals dominates; rather, they are combined to make a kind of natural supernaturalism.

5. The following characteristics tend to make a quotable phrase: brevity, point, repetition of words, alliteration, syntactic balancing, imagistic condensation, and colloquialisms. Here are a few possible candidates for quotability: "Though we march to the music of our time, our mission is timeless" (paragraph 2). "Communications and commerce are global, investment is mobile, technology is almost magical, and ambition for a better life is now universal" (paragraph 6). "Not choosing sacrifice for its own sake, but for our own sake" (paragraph 11). "Powerful people maneuver for position and worry endlessly about who is in and who is out, who is up and who is down" (paragraph 14).

PRACTICE: The Enemy of the People (p. 81)

Discussion of strategy is important here. Students should consider where they want to lead their audience--what will the final point be? Is it worthwhile to attack the other doctor's reputation? Should they attack the people who have been threatening them? What sort of audience will they be addressing? Is it hostile, unreasonable, open to reason, susceptible to emotional persuasion, or what?

PRACTICE: The Difficult Campaign Speech (p. 82)

Actually, the students who have done this assignment have not found it very difficult. The most successful papers are those with a clear sense of strategy, so class discussion should focus on that. Students should consider whether attacking their wealthy opponent will work for them or against them; how they should handle their adolescent troubles with the law (open the speech with it? end the speech with it? ignore it?); how to deal with the issue of family values; how their audience will view their accomplishments vis à vis their wealthy opponent's; and so on.

READING: The Job Letter and Résumé (p. 83)
PRACTICE: The Job Letter (p. 87)

As suggested in the text, students may want to furnish their own job descriptions or advertisements for this assignment. Your career-minded students will take this assignment very seriously and will probably do quite well with it. If your students are interested, you might consider bringing a personnel director into class to discuss what he or she looks for in a letter of application. If your school has a placement office, you might send some students over to find out what advice and information is available there.

PART FOUR
TOPIC-ORIENTED FORMS: DISCOURSE AND POWER

Chapter 6
Narration: Organizing Time

We suggest you discuss the introduction one paragraph at a time, to make sure that the concepts of scale (or level of detail), emotional effect, and point of view are understood. Make the point that narrative is used by writers of fiction and by writers of history and journalism; it is not just a "creative" kind of writing but a basic part of every writer's activity. (*Note:* Chapter 7, Description, also uses excerpts from these same writers and works. You may want to tie narration and description together directly.)

To prepare students for reading and discussing the four passages, remind them to try to keep the writer in mind. You might suggest that they pause after every sentence and ask, "Now why did the writer do it that way? Why use that level of detail, or that point of view? What effect is the writer trying to have on the reader?"

Here are our thoughts about the questions that follow the examples in the introduction.

Willa Cather, "A Shooting" (from *O Pioneers!*; p. 95)

1.   Frank's state of mind is something the reader constructs from details (such as his trembling) and from statements made by the narrator (such as "his blood was quicker than his brain" and "Either he shut his eyes or he had vertigo"). In this example the writer has indeed directed the reader, but the reader has been required to process certain details, to make interpretations.

2.   This exercise, which can be done in class in groups, is instructive in the manipulation of voice and tone: What makes language "emotional" or "unemotional"? What is the difference between presenting "just the facts" and manipulating your reader toward emotional response?

3.   This question calls for an analysis (as suggested above) of changes made.

Richard Wright, from "The Man Who Lived Underground" (p. 96)

1.   This question calls for a basic response to the text as a whole followed by a closer consideration of Wright's method of narrative manipulation.

2.   The requirement here is simply to tell what happened: to report the events as objectively as possible.

3. One of the biggest differences should be the loss of tension in an after-the-events, just-the-facts report. The issue here too is the change in time from what was happening to what happened. Consideration of Wright's rhetorical devices and descriptive language, such as his use of active verbs, should be given attention.

4. In both pieces, we see from the protagonist's point of view, but in Cather's piece, we are given authorial commentary (e.g., "Frank, who had always wanted to see things blacker than they were"). We are conscious of an author who tells us what Frank did and saw, whereas Wright puts us closer, in the protagonist's head. The intention of both writers is to build toward tension and its release, but the difference between the two situations affects the manner in which each is presented, as does the difference in each writer's style. Wright would immerse us, while Cather prefers a little distance.

Jamaica Kincaid, "The Tourist's Arrival" (from *A Small Place*; p. 98)

1. *You* are arriving (with the writer) in Antigua as a white American or European tourist. Such a point of view allows Kincaid to focus on differences in culture seen through the eyes of a person intent on pleasure.

2. The double level of irony is present here, and thus the paragraph is shaped by how you the tourist are likely to respond and the writer's knowledge of what the facts of Antiguan life are. For example, the dreadful Antiguan roads being read as "a marvelous change" from splendid American highways suggests that you the tourist do not want to admit poverty and corruption into your holiday plans.

Louise Erdrich, "Cousin Mary" (from *The Beet Queen*, p. 99)

1. This is first-person narration of simple, one might say, prosaic events. The interest is in the narrator's opinion and interpretation of those events.

2. As the beginning of the first paragraph one might simply feel sorry for Cousin Mary, who arrives with nothing. But the narrator's comment, "I was too old to be carried," sets up a tension between the narrator and her cousin. And the "lies" complicate the tension. Sita's feeling of unfair treatment is further developed in the second paragraph. Note the concise descriptive language: "crammed"; "legs dangling out," which works to engage the reader's sympathy (and amuse the reader as well).

3.   In this rewrite, one will have to judge whether Sita's mother considers Sita a testy, difficult child, or is perhaps obtuse and blind to Sita's feelings, or is patient with her.

James Joyce, "The End of Molly's Soliloquy" (from *Ulysses*; p. 101)

1.   This question works well with small groups, where results can be recorded after the group agrees on what has been narrated. The very difficulty of the passage should make this interesting. Suggest that each group begin by having one member read the passage aloud.
2.   The reading aloud works best in groups, where a reader can be chosen after discussion of tone and the effect of transforming stream-of-consciousness into "grammatically correct sentences."
3.   This assignment requires students to translate an emotional narrative into an unemotional one. Although this assignment is "creative," it runs counter to most such assignments in that students are asked to "create" something closer to standard academic prose than to literature--the kind of academic prose we usually call "objective." The deep purpose of such assignments is to persuade students that *all* writing is creative, and that there is an art to concealing art.

READING AND PRACTICE: The Life of Stephen Crane (p. 102)

The challenge to the student in this assignment lies in the comprehension of the material, the necessity to form some point of view, and the choice of material which best illustrates that point of view. Some approaches to the material might include:

--A consideration of the interaction between Crane's desire for adventure and his literary production
--The sort of education that prepared Crane for his career (his desire to learn by living life rather than by studying it)
--An analysis of the subject matter that interested Crane: common people, such as slum dwellers like Maggie; regular soldiers; war itself

     While there is plenty of material here from which to construct a narrative of Crane's life, you might consider assigning research into further biographical material or into Crane's fiction, poetry, or journalism. In Chapters 10 and 11 of this text, you will find an article by Crane ("The Last of the Mohicans") and two short stories ("The Bride Comes to Yellow Sky" and "The Blue Hotel"). R. W.

Stallman's *Stephen Crane* (rev. ed., New York: George Braziller, 1973) is a biography that also contains checklists of "Writings by Stephen Crane," "Writings on Stephen Crane," and "Related Background Writings." Stallman's *Stephen Crane: A Critical Bibliography* (Ames: Iowa State University Press, 1972) has more information.

PRACTICE: The Life of Yourself (p. 109)

Although this is not an easy assignment, you may want to use it early in the semester to enable students to get acquainted with one another and to help you get acquainted with them. Students may want to interview one another in order to add to the information in the chronologies and paragraphs.

L. L. discusses some of the pleasures and pitfalls of this assignment:

This assignment was universally appreciated and initiated a good class discussion on the subject of "nonfiction." The chronologies were indeed quite good. Most students attempted to provide a sense of their personalities as well as lifestyles in the chronologies; they included such information as "bought my first pair of painter's pants"; "refused to eat graham crackers in kindergarten." With few exceptions, the chronologies lent themselves well to the writing of interesting biographical statements. The students have led interesting lives and are accomplished in a variety of areas. It was a pleasure to read these chronologies, and it gave me a better sense of them as individuals. I recommend that this exercise be done early in the semester.

The biographies based upon these chronologies were, however, less than successful. With few exceptions, the students simply organized the chronologies into paragraphs and elaborated only upon those details which had been presented at length in the chronology itself. They organized the material in chronological sequence, and the biographer had no voice of his or her own. There were some general exceptions to this rule. Some students allowed the biographer's voice to surface in such comments as "A difficult period in his life then followed . . ." or "He will be an asset to the Brown community."

Only one woman attempted a more sophisticated ordering of material. She began by saying, "At the age of fourteen, Peter began smoking pot. This changed his outlook on life. . . ." She continued to relate Peter's life, using occasional flashbacks, with "pot smoking" and the "new outlook" as a running theme throughout.

Perhaps the assignment might be improved if a context were supplied. For example, students could be asked to choose one of these alternatives:

(1) "Special Yet One of Us": Determine a context for your biography--
for example, the student about whom you are writing has somehow
distinguished himself (pick something special from the chronology). The
local paper has asked you to provide a biography for their pages, pointing
out particularly how this person got to be where he is today. What is unique
about your subject? What obstacles has he confronted and overcome? Try
to answer the question, "How is he just like you and me?"

(2) You notice that the student whose chronology you receive is, in
some ways, representative of your generation as a whole. His or her
experiences, problems, and lifestyle may be used to illustrate and discuss
wider issues. Your biography should reflect this fact. In other words, you
wish to make some point about the category of people into which your
subject fits (this doesn't mean that you must ignore that which is special
about him or her, but you have chosen your subject in order to make your
points clear and specific through the use of examples). This biography is a
feature article for a magazine or newspaper. You must use the limited date
available to you in order to draw conclusions and convey your opinions
about the age in which you live. Above all, you want to retain your readers'
interest.

READING: Narrating an Event (p. 110)
                 Gabriel García Márquez, "A Very Old Man with Enormous
                 Wings" (p. 110)

1.   A couple living in a small town discover a very old man with enormous
wings lying in the mud in their backyard. At first, because of his strange
dialect, they think he is a sailor, but a knowledgeable neighbor woman tells
them he is an angel. The whole neighborhood comes to see this
phenomenon, whom they treat without reverence. The priest suspects an
impostor because the old man seems not to understand Latin, "the language
of God." Elisendra, the wife, decides to charge a nickel to those who wish
to see the angel. People come from all over, and the couple makes a lot of
money. At first, the people annoy the angel, but when he goes into a panic
after being burned, they leave him alone. A carnival featuring a large
tarantula "with the head of a maiden" usurps the spotlight, in part because
the angel's "miracles" have been unimpressive. Elisendra and Pelayo don't
mind being left alone, and they build a two-story mansion with the money
they've made showing the angel. Their little child plays with the angel, who
tolerates it, and they both catch chicken pox. When the child goes to
school, the angel wanders through the house, annoying Elisendra. They
send him out to a shed. He gets sick, but survives, and begins to grow new

feathers. One day Elisendra sees him trying to fly, and finally he succeeds, and she watches him go off in the distance.

2. We don't know exactly when the story took place, but judging from the child's age, the story covers about a 4- to 5-year period. García Márquez condenses time, but spends a good deal of narrative time on such things as the angel's physical qualities, the priest as representative of Catholicism, the spider with the head of a woman, and the carnival-like aspects of the situation.

3. We have an almost-omniscient narrator here who describes the actions and reactions of the characters but who can't (won't?) tell us what the angel is thinking. In that sense, the narrator's position is akin to that of the village people.

4. The story can be considered a tale for children in the sense that a child is most accepting of the angel, just as children are most accepting of fantasy. The angel's behavior after the child goes off to school suggests some attachment on the angel's part. Indeed, he acts like a child who doesn't know what to do with himself after his playmates have gone off. But this story's barbs are meant for adults: the allusions to religious arguments in paragraph 9, for example, are part of the general mockery directed at the church--especially at the bureaucracy of religion.

Chapter 7
Description: Organizing Space

The point of teaching descriptive writing is to emphasize the importance of
viewpoint. It is a point of view that literally enables one to *see*. Seeing is not just
looking; it is the selection and organization of things in the visual field. In teaching
this section, you should admit that one seldom writes a whole essay in the
descriptive mode. Practice in description is designed to improve the writer's skill
at selecting and organizing detail. Facing the difficulties of *translation* from the
visual to verbal is excellent exercise in composition.

You might also point out to students how their need to produce written
versions of visual material will actually affect what they see. In this form of
writing, composition reaches out from the necessary order of the written word
(grammar, syntax, diction) to help organize the perceived world.

READING: Point of View in Description (p. 118)
Marilynne Robinson, "A Kitchen" (from *Housekeeping*;
p. 119)
James Joyce, "A Restaurant" (from *Ulysses*; p. 119)
Kate Simon, "A Street" (from *Bronx Primitive*; p. 120)
Scott Momaday, "An Arbor" (from *The Way to Rainy
Mountain*; p. 120)

In discussing this group, use the questions posed in the introduction to the
selections. The four pieces were chosen because they present differing attitudes
toward the places described. Both the Robinson and the Joyce pieces describe
less-than-attractive locales, but there is more revulsion in Joyce, more dismay in
Robinson. The main point of reading and discussion is to see how each writer has
organized the text, so as to prepare students to write their own descriptions.
Discussion can, for example, answer the basic question, "Where do I start?"

Robinson starts by flooding her kitchen with light, then showing what the
light exposes from the first-person view of Ruthie, the narrator, who offers a bit of
commentary. Where Robinson's description is visually oriented and slightly
distanced, Joyce's immerses us in sights, sounds, and smells through eyewitness
stream-of-consciousness form. He begins in the doorway of the restaurant with
details of what the senses are immediately assaulted by. Simon runs her eye up
and down the street of her childhood, starting from her own building, while
Momaday, standing in an arbor, gives us a long landscape view before returning us
to the "hard dirt floor" of the arbor.

PRACTICE: Organizing a Space (p. 121)

Note that this is a two-stage assignment, with a choice of two directions for the second stage. If you choose to follow this pattern, make sure your students understand the sequence:

Stage 1
a. jotting, exploring
b. drafting
c. getting reactions to written draft

Stage 2
either d1. rewrite for clarity of effect
or   d2. rewrite for different effect
(choice must be indicated)

Both the draft (b) and revision (d1 or d2) should be submitted to you. You may even ask to see the exploring (a). Good discussion of the Reading will make the results of this Practice much better than they would be without it.

READING: A Place with a History (p. 121)
              Nikki Giovanni, from "400 Mulvaney Street" (p. 122)
PRACTICE: Describing a Place with a History (p. 126)

These reading and practice assignments are closely related. You should probably assign the directions for the Practice when you assign the reading, and then assign the Practice for the next class. The directions for the Practice suggest what to look for in Giovanni's text, which is meant to serve as a model for this assignment.

Giovanni provides a reflective description of the places and people of the neighborhood she grew up in, and contrasts this place in a part of Knoxville-now-gone with Knoxville present, and the neighborhood her grandmother moved to, to a house lacking the family history that made the old house a special and loved place. The many student writers who have themselves experienced moving from one place to another or who have gone back to a place after a much-loved family member has died, as Giovanni does here, will have little difficulty with this assignment.

In discussing Giovanni's text, ask students to look at the specific descriptions Giovanni gives. What does she describe? Who does she describe? How does she describe? There's enough variety in the text to provide examples for various ways of describing.

READING: Hogarth's "Noon" Described (p. 127)
PRACTICE: Describing a Hogarth Street Scene (p. 129)

The real title of Hogarth's engraving is "The Enraged Musician." We decided to omit the title from the text so as not to force "one right reading" of the picture. There are other possibilities for organizing and discussing this visual text. L. L.'s students came up with these suggestions in class discussion:

1. kinds of facial expressions represented
2. noise, sound, and music
3. a theme of poverty and people at once crowded but in isolation
4. social-class divisions
5. religious and other symbols
6. modes of amusement

This print . . . depicts the rage and frustration of an effete violinist, probably a foreigner and a court musician, at the occupational noises and common musical sounds of the London populace, their children, and their animals.

The musician stares out his window with his hands over his ears; his violin, music sheets, ink and quill surround him. A playbill outside his window announces "The Sixty Second Day . . . Comedians . . . the (Thea)re Royal . . . Beggars Opera . . . Macheath by Mr. Walker. Polly . . . by Miss Fenton. Peachum by Hippisley . . . Vivat Rex." A parrot squawks at the musician from a lamp post. Below, a ragged, pregnant woman with a crying child sings a vaguely autobiographical ballad, "The Ladies Fall." In front of her a little girl with a noisemaker drops her ball as her eyes bulge in interest at seeing a boy companion urinate down a coal hole. A writing slab is tied to the boy's belt. Both children have constructed a bird trap and have planted twigs beside it. Directly below the violinist a street musician plays an oboe.

In the center of the scene a comely milkmaid plies her trade. In front of her a little figure dressed as a soldier with a wooden sword bangs mechanically on a drum. Beside him a man sharpens a meat cleaver on a grindstone; a dog barks at him. In the background an Irish laborer (his turned-up beehive cap reveals his nationality) lays pavement, a dustman rings his bell and shouts out, a blacksmith blows a horn, and a fish seller cries out his call. Across from the musician, "John Long Pewterer" plies his noisy trade. On his roof, a sweep calls to someone, and two cats fight. A flag flies from the church to mark a holiday, suggesting more noise from the churchbells.

Sean Shesgreen, ed., *Engraving by Hogarth* (New York: Dover, 1973).

READING: A Critic Describes a Face (p. 131)
               Graham McCann, from *Marilyn Monroe* (p. 131)
PRACTICE: Describing a Famous Face (p. 132)

Careful analysis and discussion of McCann's text will be helpful when students
proceed to write their own. McCann starts with a "typical" photograph and
analyzes it, asking questions about it. He then describes it and interprets Monroe's
look. Note how aware he is of the dialogue between the object and the spectator,
with emphasis on the desires of the viewer. This descriptive exercise can give
students some experience in cultural criticism as they analyze and describe not
simply the face of a celebrity but his or her packaging and its attendant effect.

READING: "La Gioconda" (p. 133)
               Walter Pater, from *The Renaissance* (p. 134)
PRACTICE: "Il Giocondo" (p. 134)

Our smilers are new for this edition, and given the fickle world of show biz, will
both probably be replaced in the next edition of *Practice*. But Pater survives,
beautifully embalmed in his matchless prose, as does the Mona Lisa. Can students
emulate Pater's prose? Yes, indeed. Either face they work with will offer them
plenty of food for thought as "symbol of the modern idea." The students'
conception of this "modern idea" helps to organize their papers as does their
imitation of Pater's order and syntax.

     You should go over Pater's paragraph in class in order to ease the initial
syntactical shock and to suggest possibilities for the transformation of thoughts
about the Mona Lisa to thoughts about Bart and Dan. For example, Pater's
opening sentence introduces this feminine presence as an object of desire, and the
rest of the paragraph tells why by showing us what she symbolizes--according to
Pater, of course, whose fantasies may seem farfetched to the students. And
rightly so. The question for students to ponder is, "What does the masculine
presence of Bart Simpson (or Dan) symbolize for people today?" Can we consider
the popularity of both as an indication that the fantasies of the 1990s are as
bizarre as Pater's?

     In reviewing responses to this assignment, you will find that while some
students follow Pater's syntactic structure rather closely, others will deviate from it
but still maintain a similar organizational pattern. You may even receive, as we
have, amusing and thoughtful essays on "grinning" or "smiling."

Chapter 8
<u>Classification: Organizing Data</u>

This long introductory section should be assigned and studied, to ensure that your class understands the nature and function of classification. You might combine it with the short Reading from Vance Packard, to make one day's assignment and discussion. One way to start discussion would be to put on the blackboard a brief quotation from the introduction--"Those who write, rank"--and ask for comments or explication. This statement points to both the power and the nature of writing.

READING: Social Groups in a Town (p. 138)
Vance Packard, from *A Nation of Strangers* (p. 138)

1.   The businessman sees his community as simply divided between "commuters" and "locals." Packard separates the community into "three major groups": the locals, the Darien people, and the transients.
2.   The three species are each distinguished by the length of time they have lived in Darien.
3.   Those who make their living in Darien provide services for the other two groups. (Though Packard does not specify this, it is likely that these two groups commute to New York City to make their living.)
4.   To "dominate the town socially" implies that the Darien people have the largest incomes, and as a result, their needs determine the nature of the services provided by locals; further, that the wives of the Darien people would lead social and volunteer groups, thus determining who was socially acceptable and who was not. The businessman's statement suggests that the locals are seen only as those who serve the Darien people and not as social equals. The transferee's wife's statement reflects her ostracism by the social forces (e.g., country clubs, social and volunteer organizations) dominated by the Darien people.
5.   We have suggested that the Darien people dominate because of their monetary power. We might want to know what percentage of them are commuters and what percentage are professionals (i.e., doctors and lawyers) practicing in the Darien area. We might also ask if ethnic or racial background and religious persuasion are important. We might want to know how the town is divided geographically; that is, whether the Darien people live in specific neighborhoods from which they try to exclude people they consider undesirable. (You might want to return to this question after considering the kinds of information gathered by the Lynds in classifying the high-school student body of Middletown.)

PRACTICE: Social Categories in an Institution (p. 139)

This practice works well as an in-class exercise. Students can work on the practice in small groups, and then the class can come together to compare the proposed classification systems for consistency of dividing principle, exclusiveness of the classes, and completeness of the system. Since students tend to think in binary categories, problems of exclusiveness and completeness are bound to arise. You can encourage revisionary thinking by questioning the exclusiveness of proposed classes and by mentioning groups of people who have been left out (members of the custodial staff, campus visitors, and children in the day-care center are often left out). And, of course, introducing the needs of actual people such as incoming students can also lead to revision of the classificatory system.

PRACTICE: Social Types in a Particular Place (p. 140)

Observation is key to this assignment. It simply does not work as well if students rely solely on their memories--or on their preconceptions. Of course, to prepare for the observation, students will have to use their memories and preconceptions to figure out the kinds of data that are likely to be important. But they must also prepare to be surprised--to see and record data whose importance they had not anticipated. Before sending the students forth to observe, you should discuss how observations are made and recorded. We also suggest that you require students to submit their recorded observations along with the paper they develop from them.

READING: The Student Body (p. 140)
Robert and Helen Lynd, from *Middletown* (p. 141)

The Lynds provide an example of a student body classified by its organizations. You might want to make an outline of this material on the board, showing how characteristics of members of these various organizations can be compared and contrasted.

PRACTICE: Your Student Body (p. 143)

If your students have read and studied the excerpt from *Middletown*, you should ask them to think about the differences between writing an article for *Squire* magazine and writing a book-length sociological study. If *Squire*'s editors had wanted a study from the point of view of a professional sociologist, they would have asked a professional sociologist to write it. They want a student's point of view, in part because their readers are prospective college students and their parents.

Remember that students tend to think in terms of large, binary divisions such as "Greeks" (fraternity and sorority members) and "Non-Greeks" (all other students). To encourage them to complicate and refine their classification systems, you should plan to intervene in the experimenting or drafting process. Class discussion of one or two experimental classifications or paper drafts should provide numerous opportunities to consider why some classification systems work better than others. Here are L. L.'s notes about one such discussion:

A majority of students had divided the student body into athletes and nonathletes. These systems were fairly comprehensive. The athletes were divided into male and female and further subdivided into players of contact and noncontact sports. They were then described in terms of dress, strength, physique, and study habits. The nonathletes defied neat characterization. They were divided into "preppies," "fine arts students," "intellects," and "other." "Other" was generally an amusing category.

Two sets of students had classified according to campus dormitories. This classification system, the class quickly realized, failed for a number of reasons. While some dorms were easily characterized (Andrews: "girls concerned about their weight"), others housed a variety of "types." One pair of students described the population of a single dorm as containing "jocks," "nerds," "art students," "engineers," and "females." This provoked some mock outrage.

We clarified why the first system of classification was more effective than this one, and we discussed why it would be much easier to construct a coherent newspaper article form the "athlete/nonathlete" schema. While both systems aim at comprehensiveness, only the latter successfully characterizes the student body in an organized fashion. "Why do you say 'characterize,'" a student objected, "this is an exercise in stereotyping, something we should never do!" We tried to distinguish between "characterizing" and "stereotyping."

READING: Classifying Commercials (p. 144)
                John W. Wright, from "TV Commercials That Move the Merchandise" (p. 144)

I.   Music
     A.   written for ad
         1.   simple jingle
         2.   orchestrated contemporary
         3.   quiet mood
         4.   with dancing

      B.   established popular songs
           1.   nostalgic
           2.   contemporary
II.   Personality
      A.   established stars
           1.   present
           2.   past
           3.   present (again)
      B.   characters created by ads
           1.   live
               a.   present
               b.   past
           2.   animated
           3.   live (again)
               a.   present, most successful

2.   After two introductory paragraphs, Wright's paragraphing follows his classification very closely:

paragraph 3	IA, 1-3
paragraph 4	IA, 4
paragraph 5	IB
paragraph 6	IIA, 1
paragraph 7	IIA, 2
paragraph 8	IIA, 3
paragraph 9	IIB, 1
paragraph 10	IIB, 2
paragraph 11	IIB, 3

3.   Here, let the students be the experts. You will probably find that Wright's categories stand up well.

PRACTICE: The Class of Full-Page Ads (p. 148)

Note that there are two parts to this assignment. Part A is quite a bit of work in itself. You may wish to use Part B only as basis for discussion rather than requiring that a formal paper be turned in. Part A will result in a relatively short paper, but this is all right. Classification is more a tool of discourse than a form which stands well alone. This work should be seen as preparation for the analysis and synthesis material to come.

Look at the Reading "Analyzing an Advertisement" in Chapter 9. It may work well for you to assign and discuss this example while your students are thinking about collecting and classifying their own ads. The more carefully they learn to look at ads, the more likely they are to find interesting ways of classifying them.

You will want to read and discuss the most successful classifications in the classroom, passing around the ads as you do so.

READING: Classifying Forms of Power (p. 149)
Bertrand Russell, from *Power* (p. 150)

This excerpt repays careful study. While students should definitely be asked to do the first question, we suggest that you choose either the second or the third question as a follow-up.

1. An upside-down tree diagram works much better here than an outline. In working out the diagram, students sometimes discover problems with Russell's system. For example, in the "manner of influence" branch of his system, education and party politics are cited as instances of "influence by reward and punishment." However, in this "type of organization" branch of the system, education and party politics appear as examples of organizations that work by influencing opinion rather than by reward and punishment. It is worth considering why education and party politics are problems for Russell's system. In our opinion, Russell is primarily working top-down; perhaps that is one reason why the problem with education and party politics occurs.

2. In classifying "the manner of influencing individuals," Russell implicitly uses a mind-body distinction--a distinction that makes "habit" a problem. If habit is understood as a predisposition, then it would seem to belong with opinion on the mental side of the mind-body distinction. However, since habitual action does not depend on a "mental intermediary," it seems to belong on the body side of the distinction along with other effects produced by "direct physical power over [an individual's] body." Yet Russell seems unwilling to put habit in that body category (Class A), perhaps because being drilled is not as physically coercive as being "imprisoned or killed." It's possible to protect the logic of Russell's system by putting habit either into the reward and punishment class (Class B) or into the other branch of his system--the "type of organization" branch. However, it is also possible to use Russell's remarks on habit to question and revise his system, including his initial definition of power. By using the word "intended," Russell's definition implies that individual subjects first exist and then, secondarily, either wield

or yield to power. Foucault's take on power is quite different. In deciding whether to protect or to question Russell's logic, you should allow yourself to be influenced by your students' responses to this question.

3.   Like question 2, this question invites students to think critically about Russell's definition and taxonomy of power. For example, one kind of power that seems to be missing from Russell's taxonomy is the kind of reciprocal influence that characterizes dialogue--and dialogical teaching. Another is resistance, a form of power that was not entirely absent during the periods of Hitler's "rise."

PRACTICE: Power in an Institution You Know (p. 151)

Although students tend to be quite interested in--and sensitive about--power, you will need to take care to prevent them from using this practice merely to gripe about unfair treatment by X. In-depth discussion of the Russell excerpt helps; so too does in-class consideration of the classification systems that one or two students are planning to use.

PRACTICE: From Abstract to Concrete (p. 152)

In preparation for this practice, you may want to take an abstraction and work it out in class, following Russell's lead. In form, the Russell excerpt moves from abstract to concrete. Since you and the class will be engaging in a thought experiment, your way of working will necessarily be less linear and more dialectical in form than Russell's presentation. Indeed, you should use this occasion not only to point out the difference between process and product but also to show students how to move back and forth between their general ideas and specific experiences when they are defining and classifying.

Chapter 9
Analysis: Taking Things Apart

As the introduction indicates, this chapter stresses the analysis of *texts*. You should emphasize the importance of this skill in all the humanities and social sciences--and in life.

READING: Comparison and Contrast (p. 154)
              Stephen Crane, "The Last of the Mohicans" (p. 154)
PRACTICE: Analysis of a Comparative Analysis (p. 156)

In the first two paragraphs, Crane sets up the sources to be contrasted: the oral history of the nonliterary inhabitants of Sullivan County, and the popular literary version of their history written by James Fenimore Cooper--specifically, his novel *The Last of the Mohicans*. In paragraph 3, Crane sites that there is no comparison between Sullivan County's "hero" and Cooper's, and that pathos lies in the contrast between the two. In paragraphs 4 and 5, Cooper's literary last Mohican is presented. Paragraph 4 consists of a cumulative sentence extolling the qualities of Uncas (an acerbic paraphrase from Cooper), and these qualities are further reinforced by a direct quotation from Cooper's work. In paragraph 6, Crane drives home the contrast by using a reportorial tone in presenting the real last Mohican, and his tone and description serve to deflate the swollen literary hyperbole of paragraph 5.

PRACTICE: Fiction and Experience (p. 156)

Crane's short essay works well as a model for this Practice. In class, students can discuss the attributes of some popular television cop, rock star, doctor, or tycoon. These attributes should be listed on the board and discussion should emphasize the typical behavior of the character that draws on and thus reinforces popular mythology.

READING AND PRACTICE: Two Poets and a Painting (p. 157)
                    W. H. Auden, "Musée des Beaux Arts" (p. 160)
                    William Carlos Williams, "Landscape with the Fall of
                      Icarus" (p. 160)

This is a formal comparison and contrast assignment. The instructions are very specific and elaborate. We recommend that you go over them carefully with your class and discuss the poems with your students before they undertake to write.

You may find L. L.'s report on her discussion of the poems helpful in preparing your own:

By way of illustrating how to compare and contrast things which are at once different and resemble one another, we turned to the two poems on Brueghel's *The Fall of Icarus*. First I asked if anyone knew the story of Daedalus and Icarus, and we were able to piece the myth together from students' partial recollections. The two poems were read aloud. I asked the class which poem they preferred, and they agreed that they preferred the Williams poem because it is more "poetic." Auden's poem, they felt, developed an argument and imposed a judgment, while Williams left more to the reader.

In one column of their paper, students were asked to write down similarities between the two poems, and in another column, to list the differences. They seemed genuinely interested in the task; the class enjoys working with literature, and they seem to expect a certain amount of reading and interpretation in an "English class."

The first student to speak observed that "Landscape with the Fall of Icarus" could more easily be compared with the second stanza of "Musée des Beaux Arts" in that the first part of Auden's poem has little to do with either the legend or the painting. The class agreed and expanded on this observation: Auden uses the picture only as an example to support his larger thesis that "the Old Masters" understood suffering and the human position; Brueghel is just one of a number of "Old Masters." Someone else said that Auden's language is much more "powerful," in the use of such words as *suffering, torturer,* and *failure*. Another student argued that Auden's powerful language runs counter to his purpose of contrasting Icarus' drowning with everyone else's "apathy," and that Williams is more "powerful" overall because he paints a pretty picture of the landscape and then uses the word *drowning* as the final word of the poem so that it comes as a shock.

Yet another student supported this claim. She said that while Auden assumes that the reader knows the legend, Williams tells the story. Further, Williams uses words with positive connotations, such as *spring, pageantry, awake,* and *tingling*, while Auden uses negative language. This, she said, contributes to the force of the final lines of Williams's narrative because the reader is not prepared for the drowning.

As the discussion continued, someone said that Williams doesn't really place a judgment on those "concerned with themselves," but Auden "thinks that there is something deeply wrong with the fact that while some people suffer others can just continue to live normal, undisturbed lives." Still another student disagreed. He argued that the two poets pass the same judgment, but Williams expects the reader to draw the conclusion that Auden states more explicitly.

I asked two questions: (1) To which form of discourse is each of the poems most similar? and (2) Given our discussion, what are possible theses for a paper comparing the two poems? To the first question, students replied that Auden's poem is "argumentation" and Williams's poem is "description" and "narration." Finally, someone suggested that a thesis which would cover all our observations is: "Although Williams and Auden appear to treat a single subject, they do so very differently." We clarified this thesis somewhat.

This was a most successful meeting. The class enjoys working with poetry, and the discussion served as a good introduction to "synthesis" inasmuch as the exercise provides an opportunity to "compare and contrast" two things which resemble one another but turn out to be significantly different. I found this exercise a natural way to introduce the idea of formulating a thesis.

READING: Analyzing an Advertisement (p. 161)
PRACTICE: Analyzing a Magazine Advertisement (p. 163)

Advertisements that work best for this assignment usually come from general-audience, slick magazines like *Vogue*, *Elle*, *Vanity Fair*, *GQ*, or *Sports Illustrated*. Since such fashion designers as Georges Marciano, Calvin Klein, and Ralph Lauren work out their fantasies in advertising, such ads are rich in cultural codes. Marciano and Lauren--each in very different ways--flaunt stereotypes; Klein both flaunts and flouts (Obsession perfume). Cigarette and liquor ads tend to be interesting, because they must hide the dangerous qualities of their products.

Students first should read the analysis of the Marciano ad in the text; then they should find an ad they would like to analyze and bring it to class. You might have students work in groups--discussing their ads, listing their individual elements, and considering their connotations. By "elements" we mean *how* the product is displayed: the stance of the figures, the use of color or of shadow, the use of words or the lack of them; and so on. Finally, how do all the elements add up? Is the message clear, ambiguous, or mixed? What is its emotional appeal? Would you buy this product? What else is being sold along with the product?

READING: A Critic Theorizes about Advertising (p. 163)
John Berger, from *Ways of Seeing* (p. 164)

1. In paragraph 3, Berger says that while brands may compete with one another, and the customer, through advertising, is indeed offered

choices, "publicity as a system only makes a single proposal": "that we transform . . . our lives, by buying something more" (paragraphs 3 and 4). *System* is the key concept here, as a force that directs our choices.

2.   Any system will develop its own discourse (or perhaps it is the development of such discourse that creates a system). The language of publicity is both visual and verbal. As Berger points out, "every publicity image confirms and enhances every other," thus establishing the language of the system. The root, or basis, of this language is its "single proposal": Buy.

3.   Publicity directs us to transform ourselves by satisfying our desires and by being seen as enviable (like the images in the ads). Publicity offers the buyer "an image of himself made glamorous by the product." It promises a future happiness, a happiness of "being envied" by others--defined here as "glamour." But as Berger says, "Being envied is a solitary form of reassurance" (paragraph 8).

4.   For this discussion, you might ask students to bring their favorite magazines to class. They can easily find examples of states and conditions to envy, and they might consider the image that the magazine as a whole is promoting.

PRACTICE: Analyzing Images of Women in Advertising (p. 165)

We have tried to choose ads that are representative of their period. You will see that some things change, but some things remain the same in the 79-year span of American advertising presented here. Here are some notes on each ad.

1913 Shredded Wheat (p. 167)
Reflected in this ad is the influence of the women's suffrage movement, which was very active in 1913. However, not many states had approved women's right to vote, and until the Nineteenth Amendment was ratified in 1920, women suffragists engaged in a hard-fought struggle. The ad stresses that it is desirable to be emancipated. Emancipation means that a woman can vote, and moreover, in serving Shredded Wheat to her family for breakfast she is freed from "kitchen worry and household care." She need have no guilt about serving prepared food because "Every biscuit is a vote for health, happiness and domestic freedom--a vote for pure food, for clean living and clean thinking." These are all states devoutly to be desired-- unless one asks how much "domestic freedom" a little biscuit can hold.

1922 Resinol Soap (p. 168)
To be a bride is a state desired by all women, and one they fantasize about, as the picture makes clear. But the ad implies that while "beauty of feature,

becoming dress, graceful bearing, and keen wit" are desirable attributes for those who hope to become brides, they are not enough. The foremost attribute is "a clear pleasing complexion." It should be noted that "right living" is also necessary for achieving this transformation (see Shredded Wheat).

1934 Lux Soap (p. 169)

In the 1930s, Hollywood stars possessed all that was enviable, and their perfect features frequently shone out of ads during the 1930s and into the 1940s. Remind students that this was the big era of fan clubs and the glory days of the star system at all Hollywood studios. Lux ads always featured stars, and here, Irene Dunne's tea-rose complexion has given her the power to "break hearts." If you use it, you too can win "admiration . . . romance" and have the *Charm* men can't resist." The sense of active competition implied in the Resinol ad is more overt here. To have only an "average" complexion makes you a loser.

1942 General Electric (p. 170)

This ad appeared in the second year of U.S. involvement in World War II, when the government realized that the war was going to last for a while. Many ads in the 1940s featured women at work, temporarily filling "a man's job" but managing to stay lovely and desirable by using the right hand cream, shampoo, etc. This ad is representative of those praising mothers who stayed at home and took care of their children as they waited loyally for their men to return. GE is telling them they do an important job and that they shouldn't feel guilty about it. Such women are entrusted with the responsibility of keeping "dreams alive": a noble, genteel, and truly feminine thing to do. The drawing presents the purity of motherhood unsullied by any taint of the workplace. The message to married servicemen overseas was that a faithful wife was waiting in a snug little cottage for her man to return. Her dreams, of course, will be cheerful ones because GE promises things her little brain can't even imagine (what woman in 1942 could ever have imagined a *four*-cycle washing machine!). There is a patronizing tone to this ad, although most people would not have read it as such in 1942. Indeed, its message was one most Americans deeply believed in.

1954 Listerine (p. 171)

As we all know, bad breath is intolerable, and people with this noxious condition are socially doomed. In the 1950s, a girl had to be *sweet* (and not just in her mouth) to *win* the boys. Note the first paragraph of the text: life for a girl is a win-or-lose situation. If you're sweet and adorable, you get "good times, good friends . . . gaiety . . . laughter and love . . . and marriage." If you have bad breath you will not be "sweet and adorable" and you will get boredom and loneliness. Obviously, the girl in the picture uses mouthwash regularly. The big toothy smile and the gaiety symbolized by the record player confirm her sweetness. She's also fashionably dressed-- she's a winner.

1966 Cosmopolitan (p. 172)

The *Cosmo* girl invites a comparison with the 1930s and 1940s ads. How far has she come from those days? She doesn't say that *she's* brainy but that some of "the best-looking girls" she knows are--because "they work at it." We can only assume that she wishes to be included in the "brightest" category, but the pose she strikes raises some questions. We are sure that she's worked hard at being good-looking and the expanse of thigh, the peek-a-boo dress, and the little pout assert her sexuality. This ad is representative of the 1960s, when the so-called sexual revolution (which made it okay for women to say they enjoyed sex) was just beginning. At the same time, the feminist movement was beginning to assert the equality of women's brains as well. In this ad, *Cosmo* tries to play it both ways, but the use of "girl" instead of "woman" suggests that woman (girl) as sex-object still predominates. So in the end, it's most desirable to be good-looking--the brains are a little bonus.

1977 Redbook (p. 173)

In the 1970s, women were becoming liberated and entering the job market in record numbers (many, of course, out of economic necessity rather than liberation). The ads of the 1970s frequently stressed the ability of a woman to do a man's job (somewhat like the 1940s, but in the 1970s, the job was a permanent rather than a temporary one). The picture suggests a woman in a man's world, of which she is in control. Note the business suit, the attaché case, the helicopter (there seem to have been no other passengers). She has landed on top of New York--even the phallic spire of the Empire State Building is below her. Yet the text of the ad, while asserting her power quite stridently, is also stressing femininity (it's okay if you want to stay home) and the fact that women now have choices. *Redbook*, of course, wants to appeal to both young career women and young housewives. To be over 35 is *not* a desirable thing.

1987 Charlie (p. 174)

To be "Charlie" is to be sexy and successful. We are meant to read the long hair and long legs of this Charlie girl as being sexy, and sexy is the love pat she's giving her companion's business-suited rump. She, too, is dressed for business, and the attaché case she carries reinforces that image. The drama of the scarf across her body catches your eye, and it pulls your gaze diagonally across her body. Her jacket has a stylish, businesslike cut, but its black-and-white checked pattern contrasts with the man's subdued business suit. The fact that she dresses distinctively (no soft little pin-striped suit from Brooks Brothers for her) is a sign of her success in the business world. The fact that she is as tall as--or even a shade taller than--the man also asserts her power. The name "Charlie" is short for either Charlotte or Charles, more commonly the latter. It would seem, then, that to be "very Charlie" is to be one of the boys, rather than your own woman.

1993 Bisou Bisou (p. 175)

This ad for Bisou Bisou Nouvelle Couture is one of a series featuring women in various roles. The message here seems to be that maternity is both erotic and fashionable. This couture is a far cry from the wholesome cottony flaps-and-buttons stuff designed for nursing mothers. As a picture of pure pleasure, the photograph is evocative enough, but the words "A kiss is *not* just a kiss" further complicate the erotic message, since they refer to the song "As Time Goes By" (in which a kiss *is* just a kiss). The song was featured in that highly romantic movie *Casablanca*, and is about lovers' clichés (and their durability). However, the ad, while intertextually co-opting romance, rejects the song's world-weary tone and asks you to rethink not just the meaning of a kiss, but the kinds of lovers who kiss. Further, this kiss is not just a kiss because the lover/baby is being nurtured by the kiss. (Dare we say that the lover here feeds off the beloved? Or is it nicer to say that some lovers *can* live on love?) Where the usual representations of mother and child call up icons of the (original) madonna, this ad tells you that motherhood can be sexy when you wear Bisou Bisou. (We should also note that the *New York Times* "Style" section recently showed a similar ad under the heading "Fashion: Babies as accessories." In 1993, according to the *Times*, infants are appearing not only in fashion ads and layouts but also on runways.)

Chapter 10
Argumentation: Presenting a Thesis

Learning to argue well takes time and lots of practice. To get your students started, this introduction differentiates argument from both persuasion and outbursts of anger. In so doing, it also introduces three basic terms for discussing argument: thesis, evidence, and reasons. Establishing a shared vocabulary for analyzing and evaluating arguments is a must. If you prefer another vocabulary to ours, then now is the time to introduce it. For example, if you're planning to devote a substantial part of your course to argumentation, then you might want to use Stephen Toulmin's six terms (argument, claims, evidence, warrant, backing, and qualification) rather than our three. The point is to decide on a terminology and to use it relatively consistently.

We recommend that you assign one of this chapter's readings along with the introduction and that you use it to clarify and complicate our introductory remarks. Gould's essay, "Integrity and Mr. Rifkin" works well with our introduction, not only because it differentiates reasoned argument from propaganda but also because it discusses a number of logical fallacies.

READING: A Scientist Argues about Means and Ends (p. 178)
                    Stephen Jay Gould, "Integrity and Mr. Rifkin" (p. 179)
PRACTICE: Reconstructing, Summarizing, and Evaluating Gould's
                    Argument (p. 187)

When we chose this reading, we figured that the (ab)uses of biotechnology would eventually become a more public controversy. Little did we know how soon the issue would surface in the media--or how popular it would become. At this moment, Steven Spielberg's *Jurassic Park* is well on its way to becoming the most profitable film of all time. We urge you to take advantage of this situation as you prepare your students to read Gould's essay. Although Rifkin is not Spielberg, *Jurassic Park* has enough in common with *Algeny* to be used as a way into Gould's argument. It should be noted, however, that Gould has published a review of *Jurassic Park* in *The New York Review of Books* (August 12, 1993); interestingly, it is a generally positive review, even though Gould does find fault with some aspects of the film.

The practice that accompanies this reading should probably be begun, if not completed, in class. Students can be put in groups and the groups can be assigned different though related tasks. While one or two groups might try to diagram Gould's argument as a whole, other groups might work up a say/do paragraph outline for specified parts of the essay (i.e., paragraphs 1-9, 10-18, 19-26, 27-29). The groups can then share the results of their work and see if they agree about what constitutes the thesis, strategy, evidence, and reasoning of Gould's argument.

Having worked through Gould's essay, the students should be well prepared to attempt a one-paragraph summary of its argument. However, you should review summary writing with them before sending them off to write. Remind them to include Gould's name and the title of his essay somewhere in the first line of their summary and to identify the issue, strategy, and major lines of argument in the rest of the summary; evidence is usually not included in a summary. You might also refer them to Gould's one-paragraph summary of Rifkin's *Algeny* (paragraph 6), even though you'll want to point out that it doesn't include everything you'll expect in their summary.

Your students will probably be so eager to evaluate Gould's argument that they'll want to skip the first two parts of this practice. But if you have them evaluate before they've analyzed and summarized Gould's argument, you can hardly expect them to follow what Gould calls "the procedures of fair argument" and "fair scholarship."

READING: A Feminist Discusses Women and Names (p. 188)
               Dale Spender, from *Man Made Language* (p. 188)
PRACTICE: Arguing about Men and Women (p. 193)

Spender's discussion is meant to provide both a basis for reaction and a model that can be imitated in certain ways, including the citation of sources used in support of an argument, and the maintenance of a rational tone in dealing with an emotionally charged subject.

You are not required to defend the positions taken by Spender, or to present this essay as an ideal argument. It is meant to be arguable *with*, as well as a useful example. In preparing students who wish to argue against Spender, you should discuss the possibilities of (1) changing the value signs attached to "patriarchy" (that is, changing its evaluation from negative to positive) or "sexism," or (2) developing a different terminology in which to discuss the relationships between men and women. Such changes are mentioned in the directions for the Practice, but may need some discussion and illustration for students to become aware of the possibilities.

Personally, we believe that Spender's argument is reasonable and that the strongest counterposition is simply that the weight of tradition is so heavy that it will negate feminist attempts to change the practices she discusses. You may prefer to suggest that your students argue about whatever issue between men and women seems most debatable at the moment when you make the assignment.

READING: An Educator Considers Myths and Realities (p. 193)
           Gregory Mantsios, from "Class in America: Myths and
              Realities" (p. 194)

Students will have little difficulty understanding this piece, in part because of its
myth *versus* reality structure. Using this structural opposition, you might begin
discussion by asking how Mantsios gets from his list of myths to his first "reality."
Of course, he gets there through numbers--and you should follow suit by asking
the class to look closely at what numbers he uses and how he uses them. Note
especially what he chooses to report in terms of percentages, in terms of
proportions, and in terms of absolute numbers. For example, if the homeless figure
were given as a percentage of the entire population, would it have the same
rhetorical effect as the number "three million"? Similarly, if "the wealthiest 15
percent" were given as an absolute number, would it change our response to the
fact that they hold "75 percent of the total household wealth?" The point of
exploring such questions is not to indict Mantsios; nor is it to suggest that
numbers lie. The point is to demonstrate that numbers don't speak for
themselves; they must be coded in some way and thereby made meaningful.
Mantsios makes choices from the available data; codes the choices he makes in
various ways; and then makes a claim about reality. Furthermore, he has reasons--
and we think they are good reasons--for making the connections he does not only
between his claims and the numbers but also between his claims and his thesis
that "class can predict chances for both survival and success."

1.   Americans don't object to the term "middle class," probably because, as
     Mantsios points out, it has become such a part of the political lexicon and is
     meant to cover a very broad constituency. One reason the attendant terms
     "upper class" and "lower class" aren't in the American lexicon is that such
     terms are usually associated with monarchies or other nondemocratic
     countries. Since most Americans believe that social position is largely
     determined by wealth rather than birth (except for the wealthy who consider
     themselves "wellborn"), we designate as our social categories the rich, the
     middle class, and the poor. These economically based terms contribute to
     the perpetuation of the myth of success being possible for one and all.
2.   In paragraph 14, Mantsios sets out census material that shows how unequal
     the distribution of wealth is in the United States, with the "wealthiest 15
     percent" holding "nearly 75 percent of the total household wealth." Another
     15 percent live below poverty level. Such a sharp contrast makes it
     "difficult to argue we live in a classless society" (paragraph 15).
3.   The "realities" Mantsios sets out (especially 1 and 2) use statistics to show
     how radical the economic differences are and how movement among classes

tends to be downward, not upward. Statistics can be manipulated to some degree. Mantsios has drawn on a variety of statistical information (see his sources for Reality 4, for example). Here, he has emphasized the problem of physical and mental health, to highlight the basic problem of survival. He might have emphasized educational levels in various classes, or types of employment, or housing.

PRACTICE: Arguing from Statistics--The Education, Employment, and Income of Women (p. 199)

In class discussion, you should go over the charts just enough to be sure students can interpret them and can begin to see possible theses emerging from the data. Here is an overview of the tables:

Table 1: Educational Attainment. From 1970 to 1991, there was an increase in educational attainment for both men and women. However, though a higher percentage of women than men completed high school, a higher percentage of men competed four years of college. One question might be, How does the increase in educational attainment of both men and women reflect itself in the workplace?

Table 2: Occupation of Employed Civilians, by Sex, Race, and Educational Attainment: 1991. This table provides a general breakdown in *numbers* for 1991, and shows the basic sexual differences in types of employment. These later census figures now include racial differences, so that students can, if they wish, limit their theses to differences between white men and women or black men and women. There are, for example, more black women employed than men, and ot that labor force, more black women are better educated than black men. The case is different for white men and women. As for Hispanic workers, Table 4 shows that until 1990, such figures were not easily available, though students interested in pursuing information on Hispanic educational attainment and types of employment should now be able to find it.

Table 3: Women as Percent of Experienced Civilian Labor Force. There has been a steady increase in the percentage of women in professional and administrative positions. Women continue to comprise the bulk of the clerical and private household worker categories. When women dominate in a given category, the level of pay is low, and certainly lower for women than for men in those categories (Table 4 shows this to be true for clerical workers). The information in Table 3 should allow students to frame such questions as, If women have attained parity in percentage with men at the professional level, have their wages also attained parity? Or, have women's wages in female-dominated categories such as clerical or household achieved parity? If not, have such salaries increased as much percentage-wise as men's salaries?

Table 4: Full-Time Wage and Salary Workers--Number and Median Weekly Earnings. Table 4A: Female Earnings as Percentage of Male Earnings, 1991. As we note in the text, there has been a slow proportional gain in women's clerical salaries, but women are still earning only about 75 percent of what men earn in the same jobs. As for professional women and men: A simple glance at the figures shows inequity, and Table 4A shows this percentage in 1991 of women's salaries to men's to be 70 percent. In administrative positions, women earn 66 percent of what men do. The arithmetically ambitious student can go on to figure out how percentage growth or decline in wages over a 20-year period correlates with the percentage growth or decline of women in various work categories.

Tables such as these can only provide a general overview of the population of the workplace. As we have suggested, in-depth research by students interested in specific areas of employment or of issues connected with a particular segment of the working population should be encouraged to consult more specialized sources of information.

READING: **Two Positions on Bilingual Education (p. 210)**
             Diane Ravitch, from "Politicization of the Schools:
               The Case of Bilingual Education" (p. 210)
             Angelo Gonzalez, "Bilingualism Pro: The Key to Basic
               Skills," (p. 216)

1.   Gonzalez is an advocate for bilingual education. Ravitch claims that she is not specifically opposed to such education, but she is skeptical about its value and opposes having it mandated by law. She argues that we do not know that bilingual education actually achieves success. Gonzalez disagrees, arguing that we know this: Where it is well done, it works well.

2.   (and 3.) Both speakers claim very similar values, in that they want what is best for the country and for the child; but they differ about the methods that will achieve this for students who hear a foreign language in the home.

4.   Both writers depend essentially on a combination of definition and cause-and-effect reasoning. Ravitch has a double argument. First she must define "politicization" and then argue that bilingual education is a form of that rather than of improved education. This involves her in difficulties. In paragraph 19, for instance, she argues that bilingualism is a "method"--and that it is especially political for Congress to legislate about methods of teaching. In the same paragraph, however, she argues that bilingualism is

not a "technique" but a "philosophy"--and therefore is not subject to evaluation. Since "technique" and "method" are really synonyms, Ravitch is not arguing rationally. She cannot call bilingualism a method in the first part of the paragraph and then deny it in the last part without damaging her credibility.

Ravitch also must argue about the effectiveness of bilingual education in achieving the proper goal of schooling--which means that she must define or describe this goal, and she does this mainly in paragraphs 31-32: fluency in English. She does not argue, however, that we know bilingualism fails to achieve this goal; she argues only that we do not know *whether* it does or doesn't (paragraphs 23-25). She supports her case by citing three sources, in footnotes 6, 7, and 8.

Gonzalez defines his goal in paragraph 6, as development of reading skills, and cites evidence that bilingual education does, in fact, work (his sources are in paragraphs 7-9, since he could not use footnotes in a newspaper editorial). He claims that three sources show that bilingual education has contributed to improved math skills as well as better reading skills.

Both writers need to make cause-and-effect arguments, and both cite specific studies to support their positions.

5. You should get a variety of responses to these questions. Just having responses expressed will be useful, of course, but they will be most useful if you keep asking what, in particular, your students found convincing or unconvincing--and why.

PRACTICE: Arguing a Hypothetical Case of Bilingualism (p. 218)

You can, of course, choose to formulate this writing assignment differently than we have proposed, but consider our reasons for setting up the problem as we have. We wanted to leave open the choice of sides in arguing the case, so that students would have the opportunity to write well on behalf of either side. We also wanted the argument to be as rational as possible, so that it would call for serious examination of the arguments proposed by the other side. If you do use our assignment, we urge you to go over the features of the hypothetical situation with great care, so that each student sees all its features: (1) the role they will assume, (2) the audience they will address, and (3) the occasion of the debate. Success depends on students' ability to define their key terms, including what is meant by a good or successful education, and what exactly would be involved in bilingual education. Success also depends on their ability to connect a certain course of action with its probable effects. That is, bilingual education, as they have defined it, must lead either to greater success--as they have defined that--or to less success, by a chain of cause-and-effect reasoning that they must develop rationally.

In arguing either side of the case, students should take care to counter the arguments from the other side, as they are found in the essays included here. This is an important feature of the assignment. It means that the chances of writing well will be greatly improved if students understand both essays thoroughly. Remind them of this before assigning the essays and before discussing them in class. The idea is for students to discuss the essays in class knowing that their writing will depend on how well they have mastered the strengths and weakness of the positions developed in the essays. This may lead them to want further information. Since the essays are in absolute conflict about the results of bilingual education--both citing studies that seem to support their cases--this is an assignment for which research should be encouraged.

It is also possible and may be very productive, if the right material is available, to allow students to write a research paper that either defends or critiques one of the two essays. If you encourage this approach, we recommend that students directly examine the sources used by these two writers, along with the best current research available. Then your students can make their own cause-and-effect arguments about bilingual education, either refuting or drawing support from one of the essays presented here.

READING: Two Essays on Punishment of Crimes (p. 219)
Karl Menninger, "The Crime of Punishment" (p. 220)
C. S. Lewis, "The Humanitarian Theory of Punishment"
(p. 226)

These are substantial, difficult essays. They are for students who need a challenge or for classes that can devote some time to reading and discussing them before undertaking to write about them. In particular, discussions about the assumptions each writer makes about human nature and society should be explored.

Questions are meant to be answered by each student during his or her reading of the essays. They can, of course, become the focus of discussion. Since they are not the sort of questions that have answers that are simply right or wrong, it is important for you to know your own answers to each question and to realize that there is room for other answers as well. In selecting a controversial issue for this book, we have tried to find one that is truly open, allowing for strong positions to be taken on both sides. Class discussion *before* the papers are written should not be allowed to become a debate, but should be used to make sure that all students understand the two positions as clearly as possible, and that they see the assumptions and implications of both positions. After the papers are written, you might have the best on each side presented to the class and allow the inevitable debate to take place.

PRACTICE: Arguing a Hypothetical Case of Punishment or Treatment for a Convicted Criminal (p. 233)

This is a mini-research paper in the argumentative mode. Proper form for quotations and citations should be discussed. You can encourage additional research if you wish, but the assignment is designed so as *not* to need that. You should emphasize the idea of the hypothetical case, which should enable your students to avoid loose generalizations and to focus their arguments. If you have strong and well-prepared students, you may wish to allow some of them to write essays in which they directly criticize the arguments of Lewis and Menninger and write counterarguments: the hypothetical case will help to keep the less well-prepared students on the track. Above all, you should warn your students away from giving you canned essays on capital punishment or some other overworked topic.

You may well be able to design a better hypothetical case than the one we have proposed. Go right ahead. Or you may wish to have two cases discussed-- one first offender and one more habitual offender, or one young person and one older, or whatever--or to make other changes in the structure of this assignment. Feel free to do so. We think that the two essays are nicely balanced, so that they will support a variety of arguments. They will also repay careful dissection in class. Bringing out the strong and weak points in each argument, showing how the arguments are dependent upon certain assumptions about human nature and social goals--all these analytical procedures will help students when they come to write their own assignments.

This is a good place to show students that a given essay can be both strong and weak. The idea is to help them to go beyond simplistic judgments of whole texts (like it/don't like it; it's good/it's bad) to more complex analysis of what is effective or ineffective within any given text, including their own.

**READING: A Critic Reflects on the Violence of Western Reason
(p. 234)
Jane Tompkins, "Fighting Words: Unlearning to Write
the Critical Essay" (p. 235)**

Although Tompkins takes up a complex and disturbing issue, she does so in a way that students will find quite accessible. Indeed, the personal dimension of Tompkins' essay may prompt some of your students to recall experiences in school when they felt violated. If this should happen, we suggest that you allow such students to tell their stories before turning the class' attention to what Tompkins has to say about how and why such violence occurs in the realms of Western reason. Note that the issue of argumentative violence also comes up in the remarks by Feyerabend quoted in the introduction to this chapter and in Gould's essay, "Integrity and Mr. Rifkin."

1.   We take her point to be that Western reason is prone to violence because it involves a momentary feeling of self-righteous moral ecstasy. As for her aim, we think that she wants to change what we do with what we feel; instead of acting out our momentary feelings of self-righteousness, we are encouraged to pause, to reflect, to question, and to seek another, more ethical way of proceeding.
2.   Both involve a violence infused with righteousness. Tompkins is not only explicit about the basis of her analogy but also careful to acknowledge that savaging a person's book is not the same thing as murder. However, she does conflate righteousness with murder*ousness* in the realm of the feelings, thereby effacing the one difference she was so careful to acknowledge. Still, we find it hard to charge her with "false analogy" for two reasons. First, real murders do not occur in either westerns or academic critiques. And second, she uses her analogy for speculative rather than for logical purposes.
3.   Although Tompkins' essay has many of the features characteristic of an argument, its structure and purpose make it resemble reflective writing, while its style often seems designed to appeal to the reader's emotions.
4.   Although Tompkins makes value judgments, we think she avoids moralism in two ways: she implicates herself in the judgments she makes, thereby evading self-righteousness; and she displaces the standard good/bad, right/wrong distinctions with something less standard called the "better."

PRACTICE: Is There a Better Way? (p. 240)

This is a challenging practice that involves both formal and intellectual experimentation. Some students will have little trouble coming up with an interesting thesis about the means and ends of argument, while others will have difficulty articulating a thesis they feel either committed to or interested in. We suggest that you encourage the former group of students to try their hand at writing the Gould-Tompkins dialogue, an assignment that will involve them in figuring out the relationship of their thesis to the concerns and positions Gould and Tompkins articulate. The latter group of students might try a more explicitly exploratory essay in which they begin with the problem of argumentative means and ends and work towards a thesis by reflecting on Gould's and Tompkins' arguments as well as on their personal experiences with arguing. In either case, the point is to try to work with and through one's relations to others in a dialogical, nonadversarial way and in so doing, to move beyond simple good/bad, right/wrong, and pro/con models for generating and presenting a thesis.

Chapter 11
<u>Synthesis: Putting Things Together</u>

The process of writing discussed here is worth treating at length. Most amateur writers do not revise enough and are unskilled at refining their topics and starting over. They seldom reconsider their data in the light of the thesis they are developing. This is a good place to stop and review the whole process with your class.

READING AND PRACTICE: How Should Photographs Be "Read?" (p. 243)

We think this is one of the strongest assignments--but we must caution you about it. It will work only if you can give it sufficient class time so that students begin thinking seriously about interpreting photographs. You may need from 3 to 5 class hours before they will be ready to write, and all the preliminary visual and verbal material should be discussed. We recommend that you work through the preliminary material up to "Three Famous Photographs in Context," allowing students to read each piece and study each picture in class, with a discussion to follow their reading. The material on the three photographs by Doisneau, Parks, and Arnold can be studied at home, before class discussion, since it involves more reading than you may wish to do during class. We have given a lot of thought to the order in which we present this material. Reading through it in class and discussing one thing at a time is the best way to get the most out of our arrangement, and it will prepare students to write the best papers they can.

Jean Mohr, "A Photo and Some Reactions" (p. 244)

To start this exercise properly, get your students to jot down their readings of the picture the minute you draw their attention to it.

1.   This is clearly a question for group discussion. It can be done either with the whole class or in small groups. Ideally, everyone's response should be heard, and the group should select the most interesting response for further discussion.
2.   One thing that should emerge from this discussion is that there are different ways of being "good," and that correctness and imagination both play their parts.

Allan Sekula, from "On the Invention of Photographic Meaning"
  (p. 246)

This is a short selection, but it is vital to the success of this entire assignment.
Sekula offers a basic polarity that will help students see more clearly the problem
of reading photographs. As he indicates, this simple division is an
oversimplification, but it is an excellent place to start thinking about how we react
to photos.

1.   The "own words" part of this is important. We suggest having all your
      students jot down their summaries before you start discussing the passage.
2.   Sekula is talking abut two ways of seeing or reading photos; but certain
      pictures, as we shall see, lend themselves more easily to one or the other
      way of seeing.
3.   This is a very open-ended question. Your students may well have some very
      interesting things to say about photographs, and this is the place to let them
      express their ideas.

John Berger Reads a Photograph (p. 247)

We mean this to be a good example of reading, in that it pays a lot of attention to
the detail of the picture; it brings in historical background knowledge; and it enters
the lives of the people pictured by a process of imaginative sympathy.
      Both of the questions are designed to let students express themselves. You
may find that they resent Berger's bringing his knowledge of history to bear on the
picture. Many students seem to resent all knowledge of history these days. If
they feel that way, let them express those feelings so that the whole class can
examine them. (This could be the most important thing you do all year.) From our
perspective, Berger combines Sekula's two approaches--and we think this is a
good thing--but he clearly privileges the historical. In any case, class discussion
should set up the reading of the next passage from Berger.

John Berger on the Use of Photography (p. 249)

1.   Berger certainly has a political agenda. He opposes the class structure of
      society because he believes that it is the cause of much human suffering.
      Neither you nor your students need endorse this view, but you should note it
      in discussing question 1 and paragraph 2. We suggest that you draw
      students' attention to paragraph 4, to explain why Berger felt it necessary to
      bring history into his earlier discussion of the Hungarian photograph.

2.   Berger's private/public distinction is not the same as Sekula's
     document/symbol distinction, in our view. For him the private photo is
     always connected to some personal history, but the public photo has a way
     of getting disconnected. Such disconnected photos can, of course, then be
     read--and probably will be read--in what Sekula would call a symbolic way.
     So Berger and Sekula can be connected, even though they are not saying
     exactly the same things.

Three Photographs in Context (p. 250)

1.   Doisneau's title may be considered documentary, if one reads the picture as
     a typical scene in a Parisian cafe. On the other hand, Parks's title,
     "American Gothic," has a political point to make, and is, as some students
     may realize, taken from Grant Woods' well-known painting of a white farmer
     with pitchfork and his wife standing in front of an American-gothic style
     farmhouse. Arnold's title is documentary.
2.   Our first impression is that the Doisneau is more of a document than the
     Parks photo, yet the Doisneau can be read as an "equivalent," or a symbolic
     picture for the reader's mind to develop. We should keep in mind
     Doisneau's belief that photography is a "subjective document." Parks's
     photo, in comparison with the other two, looks posed, as indeed it was, and
     the black woman, the broom, and the flag resonate symbolically. The
     "casual" quality of Dietrich's pose in Arnold's photo suggests photography
     as reportage, to use Sekula's terms. Of course, the photo can be read as an
     expression of Arnold's desire to capture the "unretouched woman" at work.
3.   Some students may really want this information, and others may resent it.
     If your class splits this way, try to use the occasion to explore why students
     feel one way or the other about interpretation. Is it because they have some
     personal tendency toward the symbolic or the historical? This should be an
     open-ended discussion.
4.   There is no right answer to this question. The point is to get students to
     understand the sources of their preferences. Is it subject matter, style,
     personal associations--or what?
5.   The broadest of questions, this is really just a way of making sure that
     students are ready to begin the writing assignment. We hope that they will
     have some sense by this time of the complex possibilities of reading
     photographs: that they will see a real problem there, which requires some
     thought in order to produce a synthesis.

Writing about Photographs (p. 263)

You may or may not wish to discuss some of these photographs in class before your students write their papers or while they are writing them, but neither you nor they should feel obliged to "cover" all of them. This collection is meant as a resource, not as a chore. We have included some photos that are pretty clearly symbolic, others that are pretty clearly documents, and some that are mixed. In particular, we have tried to find pictures that will stimulate students' thinking and provide them with things to say. Following are a few comments about each photograph.

Three More Photographs by Doisneau, Parks, and Arnold

"Sidelong Glance" (p. 265)
This is certainly a provocative document of the male gaze homing in on the desired object. How one interprets the woman's gaze--does something capture her attention, or has she deliberately averted her eyes?--is worth consideration.

"Muslim School Children" (p. 266)
A document, but with symbolic weight, especially in the gaze of the smallest boy (in "manly" dress), looking so far up to the male authority figure.

"A Literacy Teacher in Abu Dhabi" (p. 267)
We may categorize this picture as photojournalism, showing us a teacher at work. But to Western eyes, the exotic dress and especially the mask carry great symbolic weight. A binary tension of concealing (the woman) and revealing (the teacher) is at work here.

Three Pictures from the Vietnam War Period

"A Paratrooper Works to Save the Life of a Buddy" (p. 268)
This is reportage--a typical moment in battle--but the picture also makes a statement about the erasure of racial difference.

Student Killed by National Guardsman (p. 269)
The girl (she was just fourteen) is caught forever in her scream in a picture that became "an emblem of the . . . antiwar movement" (Vicki Goldberg, *The Power of Photography*). As reportage, the picture displays the contrast between the girl's discovery of death and the other spectators' sudden awareness (and unawareness) that the ammunition used by the National Guard against these student demonstrators was live.

"Children Fleeing a Napalm Strike" (p. 270)
Here reportage captures the pain and terror of burned children, the boy's face frozen into a timeless mask of tragedy, the naked girl in the center a screaming crucifix. The soldiers, fully uniformed and armed, walk behind them, seeming almost unconcerned. As Vicki Goldberg points out, this photograph spoke for the helpless suffering of the Vietnam War.

A Picture Album

"Elizabeth and I" (p. 271)
This is closer to surrealism rather than to document, and invites students to speculate on the relationship between Elizabeth and "I."

"Drought Refugees Hoping for Cotton Work" (p. 272)
A document of the 1930s. The eyes are especially important in this one.

"Russian and American Troops . . ." (p. 273)
The most interesting aspect of this picture is how we can read the Russian as Russian and the American as American. It's certainly not just the uniforms. This is a document both historical and cultural.

"Athens" (p. 274)
This is a witty photo that depends on the positioning of the two contemporary and ordinary Greek women directly under the caryatids that speak of the ancient glories of Greece. Again, it is document and symbol, together.

"Mirage Jet" (p. 275)
While this photo exemplifies truly objective photography, it is certainly a highly expressive picture of technology terrifying humankind. Or, as *Life* magazine put it: "The shadow is like that of a hawk over a barnyard. An Israeli Mirage flashes over Egyptian soldiers lying in the desert during the Six-Day War."

"Tomoko in the Bath" (p. 276)
This is a historical document that figured in a legal case against the company whose pollution of the waters where Tomoko's people fished caused the mercury poisoning that led to her deformed birth--and other such births. But it is also in the ichnographic tradition of the Pietá, of Mary holding the body of her crucified son. Tomoko is a daughter not a son, of course, but the picture symbolizes a mother's love and sorrow for all children hurt by the world. It is a powerful example of how a photograph can be a document and a symbol at the same time.

"Window Dressing" (p. 277)
A (postmodern?) cultural document of complexity and expressiveness. Who's inside and who's outside? Who's the reflector, and who the reflected?

READING AND PRACTICE: Working People (p. 278)
>   Studs Terkel, from *Working* (p. 279)
>   Suzanne Reed, from *Saturday's Child* (p. 283)
>   Colin Henfrey, from *Manscapes* (p. 283)
>   Barbara Ehrenreich, from "Is Success Dangerous to Your
>   Health?" (p. 284)
>   From Interviews by Students at the University of Oklahoma
>   (p. 285)

The material presented in the text will provide a sufficient data base for simple theses such as "Respect (or lack of respect) makes for happiness (or unhappiness) in one's job," or "Pleasure in accomplishment contributes to job satisfaction."

You should analyze one of the interviews in class discussion to show how personal statements are related to larger issues. Studs Terkel's interview with Mike Lefevre is useful for this purpose. The issues he raises--respect, a sense of accomplishment--reverberate throughout the other interviews. Some students have found it amusing that Mike would like to see the names of workers on the buildings they've helped to build. You might remind such students that the stones of medieval cathedrals were autographed by the stonecutters and that such buildings were the pride of their communities in part because the people who built them felt their work acknowledged and took pride in it. Such discussion will inevitably lead to the problem of depersonalization inherent in mass production-- and eventually, to more thoughtful papers.

We have found this assignment most officient and valuable when students provide a data base with their own interviews. With more information to draw on, students have the opportunity to consider working conditions within various groups, such as blue-collar or white-collar workers, women, professionals, self-employed workers, or, depending on what the class brings in, more specialized categories (salesclerks, cafeteria workers, pharmacists, etc.). The students enjoy hearing about and reading one another's interviews, so enough class time should be set aside for each student to give a brief oral report about the interview and for students to read interviews and take notes from them or duplicate the ones they wish to use. You may find it helpful to ditto up a list, or index, of the types of interviews for your students to refer to.

READING: The Western--Theory and Practice (p. 288)
                  John Cawelti, from *The Six-Gun Mystique* (p. 288)
                  Stephen Crane, "The Bride Comes to Yellow Sky" (p. 303)
                  "The Blue Hotel" (p. 312)
PRACTICE: Stephen Crane and the Western Formula (p. 336)
PRACTICE: Crane: The Man and the Stories (p. 336)

These two assignments are candidates for your final research paper. There is enough material here for a full paper, but you can easily supplement it by ordering a formal-Western paperback by Louis L'Amour or Zane Grey, or including a Western film, or adding a creative adaptation of the Western formula like *The Ox-Box Incident*, if you are using the first Practice, or by adding more of Crane's work if you are using the second. None of this extra material is necessary, however. There is enough here to sustain a good paper by itself.

As you examine the directions for the practices with your students, you may wish to discuss the techniques of critical reading: how to take notes or how to underline, annotate, and otherwise mark up a text so as to facilitate retrieving information from it. Here your own experience as a serious reader of texts can be drawn upon for methods and examples. The point is to help students move from being passive consumers of texts to being active readers with a viewpoint of their own. They should not just be reading but reading *for* something, looking for confirmation or qualification of a tentative thesis about what they are reading. If you can get them to read this way, they will discover that they will remember their reading better and that it is more fun.

The two practices offer quite different approaches to the material. The first is an exercise in literary theory. The kind of synthesis it requires will be something like that used in the social sciences. The material is literary, but it is being approached in cultural terms. The cultural material can then be used to make critical judgments. One of the ways to evaluate Crane's achievement as a writer is through his relation to the formulas of the Western. One issue is whether Crane works within the formulas or around and through the formulas. Extending or subverting a formula is one of our measures of literary creativity.

The second Practice is more oriented to literary history and biography. It asks for a synthesis of the man and the work. This kind of writing is used in literary and historical study. It presents a kind of equation in which either term can be emphasized. One can work from the texts toward the man, or from biographical information toward the work--or back and forth. Both these practices are designed to accomplish what the research paper is supposed to do--teach students how to generate and support a thesis from a body of data. It will not hurt to emphasize once again the importance of generating a thesis during the prewriting phase of the work.

In your discussion of the material, of course, you are free to make your study as literary as you wish. Depending on your assessment of your students' abilities, you may treat this material as if it were all "research," to be done outside class, or you may assign and discuss each story and the selections from Cawelti. One of our aims throughout this book has been to give you the maximum amount of flexibility. We have chosen primarily literary material for these two synthesis projects, because we believe that many writing instructors will be comfortable with this kind of material, and the synthetic skills that can be developed in writing about this material should be widely useful to the students who develop them.

In addition to the biographical material on Crane in Chapter 6, you should be aware of an early essay of Crane's (in Chapter 9) on the myth and the reality of the last of the Mohicans. Obviously, whichever of the two practices your students undertake, this essay will be useful to them.

We have chosen the combination of Cawelti and Crane because Crane's writing is both like and unlike the Western formulas described by Cawelti. You can help your students to see this by encouraging them to look at the fights in the two stories in the light of Cawelti's discussion of the Western hero as gunfighter. Crane gives us a shootout that doesn't take place, a fistfight, and a fatal stabbing: everything *but* a classic gunfight, yet the Western atmosphere of fatal violence is one of his major themes. Your students should find many things to write about, whichever practice they undertake.

READING AND PRACTICE: Men and Women on Love: A Collection of Poems (p. 337)

Although diverse in discursive orientation and point of view, these poems pose a set of related problems or issues about the (lack of) distinction between self and other, men and women, body and soul, truth and lie, appearance and reality, pain and pleasure, unity and duplicity, and presence and absence. As our introduction to this assignment indicates, we think that students should be encouraged to analyze these poems dialectically and comparatively (see Chapter 9). In this instance, an appropriate framework for dialectical analysis would be the communications framework we present in Chapter 1, "Writing as a Human Act." Within this framework, a love poem would be considered as a discursive act that involves not only a sender (writer/speaker), a receiver (a loved one and/or a third party), and a topic (love as experience and/or idea) but also a rhetorical orientation with formal consequences. Using this framework, students might inquire about the dominant orientation of a poem. To what extent is it oriented toward representing an expressive or reflective self? toward directing or moving a loved one or a third party? toward an intellectual understanding of love? To answer such questions, students will have to consider the formal features of a poem, most especially its organizational mode, its tropes, and its diction. However, it is important that these formal features be considered rhetorically rather than in isolation; that is, they should be analyzed as reflective, persuasive, and interpretive strategies that expose the discursive issues through which the subject of love has been historically and culturally constructed.

To help your students get started on this assignment, we suggest that you do a dialectical analysis of at least one poem with them and then engage them in a comparative analysis of two additional poems. Here are some brief notes about what we take to be the dominant orientation and significant formal features of each poem; we hope that you will find these brief remarks to be both useful and debatable.

William Shakespeare, "Sonnet 138" (p. 338)
In this self-reflective sonnet, Shakespeare works through metaphors of age, education, economic exchange, and dress not only to subvert the distinction between truth/lie but also to embrace the cunning and punning truth of that inter-subjective love that is made when two people enjoy lying together.

Ann Bradstreet, "To My Dear and Loving Husband" (p. 338)
This short lyric strikes us as subtly but surely directive in orientation. Both the husband and "ye women" are directly addressed; and both are invited to see the "I" as an exemplary guide whose way of loving shows how one turns an earthly treasure into a heavenly reward. In this regard, both the abstract diction and the word "persevere" are worth considering.

Andrew Marvell, "To His Coy Mistress" (p. 339)
This is definitely a persuasive piece. Here's a speaker who knows not only what he's conventionally supposed to express but also what conventionally constitutes a logical argument. However his threatening imagery, hyperbolic diction, and driving rhythm suggest that he's much more interested in making time than either expressing love or understanding the personal, social, and metaphysical issues posed by his relation to an other--to a virgin woman. Be prepared to find your students absolutely persuaded by this poem.

Charlotte Lennox, "A Song" (p. 340)
This is an expressive lyric with a reflective edge that raises the issue of virginity in ways that Marvell has neither the time nor the interest in considering. This virgin feels passion, but note the positive and negative terms she uses to express her feelings as well as her lack of a name for her desire. It is interesting to compare this poem with Shakespeare's "Sonnet 138" and with Rich's "Living in Sin."

Percy Bysshe Shelley, "Love's Philosophy" (p. 341)
Although most of this lyric is organized as a description, we think its orientation is more persuasive than interpretive. As the unusual use of the word "emotion" in line 4 suggests, Shelley uses description of what "is" as a way of moving the receiver of his message (that "sister-flower"?) to give him what he wants. He wants a kiss and we think he knows how to go about getting one. Comparing his persuasive appeals with Marvell's in "To His Coy Mistress" can be enlightening-- and fun.

Elizabeth Barrett Browning, "Sonnet 43" (p. 341)
Although this poem is much more explicitly self-expressive than Bradstreet's poem, the two raise similar thematic issues about the relation of earth and heaven or body and soul and what it takes in the here and now to turn love into an immortal, if not infinite (uncountable?), treasure.

Gwendolyn Brooks, "When You Have Forgotten Sunday: A Love Story"
(p. 342)
As its concern with forgetting and remembering suggest, this poem is self-reflective in orientation. However, Brooks's self (or "me") is sort of like Shakespeare's: that is, it emerges in and through the truly inter-subjective love that is made when two people really enjoy living together. Since Brooks prefers living together over Shakespeare's lying together, she downplays tropes and emphasizes the seemingly prosaic details (description) and everyday events (narration) of an especially poetic time: the memory of Sundays. It is worthwhile comparing Brooks's use of details with Rich's in "Living in Sin."

John Frederick Nims, "Love Poem" (p. 342)
Even though this lyric includes a humorous directive ("Smash glasses") and some heart-wrenching self expression (lines 23-24), both its title and its contrastive mode of organization lead us to believe that it is primarily oriented toward (re)interpreting the subject of love. Rather than being perfectly ideal, Nims's love actually disrupts the prevailing aesthetic, spatial, and temporal orders, thereby making people more at home in the world--and the world more humanely wry in spirit. Compared to Bradstreet's and Browning's hereafter, Nims's "unbreakable heaven" seems to be quite untraditional. Yet Nims's (re)interpretation of love relies on many traditional gender stereotypes; in this regard, it warrants comparison with Shakespeare's sonnet.

Adrienne Rich, "Living in Sin" (p. 343)
This is a topic-oriented poem that works through description and narration to create the impression of a woman who is benighted by love yet disturbingly aware of the dehumanizing banality of her existence. Level of detail, point of view, and affect are worth considering, as is the relationship between this poem's interpretation of love and Nims's interpretation of the subject. Comparing Rich's version of a woman in love with Lennox's in "A Song" can also be quite interesting.

Alan Dugan, "Love Song: I and Thou" (p. 344)
In this poem description and narration serve the purposes of self-expression. The last few lines should shock the reader, even though the earlier references to maggots, Christ, carpenters, God, and hell anticipate the poem's final turn to crucifixion. It is interesting to compare this poem with Marvell's "To His Coy Mistress," as well as to Bradstreet and Browning on resurrection and love.

Carolyn M. Rodgers, "Now Ain't That Love?" (p. 345)
Although this poem is definitely self-expressive in orientation, both its title and its final question pose an explicit problem for reflection, a problem that is related to-- yet not quite the same as--the one raised and dismissed in the lines proclaiming that the "whole scene is not/cool, but it's real!" Colloquial diction and syntax support the claim to reality. But the question remains: this is real--but is it love? For the purposes of comparison, this poem works well with Ponsot's "Unabashed."

Marie Ponsot, "Unabashed" (p. 345)
In this quintessentially interpretive poem, human love appears as an invention, invention appears as a way of discoursing or "saying," and saying appears as the making of a metaphor. Since Ponsot unabashedly demonstrates how one metaphor is produced (i.e., the "lakeshape" metaphor) and how another metaphor works (i.e., the angel metaphor), it's probably a good idea to analyze this poem in class and to take up one of the questions it raises: what, if anything, is real in the appearances this poem inscribes? Some answers worth considering are "landscapes," the imagination (line 12), and hoping (line 13).

St. Martin's